Dagger by Tutorials

First Edition

By Massimo Carli

Dagger by Tutorials

By Massimo Carli

Notice of Rights

Notice of Liability

Trademarks

ISBN: 978-1-950325-17-7

About the Author

Massimo Carli is the author of this book. Massimo has been working with Java since 1995 when he co-founded the first Italian magazine about this technology (http://www.mokabyte.it). After many years creating Java desktop and enterprise application, Massimo started to work in the mobile world. In 2001 he wrote his first book about J2ME. After many J2ME and Blackberry applications, he then started to work with Android in 2008. The same year Massimo wrote the first Italian book about Android; best seller on Amazon.it. That was the first of a series of 12 books. Massimo worked at Yahoo and Facebook and he's actually working as Senior Engineer at Spotify. Massimo is a musical theatre lover and a supporter of the soccer team S.P.A.L.

About the Editors

Gordan Glavaš is the tech editor of this book. Gordan is a mobile architect with over 10 years of Android and iOS experience. He's also a big fan of code reusability through annotation processing and enjoys designing programming languages. In his free time, he's always up for cooking, playing sports or a pint of good pale ale.

Martyn Haigh is the other tech editor of this book. Martyn started hacking on Android in 2008 and enjoyed it so much that he went on to make a career out of it for names like Mozilla and Meet-up. After over a decade of consulting, he's currently working as a senior developer at Facebook. He loves snowboarding, banging coffee, amazing food and his gorgeous family.

Sandra Grauschopf is the editor of this book. She is a freelance writer, editor, and content strategist as well as the Editing Team Lead at raywenderlich.com. She loves to untangle tortured sentences and to travel the world with a trusty book in her hand.

Dean Djermanović is final pass editor of this book. He's an experienced Android developer from Croatia working at the Five agency where he worked on many interesting apps like the Rosetta Stone app for learning languages which has over 10 million downloads. Previously, he's been a part of two other mobile development agencies in Croatia where he worked on many smaller custom mobile solutions for various industries. He's was also a part-time Android lecturer at the Algebra University College in Zagreb. Very passionate about Android, software development, and technology in general. Always trying to learn more, exchange knowledge with others, and improve in every aspect of life. In his free time, Dean likes to work out at the gym, ride a bike, read a good book or watch a good movie.

About the Artist

Vicki Wenderlich is the designer and artist of the cover of this book. She is Ray's wife and business partner. She is a digital artist who creates illustrations, game art and a lot of other art or design work for the tutorials and books on raywenderlich.com. When she's not making art, she loves hiking, a good glass of wine and attempting to create the perfect cheese plate.

Table of Contents

Book License

Before You Begin

This section tells you a few things you need to know before you get started, such as what you'll need for hardware and software, where to find the project files for this book, and more.

What You Need

To follow along with this book, you'll need the following:

- **IntelliJ IDEA Community Edition 2020.2.x**: Available at https://www.jetbrains.com/idea/.
- **Android Studio 4.1.x**: Available at https://developer.android.com/studio/. This is the environment in which you'll develop most of the sample code in this book.

Book Source Code & Forums

Where to download the materials for this book

The materials for this book can be cloned or downloaded from the GitHub book materials repository:

- https://github.com/raywenderlich/dag-materials/tree/editions/1.0

Forums

We've also set up an official forum for the book at https://forums.raywenderlich.com/c/books/dagger-by-tutorials/. This is a great place to ask questions about the book or to submit any errors you may find.

About the Cover

Dagger by Tutorials

The cassowary is the large bird most closely related to the emu. It's considered the most dangerous bird in the world. The dagger-like claw on the inner toe of each foot is what's making cassowaries so dangerous. The cassowary can slice open any predator or potential threat with a single swift kick.

Dagger by Tutorials illustrates the use of the Dagger library to manage dependencies in the app. It's not possible to create an application without dependencies. After reading Dagger by Tutorials, you'll be armed with Dagger and ready to make your app testable and maintainable with a single dependency injection library.

Introduction

Dagger is a library for dependency injection on JVM-based systems, including Android. Dependency injection is an important technique for building software systems that are maintainable and testable.

You're likely already doing dependency injection, maybe without even realizing it. Dependency injection is nowhere near as complex as its name implies.

In this book, you'll update an existing app named Busso to use dependency injection with Dagger and Hilt. The Busso app is a simple app that allows you to find bus stops near you and information about arrival times.

This book will serve you as a central point that holds all the information you need to dive deep into Dagger and Hilt, to apply it to your personal and production level projects.

How to read this book

The book is aimed at Android developers who aren't familiar with dependency injection and libraries like Dagger and Hilt, or developers who know little about the libraries but haven't had the chance to use it in real projects.

If you're completely new to dependency injection, we recommend reading it one chapter at a time, in the order of sections and chapters as available in the table of contents.

If you're familiar with the fundamentals of dependency injection, you can skip to "Section II: Introducing Dagger" instead, and continue learning about dependency injection with Dagger library.

If you're already using Dagger in your projects, but want to know more about complex topics, jump over to "Section IV: Advanced Dagger". You'll build complex use cases there on a real-world project, learn about multi-binding and modularization.

If you're already proficient with Dagger library, you can skip to "Section V: Introducing Hilt" and learn about dependency injection with Hilt on Android.

This book is split into five main sections:

Section I: DI Fundamentals

In this section, you'll get motivated to use a Dependency Injection (DI) library like Dagger by learning all about the problem you need to solve: dependency.

You'll understand what dependencies are and why you need to control them to create successful apps. You'll get to know the Busso App, which you'll work on, and improve throughout this book. It's a client-server app where the server is implemented using Ktor.

You'll take your next step toward implementing better apps that are easier to test and modify. You'll keep the concept of mass of the project in mind. In the process, you'll learn more about Scope and see how it relates to dependency.

You'll also use techniques that would work in a world without frameworks like Dagger or Hilt to create a fully testable app.

Section II: Introducing Dagger

In this section, you'll learn what Dagger is, how it works, and how it slashes the amount of code you need to write by hand when you implement dependency injection in your app.

You'll learn how to deal with constructor, field and method injection with Dagger, how to simplify the implementation of @Module by using @Binds in cases when you have abstraction and its implementation, and how to use @Singleton to solve a very common problem.

You'll learn everything you need to know about Dagger @Modules and you'll experiment with using different fundamental annotations like @Binds, @Provides and BindsOptionalOf as well as useful interfaces like dagger.Lazy and Provider.You'll also learn what qualifiers are, how to implement them with @Named and how to use custom @Qualifiers.

Section III: Components and Scope management

In this section, you'll migrate the Busso App from the homemade framework to Dagger. In the process, you'll learn how to migrate the existing ServiceLocators and Injectors to the equivalent Dagger @Modules and @Components, how to provide existing objects with a customized Builder for the @Component using @Component.Builder, and how to use @Component.Factory as a valid alternative to @Component.Builder.

The first migration will not be optimal — there will still be some fundamental aspects you will improve.

Later, you'll learn even more about @Components and dependencies. In particular, you'll learn why @Singleton is not so different from the other @Scopes, why you might need a different approach in managing component dependencies, what type of dependency exist between @Components with @Singleton, @ActivityScope and @FragmentScope scope, etc.

Section IV: Advanced Dagger

In this section, you'll dive deeper into the advanced features of Dagger like multi-binding. Multibinding is a very interesting feature of Dagger because it simplifies the integration of new features using a plugin pattern you'll learn in this section.

You'll implement a simple framework that allows you to integrate new services in the Busso app in a very simple and declarative way. You'll learn all you need to know about multi-binding with Set and Map.

Section V: Introducing Hilt

In the last section, you'll learn everything you need to know about Hilt. Hilt is a dependency injection library for Android that reduces the boilerplate of doing manual dependency injection in your project.

Hilt is built on top of the DI library Dagger to benefit from the compile-time correctness, runtime performance, scalability, and Android Studio support that Dagger provides.

You'll migrate the existing Busso app to use Hilt library.

Section I: DI Fundamentals

In this section, understand why you should use a dependency injection (DI) library like Dagger by learning all about the problem you need to solve: dependency.

You'll understand what dependencies are and why you need to control them to create successful apps. You'll get to know the Busso App, which you'll work on, and improve throughout this book. And you'll take your next step toward implementing better apps that are easier to test and modify.

Chapter 1: Design Principles

By Massimo Carli

In this chapter, you'll get motivated to use a **Dependency Injection** (DI) library like Dagger by learning all about the problem you need to solve: **dependency**. You'll understand what dependencies are and why you need to control them to create successful apps.

> **Note**: This first chapter describes all the main concepts about object-oriented programming using a dependency management focus. Go to the next chapter if you're already familiar with this topic.

Dependency Injection is one of the most important patterns to use in the development of a modern professional app, and frameworks like Dagger and Hilt help implement it in Android.

When you thoroughly understand the object-oriented principles of this chapter, the learning curve of those frameworks, initially steep, becomes flatter and everything gets easier.

> **Note**: You can find all the code for this chapter in the material section of this book. It's a good idea to follow along by adding the code to the **starter** project with IntelliJ. You can also check out the complete code in the **final** project. The **challenge** project contains the solutions to the challenges at the end of the chapter.

What dependency means

Dependency is a fancy way of saying that one thing relies on another in order to do its job. You can use the term in different ways for different contexts: One person might depend on another. A project might depend on a budget. In math, given `y = f(x)`, you can say that **y** depends on **x**.

But what does dependency mean? In the previous examples, it means that if the person you depend on is not available anymore, you need to change your way of life. If the dependency is economic, you have to reduce your expenses.

Similarly, if the business cuts the budget, you have to change the requirements for your project or cancel it.

This concept is obvious in the last example because if **x** changes, **y** changes as well.

But why are changes important? Because it takes effort to make changes.

The previous examples showed how dependencies can cause changes, and you can even prove this using physics. Consider the famous principle, **Newton's second law**, shown in Figure 1.1:

$$\vec{F} = m \cdot \vec{a}$$

Figure 1.1 - Newton's second law

In that formula, **F** is the force you need to apply if you want the equation to be true with **a**, which is acceleration. Acceleration is a change in speed that, again, is a measure of how the position changes in time.

This doesn't mean that change is bad. It just says that if you want to change, you need to apply effort that's as big or bigger than the mass **m**.

Hey, but this is a book about Dagger and Hilt! What does this have to do with your code?

In the context of coding, dependency is inevitable, and applying changes will always take some effort. But there are also ways to reduce the **mass of your code**, reducing the effort, even for big changes.

This is what you're going to learn in the following paragraphs. Mastering this skill will allow you to use tools like Dagger and Hilt effectively and productively.

A formal definition of dependency

In the previous paragraph, you learned what dependency means in your real life, but in the context of computer science, you need a more formal definition:

Entity A depends on entity B if a change in B can imply a change in A.

Note the **"can"** because this is something that could, but shouldn't necessarily, happen. In the previous examples, **A** can be you, your project or **y**. In the same examples, **B** can be the person you depend on, the budget of your project or, simply, **x**.

Figure 1.2 - Real life dependencies

It's a relationship that, in the object-oriented (OO) context, you can represent using the following **Unified Modeling Language** (UML) diagram:

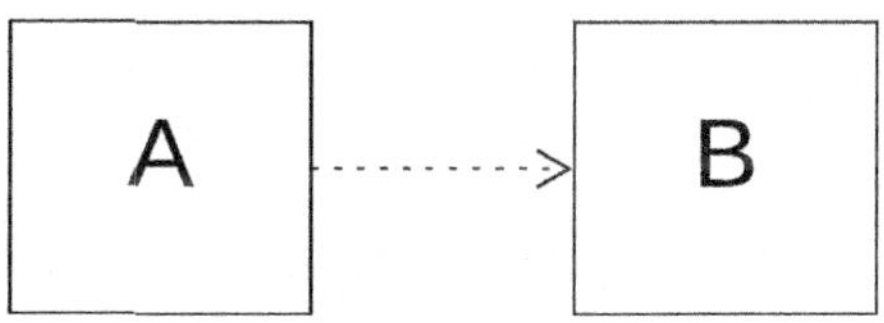

Figure 1.3 - Dependency relation in UML

In UML, you represent a dependency between entity A and entity B by showing an open arrow with a dotted line from A to B. This is how you indicate that a change in B can result in a change of A.

In these diagrams, A and B can be different things like objects, classes or even packages or modules. This is a model that reflects what happens in software development, where many components interact with many others in different ways.

If a change in a component triggers a change in all its dependents, you end up changing a lot of code — which increases the probability of introducing new bugs. Additionally, you need to rewrite and run the tests. This takes time, which translates into money.

On the other hand, it's not possible to create an app without dependencies. If you tried, you'd have the opposite problem of a monolithic app: All the code would be in a single point, making writing code in large teams difficult and testing almost impossible.

As a developer, one possible solution is to use patterns and practices that allow the adoption of *benign* types of dependencies, which is the topic of the following paragraphs.

Types of dependencies

Figure 1.3 above depicts a generic type of dependency, where the arrow simply indicates that A depends on B without going into detail. It doesn't show what A and B are, or how the dependency looks in code.

Using object-oriented language, you can define relationships more precisely, and you can do it in different ways for different types of dependencies. In the following paragraphs you'll learn about:

1. Implementation Inheritance
2. Composition
3. Aggregation
4. Interface Inheritance

You'll also learn how **abstraction** can limit the impact of dependency.

Implementation inheritance

Implementation Inheritance is the strongest type of dependency. You describe it using the UML diagram in Figure 1.4 below:

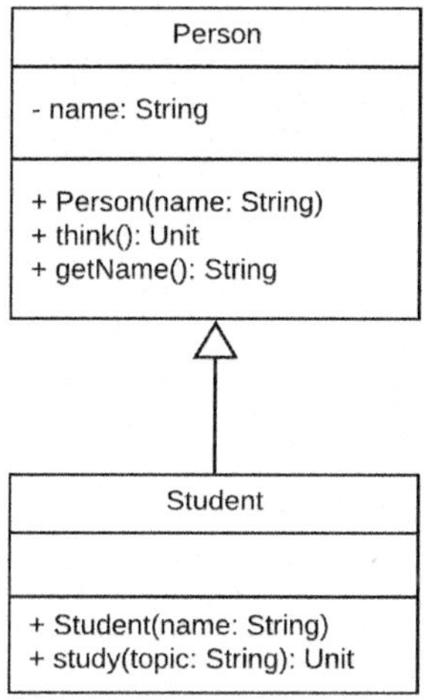

Figure 1.4 - Implementation Inheritance; the strongest level of dependency

You represent this relationship by using a continuous arrow with the tip closed and empty. Read the previous diagram by saying that **Student IS-A Person**. This means that a student has all the characteristics of a person and does all the things a person does.

The `Student` class depends on the `Person` class because a change of the former has, as an obvious consequence, a change in the latter — which is the very definition of dependency.

For example, if you change the `Person` class by adding `eat` function, the `Student` class now also has the ability to eat.

A `Student` differs from a generic `Person` because they study a particular subject. You need both `Person` and `Student` classes due to two fundamental object-oriented concepts: The first is that not all people study. The second, more important, concept is that the fact that some people study may not interest you at all.

You have a `Person` class so you can generalize people of different types when the only thing that interests you is that they are people.

For this reason, the statement **Student IS-A Person** is not the most correct way of phrasing it. To be more accurate, you'd say: **Person is a generalization or abstraction of Student** instead.

This app probably started with `Student`, then the developers added `Person` to limit dependency. As you'll see in the following paragraphs, they introduced a level of abstraction to limit the dependency relationship.

Implementation inheritance in code

To define that `Student` depends on `Person` through an **implementation inheritance** relationship, simply use the following code:

```
open class Person(val name: String) {
  fun think() {
    println("$name is thinking...")
  }
}

class Student(name: String) : Person(name) {
  fun study(topic: String) {
    println("$name is studying $topic")
  }
}
```

Here, you can see that `Person` describes objects with a name and that they can `think()`. A **Student IS-A Person** and so they can `think()` but they also study some topics. All students are persons but not all persons are students.

Abstraction reduces dependency

The discussion of when to use **implementation inheritance**, although interesting, is beyond the scope of this book. It's important to say that merely introducing `Person`-type abstraction is a step toward reducing dependency. You can easily prove it with a story.

The first implementation

Suppose you're starting a new project from scratch and you want to print the names of a list of students for a university. After some analysis, you write the code for `Person` like this:

```
class Student(val name: String) {
  fun study(topic: String) {
    println("$name is studying $topic")
  }

  fun think() {
    println("$name is thinking...")
  }
}
```

A `Student` has a name, can think and studies a topic. In Figure 1.5 below, you have its UML representation.

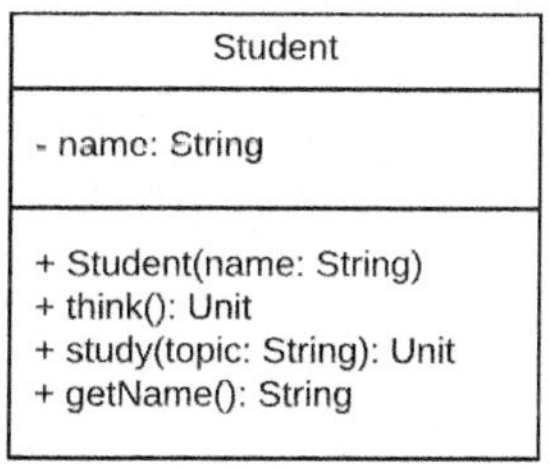

Figure 1.5 - Initial implementation for the Student class

Your program wants to print all the names of the students; you end up with the following code:

```
fun printStudent(students: List<Student>) = students.forEach
{ println(it.name) }
```

You can then test `printStudent()` with the following code:

```
fun main() {
  val students = listOf<Student>(
    Student("Mickey Mouse"),
    Student("Donald Duck"),
    Student("Minnie"),
    Student("Amelia")
  )
  printStudent(students)
}
```

Build and run `main()` and you get this output:

```
Mickey Mouse
Donald Duck
Minnie
Amelia
```

Your program works and everybody is happy... for now. But something is going to change.

Handling change

Everything looks fine, but the university decided to hire some musicians and create a band. They now need a program that prints the names of all the musicians in the band.

You're an expert now and you know how to model this new item, so you create the `Musician` class like this:

```
class Musician(val name: String) {
  fun think() {
    println("$name is thinking...")
  }

  fun play(instrument: String) {
    println("$name is playing $instrument")
  }
}
```

Musicians have a name, they think and play a musical instrument. The UML diagram is now this:

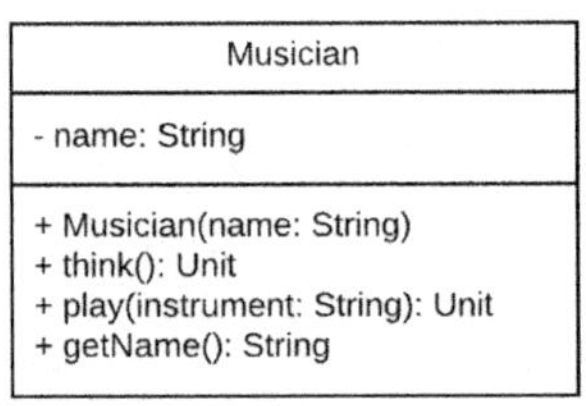

Figure 1.6 - Initial implementation for the Musician class

You also write the `printMusician()` function like this:

```
fun printMusician(musicians: List<Musician>) = musicians.forEach
{ println(it.name) }
```

Then you can test it with the following code:

```
fun main() {
  val musicians = listOf<Musician>(
    Musician("Mozart"),
    Musician("Andrew Lloyd Webber"),
    Musician("Toscanini"),
    Musician("Puccini"),
    Musician("Verdi")
  )
  printMusician(musicians)
}
```

Build and run `main()` and you'll get this output:

```
Mozart
Andrew Lloyd Webber
Toscanini
Puccini
Verdi
```

Everything looks fine and everybody is still happy. A good engineer should smell that something is not ideal, though, because you copy-pasted most of the code. There's a lot of repetition, which violates the **Don't Repeat Yourself** (DRY) principle.

Keeping up with additional changes

The university is happy with the system you created and decides to ask you to do the same thing for the teachers, then for the teacher assistants, and so on.

Following the same approach, you ended up creating N different classes with N different methods for printing N different lists of names.

Now, you've been asked to do a "simple" task. Instead of just printing the name, the University asked you to add a `Name:` prefix. In code, instead of using:

```
println(it.name)
```

they asked you to use:

```
println("Name: $it.name")
```

> **Note**: It's curious how the customer has a different perception of what's simple and what isn't.

Because of this request, you have to change N printing functions and the related tests. You need to apply the same change in different places. You might miss some and misspell others.

The probability of introducing bugs increases with the number of changes you need to make.

If something bad happens, you need to spend a lot of time fixing the problem. And even after that, you're still not sure everything's fine.

Using your superpower: abstraction

If you end up in the situation described above, you should immediately stop coding and start thinking. Making the same change in many different places is a signal that something is wrong.

> **Note**: There's a joke about a consultant who wanted to make their employer dependent on them. To do that, they only needed to implement the same feature in many different ways and in many different places. This is *no bueno*!

The solution, and the main weapon in your possession, is **abstraction**.

To print names, you're not interested in whether you have `Student` or `Musician`. You don't care if they study a topic or play an instrument. The only thing that interests you is that *they have a name.*

You need a way to be able to see all the entries as if they were the **same type**, containing the only thing that interests you: the name.

Here, the need to remove the superfluous leads you to the definition of the following abstraction, which you call `Person`:

```
abstract class Person(val name: String) {
  fun think() {
    println("$name is thinking...")
  }
}
```

Abstraction means considering only the aspects that interest you by eliminating everything superfluous. **Abstraction is synonymous with reduction**.

Knowing how to abstract, therefore, means knowing how to eliminate those aspects that don't interest you and, therefore, you don't want to depend upon.

Creating `Person` means that you're interested in the fact that a person can think and you don't care whether this person can study.

This is an **abstract class**. It allows you to define the `Person` type as an abstraction only, thus preventing you from having to create an instance of it.

`think()` is present in both classes, which makes it part of the abstraction. As defined, every person is able to think, so it's a logical choice.

Now, `Student` and `Musician` become the following:

```
class Student(name: String) : Person(name) {
  fun study(topic: String) {
    println("$name is studying $topic")
  }
}

class Musician(name: String) : Person(name) {
  fun play(instrument: String) {
    println("$name is playing $instrument")
  }
}
```

Now that you've put in the effort, you can reap the benefits of simplifying the method of displaying names, which becomes:

```
fun printNames(persons: List<Person>) = persons.forEach
{ println(it.name) }
```

The advantage lies in the fact that you can print the names of all the objects that can be considered `Person` and, therefore, include both `Student` and `Musician`.

Because of that, you can run the following code:

```
fun main() {
  val persons = listOf(
    Student("Topolino"),
    Musician("Bach"),
    Student("Minnie"),
    Musician("Paganini")
  )
  printNames(persons)
}
```

And that's not all. Returning to the concept of dependency, you can see that adding a further specialization of `Person` does not imply any change in the printing function. That's because the only thing this depends on is the generalization described by `Person`.

With this, you've shown how the definition of an abstraction can lead to a reduction of dependency and, therefore, to changes having a smaller impact on the existing code.

Abstraction & UML

Explain the level of dependency using the following UML diagram, Figure 1.7:

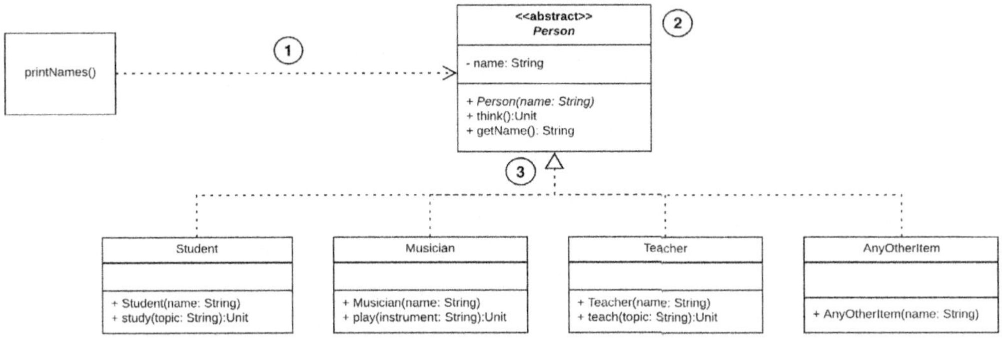

Figure 1.7 - The abstract Person class

Here, you can see many important things:

1. `printNames()` now depends on the `Person` abstraction. Even if you add a new `Person` specialization, you won't need to change `printNames()`.

2. `Person` is **abstract**. It's now the description of an abstraction and not of a specific object. In UML, you represent this using a **stereotype** which is the *abstract* word between « ». Alternatively, you can use an **italic** font.

3. `Student`, `Musician` and `Teacher` are some of the **realizations** of the `Person` abstract class. These are concrete classes that you can actually instantiate. `AnyOtherItem` is an example of a concrete class you can add without impacting `printNames()` in any way.

Finding the right level of abstraction

Reading the previous code, you'll notice there are still some problems. That's because what `printNames()` really needs, or depends on, are objects with a name. Right now, however, you're forcing it to care that the name belongs to a person.

But what if you want to print the names for a list of objects for whom the **IS-A** relation with `Person` is not true? What if you want to name cats, vehicles or food? A cat is not a person, nor is food.

The current implementation of `printNames()` still has an unnecessary dependency on the `Person` class. How can you remove that dependency? You already know the answer: **abstraction**.

So now, define the following `Named` interface:

```
interface Named {
  val name: String
}
```

and change `Person` to:

```
abstract class Person(override val name: String) : Named {
  fun think() {
    println("$name is thinking...")
  }
}
```

Now, each person implements the `Named` interface. So do the `Student`, `Musician`, `Teacher` and other realizations of the `Person` abstract class.

Now, change `printNames()` to:

```
fun printNames(named: List<Named>) = named.forEach
{ println(it.name) }
```

The good news is that now you can create `Cat` like this:

```
class Cat(override val name: String) : Named {
  fun meow() {
    println("$name is meowing...")
  }
}
```

and successfully run the following code:

```
fun main() {
  val persons = listOf(
    Student("Topolino"),
    Musician("Bach"),
    Student("Minnie"),
    Musician("Paganini"),
    Cat("Silvestro")
  )
  printNames(persons)
}
```

getting this as output:

```
Topolino
Bach
Minnie
Paganini
Silvestro
```

In the context of printing names, all the objects are exactly the same because they all provide a name through a **name** property defined by the **Named** interface they implement.

This is the first example of dependency on what a specific object **DOES** and not on what the same component **IS**. You'll learn about this in detail in the following paragraphs.

The named interface in UML

It's interesting to see how you represent the solution of the previous paragraph in UML:

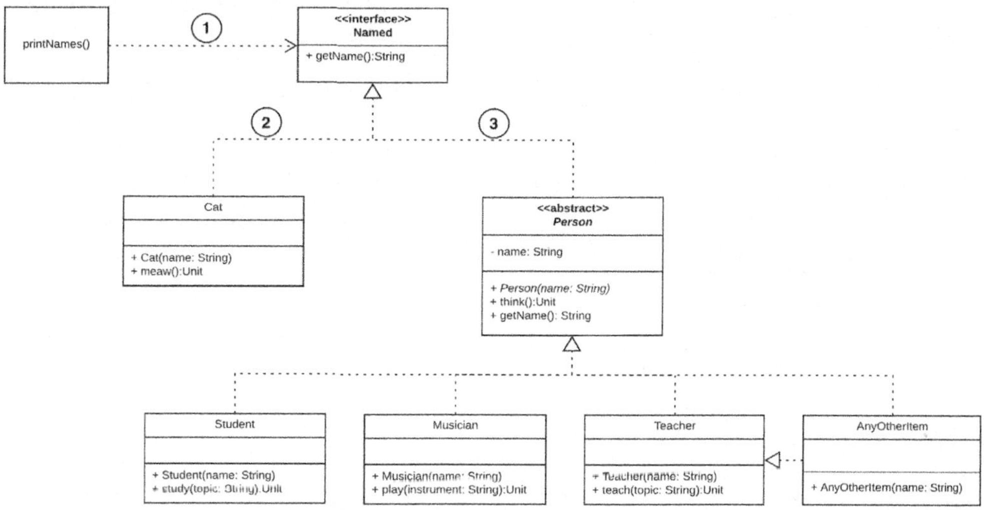

Figure 1.8 - The Named interface

Here you can see that:

1. `printNames()` now depends only on the `Named` interface.
2. `Person` implements the `Named` interface and you can now use each of its realizations in `printNames()`.
3. `Cat` implements the `Named` interface, `printNames()` can use it and it has nothing to do with the `Person` class.

Now you can say that `Cat` as well as `Student`, `Musician`, `Teacher` and any other realization of `Person` IS-A `Named` and `printNames()` can use them all.

What's described here is an example of Open Closed Principle (https://en.wikipedia.org/wiki/Open%E2%80%93closed_principle). It's one of the SOLID (https://en.wikipedia.org/wiki/SOLID) principles and it states: **software entities should be open for extension, but closed for modification**.

This means that if you want to implement a new feature, you should add the new thing without changing the existing code.

In the previous example, to add a new object compatible with `printNames()`, you just need to make a new class that implements the `Named` interface. None of the existing code needs to be changed.

Composition over (implementation) inheritance

In the previous paragraph, you saw how you can remove the dependency between `printNames()` and realizations for the `Person` abstract class by introducing the `Named` interface.

This change is actually a big thing, because it's your first example of dependency on what an object **DOES** and not on what the same object **IS**.

In the `printNames()` example, this further reduced the dependency on the `Person` abstraction.

This is a very important principle you should always consider in your app: **Program to an interface, not an implementation**.

This principle is also true in real life. If you need a plumber, you don't usually care who that plumber *is*. What's important is what they *do*. You want to hire the plumber who can fix the pipes in your house.

Because of this, you can change who you use as your plumber if you have to. If you need a specific plumber because of who they are, you need to consider a course of action if they aren't available anymore.

Composition

A classic example of dependency on what an object does is **persistence management**.

Suppose you have a server that receives requests from clients, collects information then stores it within a repository.

In this case, it would be completely wrong to say the **Repository IS-A Server** or the **Server IS-A Repository**.

So if you were to represent the relationship between `Server` and `Repository`, you could say that the former uses the latter, as the UML diagram in Figure 1.9 shows:

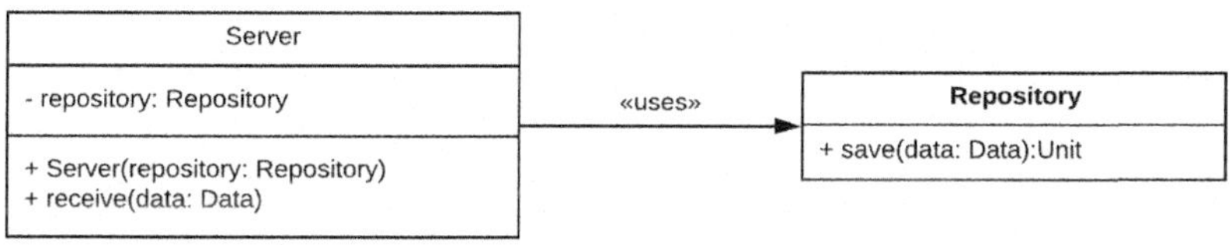

Figure 1.9 - The Server uses a Repository

This diagram just says that `Server` uses `Repository`, but it doesn't say how.

How do different entities communicate? In this case, `Server` must have a reference to `Repository` and then invoke one or more methods on it. Here, you can suppose it invokes `save(Data)` with a parameter of type `Data`.

You can represent the previous description with the following code:

```
data class Data(val value: Int)

class Repository {
    fun save(data: Data) {
        // Save data
    }
}

class Server {
    private val repository = Repository()

    fun receive(data: Data) {
        repository.save(data)
    }
}
```

Note: `Data` is not important; it simply represents the information `Server` receives and saves into `Repository` without any transformation using `save()`.

Everything looks perfect, but a problem arises as soon as you represent the previous relationship through the UML diagram in Figure 1.10:

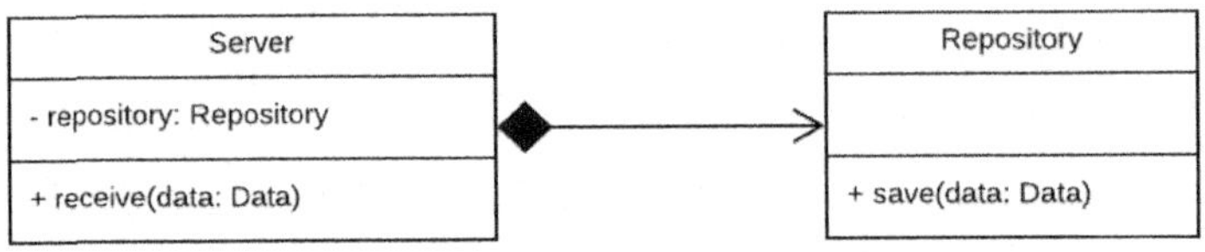

Figure 1.10 - Composition

The dependency between `Server` and `Repository` is a **composition**, which has a UML representation of an arrow starting with a full diamond.

You can say that `Server` composes `Repository`. As you can see in the previous code, `Server` has a private local variable of `Repository`. It initializes with an instance of the `Repository` class itself.

This means that:

- `Server` **knows exactly** what the implementation of `Repository` is.
- `Repository` and `Server` have the **same lifecycle**. The `Repository` instance is created at the same time as the `Server` instance. `Repository` dies when `Server` does.
- A particular instance of `Repository` belongs to **one and only one** instance of `Server`. Therefore, **it cannot be shared**.

In terms of dependency, if you wanted to modify the `Repository` implementation, you'd have to modify all the classes, like `Server`, that use it in this way. Ring a bell? Once again, you're duplicating a lot of work — and running the risk of introducing bugs.

You now understand that if a change of `Repository` leads to a change of `Server`, then there's a dependency between these two entities. How can you reduce that? A different kind of dependency will help.

Aggregation

For a better solution to this problem, you can use a different type of dependency: **aggregation**. You represent it as in the UML diagram in Figure 1.11:

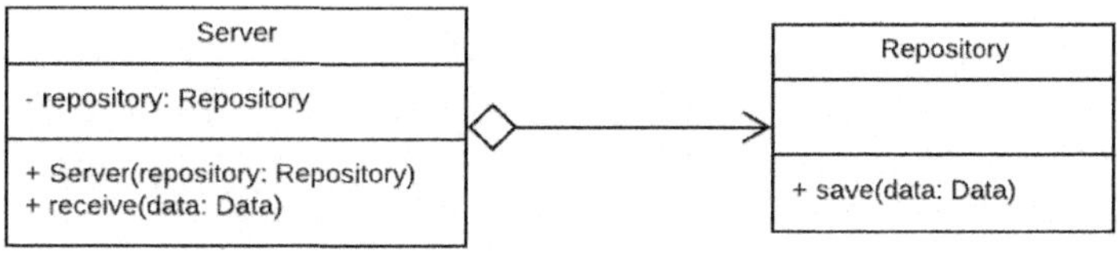

Figure 1.11 - Aggregation

This leads to the following code, where the `Server`, `Repository` and `Data` classes remain the same.

```
class Server(val repository: Repository) {

  fun receive(data: Data) {
    repository.save(data)
  }
}
```

In this case, you pass the reference to a `Repository` instance in the constructor of the `Server` class.

This means that `Server` is no longer responsible for creating the particular `Repository`. This (apparently simple) change greatly improves your dependency management.

You can now make `Server` use different `Repository` implementations simply by passing a different instance in the constructor.

Now:

- `Server` **doesn't know exactly** which implementation of the `Repository` it's going to use.
- `Repository` and `Server` may have **different lifecycles**. You can create the `Repository` instance before the `Server`. `Repository` doesn't necessarily die when `Server` does.
- You can use a particular instance of `Repository` in **many** different instances of `Server` or similar classes; therefore, **it can be shared**.

Using a **composition** or **aggregation** doesn't change the fact that `Server` depends on `Repository`. The difference is in the *type* of dependency.

Using **composition**, `Server` depends on what `Repository` **IS**. With **aggregation**, `Server` depends on what `Repository` **DOES**.

In the latter case, `Repository` can be an abstraction. This isn't possible with **composition** because you need to create an instance.

> **Note**: You might ask why you need to support different `Repository` implementations. As you'll see in the following chapters, any abstraction always has at least one additional implementation: the one you use in testing.

Interface inheritance

In the previous paragraphs, you learned the importance of abstractions and, specifically, of using interfaces. In the `Server` and `Repository` example, you use an aggregation relationship to make `Repository` an abstraction instead of using a concrete class. This is possible because what the `Server` really needs is not an instance of `Repository` but something that allows it to save some `Data`.

> **Note**: The dependency is based on what the `Repository` **DOES** and not on what the `Repository` **IS**.

For this reason, you can implement the following solution, where the `Repository` is now an interface that might have different implementations, including the one you can describe using the following `RepositoryImpl` class:

```
interface Repository {
  fun save(data: Data)
}

class RepositoryImpl : Repository {
  override fun save(data: Data) {
    // Save data
  }
}
```

You don't need to change `Server` — it continues to depend on `Repository`, which is now an interface. Now, you can pass any implementation of `Repository` to `Server` and, therefore, any class capable of making a `Data` object persistent.

You usually refer to this kind of dependency between `Server` and `RepositoryImpl` as **loosely coupled** and describe it with the UML diagram in Figure 1.12:

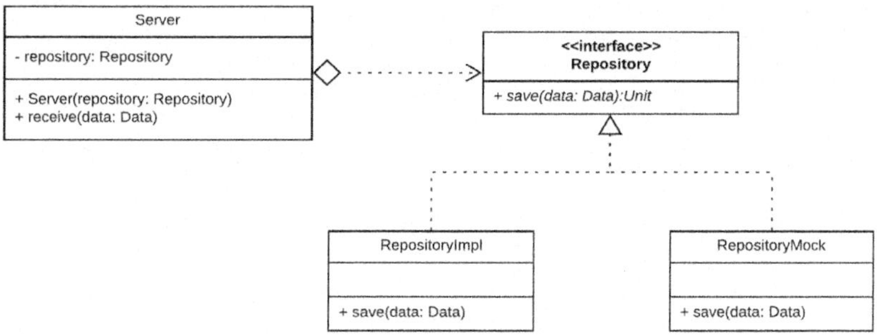

Figure 1.12 - Loosely Coupled

This is an ideal situation in which the `Server` class does not depend on the particular `Repository` implementation, but rather on the abstraction that the interface itself describes.

This describes a fundamental principle: the **Dependency Inversion Principle**, which says that:

- **High-level** modules should not depend on **low-level** modules. Both should depend on **abstractions** like the `Repository` interface.
- **Abstractions** should not depend on details. **Details** (concrete implementations) should depend on abstractions.

But why inversion? What, exactly, are you inverting?

In Figure 1.10, `Server` had a dependency on `Repository`, which contains implementation details. Instead, `Server` should have a dependency on the `Repository` interface. Now, all the `Repository` implementations depend on the same interface — and the dependency is reversed, as you can see in Figure 1.12.

Why abstraction is important

What you've learned in the previous paragraphs looks theoretical, but it has important practical consequences.

> **Note**: In theory, there's no difference between theory and practice, but in practice, there is :]

You might ask, why do you need to manage different implementations for the `Repository` abstraction? This is usually an interface to a database, the part of a project that changes less frequently compared to the UI.As mentioned in a previous note, you should always have at least one implementation of any abstraction for testing. In Figure 1.12, this is called `RepositoryMock`.

How would you test the `Server` class you wrote for the composition case described in Figure 1.10?

```
class Server {
    private val repository = Repository()

    fun receive(data: Data) {
        repository.save(data)
    }
}
```

If you want to test this class, you need to change it. If you change it, then this is not the same class anymore. Consider, then, **interface inheritance** and the following implementation:

```
class Server(val repository: Repository) {
  fun receive(data: Data) {
    repository.save(data)
  }
}
```

Now, in your test, you just have to pass the mock implementation of the `Repository` instance. If you use Mockito, this looks something like the following:

```
class ServerTest {
  @Test
  fun `When Data Received Save Method is Invoked On
Repository`() {
    // 1
    val repository = mock<Repository>()
    // 2
    val server = Server(repository)
    // 3
    val dataToBeSaved = Data(10)
    server.receive(dataToBeSaved)
    // 4
    verify(repository).save(dataToBeSaved)
  }
}
```

Here you:

1. Use Mockito to create an instance of the mock implementation of the `Repository` interface to use for testing.
2. Instantiate the `Server`, passing the previously-created mocked instance of `Repository` as a parameter for the primary constructor.
3. Create `Data()`, which you pass as a parameter for `receive()`.
4. Verify that you've invoked `save()` on the `Repository` mock with the expected parameter.

> **Note**: The previous code uses the Mockito testing framework, which is outside the scope of this book. If you want to learn more about testing, read the **Android Test-Driven Development by Tutorials** book. You can implement the same test without Mockito, as you'll see in the **Challenge 3** for this chapter.

This is a typical example of how thinking in terms of abstraction can help in the creation, modification and testing of your code.

Challenges

Now that you've learned some important theory, it's time for a few quick challenges.

Challenge 1: What type of dependency?

Have a look at this UML diagram in Figure 1.13. What type of dependency is described in each part?

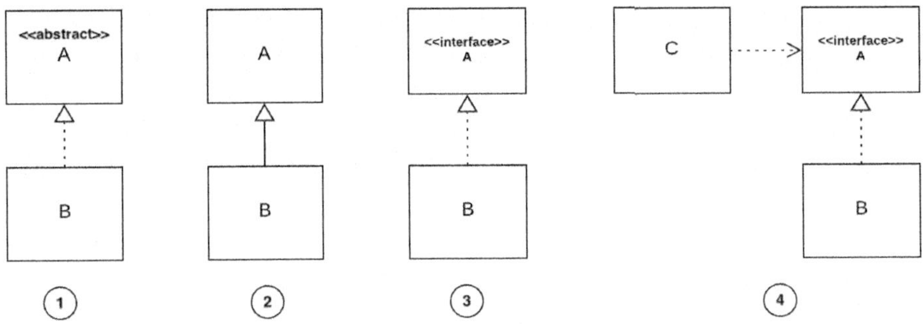

Figure 1.13 - Challenge 1 - Type of dependency

Challenge 2: Dependency in code

How would you represent the dependencies in Figure 1.13 in code? Write a Kotlin snippet for each one.

Challenge 3: Testing without Mockito

Earlier in this chapter, you learned that `RepositoryMock` is an implementation of `Repository` to use for testing. How would you implement it to test `Server` without the Mockito framework?

Challenge solutions

Challenge solution 1: What type of dependency?

In Figure 1.13, you have different types of dependency. Specifically:

1. This is an **implementation inheritance**. Class B is a realization of the abstract class A.
2. This is also an **implementation inheritance** between two concrete classes, A and B. If using Kotlin, class A might also have an «open» stereotype. UML is extensible, so nobody can prevent you from using the stereotype you need as soon as it has a simple and intuitive meaning.
3. The third dependency is an **interface inheritance**. This shows class B implementing interface A.
4. The last dependency is a **loosely coupled** dependency. Class C depends on abstraction A. Class B is a realization of A.

Challenge solution 2: Dependency in code

If you did the previous challenge, this should be a piece of cake. The code for each case is:

Case 1

```
abstract class A

class B : A()
```

Case 2

```
open class A

class B : A()
```

Case 3

```
interface A

class B : A
```

Case 4

```
interface A

class B : A

class C(val a: A)

fun main() {
  val a: A = B()
  val c = C(a)
}
```

Challenge solution 3: Testing without Mockito

The testing code in the **Why abstraction is important** paragraph is:

```
class ServerTest {
  @Test
  fun `When Data Received Save Method is Invoked On
Repository`() {
    // 1
    val repository = mock<Repository>()
    // 2
    val server = Server(repository)
    // 3
    val dataToBeSaved = Data(10)
    server.receive(dataToBeSaved)
    // 4
    verify(repository).save(dataToBeSaved)
  }
}
```

If the Mockito framework is not available, you need to define a mock implementation for the `Repository` interface, then create `RepositoryMock`. A possible solution is:

```
// 1
class RepositoryMock : Repository {
  // 2
  var receivedData: Data? = null

  override fun save(data: Data) {
    // 3
    receivedData = data
  }
}
```

Here you:

1. Create `RepositoryMock`, implementing the `Repository` interface.
2. Define the public `receivedData` variable.
3. Implement `save()`, saving the received parameter `data` to the local variable `receivedData`.

Now, the testing code can be:

```
fun main() {
  val repository = RepositoryMock()
  val server = Server(repository)
  val dataToBeSaved = Data(10)
  server.receive(dataToBeSaved)
  assert(repository.receivedData == dataToBeSaved) // HERE
}
```

The test is successful if the value of the `receivedData` equals the value passed to the `receive()` function of the server. Of course, using a framework like JUnit or Mockito makes the testing experience better from the engineering tools perspective, but the point doesn't change.

Note: In this case, you're not actually testing interaction but state, so the proper name for `RepositoryMock` should be `RepositoryFake`.

Key points

- Dependency is everywhere — you can't avoid it altogether.
- In computer science, you need to control dependency using the proper patterns.
- Implementation inheritance is the strongest type of dependency.
- Program to an interface, not an implementation.
- Interface inheritance is a *healthy* type of dependency.
- It's better to depend on what an entity **DOES** rather than what an entity **IS**.

Where to go from here?

In this first chapter, you learned what dependency means and how you can limit its impact. You've seen that a good level of abstraction allows you to write better code. Good code is easy to change.

If you want to learn more about the concepts and libraries of this chapter, take a look at:

- The SOLID Principles (https://en.wikipedia.org/wiki/SOLID) and, in particular, the Dependency Inversion Principle (https://en.wikipedia.org/wiki/Dependency_inversion_principle)
- Android Test-Driven Development By Tutorials (https://www.raywenderlich.com/books/android-test-driven-development-by-tutorials)
- [Advanced Android App Architecture] (https://www.raywenderlich.com/books/advanced-android-app-architecture)
- Mockito Testing Framework (https://site.mockito.org/)

Now, it's time for some code!

Chapter 2: Meet the Busso App

By Massimo Carli

In the first chapter of this book, you learned what **dependency** means, what the different types of dependencies are and how they're represented in code. You learned details about:

- Implementation Inheritance
- Composition
- Aggregation
- Interface Inheritance

You saw examples of each type of dependency and you understood which works better in various situations. Using UML diagrams, you also learned why dependency is something you need to control if you want your code to be maintainable. You saw why applying these principles using design patterns is important to make your code testable.

So far, this book has contained a lot of theory with many concepts you need to master if you want to successfully use libraries like Dagger or Hilt for Dependency Injection (**DI**) on Android. Now, it's time to move beyond theory and start coding.

In this chapter, you'll get to know the **Busso App**, which you'll work on and improve throughout this book. It's a client-server app where the server is implemented using **Ktor**.

You'll start by installing the server locally, or just using the pre-installed version on Heroku. Then you'll configure, build and run the Busso Android App.

The version of the app you start with is basic, not something to be proud of. You'll spend the last part of the chapter understanding why and taking the first steps to improve it.

The Busso App

Throughout this book, you'll implement the Busso App, which allows you to find bus stops near you and information about arrival times. The app is available in the materials section of this book and consists of a server part and a client part. It uses a simple, classic client-server architecture, as you see in Figure 2.1:

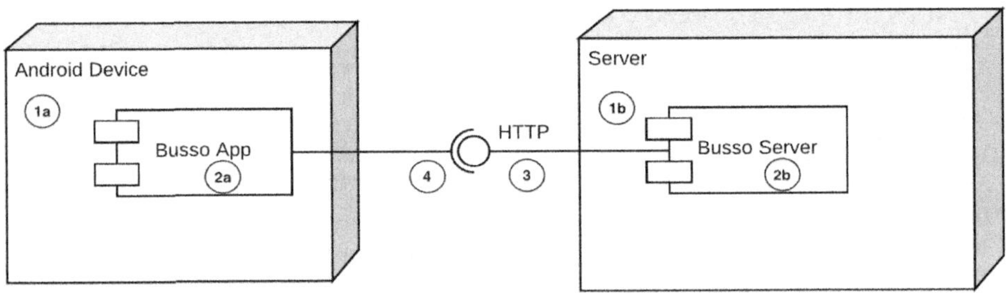

Figure 2.1 — Client Server Architecture

The UML diagram in Figure 2.1 is a **deployment diagram** that shows you many interesting bits of information:

1. The big boxes represent physical machines like computers, devices or servers. You call them **nodes**.
2. The boxes with the two small rectangles on the left edge are **components**. The **Busso App** component lives in the device while the **Busso Server** lives on a server machine, probably in the cloud.
3. The **Busso Server** exposes an interface you represent using something called a **lollipop**. You can use a label to give information about the specific protocol used in the communication — in this case, HTTP.
4. The **Busso App** interacts with the HTTP interface the **Busso Server** provides. Represent this with a semicircle embracing the lollipop.

Before going into the details of these components, run the app using the following steps.

Installing and running the Busso Server

Busso Server uses **Ktor**, which you can open using IntelliJ.

> **Note**: You don't need to know the details now, but if you're curious, you can read more about Busso Server in the Appendix of this book.

> **Note**: If you don't want to run the Busso Server **locally**, there's an existing installation running on **Heroku**. Just skip to the next section to find out how to use it.

Open the **BussoServer** project and you'll get the following structure of directories:

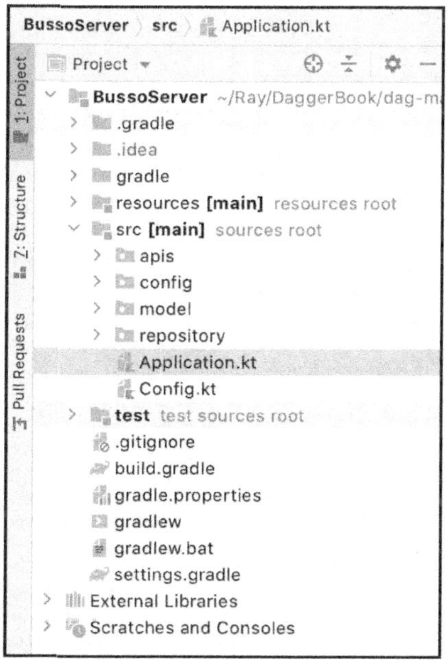

Figure 2.2 — Busso Server File Structure

Now, open **Application.kt** and find `main` function, which looks like this:

```
fun main(args: Array<String>): Unit =
io.ktor.server.netty.EngineMain.main(args)
```

Click on the arrow on the left of the code, as in Figure 2.3:

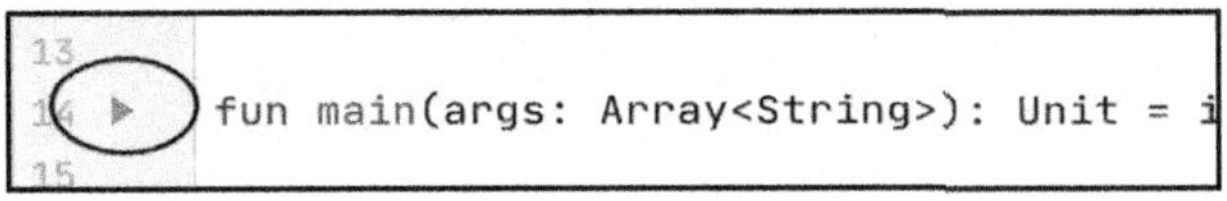

Figure 2.3 — Run Busso Server from the code

Alternatively, you can use the same icon in the **Configurations** section of the IntelliJ toolbar, as shown in Figure 2.4:

Figure 2.4 — Run Busso Server from Configurations

Now the server starts and you'll see some log messages in the **Run** section of IntelliJ, ending with something like:

```
2020-07-30 01:12:01.177 [main] INFO  Application - No
ktor.deployment.watch patterns specified, automatic reload is
not active
2020-07-30 01:12:03.320 [main] INFO  Application - Responding at
http://0.0.0.0:8080
```

If you get this, the Busso Server is running. Congratulations!

Now, your next step is to connect the server to the Busso Android App.

Building and running the Busso Android App

In the previous section, you started the Busso Server. Now it's time to build and run the Busso Android App. For this, you need to:

1. Define the address of the server
2. Configure network security
3. Build and run the app

> **Note**: If you use the Busso Server on Heroku, you can skip this configuration and follow the instructions in the section, "Running the Busso Server on Heroku".

Defining the server address

Use **Android Studio** to open the **Busso** project in the **starter** folder of the material for this chapter. You'll see the file structure in Figure 2.5.

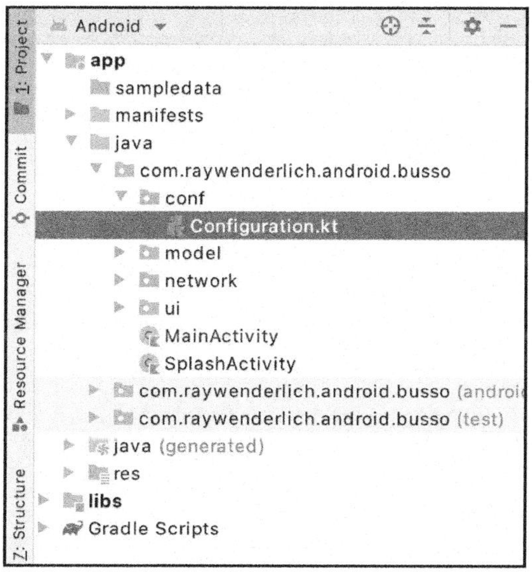

Figure 2.5 — Busso Android File Structure

Configuration.kt contains the following code:

```
// INSERT THE IP FOR YOUR SERVER HERE
const val BUSSO_SERVER_BASE_URL = "http://<YOUR SERVER IP>:8080/
api/v1/"
```

The Busso App doesn't know where to connect yet. You need to change this to include the IP of your server. But how do you determine what that IP is? You need to find the IP of your server machine in your local network.

> **Note**: You can't just use **localhost** or **127.0.0.1** because that would be the IP address of your Android device, not the device where the Busso Server is running.

If you're using a Mac, open a terminal and run the following command if you're using ethernet:

```
# ipconfig getifaddr en0
```

Or this, if you're on wireless:

```
# ipconfig getifaddr en1
```

You'll get an IP like this:

```
# 192.168.1.124
```

Remember that your specific IP will be different from the one shown above.

On Windows, run the `ifconfig` command to get the same information from a terminal prompt.

Now, in **Configuration.kt**, replace <`YOUR SERVER IP`> with your IP. With the previous value, your code would be:

```
// INSERT THE IP FOR YOUR SERVER HERE
const val BUSSO_SERVER_BASE_URL = "http://192.168.1.124:8080/
api/v1/"
```

Great, you've completed the first step!

Configuring network security

As you can see, the local server uses the HTTP protocol, which requires additional configuration on the client side. Locate and open **network_security_config.xml** as a resource of XML type, like in Figure 2.6:

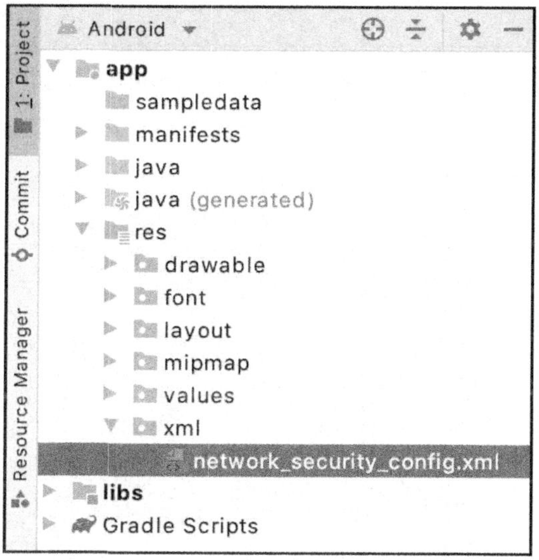

Figure 2.6 – Allow the HTTP protocol from the Android Client

You'll get the following XML content:

```
<?xml version="1.0" encoding="utf-8"?>
<network-security-config>
  <domain-config cleartextTrafficPermitted="true">
    <domain includeSubdomains="true"><!-- YOUR SERVER IP --></
domain>
  </domain-config>
</network-security-config>
```

Next, replace `<!-- YOUR SERVER IP -->` with the same IP you got earlier.

Using the IP value from the previous example, you'd end up with:

```
<?xml version="1.0" encoding="utf-8"?>
<network-security-config>
  <domain-config cleartextTrafficPermitted="true">
    <domain includeSubdomains="true">192.168.1.124</domain>
  </domain-config>
</network-security-config>
```

Now, everything's set up and you're ready to build and run.

Building and running the app

Now, you can run the app using an emulator or a real device by selecting the arrow shown in Figure 2.7:

Figure 2.7 — Run the Busso Android App

When the app starts for the first time, it'll show the **Splash Screen** and then the dialog asking for location permissions, as in Figure 2.8:

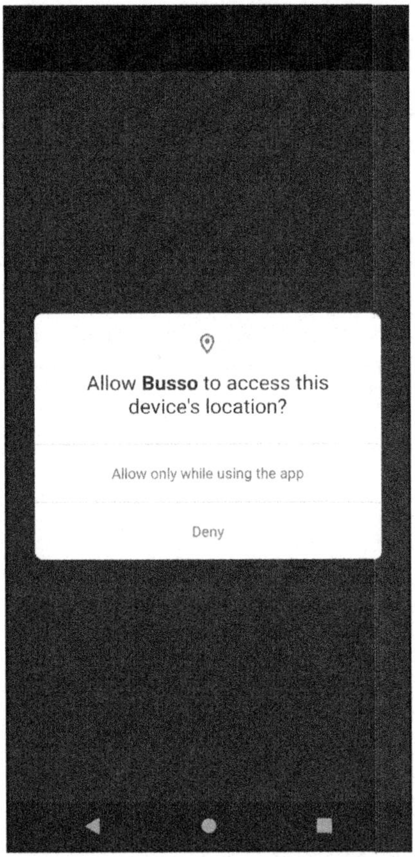

Figure 2.8 — Asking for Permission

Of course, if you want to use the app, you have to select the **Allow while using the app** option. This will bring you to the screen shown in Figure 2.9:

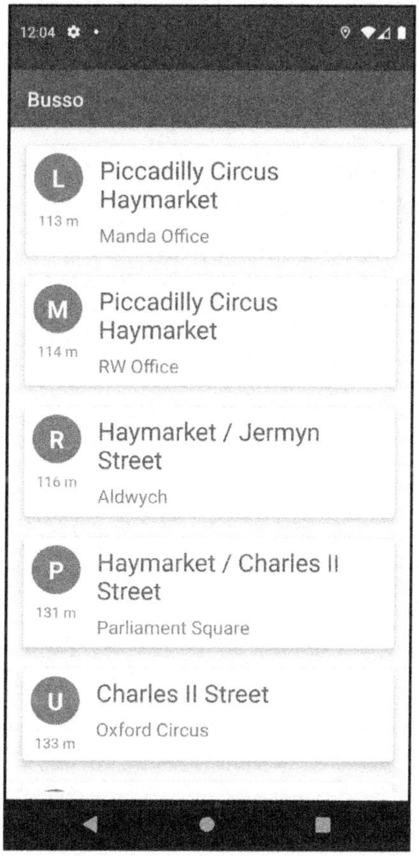

Figure 2.9 — Bus Stops close to you

If you have a similar result, great job! You've successfully run the Busso Android App.

You're getting fake data — you're not necessarily in London :] — but that data comes from the Busso Server. For each bus stop, you'll see something similar to Figure 2.10:

Figure 2.10 — Bus Stop data

You can see:

- An **indicator** of the bus stop, like **M** in the picture.
- Your **distance** from the bus stop in meters, like **114 m**.
- The name of the bus stop. For example, **Piccadilly Circus Haymarket**.
- The destination: **RW Office**

Now, select one of the cards and you'll come to a second screen:

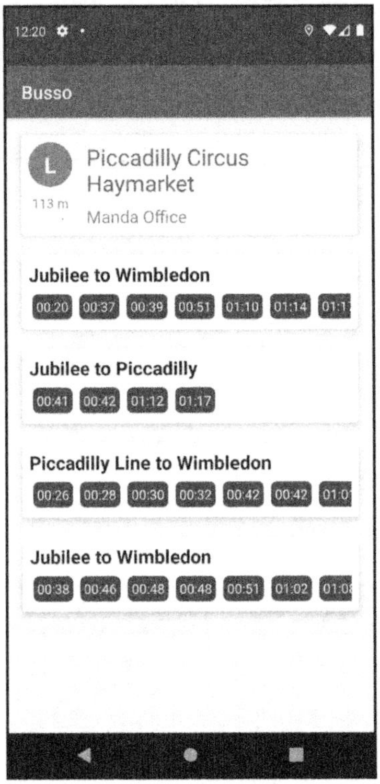

Figure 2.11 — Arrival time for the Bus

Below the information regarding the selected bus stop in the header, you can see a list of all the lines with their destinations, as well as a list of arrival times. Again, the data is fake but comes from the Busso Server.

The Busso App is now running and you're ready to start the journey through design principles and, specifically, dependency injection.

Running the Busso Server on Heroku

As mentioned earlier, you might not want to build and run the Busso Server on your own machine. Instead, you can use a running app that's available on Heroku at the following address:

```
https://busso-server.herokuapp.com/
```

Using this server has two main advantages:

- You don't overload your machine running the **Busso Server Process**.
- The app can use the **HTTPS** protocol, while the local installation uses **HTTP**. Using the **HTTPS** protocol, you don't need the configuration in Figure 2.6 anymore.

You can easily verify that the server is up and running by accessing the previous URL with your favorite browser. If you use Chrome, you'll get what is shown in Figure 2.12:

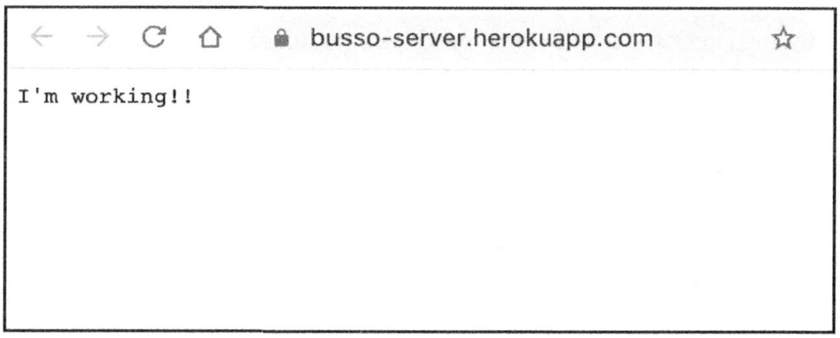

Figure 2.12 — Accessing the public Busso Server

Configuring the Busso App for the Heroku server

To use the server installation on Heroku, you need to enter the following code into **Configuration.kt**:

```
const val BUSSO_SERVER_BASE_URL = "https://busso-
server.herokuapp.com/api/v1/"
```

Next, you need to put a valid value into the **xml** resource folder in **network_security_config.xml**, like this:

```
<?xml version="1.0" encoding="utf-8"?>
<network-security-config>
```

```
    <domain-config cleartextTrafficPermitted="true">
      <domain includeSubdomains="true">0.0.0.0</domain>
    </domain-config>
  </network-security-config>
```

The specific IP you use here isn't important as long as it's a valid IP address.

Improving the Busso App

Do you like the Busso App? Well, it works, but you can't say the quality is the best. But what are the problems, and how can you fix them?

Specifically, the Busso App has:

- A lot of copied and pasted code that leads to repetition you should avoid.
- No concept of lifecycle or scope.
- No unit tests.

In the following sections, you'll learn more about these problems and get some ideas for solving them.

Reducing repetition

SplashActivity.kt contains the following code:

```
override fun onCreate(savedInstanceState: Bundle?) {
  super.onCreate(savedInstanceState)
  makeFullScreen()
  setContentView(R.layout.activity_splash)
  // 1
  locationManager = getSystemService(Context.LOCATION_SERVICE)
as LocationManager
  // 2
  locationObservable =
provideRxLocationObservable(locationManager, permissionChecker)
  // 3
  navigator = NavigatorImpl(this)
}
```

Here, you:

1. Get the reference to `LocationManager` using `getSystemService()`.
2. Invoke `provideRxLocationObservable()` to get a reference to `Observable<LocationEvent>`, which you'll subscribe to later. This will provide location events.
3. Instantiate `NavigatorImpl`, passing the reference to `Activity` as the primary constructor parameter.

In **BusStopFragment.kt**, you'll find the following code:

```
override fun onAttach(context: Context) {
  super.onAttach(context)
  // 1
  locationManager =
context.getSystemService(Context.LOCATION_SERVICE) as
LocationManager
  // 2
  locationObservable =
provideRxLocationObservable(locationManager,
grantedPermissionChecker)
  navigator = NavigatorImpl(context as Activity)
}
```

The code in `onAttach()` does basically the same thing as the previous example, because it:

1. Gets the reference to `LocationManager`.
2. Invokes `provideRxLocationObservable()` to get `Observable<LocationEvent>`.
3. Creates another instance of `NavigatorImpl`, passing the reference to the same `Activity` as in the previous example.

Better would be to share some of the objects between different components to reduce code duplication. This is a problem that dependency injection helps solve, as you'll see in the following chapters.

Taking scope and lifecycle into consideration

In any Android app, all the other components of the same app should share some objects, while other objects should exist while a specific `Activity` or `Fragment` exists. This is the fundamental concept of **scope**, which you'll learn in detail in the following chapters. Scope is a vital part of resource management.

Adding application scope

Look at `useLocation()` in **BusStopFragment.kt**:

```
private fun useLocation(location: GeoLocation) {
  context?.let { ctx ->
    disposables.add(
        provideBussoEndPoint(ctx) // HERE
            .findBusStopByLocation(location.latitude,
location.longitude, 500)
            .subscribeOn(Schedulers.io())
            .observeOn(AndroidSchedulers.mainThread())
            .map(::mapBusStop)
            .subscribe(busStopAdapter::submitList, ::handleBusSt
opError)
    )
  }
}
```

Every time you invoke `provideBussoEndPoint(ctx)`, you create a different instance of the implementation of the `BussoEndpoint` interface that **Retrofit** provides.

> **Note**: Retrofit (https://github.com/square/retrofit) is a library created by **Square** that allows you to implement the network layer in a declarative and easy way.

This also happens in `getBusArrivals()` in **BusArrivalFragment.kt**.

```
private fun getBusArrivals() {
  val busStopId = arguments?.getString(BUS_STOP_ID) ?: ""
  context?.let { ctx ->
    disposables.add(
        provideBussoEndPoint(ctx)
            .findArrivals(busStopId)
            .subscribeOn(Schedulers.io())
            .observeOn(AndroidSchedulers.mainThread())
            .map(::mapBusArrivals)
            .subscribe(::handleBusArrival, ::handleBusArrivalErr
```

```
or)
      )
    }
  }
```

Only one instance of a `BussoEndpoint` implementation should exist, and `BusStopFragment`, `BusArrivalFragment` and all the other places where you need to access the server should all share it.

`BussoEndpoint` should have **the same lifecycle as the app**.

Adding activity scope

Other objects should have a different lifecycle, such as the `Navigator` implementation in **NavigatorImpl.kt** located in **libs/ui/navigation**, as shown in Figure 2.13:

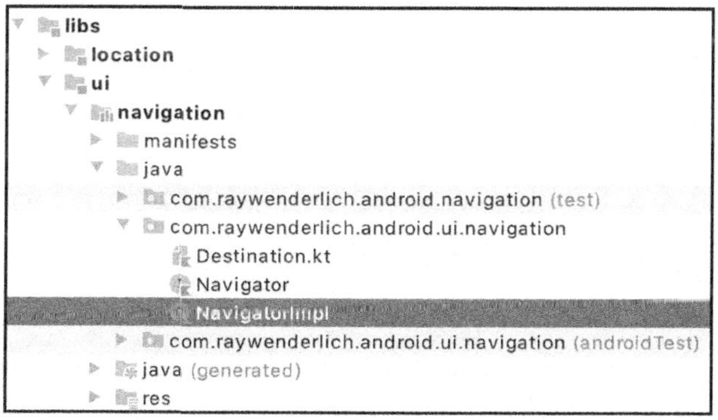

Figure 2.13 — The NavigatorImpl class

```
class NavigatorImpl(private val activity: Activity) : Navigator
{
  override fun navigateTo(destination: Destination, params:
Bundle?) {
    // ...
  }
}
```

As you can see, `NavigatorImpl` depends on the `Activity` that it accepts as the parameter in its primary constructor.

This means that `NavigatorImpl` should have the same lifecycle as the `Activity` you use for its creation. This currently isn't happening, as you can see in `onAttach()` in **BusStopFragment.kt**:

```
override fun onAttach(context: Context) {
```

```
    super.onAttach(context)
    locationManager =
context.getSystemService(Context.LOCATION_SERVICE) as
LocationManager
    locationObservable =
provideRxLocationObservable(locationManager,
grantedPermissionChecker)
    navigator = NavigatorImpl(context as Activity) // HERE
}
```

This is something else you'll fix in the following chapters.

The importance of scope

The concept of **scope** is fundamental, and you'll read a lot about it in the following chapters.

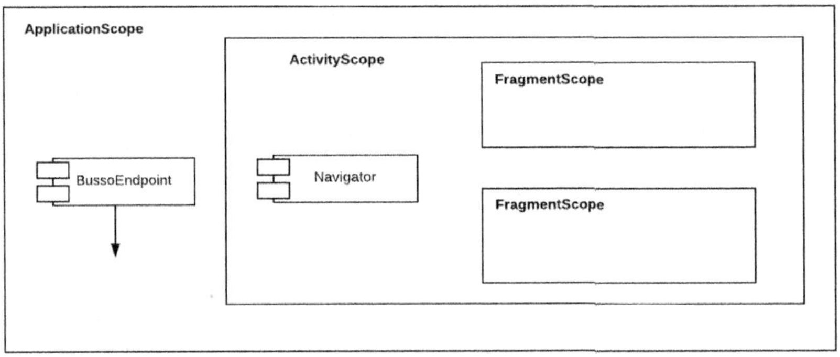

Figure 2.14 — Different scopes for different components

The diagram in Figure 2.14 gives you an idea about what the scope of the Busso App should be. `BussoEndpoint` should have the same scope as the app, while the `Navigator` should have the same scope as the `Activity`.

What isn't obvious in the diagram is that each component living within a scope should have access to the instance living in an external scope.

For instance, any component should be able to access the same `BussoEndpoint` implementation, `Fragments` living in a specific `Activity` should share the same instance of the `Navigator` implementation, and so on.

Don't worry if this isn't clear yet. You'll learn a lot about this concept in the following chapters.

Adding unit tests

The current implementation of the Busso App doesn't contain any unit tests at all. What a shame! Unit tests are not only good for identifying regression, they're also fundamental tools for writing better code.

> **Note**: As you'll see later in this chapter, the Rx Module for Location contains some tests. They're in a different module, though.

As it is now, the Busso App is almost impossible to test. Just have a look at **BusStopFragment.kt**. How would you test a function like this?

```
private fun useLocation(location: GeoLocation) {
  context?.let { ctx ->
    disposables.add(
        provideBussoEndPoint(ctx)
            .findBusStopByLocation(location.latitude,
location.longitude, 500)
            .subscribeOn(Schedulers.io())
            .observeOn(AndroidSchedulers.mainThread())
            .map(::mapBusStop)
            .subscribe(busStopAdapter::submitList, ::handleBusSt
opError)
    )
  }
}
```

In the following chapters, you'll see how using dependency injection and other design patterns will make the Busso App easy to test.

The Rx Module for location

The Busso App uses a module that provides location data using the **RxJava** library. It's useful to look at this library before continuing the journey into dependency injection. It's the module located in the directory structure in Figure 2.15.

Figure 2.15 — The RxLocationObservable.kt file

The same module also contains some unit tests, implemented in **RxLocationObservableKtTest**, which uses the **Robot Pattern**. This is actually the only module with some tests in the project so far.

The **Rx** module contains an implementation of the **APIs** defined in the **location/api** module in the **libs** folder, as you can see in Figure 2.16:

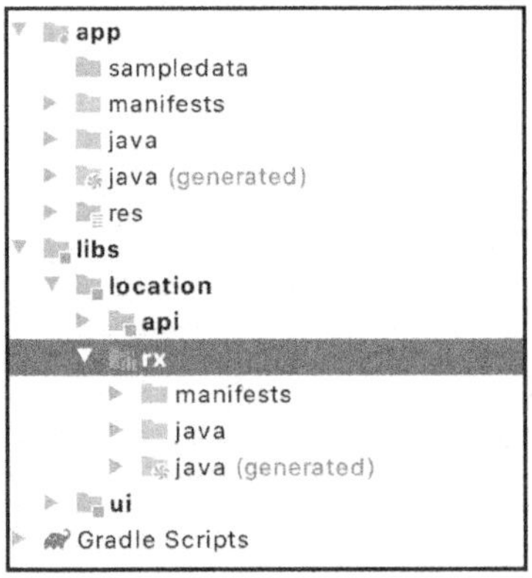

Figure 2.16 — RX implementation for the Location API

The API contains some basic definitions and abstractions that all the different implementations can use. In the **api** module, you'll find the `GeoLocation` data class, which describes a location in terms of latitude and longitude.

```
data class GeoLocation(
    val latitude: Double,
    val longitude: Double
)
```

Every **API** implementation should provide some events of the `LocationEvent` type in **LocationEvent.kt**. This is a sealed class that defines the following specific subtypes:

- `LocationPermissionRequest`
- `LocationPermissionGranted`
- `LocationNotAvailable`
- `LocationData`
- `LocationStatus`
- `LocationProviderEnabledChanged`

The events' names are self-explanatory but it's important to note that `LocationPermissionRequest` is an event that fires when the permission to access the user's location is missing, and that you need to put some request permission procedure in place.

On the other hand, `LocationPermissionGranted` fires if you've already obtained the permission.

The most important event is `LocationData`, which contains the information about the location in an object of type `GeoLocation`.

Permission can be granted in many ways, so you need an abstraction like the one defined by:

```
interface GeoLocationPermissionChecker {
  val isPermissionGiven: Boolean
}
```

The **Rx** module contains an implementation of the previous APIs that use **RxJava** or **RxKotlin**. You can take a look at its logic in **RxLocationObservable.kt**.

> **Note**: RxJava is a library that implements the React specification. It's used in many commercial apps. This book is not about RxJava, but you can learn all about it in the **Reactive Programming With Kotlin** book.

Testing the RxLocation module

The **Rx** module is fairly well tested. Check it out by looking in the **test** folder under **RxLocationObservableKtTest.kt** and taking a quick look at the following test:

```
@Test
fun
whenPermissionIsDeniedLocationPermissionRequestIsSentAndThenComp
letes() {
  rxLocationTest(context) {
    Given {
      permissionIsDenied()
    }
    When {
      subscribeRx()
    }
    Then {
      permissionRequestIsFired()
      isComplete()
    }
  }
}
```

It verifies that you receive a `LocationPermissionRequest` when you subscribe to the `RxLocationObservable` without having the necessary permissions. After that, `Observable` will complete.

> **Note**: The Robot Pattern is a useful testing pattern that allows you to write more readable tests. You can learn all about the Robot pattern and other testing procedures in the Android Test-Driven Development by Tutorials (https://www.raywenderlich.com/books/android-test-driven-development-by-tutorials) book.

Challenge

Challenge 1: Some unit tests as a warm-up

After building and running the Busso App, it's time for a nice challenge.As you know, the Busso App doesn't have unit tests. Can you write some for the code related to the **BusStopMapper.kt** and **BusArrivalMapper.kt** files, as shown in Figure 2.17?

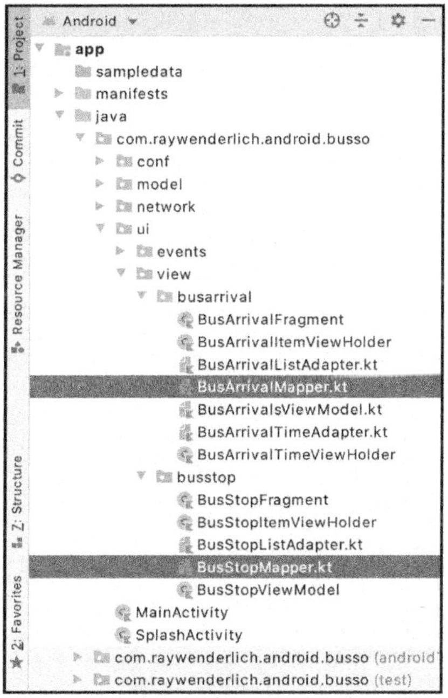

Figure 2.17 — The Mapper classes

These files contain simple functions for mapping the `Model` you get from the network, with the `ViewModel` you use to display information in the UI.

Challenge solution: Some unit tests as a warm-up

BusStopMapper.kt contains `mapBusStop()`, which you use to convert a `BusStop` model into a `BusStopViewModel`. What's the difference?

`BusStop` contains pure data about a bus stop, which you get from the server. It looks like this:

```
data class BusStop(
    val id: String,
    val name: String,
    val location: GeoLocation,
    val direction: String?,
    val indicator: String?,
    val distance: Float?
)
```

`BusStopViewModel` contains the information that's actually displayed in the app, such as information about the locale or some I18N (Internationalization) Strings. In this case, it's:

```
data class BusStopViewModel(
    val stopId: String,
    val stopName: String,
    val stopDirection: String,
    val stopIndicator: String,
    val stopDistance: String
)
```

For instance, `BusModel`'s distance property is mapped onto the `stopDistance` property of `BusStopViewModel`. The former is an optional `Float` and the latter is a `String`. Why do you need to test these?

Tests allow you to write better code. In this case, `mapBusStop()` is pure, so you have to verify that for a given input, the output is what you expect.

Open **BusStopMapper.kt** and select the name of `mapBusStop()`. Now, open the quick actions menu with **Control - Enter** to what's shown in Figure 2.18:

Figure 2.18 — Create a new Unit Test

Select the **Test...** menu item and the dialog in Figure 2.19 will appear:

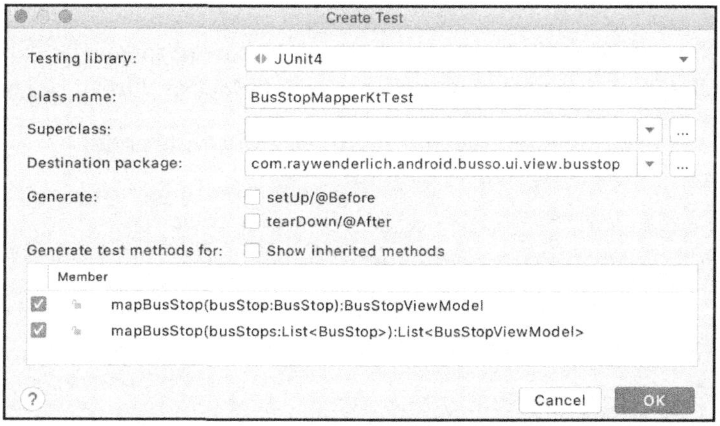

Figure 2.19 — Create Test information

Now, press the **OK** button and a new dialog will appear, asking where to put the test you're going to create. In this case, you're creating a unit test, so select the **test** folder and select the **OK** button again:

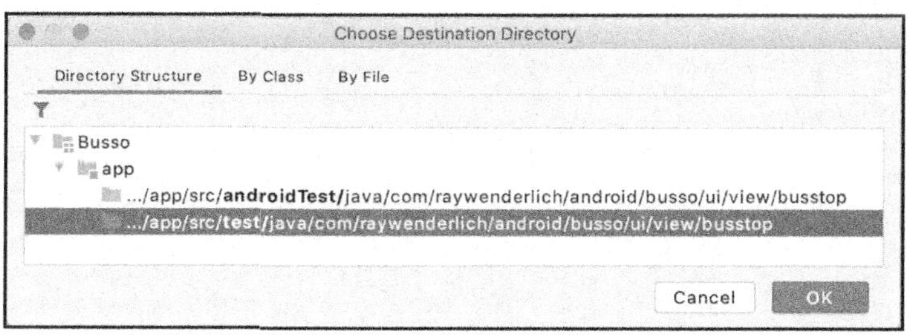

Figure 2.20 — Select the test folder

Now, Android Studio will create a new file for you, like this:

```
class BusStopMapperKtTest {
  @Test
  fun mapBusStop() {
  }

  @Test
  fun testMapBusStop() {
  }
}
```

The first question you need to ask yourself when writing a unit test is: **What am I testing?**

In this case, the answer is that, given a `BusStop`, you need to get the expected `BusStopViewModel`. This must be true in the happy case and in all the edge cases.

Now, replace the existing `mapBusStop()` with the following code:

```
@Test
fun
mapBusStop_givenCompleteBusStop_returnsCompleteBusStopViewModel(
) {
  // 1
  val inputBusStop = BusStop(
      "id",
      "stopName",
      GeoLocation(1.0, 2.0),
      "direction",
      "indicator",
      123F
  )
  // 2
  val expectedViewModel = BusStopViewModel(
      "id",
      "stopName",
      "direction",
      "indicator",
      "123 m"
  )
  // 3
  assertEquals(expectedViewModel, mapBusStop(inputBusStop))
}
```

In this test, you:

1. Create a `BusStop` object to use as input for the function.
2. Define an instance of `BusStopViewModel` like the one you expect as result.
3. Use JUnit to verify the result is what you expected.

Now, you can run the test selecting the arrow as in Figure 2.21:

Figure 2.21 — Run the Unit Test

If everything is fine, you'll get a checkmarks as a result like the following:

Figure 2.22 — Successful test

Congratulations and thank you! You've improved the Busso App — but there's still a lot to do.

As an exercise, add the missing tests and check if they're similar to the ones you'll find in the final project for this chapter.

Key points

- The Busso App is a **client-server** app.
- The Busso Server has been implemented with **Ktor**. You can run it locally or use the existing Heroku installation.
- The Busso App works, but you can improve it by removing code duplication and adding unit tests.
- The concept of **scope** or **lifecycle** is fundamental and you'll learn much more about it throughout this book.

Chapter 3: Dependency Injection

By Massimo Carli

In the first chapter, you learned what **dependency** means and how you can limit its impact during the development of your app. You learned to prefer **aggregation** over **composition** because that allows you to change the implementation of `Repository` without changing the implementation of `Server`, as described by the following UML diagram:

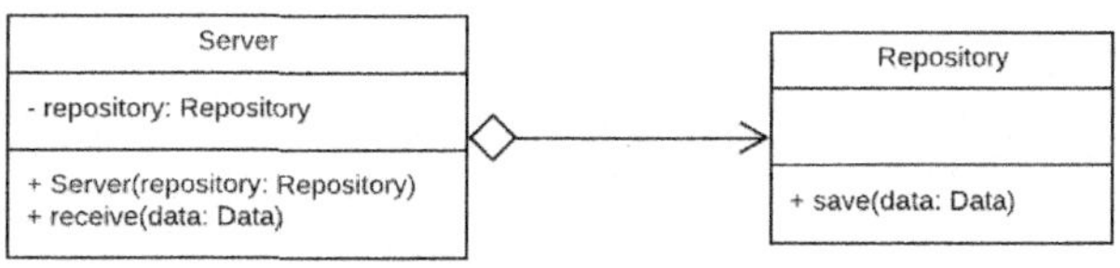

Figure 3.1 - Aggregation

In code, you can represent that concept like this:

```
class Server(val repository: Repository) {
  fun receive(data: Data) {
    repository.save(data)
  }
}
```

With this pattern, `Server` has no responsibility for the creation of the specific `Repository`. That syntax is just saying that `Server` needs a `Repository` to work. In other words, `Server` **depends on** `Repository`.

In the second chapter, you looked at the **Busso App**. You learned how to build and run both the server and the Android app. You also looked at its code to understand how the **RxLocation** and **Navigator** modules work. More importantly, you learned why the architecture for the Busso App is not the best and what you could do to improve its quality.

In this chapter, you'll take your next step toward implementing a better app that's easier to test and modify. You'll keep the concept of **mass of the project** in mind, which you saw in the first chapter.

You'll start by refactoring the Busso App in a world without Dagger or Hilt. This is important if you want to really understand how those frameworks work and how you can use them to solve the dependency problem in a different, easier way.

Dependency injection

Looking at the previous code, which component is responsible for the creation of the `Repository` implementation you need to pass as parameter of the `Server` primary constructor?

It's **Main**, which contains all the "dirty" code you need to create the necessary instances for the app, binding them according to their dependencies.

OK, so how do you describe a dependency between different objects? You just follow some coding rules, like the one you already used in the `Server`/`Repository` example. By making `Repository` a primary constructor parameter for `Server`, you explicitly defined a dependency between them.

In this example, a possible **Main** component is the following `main()` function:

```
fun main() {
  // 1
  val repository = RepositoryImpl()
  // 2
  val server = Server(repository)
  // ...
  val data = Data()
  server.receive(data)
  // ...
}
```

This code creates:

1. The instance of the `RepositoryImpl` as an implementation of the `Repository` interface.
2. A `Server` that passes the repository instance as a parameter of the primary constructor.

You can say that the **Main** component **injects** a `Repository` into `Server`.

This approach leads to a technique called **Dependency Injection (DI)**, which describes the process in which an external entity is responsible for **creating** all the instances of the components an app requires. It then **injects** them according to some dependency rules.

By changing **Main**, you modify what you can inject. This reduces the impact of a change, thus reducing dependency.

> **Note**: Spoiler alert! Looking at the previous code, you understand that `Server` needs a `Repository` because it's a required parameter of its primary constructor. The `Server` depends on the `Repository`. Is this enough to somehow generate the code you have into `main()`? Sometimes yes, and sometimes you'll need more information, as you'll see in the following chapters.

Currently, the Busso App doesn't use this method, which makes testing and changes in general very expensive.

In the following sections of this chapter, you'll start applying these principles to the Busso App, improving its quality and reducing its mass.

Types of injection

In the previous example, you learned how to define a dependency between two classes by making `Repository` a required constructor parameter for `Server`. This is just one way to implement dependency injection. The different types of injection are:

- **Constructor** injection
- **Field** injection
- **Method** injection

Take a closer look at each of these now so you can use them in the Busso App later.

Constructor injection

This is the type of injection you saw in the previous example, where the **dependent type** (`Server`) declares the dependency on a **dependency type** (`Repository`) using the primary constructor.

```
class Server(private val repository: Repository) {
  fun receive(data: Date) {
    repository.save(date)
  }
}
```

In the code above, you can't create a `Server` without passing the reference of a `Repository`. The former depends on the latter.

Also, note the presence of the **private** visibility modifier, which makes the `repository` property **read-only** and `Server` class **immutable**. This is possible because the binding between the two objects happens during the creation of the dependent one — `Server`, in this case.

For the same reason, **this is the best type of injection you can achieve if you have control over the creation of the components in the dependency relation.**

Field injection

Constructor injection is the ideal type of injection but, unfortunately, it's not always possible. Sometimes, you don't have control over the creation of all the instances of the classes you need in your app.

This is strongly related to the definition of a **component**, which is something whose lifecycle is managed by a **container**. There's no component without a container. This is the case, for example, of `Activity` instances in any Android app.

> **Note**: The same is true for the other Android standard components represented by classes like `Service`, `ContentProvider` and `BroadcastReceiver`. If you think about it, these are the things you describe to the Android container using the **AndroidManifest.xml** file.

A possible alternative is to define **a property whose value is set after the creation of the instance it belongs to**. The type of the property is the dependency. This is called a **property injection**, which you can implement with the following code:

```
class Server () {
  lateinit var repository: Repository // HERE

  fun receive(data: Date) {
    repository.save (date)
  }
}
```

Using `lateinit var` ensures you've initialized the corresponding property before you use it. In this case, **Main** must obtain the reference to the **Repository** and then assign it to the related property, as in the following code:

```
fun main() {
  // 1
  val repository = RepositoryImpl()
  // 2
  val server = Server()
  // 3
  server.repository = repository
  // ...
  val data = Data()
  server.receive(data)
  // ...
}
```

Here you:

1. Create the instance of `RepositoryImpl` as an implementation of the `Repository` interface.
2. Create the instance for `Server`, whose primary constructor is the default one — the one with no parameters.
3. Assign the repository to the related `Server` property.

A possible hiccup is that `Server`'s state is inconsistent between points 2 and 3. This might cause problems in concurrent systems.

> **Note**: This book uses Kotlin, which doesn't have the concept of an **instance variable** of a class; it allows you to define **properties** instead. A property is the characteristic of an object that can be seen from the outside. This happens by using particular methods called **accessor** and **mutator**. The former are usually (but not necessarily) methods with the prefix **get**, while the latter methods start with **set**.
>
> For this reason, the definition of **field injection** in Kotlin can be a bit confusing. Don't worry, everything will be clear when you learn how to implement this with Dagger.

As mentioned, **field injection** is very important. It's the type of injection you'll often find when, while developing Android apps, you need to inject objects into `Fragment` or other standard components, like the ones mentioned earlier.

Method injection

For completeness, take a brief look at what **method injection** is. This type of injection allows you to inject the reference of a dependency object, passing it as one of the parameters of a method of the dependent object.

This code clarifies the concept:

```
class Server() {
  private var repository: Repository? = null

  fun receive(data: Date) {
    repository?.save(date)
  }

  fun fixRepo(repository: Repository) {
    this.repository = repository
  }
}
```

Using method injection, you assume that `null` is valid as an initial value for the `repository` property. In this case, you declare that `Server` can use a `Repository`, but it doesn't need to. This is why you don't use a `lateinit var`, like you would with a **field injection**, and you use the `?.` (safe call operator) while accessing the `repository` property into the `receive()` function.

In this example, **Main** can invoke `fixRepo()` to set the dependency between `Server` and `Repository`, as in the following code:

```
fun main() {
  val repository = RepositoryImpl()
  val server = Server()
  server.fixRepo(repository) // HERE
  // ...
  val data = Data()
  server.receive(data)
  // ...
}
```

Unlike field injection, method injection gives you the ability to inject multiple values with the same method, in case the method has more than one parameter. For instance, you might have something like:

```
class Dependent() {
  private var dep1: Dep1? = null
  private var dep2: Dep2? = null
  private var dep3: Dep3? = null

  fun fixDep(dep1: Dep1, dep2: Dep2, dep3: Dep3) {
    this.dep1 = dep1
    this.dep2 = dep2
    this.dep3 = dep3
  }
}
```

In this case, the problem is that you need to pass all the dependencies, even when you only need to set some of them.

Busso App dependency management

In the previous sections, you learned all the theory you need to improve the way the Busso App manages dependencies. Now, it's time to get to work.

Use **Android Studio** and open the **starter project** that's in the material for this chapter.

> **Note**: The starter project uses the existing Heroku server, but you can configure it for using a local server using the instructions in Chapter 2, "Meet the Busso App".

Build and run the Busso App, checking everything works as expected and you get what's shown in Figure 3.2:

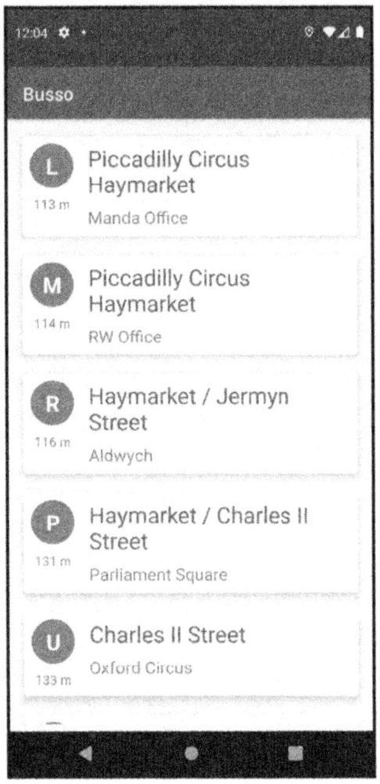

Figure 3.2 - The Busso App

Now, you're ready to start. There's a lot of work to do!

Dependency graph

When you want to improve the quality of any app, a good place to start is by defining the **dependency graph**.

In the examples above, you only had two objects: `Server` and `Repository`. In a real app, you often have more classes that depend on each other in many different ways.

To better understand this, open **SplashActivity.kt** and check the dependencies between the different classes or interfaces.

> **Note**: As a useful exercise, try to find the dependencies between different classes or interfaces in the **SplashActivity.kt**. Then compare your results with the description below.

In the previous chapter, you learned how to represent dependencies using a UML diagram. With the same language, you can create the **dependency diagram** in Figure 3.3:

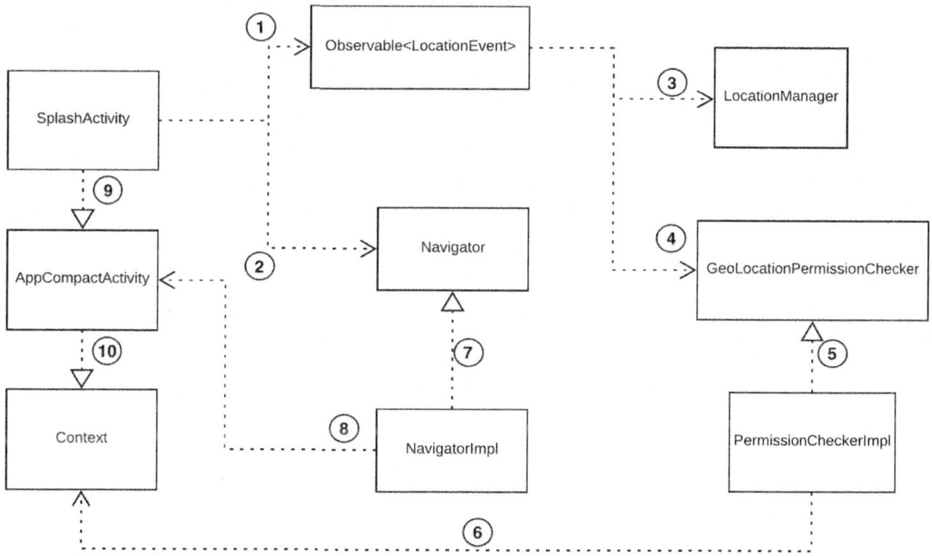

Figure 3.3 - SplashActivity dependency diagram

In this diagram, you can see many interesting things:

1. `SplashActivity` needs the reference to — and so **depends on** — an `Observable<LocationEvent>` to get information about the user's location and related permission requests.
2. The same activity also depends on the `Navigator` interface.
3. `Observable<LocationEvent>` depends on `LocationManager`.
4. To manage the permissions, `Observable<LocationEvent>` depends on a `GeoLocationPermissionChecker` implementation of `PermissionChecker` interface.
5. The component named `PermissionCheckerImpl` in the diagram was actually developed as an **object** but it definitely implements the `GeoLocationPermissionChecker` interface.
6. `PermissionCheckerImpl` defines an implementation of the `GeoLocationPermissionChecker` interface and depends on the `Context` abstraction.

7. `NavigatorImpl` is an implementation of the `Navigator` interface.
8. As you'll see in code later, `NavigatorImpl` depends on `AppCompactActivity`.
9. `AppCompactActivity` is as abstraction of `SplashActivity`.
10. This relationship represents `Context` as an abstraction of `AppCompactActivity`.

This diagram represents the dependency graph for `SplashActivity`. It contains different types of dependencies but it can't contain cycles. You can see that the dependencies in points 5 and 7 use **interface inheritance** and numbers 9 and 10 are examples of **implementation inheritance**, because `Context` is an abstraction the Android environment provides.

> **Note**: The diagram in Figure 3.3 is the representation of a **Direct Acyclic Graph, DAG** for short. It's the inspiration for the name **Dagger**.

This dependency diagram is the map you need to refer to when you want to manage dependencies in your app. It's a representation of a **dependency graph**, which is the set of all the objects an app uses, connected according to their dependencies.

In the next section, you'll learn how to use this diagram in the Busso App.

The service locator pattern

Now, you have the dependency diagram for `SplashActivity` and you've learned how dependency injection works. Now, it's time to start refactoring the Busso App.

A good place to start is with the definition of the **Main** object. This is the object responsible for the creation of the **dependency graph** for the app.

In this case, you're working on an `Activity`, which is a standard Android component. Because the Android environment is responsible for the lifecycle of any standard component, you can't use constructor injection. Instead, you need to implement something similar to field injection.

To do this, you need a way to:

1. Get a reference to the objects the app needs to do its job.
2. Assign the reference to these objects to the `lateinit var` properties of `SplashActivity`.

Start with a component responsible for providing the reference to the objects you need. This is the idea behind the **service locator** design pattern.

The ServiceLocator interface

Next, create a new package named **di** in the **com.raywenderlich.android.busso** package for the Busso app. Then add the following to **ServiceLocator.kt**:

```
interface ServiceLocator {
  /**
   * Returns the object of type A bound to a specific name
   */
  fun <A : Any> lookUp(name: String): A
}
```

In the first chapter, you learned to always **think of interface**. That's what you've done with the `ServiceLocator` interface, which is the abstraction for the homonym design pattern. This interface defines the `lookUp()` operation, which, given a specific object's name, returns its reference.

The initial ServiceLocator implementation

Now you can also provide an initial implementation for the `ServiceLocator` interface. Create **ServiceLocatorImpl.kt** in the same package of the interface with the following code:

```
class ServiceLocatorImpl : ServiceLocator {
  override fun <A : Any> lookUp(name: String): A = when (name) {
    else -> throw IllegalArgumentException("No component lookup
for the key: $name")
  }
}
```

At the moment, `ServiceLocatorImpl` throws an exception when you invoke `lookUp()` because it can't provide an object yet.

After this, the project should have a structure like in Figure 3.4:

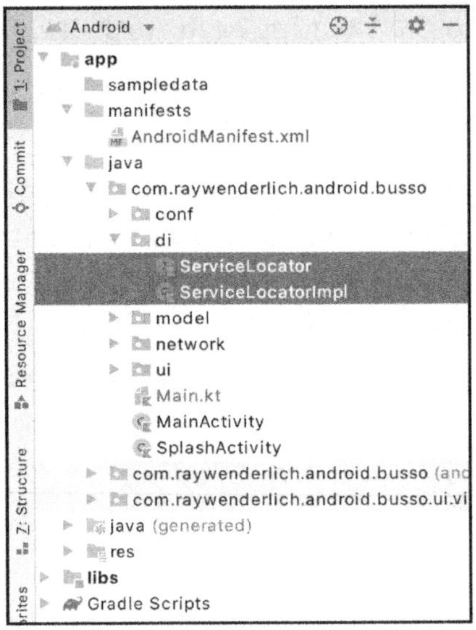

Figure 3.4 - Creation of the ServiceLocator.kt file into the di package

A **ServiceLocator** is a simple abstraction for any service that allows you to get the reference to a specific object given its name.

> **Note**: When you assign the value you get from a `ServiceLocator` using its `lookUp()` operation to a `lateinit var`, you're not actually using **injection**. Rather, you're using **dependency lookup**. You usually do this on the server side with abstractions like **Java Naming and Directory Interface** (JNDI).

Now you can start using the **ServiceLocator** in the Busso App.

Using ServiceLocator in your app

Start by creating a new **Main.kt** file in the main package for the Busso App, then add the following content:

```
class Main : Application() {
  // 1
  lateinit var serviceLocator: ServiceLocator

  override fun onCreate() {
    super.onCreate()
    // 2
    serviceLocator = ServiceLocatorImpl()
```

```
    }
}

// 3
internal fun <A: Any> AppCompatActivity.lookUp(name: String): A
=
  (applicationContext as Main).serviceLocator.lookUp(name)
```

This is the `Main` class where you:

1. Define a `lateinit var` for the reference to a `ServiceLocator` implementation.
2. Create an instance of `ServiceLocatorImpl` and assign it to the `serviceLocator` property.
3. Define the `lookUp()` **extension function** for `AppCompatActivity`, which allows you to easily look up components from any class that **IS-A** `AppCompatActivity`, like `SplashActivity`.

> **Exercise 3.1**: If you want to use TDD, you should already start writing the unit test for `ServiceLocatorImpl`.

`Main` is a custom `Application` for the Busso App that you need to declare to the Android environment by adding the following definition to **AndroidManifest.xml**, which is in the **manifests** folder in Figure 3.5:

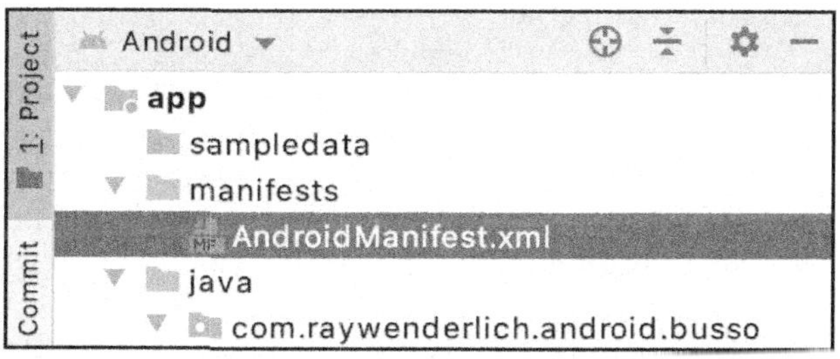

Figure 3.5 - Location for the AndroidManifest.xml file

```
<?xml version="1.0" encoding="utf-8"?>
<manifest xmlns:android="http://schemas.android.com/apk/res/
android"
  xmlns:tools="http://schemas.android.com/tools"
  package="com.raywenderlich.android.busso">

  <uses-permission android:name="android.permission.INTERNET" />
  <uses-permission
android:name="android.permission.ACCESS_FINE_LOCATION" />
```

```
  <application
    android:name=".Main" <!-- The Main component-->
    android:allowBackup="false"
    android:icon="@mipmap/ic_launcher"
    android:label="@string/app_name"
    android:networkSecurityConfig="@xml/network_security_config"
    android:roundIcon="@mipmap/ic_launcher_round"
    android:supportsRtl="true"
    android:theme="@style/AppTheme"
    tools:ignore="GoogleAppIndexingWarning">
    <!-- ... -->
  </application>

</manifest>
```

Now you're ready to:

1. Create the instances your app needs.
2. Register those objects with the `ServiceLocator` for a given name.
3. Use the same name to look up the reference to the registered objects from any of the Busso App activities.

Next, you'll start with a simple one: `LocationManager`.

Using ServiceLocator with LocationManager

You're now ready to use **ServiceLocator** to manage the instances of your app in a single place, thus simplifying its code.

Look at the diagram in Figure 3.2. This shows you can start with `LocationManager` which you don't use directly from the `SplashActivity`. Instead, `Observable<LocationEvent>` depends on `LocationManager`.

Then, open **ServiceLocatorImpl.kt** and replace the current code with the following:

```
// 1
const val LOCATION_MANAGER = "LocationManager"

class ServiceLocatorImpl(
  // 2
  val context: Context
) : ServiceLocator {
  // 3
  @Suppress("UNCHECKED_CAST")
  @SuppressLint("ServiceCast")
  override fun <A : Any> lookUp(name: String): A = when (name) {
    // 4
```

```
    LOCATION_MANAGER ->
context.getSystemService(Context.LOCATION_SERVICE)
    else -> throw IllegalArgumentException("No component lookup
for the key: $name")
  } as A
}
```

You've made some important changes:

1. You define `LOCATION_MANAGER` to use as the name for the lookup of `LocationManager`.
2. `ServiceLocatorImpl` needs — and so depends on — the `Context` you pass as the primary constructor parameter.
3. You need to challenge the Kotlin inference mechanism here a little bit, forcing the cast to the generic type `A` by adding `@Suppress("UNCHECKED_CAST")` and `@SuppressLint("ServiceCast")` annotations.
4. You just need to add the entry for the `LOCATION_MANAGER`, returning what you get from the `Context` through `getSystemService()`.

> **Note**: Oh, look! Android already uses the `ServiceLocator` pattern with `Context` and `getSystemService()`.

Now, you need a small change in **Main.kt**, too. Now that the `ServiceLocatorImpl` primary constructor needs the `Context`, you need to change it like this:

```
class Main : Application() {
  lateinit var serviceLocator: ServiceLocator

  override fun onCreate() {
    super.onCreate()
    serviceLocator = ServiceLocatorImpl(this) // HERE
  }
}
// ...
```

This is possible because the `Application` **IS-A** `Context`. Now you have an object responsible for the creation of the instances of the classes the Busso App needs.

At the moment, this is only true for the `LocationManager`. For your next step, you'll start using it in the `SplashActivity`.

Using ServiceLocator in SplashActivity

Now, you can use `ServiceLocator` for the first time in `SplashActivity`, completing the **field injection**. First, open **SplashActivity.kt** and remove the definition you don't need anymore:

```
private lateinit var locationManager: LocationManager // REMOVE
```

Then replace `onCreate()` with this:

```
  override fun onCreate(savedInstanceState: Bundle?) {
    super.onCreate(savedInstanceState)
    makeFullScreen()
    setContentView(R.layout.activity_splash)
    val locationManager: LocationManager =
lookUp(LOCATION_MANAGER) // HERE
    locationObservable =
provideRxLocationObservable(locationManager, permissionChecker)
    navigator = NavigatorImpl(this)
  }
```

This lets you get `LocationManager` using `lookUp()` with the proper parameter.

> **Note**: It's important that the type for the local variable `locationManager` must be explicit to help Kotlin in the type inference of the value you get from the lookup.

Build and run. The app works as usual:

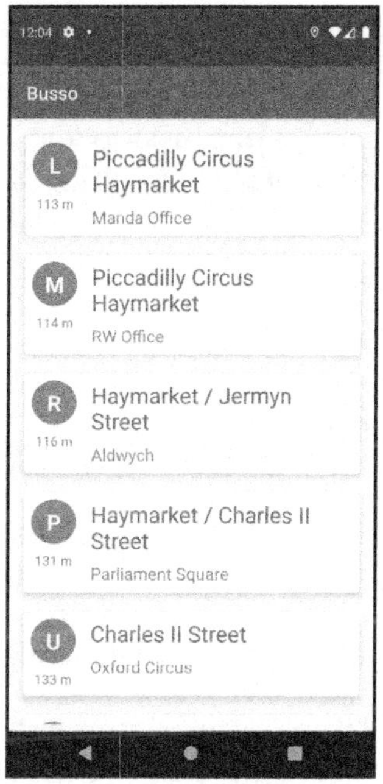

Figure 3.6 - The Busso App

Congratulations! You've started to implement the `ServiceLocator` pattern, which is the first step toward a better architecture for the Busso App. It looks a small change but the benefits are huge, as you'll see very soon.

Adding the GeoLocationPermissionChecker implementation

To prove that the small change you just made has a huge impact, just repeat the same process for the `GeoLocationPermissionChecker` implementation.

Do this by creating a package named **permission** and a new file named **GeoLocationPermissionCheckerImpl.kt**, resulting in the structure in Figure 3.7:

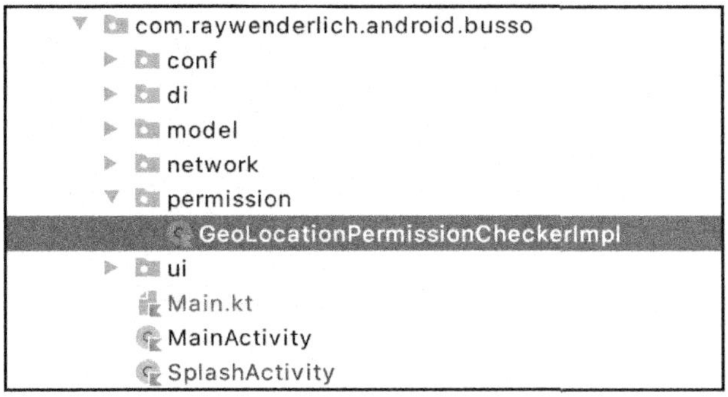

Figure 3.7 - The GeoLocationPermissionCheckerImpl.kt file

Now add the following code to it:

```
class GeoLocationPermissionCheckerImpl(val context: Context) :
GeoLocationPermissionChecker {
  override val isPermissionGiven: Boolean
    get() = ContextCompat.checkSelfPermission(
      context,
      Manifest.permission.ACCESS_FINE_LOCATION
    ) == PackageManager.PERMISSION_GRANTED
}
```

Here, you create an implementation for the `GeoLocationPermissionChecker` interface, passing the `Context` as a parameter.

Next, you need to include this component into your **ServiceLocator** implementation. Open **ServiceLocatorImpl.kt** and add the following code:

```
const val LOCATION_MANAGER = "LocationManager"
// 1
const val GEO_PERMISSION_CHECKER = "GeoPermissionChecker"

/**
 * Implementation for the ServiceLocator
 */
class ServiceLocatorImpl(
  val context: Context
) : ServiceLocator {
  @Suppress("UNCHECKED_CAST")
```

```
  @SuppressLint("ServiceCast")
  override fun <A : Any> lookUp(name: String): A = when (name) {
    LOCATION_MANAGER ->
context.getSystemService(Context.LOCATION_SERVICE)
    // 2
    GEO_PERMISSION_CHECKER ->
GeoLocationPermissionCheckerImpl(context)
    else -> throw IllegalArgumentException("No component lookup
for the key: $name")
  } as A
}
```

In this code, you:

1. Define the `GEO_PERMISSION_CHECKER` constant that you'll use as a key.

2. Add the related case option, returning `GeoLocationPermissionCheckerImpl`.

Now, you can edit **SplashActivity.kt** by removing the following definition:

```
  // TO BE REMOVED
  private val permissionChecker = object :
GeoLocationPermissionChecker {
    override val isPermissionGiven: Boolean
      get() = ContextCompat.checkSelfPermission(
        this@SplashActivity,
        Manifest.permission.ACCESS_FINE_LOCATION
      ) == PackageManager.PERMISSION_GRANTED
  }
```

Then change `onCreate()` like this:

```
  override fun onCreate(savedInstanceState: Bundle?) {
    super.onCreate(savedInstanceState)
    makeFullScreen()
    setContentView(R.layout.activity_splash)
    val locationManager: LocationManager =
lookUp(LOCATION_MANAGER)
    val permissionChecker: GeoLocationPermissionChecker =
lookUp(GEO_PERMISSION_CHECKER) // HERE
    locationObservable =
provideRxLocationObservable(locationManager, permissionChecker)
    navigator = NavigatorImpl(this)
  }
```

Here, you're using `lookUp()` to get the reference to the `GeoLocationPermissionChecker` implementation you previously created and registered in `ServiceLocatorImpl`.

Build and run and you'll get the result shown in Figure 3.8:

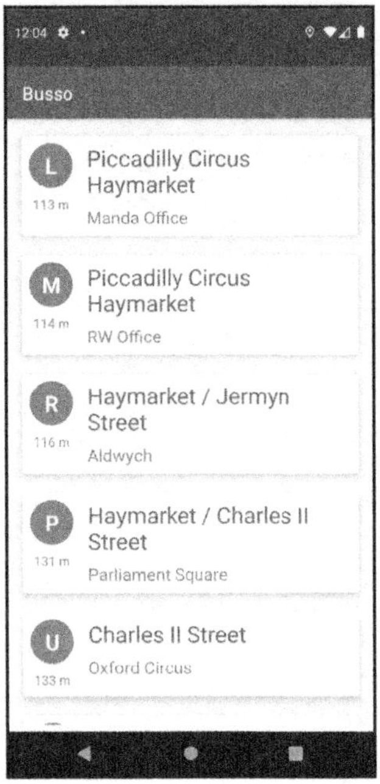

Figure 3.8 - The Busso App

At this point, you might notice that `LocationManager` and `GeoLocationPermissionChecker` are not directly used in `SplashActivity`. However, `provideRxLocationObservable()` needs them to provide the `Observable<LocationEvent>`. This lets you write even better code since the `SplashActivity` doesn't need to know for the `LocationManager` and `GeoLocationPermissionChecker`. You can hide these objects from the `SplashActivity`.

Refactoring Observable<LocationEvent>

As mentioned above, the dependency diagram is useful when you need to improve the quality of your code. Look at the detail in Figure 3.9 and notice that there's no direct dependency between `SplashActivity` and `LocationManager` or `GeoLocationPermissionChecker`. `SplashActivity` shouldn't even know these objects exist.

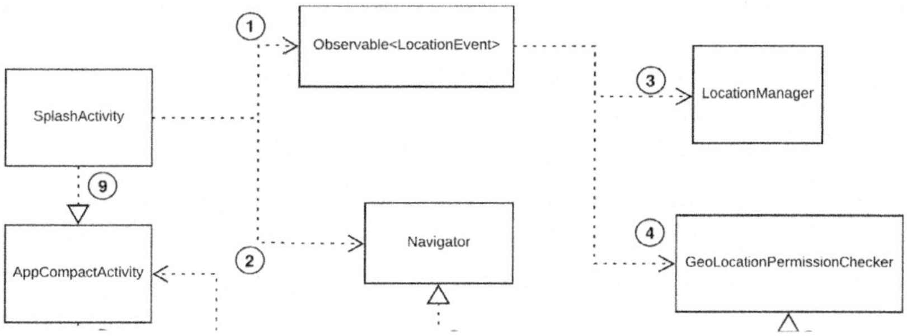

Figure 3.9 - Dependency between SplashActivity and Observable<LocationEvent>

> **Note**: Remember, in object-oriented programming, what you hide is more important than what you show. That's because you can change what's hidden (or unknown) with no consequences.

You can easily fix this problem by changing the code in **ServiceLocatorImpl.kt** to the following:

```
// 1
const val LOCATION_OBSERVABLE = "LocationObservable"

class ServiceLocatorImpl(
  val context: Context
) : ServiceLocator {

  // 2
  private val locationManager =
    context.getSystemService(Context.LOCATION_SERVICE) as
LocationManager
  // 3
  private val geoLocationPermissionChecker =
GeoLocationPermissionCheckerImpl(context)
  // 4
  private val locationObservable =
    provideRxLocationObservable(locationManager,
geoLocationPermissionChecker)

  @Suppress("UNCHECKED_CAST")
  @SuppressLint("ServiceCast")
  override fun <A : Any> lookUp(name: String): A = when (name) {
    // 5
    LOCATION_OBSERVABLE -> locationObservable
    else -> throw IllegalArgumentException("No component lookup
for the key: $name")
  } as A
}
```

In this code, there are some important things to note. Here, you:

1. Define `LOCATION_OBSERVABLE`, which is now the only dependency you'll need for the lookup.

2. Initialize `LocationManager` into a private property.

3. Save the instance of `GeoLocationPermissionCheckerImpl` in the local property, `geoLocationPermissionChecker`.

4. Invoke `provideRxLocationObservable()`, passing the previous objects to get the instance of `Observable<LocationEvent>` you need.

5. Delete the existing cases and add the one related to `LOCATION_OBSERVABLE`.

Due to point 4, when you invoke `lookUp()`, you always return the reference to the same object.

Now, you just need to add this to **SplashActivity.kt**, changing `onCreate()` like this:

```
  override fun onCreate(savedInstanceState: Bundle?) {
    super.onCreate(savedInstanceState)
    makeFullScreen()
    setContentView(R.layout.activity_splash)
    locationObservable = lookUp(LOCATION_OBSERVABLE) // HERE
    navigator = NavigatorImpl(this)
  }
```

Finally, build and run again and check again that everything works as expected.

Challenge

Challenge 1: Testing ServiceLocatorImpl

By following the same process you saw in the previous chapter, create a test for `ServiceLocatorImpl`. At this moment, you can implement the test as:

```
@RunWith(RobolectricTestRunner::class)
class ServiceLocatorImplTest {
  // 1
  @Rule
  @JvmField
  var thrown: ExpectedException = ExpectedException.none()

  // 2
  lateinit var serviceLocator: ServiceLocatorImpl

  @Before
  fun setUp() {
    // 3
    serviceLocator =
ServiceLocatorImpl(ApplicationProvider.getApplicationContext())
  }

  @Test
  fun lookUp_whenObjectIsMissing_throwsException() {
    // 4
    thrown.expect(IllegalArgumentException::class.java)
    // 5
    serviceLocator.lookUp<Any>("MISSING")
  }
}
```

In this code, you:

1. Use the `ExpectedException` JUnit rule to manage expected exceptions in tests. Here, it's important to note the usage of the `@JvmField` annotation, which lets you apply the `@Rule` to the generated instance variable and not to the getter or setter.
2. Define a property for the object under test, which is an instance of `ServiceLocatorImpl`.
3. Implement `setUp()` annotated with `@Before` to initialize `serviceLocator`.
4. Then, you implement the function for the test annotated with `@Test`, starting with the definition of the expected exception.
5. Finally, you invoke `lookUp()` for a missing object.

Now, run the tests and, if successful, you'll get a green bar!

> **Note**: Throughout the chapter, the implementation of `ServiceLocatorImpl` changes and so does its test. In the **challenge** folder in this chapter's material, you'll also find this test adapter for the last `ServiceLocatorImpl` implementation. That test uses the Robolectric (http://robolectric.org/) testing library, which is outside the scope of this book. You can learn all about Android Testing in the Android Test-Driven Development by Tutorials (https://www.raywenderlich.com/books/android-test-driven-development-by-tutorials) book.

Key points

- **Dependency Injection** describes the process in which an external entity is responsible for creating all the instances of the components an app requires, injecting them according to the dependency rules you define.
- **Main** is the component responsible for the creation of the dependency graph for an app.
- You can represent the **dependency graph** with a **dependency diagram**.
- The main type of injections are **constructor injection**, **field injection** and **method injection**.
- **Constructor injection** is the preferable injection type, but you need control over the lifecycle of the object's injection destination.
- **Service Locator** is a pattern you can use to access the objects of the dependency graph, given a name.

In this chapter, you learned what **dependency injection** means and what the different types of injections you can use in your code are. You also started to refactor the Busso App in a world where frameworks like Dagger and Hilt don't exist.

In that world, you defined a simple implementation for the **ServiceLocator** pattern and you started using it in the Busso App for `LocationManager`, `GeoLocationPermissionChecker` and, finally, `Observable<LocationEvent>`.

Is this process still valid for components like `Navigator`? Are the lifecycles of all the objects the same? In the next chapter, you'll find that there are still things to improve in the app.

Chapter 4: Dependency Injection & Scopes

By Massimo Carli

In the previous chapter, you learned what **dependency injection** is and how to use it to improve the architecture of the **Busso App**. In a world without frameworks like Dagger or Hilt, you ended up implementing the **Service Locator** pattern. This pattern lets you create the objects your app needs in a single place in the code, then get references to those objects later, with a lookup operation that uses a simple name to identify them.

You then learned what **dependency lookup** is. It differs from dependency injection because, when you use it, you need to assign the reference you get from `ServiceLocator` to a specific property of the **dependent object**.

Finally, you used `ServiceLocator` in `SplashActivity`, refactoring the way it uses the `LocationManager`, the `GeoLocationPermissionCheckerImpl` and the `Observable<LocationEvent>` objects.

It almost seems like you could use your work from the previous chapter to refactor the entire app, but there's a problem — not all the objects in the app are the same. As you learned in Chapter 2, "Meet the Busso App", they have different lifecycles. Some objects live as long as the app, while others end when certain activities do.

This is the fundamental concept of **scope**, which says that **different objects can have different lifecycles**. You'll see this many times throughout this book.

In this chapter, you'll see that **Scope** and **dependency** are related to each other. You'll start by refactoring how `SplashActivity` uses `Navigator`. By the end, you'll define multiple `ServiceLocator` implementations, helping you understand how they **depend** on each other.

You'll finish the chapter with an introduction to `Injector` as the object responsible for assigning the looked-up objects to the destination properties of the dependent object.

Now that you know where you're heading, it's time to get started!

Adding ServiceLocator to the Navigator implementation

Following the same process you learned in the previous chapter, you'll now improve the way `SplashActivity` manages the `Navigator` implementation. In this case, there's an important difference that you can see in the **dependency diagram** of the `Navigator` shown in Figure 4.1:

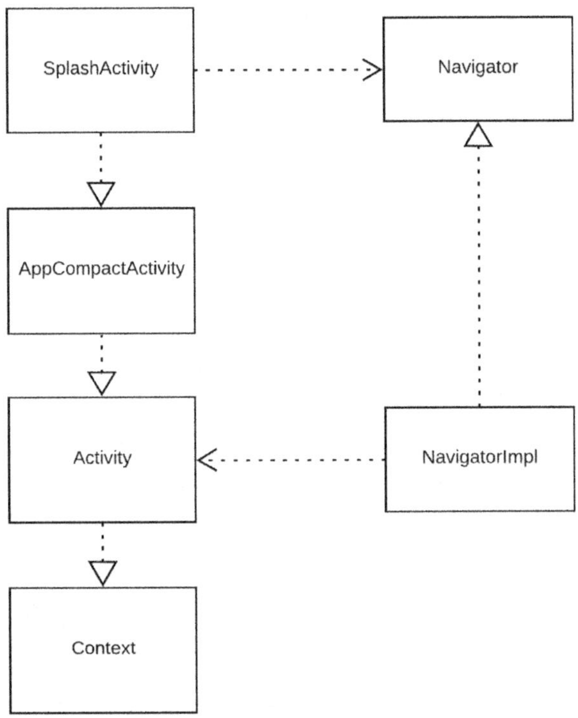

Figure 4.1 — The dependency between Navigator and SplashActivity

In the dependency diagram, you see that `NavigatorImpl` depends on `Activity`, which **IS-A** `Context` but also an abstraction of `AppCompatActivity`. This is shown in the **class diagram** in Figure 4.2:

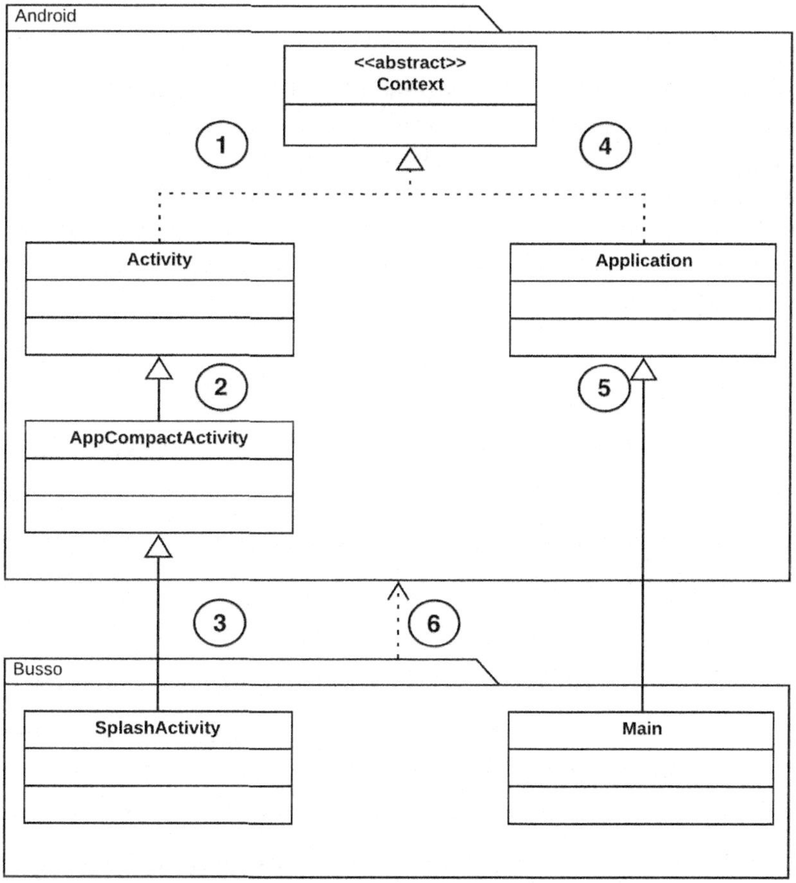

Figure 4.2 — Class Diagram for the Main and SplashActivity classes

In this class diagram, note that:

1. `Activity` extends the `Context` abstract class. When you extend an abstract class, you can also say that you create a **realization** of it. `Activity` is, therefore, a **realization** of `Context`.

2. `AppCompactActivity` extends `Activity`.

3. `SplashActivity` **IS-A** `AppCompactActivity` and so **IS-A** `Activity`. Thus, it also **IS-A** `Context`.

4. `Application` **IS-A** `Context`.
5. `Main` **IS-A** `Application` and so **IS-A** `Context`.
6. Busso **depends on** the Android framework.

> **Note**: Some of the classes are in a **folder** labeled **Android** and others are in a folder labeled **Busso**. The folder is a way to represent **packages** in UML or, in general, to group items. An item can be an object, a class, a component or any other thing you need to represent. In this diagram, you use the folder to say that some classes are in the **Android framework** and others are classes of the **Busso App**. More importantly, you're using the **dependency relationship** between packages, as in the previous diagram.

The class diagram also explicitly says that `Main` **IS-NOT-A** `Activity`.

You can see the same in **NavigatorImpl.kt** inside the **libs/ui/navigation** module:

```
class NavigatorImpl(private val activity: Activity) : Navigator
{
  override fun navigateTo(destination: Destination, params:
Bundle?) {
    // ...
  }
}
```

From `Main`, you don't have access to the `Activity`. The `Main` class **IS-A** `Application` that **IS-A** `Context`, but it's **not** an `Activity`. The lifecycle of an `Application` is different from the `Activity`'s.

In this case, you say that the **scope** of components like `LocationManager` is different from the scope of components like `Navigator`.

But how can you manage the injection of objects with different scopes?

> **Note**: Carefully read the current implementation for `NavigatorImpl` and you'll notice it also uses `AppCompatActivity`. That means it depends on `AppCompatActivity`, as well. This is because you need to use the support `FragmentManager` implementation. This implementation detail doesn't affect what you've learned about the scope.

Using ServiceLocator with different scopes

The **ServiceLocator** pattern is still useful, though. In **ServiceLocator.kt** in the **di** package, add the following definition, just after the `ServiceLocator` interface:

```
typealias ServiceLocatorFactory<A> = (A) -> ServiceLocator
```

This is a simple `typealias`. Type aliases are a way to provide a shorter or more meaningful name for an existing type. This typealias provides a shorter name to the type of a **factory function** from an object of type `A` to an implementation of `ServiceLocator`. In the same **di** package, create a new file named **ActivityServiceLocator.kt** and enter the following code:

```
// 1
const val NAVIGATOR = "Navigator"

// 2
val activityServiceLocatorFactory:
ServiceLocatorFactory<AppCompatActivity> =
  { activity: AppCompatActivity ->
ActivityServiceLocator(activity) }

class ActivityServiceLocator(
  // 3
  val activity: AppCompatActivity
) : ServiceLocator {

  @Suppress("IMPLICIT_CAST_TO_ANY", "UNCHECKED_CAST")
  override fun <A : Any> lookUp(name: String): A = when (name) {
    // 4
    NAVIGATOR -> NavigatorImpl(activity)
    else -> throw IllegalArgumentException("No component lookup
for the key: $name")
  } as A
}
```

This is another implementation of `ServiceLocator`. It contains the references to the objects with a dependency on the `Activity` or, as you've seen earlier, with the same **scope**. Here you:

1. Define a new `NAVIGATOR` constant to use as a key for the `Navigator` implementation.

2. Create `activityServiceLocatorFactory` as an implementation for `ServiceLocatorFactory<AppCompatActivity>`. It's basically a function from an `AppCompatActivity` to the `ActivityServiceLocator` you'll create in the next point.

3. Create `ActivityServiceLocator` as a new implementation for the `ServiceLocator` interface with `AppCompatActivity` as a parameter of its primary constructor.
4. Add the case for `Navigator` for the given constant, returning an instance of `NavigatorImpl` that uses the `Activity` you pass in the primary constructor of `AppCompatActivity`.

How can you get the reference to the `ActivityServiceLocator` implementation? You already know the answer: Use `ServiceLocator` from `Main`.

Accessing ActivityServiceLocator

As noted in the last paragraph, you can get the reference to `ActivityServiceLocator` using the same **Service Locator** pattern.

Open **ServiceLocatorImpl.kt** and replace its content with the following code:

```
const val LOCATION_OBSERVABLE = "LocationObservable"
// 1
const val ACTIVITY_LOCATOR_FACTORY = "ActivityLocatorFactory"

class ServiceLocatorImpl(
  val context: Context
) : ServiceLocator {

  private val locationManager =
    context.getSystemService(Context.LOCATION_SERVICE) as
LocationManager
  private val geoLocationPermissionChecker =
GeoLocationPermissionCheckerImpl(context)
  private val locationObservable =
    provideRxLocationObservable(locationManager,
geoLocationPermissionChecker)

  @Suppress("IMPLICIT_CAST_TO_ANY", "UNCHECKED_CAST")
  override fun <A : Any> lookUp(name: String): A = when (name) {
    LOCATION_OBSERVABLE -> locationObservable
    // 2
    ACTIVITY_LOCATOR_FACTORY -> activityServiceLocatorFactory
    else -> throw IllegalArgumentException("No component lookup
for the key: $name")
  } as A
}
```

Here you:

1. Define a new constant, ACTIVITY_LOCATOR_FACTORY, to use to look up the ServiceLocatorFactory<AppCompatActivity> instance.
2. Add the case for the activityServiceLocatorFactory, giving it a lookup key equal to ACTIVITY_LOCATOR_FACTORY.

Using ActivityServiceLocator

For your last step, you need to use ActivityServiceLocator. Open **SplashActivity.kt** and apply the following changes:

```
// ...
private val handler = Handler()
private val disposables = CompositeDisposable()
private lateinit var locationObservable:
Observable<LocationEvent>
// 1
private lateinit var activityServiceLocator: ServiceLocator
private lateinit var navigator: Navigator

override fun onCreate(savedInstanceState: Bundle?) {
  super.onCreate(savedInstanceState)
  makeFullScreen()
  setContentView(R.layout.activity_splash)
  locationObservable = lookUp(LOCATION_OBSERVABLE)
  // 2
  activityServiceLocator =

lookUp<ServiceLocatorFactory<AppCompatActivity>>(ACTIVITY_LOCATO
R_FACTORY)
      .invoke(this)
      // 3
  navigator = activityServiceLocator.lookUp(NAVIGATOR)
}
// ...
```

In this code, you:

1. Create activityServiceLocator for the ServiceLocator implementation with Activity as its scope.
2. Initialize activityServiceLocator with the object you get from the global ServiceLocator, using the ACTIVITY_LOCATOR_FACTORY key.
3. Use the activityServiceLocator, using the NAVIGATOR key to get the reference to the Navigator implementation.

Now you can build and run Busso and see that everything works, as shown in Figure 4.3:

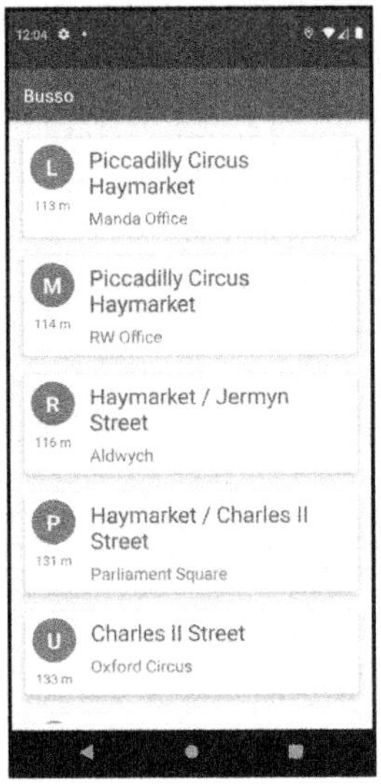

Figure 4.3 — The Busso App

Using multiple ServiceLocators

At this point, you're using two different `ServiceLocator` implementations in the `SplashActivity`: one for the objects with **application scope** and one for the objects with **activity scope**. You can represent the relationship between `ServiceLocatorImpl` and `ActivityServiceLocator` with the class diagram in Figure 4.4:

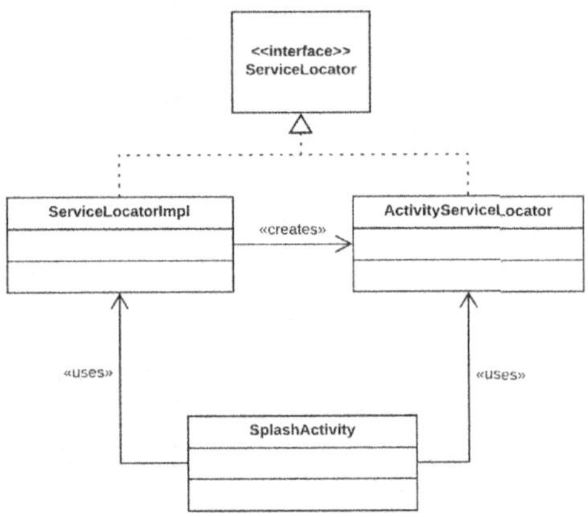

Figure 4.4 — ServiceLocator's usage in SplashActivity

The main things to note in this diagram are:

- `SplashActivity` uses both of the existing implementations for the `ServiceLocator` interface: `ActivityServiceLocator` and `ServiceLocatorImpl`.
- You create the `ActivityServiceLocator` instance through a factory you get from a lookup on the `ServiceLocatorImpl`. In short, you need `ServiceLocatorImpl` to create an `ActivityServiceLocator` to look up the `Navigator` implementation.

You can describe the logic better by using a **sequence diagram**, like the one in Figure 4.5.

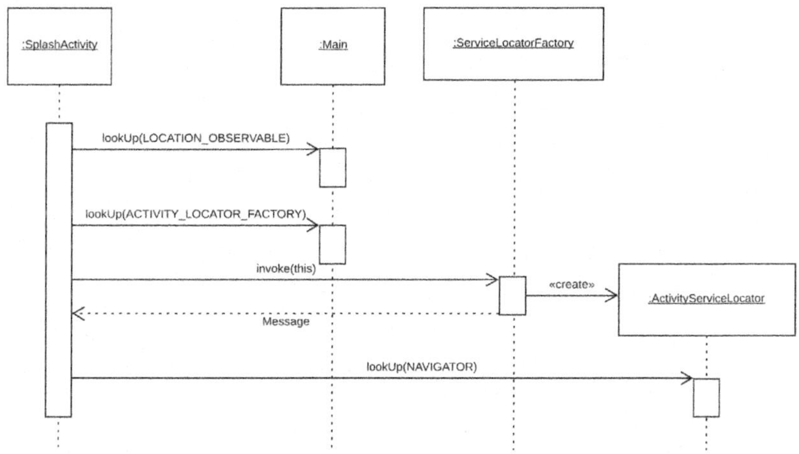

Figure 4.5 — ServiceLocator's usage in SplashActivity

This diagram better represents the sequence of instructions that you execute in `SplashActivity`'s `onCreate()`.

As you see, there's some sort of dependency between the different `ServiceLocator` implementations. The good news is that this is something you can improve, making the code much simpler. You'll do that in the next section.

ServiceLocator dependency

You can create a diagram to see the different objects within their scope, just as you did in Figure 2.14 of Chapter 2, "Meet the Busso App". In this case, the result is the following:

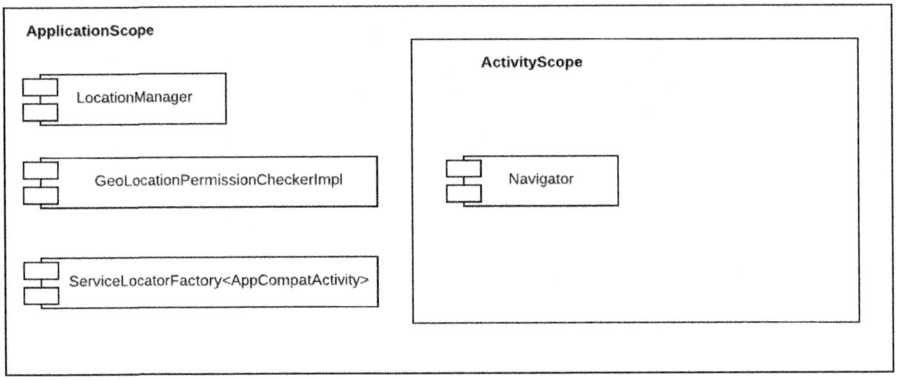

Figure 4.6 — Busso App's ServiceLocator Scopes

In this diagram:

- `LocationManager` and `GeoLocationPermissionCheckerImpl` have the same lifecycle as the app, so they're also inside the `ApplicationScope` box.
- The same is true for `ServiceLocatorFactory<AppCompactActivity>`, which is the factory for `ActivityServiceLocator`.
- `NavigatorImpl` has the same lifecycle as the `Activity`, so it's in the `ActivityScope` box.

What isn't obvious here is the relationship between the objects in the two different scopes that you represented using the sequence diagram in Figure 4.5. That diagram is just the representation of the following lines of code in `onCreate()` in **SplashActivity.kt**:

```
    // ...
    // 1
    locationObservable = lookUp(LOCATION_OBSERVABLE)
    // 2
    activityServiceLocator =

  lookUp<ServiceLocatorFactory<AppCompatActivity>>(ACTIVITY_LOCATO
  R_FACTORY)
        .invoke(this)
    // 3
```

```
    navigator = activityServiceLocator.lookUp(NAVIGATOR)
    // ...
```

Here you:

1. Use `ServiceLocator` to look up `Observable<LocationEvent>`.
2. Again, use `ServiceLocator` to look up `ServiceLocatorFactory<AppCompactActivity>`, which creates the `ActivityServiceLocator`, passing the reference to the `Activity` itself.
3. Use the `ServiceLocatorFactory` to look up the `Navigator` implementation.

Now, you might wonder why you need two different `ServiceLocator` implementations to execute basically the same operation: looking up the instance of a class, given a name. Wouldn't be useful to use a single `ServiceLocator` implementation to handle the different scopes?

Creating a ServiceLocator for objects with different scopes

In the last paragraph, you learned how to access objects with different scopes using different `ServiceLocator` implementations. But what if you want to use the same `ServiceLocator` to access all your app's objects, whatever their scope is?

Open **ActivityServiceLocator.kt** and replace `ActivityServiceLocator` with the following:

```
// ...
class ActivityServiceLocator(
  val activity: AppCompatActivity
) : ServiceLocator {

  // 1
  var applicationServiceLocator: ServiceLocator? = null

  @Suppress("IMPLICIT_CAST_TO_ANY", "UNCHECKED_CAST")
  override fun <A : Any> lookUp(name: String): A = when (name) {
    NAVIGATOR -> NavigatorImpl(activity)
    // 2
    else -> applicationServiceLocator?.lookUp<A>(name)
      ?: throw IllegalArgumentException("No component lookup for
the key: $name")
  } as A
}
```

Here you:

1. Define applicationServiceLocator with null as its initial value.
2. If present, use the applicationServiceLocator as a fallback for cases where the requested object is missing.

With this simple change, you delegate the look-up of objects not present in the current implementation to an optional ServiceLocator.

Also in **ActivityServiceLocator.kt**, you need to change the definition of activityServiceLocatorFactory(), like this:

```
// 1
val activityServiceLocatorFactory: (ServiceLocator) ->
ServiceLocatorFactory<AppCompatActivity> =
  // 2
  { fallbackServiceLocator: ServiceLocator ->
    // 3
    { activity: AppCompatActivity ->
      ActivityServiceLocator(activity).apply {
        applicationServiceLocator = fallbackServiceLocator
      }
    }
  }
```

This change isn't obvious and requires some functional programming knowledge.

> **Note**: activityServiceLocatorFactory() is an **High Order Function**, which is a type of function that can accept other functions as parameters and/or as return values. In this case, activityServiceLocatorFactory() is a function that accepts a ServiceLocator as input and returns a function with type ServiceLocatorFactory<AppCompatActivity>.

In the code above, activityServiceLocatorFactory:

1. Receives a ServiceLocator and returns a ServiceLocatorFactory<AppCompatActivity>.
2. Is implemented with a lambda whose parameter is the ServiceLocator to use as fallback.
3. Contains simple logic that assigns the fallbackServiceLocator to the related property of the ActivityServiceLocator.

As your final step, open **ServiceLocatorImpl.kt** and change `lookUp()`'s implementation to the following code:

```
  // ...
  @Suppress("IMPLICIT_CAST_TO_ANY", "UNCHECKED_CAST")
  override fun <A : Any> lookUp(name: String): A = when (name) {
    LOCATION_OBSERVABLE -> locationObservable
    ACTIVITY_LOCATOR_FACTORY ->
activityServiceLocatorFactory(this) // HERE
    else -> throw IllegalArgumentException("No component lookup
for the key: $name")
  } as A
  // ...
```

`activityServiceLocatorFactory()` now accepts the current `ServiceLocator` implementation as a parameter.

Using a single serviceLocator

You're now ready to simplify the code in `SplashActivity`. Open **SplashActivity.kt** and change the implementation of `onCreate()` to this:

```
override fun onCreate(savedInstanceState: Bundle?) {
  super.onCreate(savedInstanceState)
  makeFullScreen()
  setContentView(R.layout.activity_splash)
  activityServiceLocator =

lookUp<ServiceLocatorFactory<AppCompatActivity>>(ACTIVITY_LOCATO
R_FACTORY)
      .invoke(this)
  // 1
  locationObservable =
activityServiceLocator.lookUp(LOCATION_OBSERVABLE)
  // 2
  navigator = activityServiceLocator.lookUp(NAVIGATOR)
}
```

With this code, you use the same `ServiceLocator` implementation to:

1. Get the reference to `Observable<LocationEvent>`.
2. Obtain the instance of the `Navigator` implementation.

After implementing this change, you use a simple `ServiceLocator` implementation to access all the components you need in `SplashActivity`. To do this, the only thing you need is the reference to the current `Activity`. You then assign the response from `ServiceLocator` to the related property.

As you saw earlier, this is **dependency lookup**. But how can you implement this as actual **dependency injection**? Before proceeding to the next step, build and run Busso and verify that everything works as expected.

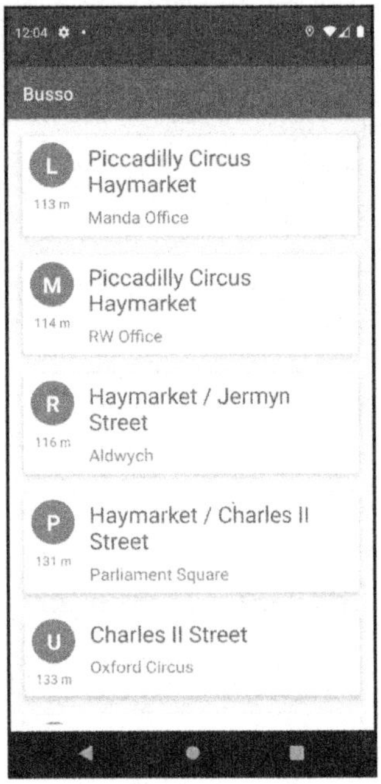

Figure 4.7 — The Busso App

Going back to injection

Dependency lookup is not exactly the same as **dependency injection**. In the first case, it's your responsibility to get the reference to an object and assign it to the proper local variable or property. This is what you've done in the previous paragraphs. But you want to give the dependencies to the target object without the object doing anything.

The injector interface

Create a new file named **Injector.kt** in the **di** package and enter the following code:

```
interface Injector<A> {
  fun inject(target: A)
}
```

This is the interface of any object that can inject references into others. For example, create a new file, **SplashActivityInjector.kt** in the **di** package and give it the following code:

```
class SplashActivityInjector : Injector<SplashActivity> {
  override fun inject(target: SplashActivity) {
    // TODO
  }
}
```

This is just a simple implementation for the `Injector` interface... but what should it do? What do you need to implement the `inject()` operation?

An injector for SplashActivity

From the type parameter, you know that the target of the injection for the `SplashActivityInjector` is `SplashActivity`. You can then replace the code in **SplashActivityInjector.kt** with this:

```
// 1
object SplashActivityInjector : Injector<SplashActivity> {
  override fun inject(target: SplashActivity) {
    // 2
    val activityServiceLocator =

target.lookUp<ServiceLocatorFactory<AppCompatActivity>>(ACTIVITY
_LOCATOR_FACTORY)
        .invoke(target)
    // 3
    target.locationObservable =
activityServiceLocator.lookUp(LOCATION_OBSERVABLE) // ERROR
    // 4
    target.navigator =
activityServiceLocator.lookUp(NAVIGATOR) // ERROR
  }
}
```

In this simple code, you:

1. Define `SplashActivityInjector` as an object using the syntax Kotlin provides for creating instances of implementation for interfaces with one abstract method (SAM).
2. Use the target (`SplashActivity`) to get the reference to `ActivityServiceLocator`.

3. Invoke `lookUp()` on `activityServiceLocator` and assign the return value to the target's `locationObservable`.

4. Do the same for `navigator`.

> **Note**: An interface with only one abstract method is called a functional interface or a **Single Abstract Method** (SAM) interface.

Unfortunately, `SplashActivityInjector` needs to access the target properties, which isn't possible at the moment because they're private.

> **Note**: **Constructor injection** doesn't have this problem because you pass the value to the primary constructor when you create the instance of the dependent object.

In this example, you need to change the code in **SplashActivity.kt** by removing the `private` visibility modifier from `locationObservable` and `navigator` and removing `activityServiceLocator`, like this:

```
  // ...
  lateinit var locationObservable: Observable<LocationEvent>
  lateinit var navigator: Navigator
  // ...
```

To use `SplashActivityInjector`, you also need to refactor the `onCreate()` in **SplashActivity.kt** to look like this:

```
// ...
  override fun onCreate(savedInstanceState: Bundle?) {
    super.onCreate(savedInstanceState)
    makeFullScreen()
    setContentView(R.layout.activity_splash)
    SplashActivityInjector.inject(this) // HERE
  }
// ...
```

Now, everything compiles. Build and run Busso, getting what's shown in Figure 4.8:

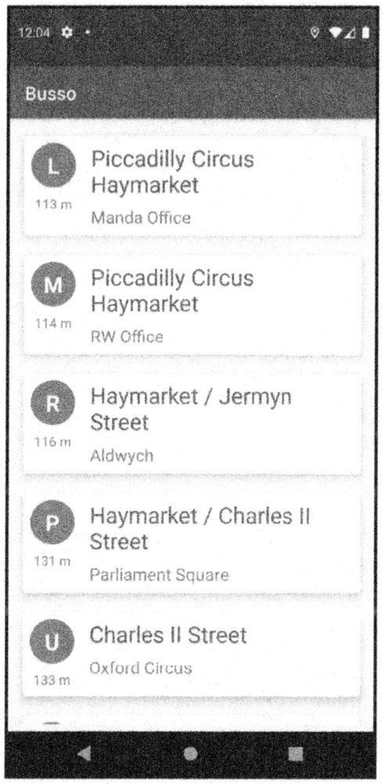

Figure 4.8 — The Busso App

Now, you might wonder if a class like `SplashActivityInjector` could be generated, and what the code generator would need to know to do that. That's a very important question, and you'll answer it in the following chapters of this book.

Key points

- Not all the objects you look up using `ServiceLocator` have the same lifecycle.
- The lifecycle of an object defines its scope.
- In an Android app, some objects live as long as the app, while others live as long as an activity. There's a lifecycle for each Android standard component. You can also define your own.
- **Scope** and **dependency** are related topics.
- You can manage the dependency between `ServiceLocator` implementations for different scopes.
- `ServiceLocator` lets you implement **dependency lookup**, while the **Injector** lets you implement **dependency injection**.

Congratulations on finishing the chapter! By doing so, you learned how to implement the **ServiceLocator** design pattern in a scope-dependent way. You have a better understanding of the difference between **dependency lookup** and **dependency injection** and you created an implementation of the `Injector` interface to connect the dots between them.

You improved Busso's code, focusing on `SplashActivity`. However, you can use the same approach through all the app by also managing the **fragment scope**. Don't worry you'll get there.

In the next chapter, you'll solve another problem, **testability**, before starting your journey to using Dagger and then Hilt.

Chapter 5: Dependency Injection & Testability

By Massimo Carli

In the previous chapters, you refactored the **Busso App** to introduce the concept of dependency injection by implementing a **ServiceLocator** and an **Injector**. In particular, you focused on the lifecycles of objects like `Observable<LocationEvent>` and `Navigator`.

This has simplified the code a bit, but there's still a lot of work to do. Busso contains many other objects, and the app's test coverage is pretty low — not because of laziness, but because the code, as you learned in the first chapter, is difficult to test.

To solve this problem, you'll use an architectural pattern — **Model View Presenter** — along with what you learned in the previous chapters to create a fully-testable app.

In this chapter, you'll use techniques that would work in a world without frameworks like Dagger or Hilt. Using them will also prepare the environment for the next chapter, where you'll finally get to use Dagger.

> **Note**: In this chapter, you'll prepare Busso for Dagger and, later, Hilt. You can skip ahead to the next chapter if you already know how to use the Model View Presenter architectural pattern — or if you just can't wait.

Model View Presenter

Maintainability, testability and making changes easy to apply are some of the main reasons to use an **architectural pattern**. Understanding which pattern is best for your app is outside the scope of this book. For Busso, you'll use **Model View Presenter** (**MVP**).

> **Note**: To learn all about architectural patterns in Android, read our book, Advanced Android App Architecture (https://www.raywenderlich.com/books/advanced-android-app-architecture).

As the name implies, **MVP** is a pattern that defines the following main components:

- Model
- View
- Presenter

A pattern gives you some idea about the solution to a specific problem. Different projects implement patterns in different ways. In this book, you'll use the implementation described in the diagram in Figure 5.1:

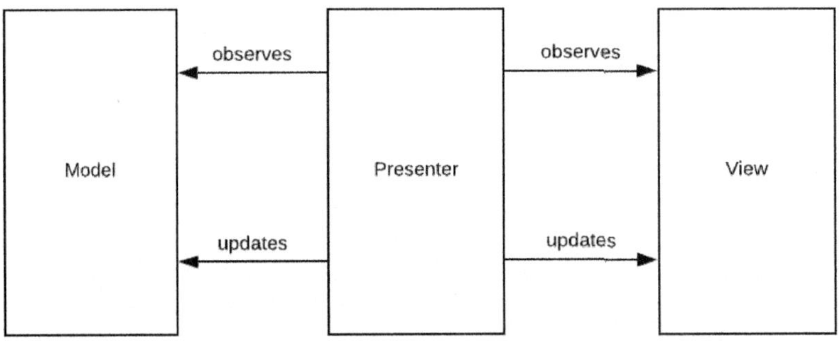

Figure 5.1 — The Model View Presenter Architectural Pattern

Before you move on, take a quick look at the responsibilities of each component and how you use them to define the main abstractions in code.

Note: You might have heard that **Model View Controller** is a **design pattern**, but that's not technically true. Historically, the only design patterns are the ones listed in the famous book, *Design Patterns: Elements of Reusable Object-Oriented Software* by Erich Gamma, Richard Helm, Ralph Johnson and John Vlissides, also known as "The Gang Of Four".

Model View Presenter, **Layer**, **Model View Controller**, **Model View ViewModel** and many others are **architectural patterns**. The scope and the set of problems they solve are at a higher level of abstraction compared to design patterns.

Next, you'll take a closer look at each of the components that compose **MVP**.

Model

The **Model** is the **data layer** — the module responsible for handling the business logic and communication with the network or database layers. In Figure 5.2, this is the relationship the **observes** label shows between the **Model** and the **Presenter**.

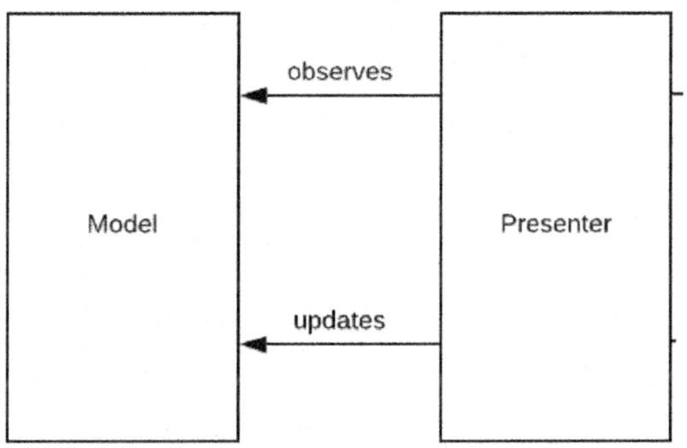

Figure 5.2 — The Model interactions

It might be a little confusing to see that the arrow points from the Presenter to the Model. That's because if **A observes B** it means that the data goes **from B to A**. Consider that in real life, if a person is listening to the radio, it means that the sound is going from the radio to the person.

The Model state changes in response to external events or events from the user. The **updates** label shows that relationship.

But what is the Model in Busso?

Busso App's Model

In Busso, the Model contains:

1. `BussoEndpoint` implementation, which accesses the network.
2. `Observable<LocationEvent>`, an `Observable` that passes updates about the current location.

Busso's starter project contains an implementation to manage the Model. Open **ServiceLocatorImpl.kt** in the **di.locators** package of the **app** module and you'll see the following code:

```
// 1
const val BUSSO_ENDPOINT = "BussoEndpoint"
const val LOCATION_OBSERVABLE = "LocationObservable"
const val ACTIVITY_LOCATOR_FACTORY = "ActivityLocatorFactory"

class ServiceLocatorImpl(
  val context: Context
) : ServiceLocator {

  private val locationManager =
    context.getSystemService(Context.LOCATION_SERVICE) as
LocationManager
  private val geoLocationPermissionChecker =
GeoLocationPermissionCheckerImpl(context)
  private val locationObservable =
    provideRxLocationObservable(locationManager,
geoLocationPermissionChecker)
  private val bussoEndpoint = provideBussoEndPoint(context)

  @Suppress("IMPLICIT_CAST_TO_ANY", "UNCHECKED_CAST")
  override fun <A : Any> lookUp(name: String): A = when (name) {
    // 2
    LOCATION_OBSERVABLE -> locationObservable
    // 3
    BUSSO_ENDPOINT -> bussoEndpoint
    ACTIVITY_LOCATOR_FACTORY ->
activityServiceLocatorFactory(this)
    else -> throw IllegalArgumentException("No component lookup
for the key: $name")
  } as A
}
```

Here, you can see that you:

1. Have the constants for the name you'll use to look up the `BussoEndpoint` and the `Observable<LocationEvent>`.
2. If you have `LOCATION_OBSERVABLE`, you return `Observable<LocationEvent>`.
3. In the `BUSSO_ENDPOINT` case, you return `BussoEndpoint`.

It's important to remember that these objects have the same lifecycle as the app.

Testing Busso's Model

Thinking about the Model components this way makes the test implementation easier. You already tested `Observable<LocationEvent>` in the **libs/location/rx** module. But what about the test for `BussoEndpoint`?

As you learned in Chapter 2, "Meet the Busso App", the `BussoEndpoint` implementation uses **Retrofit**, which is a fully-tested framework by **Square**. Because of that, you don't need to do anything now.

> **Note**: The interesting part about the test for `BussoEndpoint` is the implementation of a mock for it, as you'll see later in this chapter.

At this point, you should have a better understanding of the Model. Next, you'll take a deeper look at the **View** component.

View & ViewBinder

The **View** component is the **UI Layer**. It has a bidirectional interaction with the **Presenter**. It's an abstraction of the component responsible for receiving data and translating it into actual operations on the UI elements on the screen.

Figure 5.3 shows the relationship the View has with the Presenter, under the **updates** label.

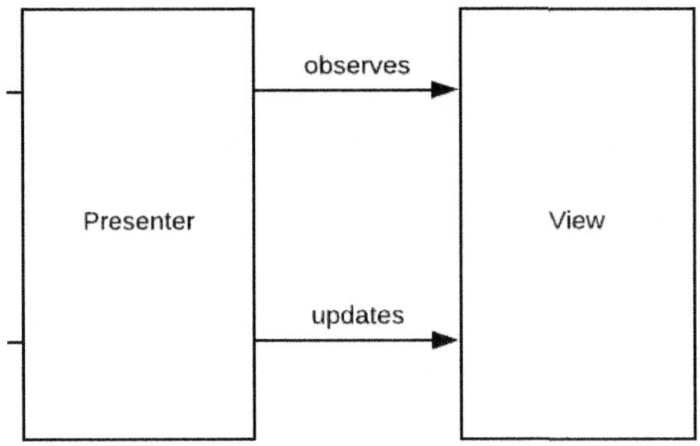

Figure 5.3 — View interaction

The View has the fundamental responsibility of handling how the user events affect the UI elements, translating them to actions in the **Presenter**. In Figure 5.3, this is the relationship with the label, **observes**.

In some Model View Presenter implementations, the Presenter interacts with the View through the `ViewBinder` abstraction. Using a `ViewBinder` has two main advantages. It:

1. Decouples the Presenter from the actual View implementation, which is usually an Activity or a Fragment.

2. Avoids using the name **View**, which is also the name of one of the most important classes in Android. The `View` class is the base class for all the UI Android widgets.

For type safety, it's useful to define an abstraction for the `ViewBinder`. In Figure 5.4, you can see the `ViewBinder` interface from **libs/mvp**:

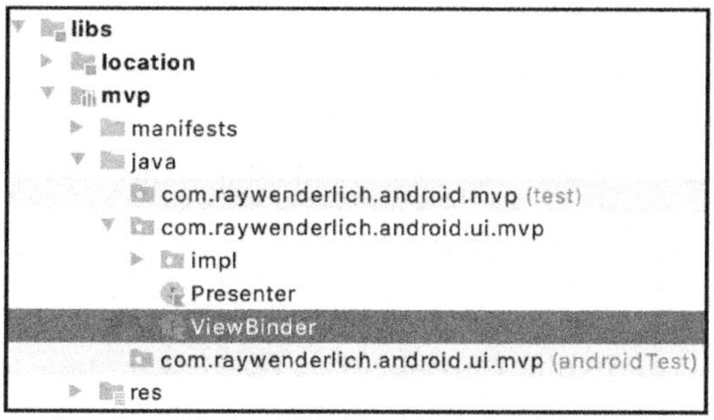

Figure 5.4 — The ViewBinder abstraction in the Busso Project

The code is very simple:

```
// 1
interface ViewBinder<V> {
  // 2
  fun init(rootView: V)
}
```

`ViewBinder` is an interface with two important things to note:

1. It's a **generic** interface in the generic type variable `V`. This represents the type for the actual **View** or for another object that lets the `ViewBinder` implementation access all the UI components. Using generics allows you to avoid any dependencies with the Android framework.

2. It defines `init()`, accepting a parameter of type `V`. That's because most of the `ViewBinder` implementations need an entry point where they get the reference to the actual UI components of the screen they represent.

How do you implement the `ViewBinder` interface? Busso gives you a very good opportunity to find out.

Using ViewBinder for the BusStopFragment

Open **BusStopFragment.kt** and look at the code. Keeping the **View** responsibility in Figure 5.3 in mind, find the place in the code where you:

1. Create the UI components or get references to the existing ones.

2. Use the UI components to display some information.

3. Observe user events.

> **Note**: For this chapter, you'll need to read the code of the existing Busso project directly in Android Studio. Copying all the code into the chapter would take too much space.

Looking at the structure of `BusStopFragment`, note that:

- `onCreateView()` is where you inflate the layout for `Fragment` and prepare the UI to display the **BusStop** information.
- In `useLocation()`, you display the `BusStop` data by invoking `submitList()` on `Adapter`.
- You have some operations to manage errors, like `handleBusStopError()` and `displayLocationNotAvailable()`.
- For user events, you need to manage the selection of a `BusStop` in the list to navigate to the arrivals information.

Now, you have all the information you need to define the specific `ViewBinder` interface for the `BusStopFragment`.

Create a new file named **BusStopListViewBinder.kt** in the **ui.view.busstop** package and give it the following code:

```
// 1
interface BusStopListViewBinder : ViewBinder<View> {
  // 2
  fun displayBusStopList(busStopList: List<BusStopViewModel>)
  // 3
  fun displayErrorMessage(msg: String)
  // 4
  interface BusStopItemSelectedListener {
    // 5
    fun onBusStopSelected(busStopViewModel: BusStopViewModel)
    // 6
    fun retry()
  }
}
```

This is the translation, in code, of the previous bullet points. In particular:

1. `BusStopListViewBinder` is an interface that extends the `ViewBinder` using `View` (the Android one) as the actual type for the generic type variable `V`. Here, you inherit the definition for `init` with a `View` as the parameter.
2. You define the `displayBusStopList()` operation you'll invoke to display the `BusStop` data onscreen.
3. You invoke `displayErrorMessage()` to display alerts in case of errors or warnings.
4. To monitor the events the user can generate from the UI, you define the `BusStopItemSelectedListener`. You implement this interface to observe the `BusStop` a user selects.
5. You use `onBusStopSelected()` to receive the information about the selected `BusStop`.
6. You also provide `retry()`, which lets the user attempt to fetch the `BusStop` information again if an error occurs.

For your next step, you'll create the `BusStopListViewBinder` implementation — which will make everything clearer.

Implementing BusStopListViewBinder

Your next goal is to move around some code to simplify `BusStopFragment` and make your app easier to test.

Create a new file named **BusStopListViewBinderImpl.kt** in the **ui.view.busstop** package and enter the following code:

```
class BusStopListViewBinderImpl : BusStopListViewBinder {
  override fun init(rootView: View) {
    TODO("Not yet implemented")
  }

  override fun displayBusStopList(busStopList:
List<BusStopViewModel>) {
    TODO("Not yet implemented")
  }

  override fun displayErrorMessage(msg: String) {
    TODO("Not yet implemented")
  }
}
```

This is a skeleton for a class that implements the `BusStopListViewBinder` interface, allowing you to start addressing the responsibilities listed above.

Creating the UI components

`init()`'s implementation is very simple. All it needs to do is to create the UI for the list of `BusStops`. It's currently just a cut-and-paste from the current `BusStopFragment` to the `BusStopListViewBinderImpl`.

Replace the existing `init()` implementation with the following code:

```
class BusStopListViewBinderImpl : BusStopListViewBinder {
  // 1
  private lateinit var busStopRecyclerView: RecyclerView
  private lateinit var busStopAdapter: BusStopListAdapter
  // 2
  override fun init(rootView: View) {
    busStopRecyclerView =
rootView.findViewById(R.id.busstop_recyclerview)
    busStopAdapter = BusStopListAdapter()
    initRecyclerView(busStopRecyclerView)
  }
  // 3
  private fun initRecyclerView(busStopRecyclerView:
RecyclerView) {
    busStopRecyclerView.apply {
      val viewManager =
LinearLayoutManager(busStopRecyclerView.context)
      layoutManager = viewManager
      adapter = busStopAdapter
    }
  }
  // ...
}
```

In this code, you simply:

1. Define the private properties for the `RecyclerView` and the `BusStopListAdapter`. You'll initialize these in the `init()` function implementation.
2. Implement `init()`, saving the reference to the `RecyclerView` in the private `busStopRecyclerView` property and creating the `BusStopListAdapter`. Here, you also initialize the `RecyclerView`, moving the code for the private `initRecyclerView()` function from the `BusStopFragment`.

> **Note**: Throughout the process of switching to the Model View Presenter architectural pattern, you'll break Busso repeatedly. Don't worry, everything will be fine in the end.

The next step is to implement the function that updates the UI components.

Displaying information in the UI components

In the `BusStopListViewBinder` interface, you now need to do two things: Implement the operation that displays the list of `BusStops` onscreen and show an error message.

Start by replacing the implementation of the `displayBusStopList()` and `displayErrorMessage()` operations with the following code:

```
class BusStopListViewBinderImpl : BusStopListViewBinder {
  // ...
  override fun displayBusStopList(busStopList:
List<BusStopViewModel>) {
    // 1
    busStopAdapter.submitList(busStopList)
  }

  override fun displayErrorMessage(msg: String) {
    // 2
    Snackbar.make(
      busStopRecyclerView,
      msg,
      Snackbar.LENGTH_LONG
    ).show()
  }
  // ...
}
```

The code above is very simple. It:

1. Invokes the `submitList()` on the `BusStopAdapter`, passing the parameter you received in `displayBusStopList()`.
2. Displays a snackbar with the error message you received as its parameter.

This is quite straightforward. But you still need to handle the events.

Observing user events

Your `BusStopListViewBinder` implementation needs to manage two events:

1. The user selects a `BusStop` from the list.
2. A `retry()` option, if something goes wrong.

To do this, you need to apply the following changes to the existing code for `BusStopListViewBinderImpl`, leaving the rest as it is:

```
class BusStopListViewBinderImpl(
  // 1
  private val busStopItemSelectedListener:
BusStopListViewBinder.BusStopItemSelectedListener? = null
) : BusStopListViewBinder {

  private lateinit var busStopRecyclerView: RecyclerView
  private lateinit var busStopAdapter: BusStopListAdapter

  override fun init(rootView: View) {
    busStopRecyclerView =
rootView.findViewById(R.id.busstop_recyclerview)
    // 2
    busStopAdapter = BusStopListAdapter(object :
OnItemSelectedListener<BusStopViewModel> {
      override fun invoke(position: Int, selectedItem:
BusStopViewModel) {

busStopItemSelectedListener?.onBusStopSelected(selectedItem)
      }
    })
    initRecyclerView(busStopRecyclerView)
  }

  // ...

  override fun displayErrorMessage(msg: String) {
    Snackbar.make(
      busStopRecyclerView,
      msg,
      Snackbar.LENGTH_LONG
      // 3
    ).setAction(R.string.message_retry) {
      busStopItemSelectedListener?.retry()
    }.show()
  }
}
```

As you can see, you now:

1. Define an optional primary constructor parameter of type `BusStopListViewBinder.BusStopItemSelectedListener`.
2. Pass an implementation of the `OnItemSelectedListener` interface as a parameter to the existing `BusStopListAdapter`. Here, you just invoke the callback on the `BusStopListViewBinder.BusStopItemSelectedListener`.
3. Add an action to the `Snackbar` that displays the error message. When the user selects the action, you invoke the `retry()` callback operation on the `BusStopListViewBinder.BusStopItemSelectedListener`.

Great job! You've just made a big improvement by implementing a `ViewBinder` for the `BusStopFragment`. You did this for a reason: testing! Next, you'll put that test into place.

Testing BusStopListViewBinderImpl

The `BusStopListViewBinderImpl` you just implemented isn't difficult to test. Create the test class with Android Studio, just as you learned in Chapter 2, "Meet the Busso App", and add the following code:

```
@RunWith(RobolectricTestRunner::class)
@Config(sdk = [Build.VERSION_CODES.P])
class BusStopListViewBinderImplTest {

  private lateinit var busStopListViewBinder:
BusStopListViewBinder
  private lateinit var fakeBusStopItemSelectedListener:
FakeBusStopItemSelectedListener
  private lateinit var activityController:
ActivityController<Activity>
  private lateinit var testData: List<BusStopViewModel>

  @Before
  fun setUp() {
    activityController = Robolectric.buildActivity(
      Activity::class.java
    )
    testData = createTestData()
    fakeBusStopItemSelectedListener =
FakeBusStopItemSelectedListener()
    busStopListViewBinder =
BusStopListViewBinderImpl(fakeBusStopItemSelectedListener)
  }

  // 1
```

```
  @Test
  fun displayBusStopList_whenInvoked_adapterContainsData() {
    val rootView = createLayoutForTest(activityController.get())
    with(busStopListViewBinder) {
      init(rootView)
      displayBusStopList(testData)
    }
    val adapter =
rootView.findViewById<RecyclerView>(R.id.busstop_recyclerview).a
dapter!!
    assertEquals(3, adapter.itemCount)
  }

  // 2
  @Test
  fun
busStopItemSelectedListener_whenBusStopSelected_onBusStopSelecte
dIsInvoked() {
    val testData = createTestData()
    val activity = activityController.get()
    val rootView = createLayoutForTest(activity)
    activity.setContentView(rootView)
    activityController.create().start().visible();
    with(busStopListViewBinder) {
      init(rootView)
      displayBusStopList(testData)
    }

rootView.findViewById<RecyclerView>(R.id.busstop_recyclerview).g
etChildAt(2).performClick()
    assertEquals(testData[2],
fakeBusStopItemSelectedListener.onBusStopSelectedInvokedWith)
  }

  private class FakeBusStopItemSelectedListener :
    BusStopListViewBinder.BusStopItemSelectedListener {

    var onBusStopSelectedInvokedWith: BusStopViewModel? = null
    var retryInvoked = false

    override fun onBusStopSelected(busStopViewModel:
BusStopViewModel) {
      onBusStopSelectedInvokedWith = busStopViewModel
    }

    override fun retry() {
      retryInvoked = true
    }
  }

  private fun createTestData() = listOf(
    createBusStopViewModelForTest("1"),
    createBusStopViewModelForTest("2"),
```

```
    createBusStopViewModelForTest("3"),
  )

  private fun createBusStopViewModelForTest(id: String) =
BusStopViewModel(
    "stopId $id",
    "stopName $id",
    "stopDirection $id",
    "stopIndicator $id",
    "stopDistance $id"
  )

  private fun createLayoutForTest(context: Context) =
LinearLayout(context)
    .apply {
      addView(RecyclerView(context).apply {
        id = R.id.busstop_recyclerview
      })
    }
}
```

Aside from a lot of scaffolding, this class allows you to test that when:

1. You invoke the `displayBusStopList()`, the app displays the data you pass as a parameter in a `RecyclerView`.
2. The user selects an item, it calls the callback function `onBusStopSelected()` with the selected `BusStop`.

These tests use **Roboletric**, which is outside the scope of this book, but it's good to prove that `BusStopListViewBinderImpl` contains code you can simply test in isolation.

> **Note**: Robolectric (http://robolectric.org/) is a testing framework that allows you to test Android classes without the actual Android environment. This allows you to run tests more quickly, saving a lot of time.

At this point, Busso has a **Model** and a **ViewBinder** but you still need to connect all the dots. To do this you need a **Presenter** — a kind of mediator between the **Model** and the **View**. You'll learn about Presenters next.

Presenter

As a mediator, the Presenter has two jobs. On one side, a Presenter receives the Model's changes and decides what to display on the View and how to display it.

On the other side, the Presenter receives user events from the View and decides how to change the Model accordingly.

You can abstract the Presenter in different ways. Open **Presenter.kt** into the **libs/mvp** module, as shown in Figure 5.5.

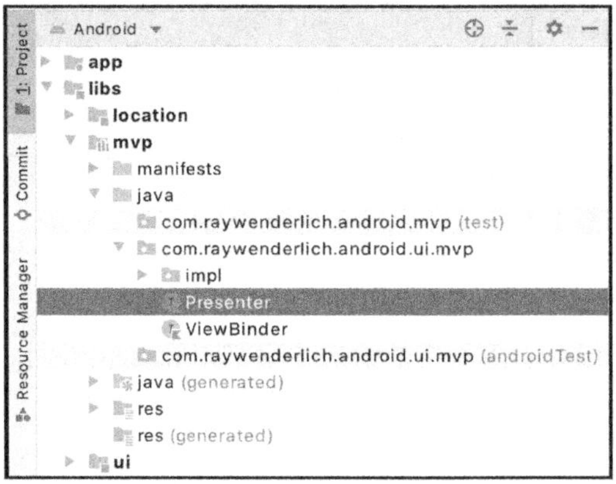

Figure 5.5 — The Presenter abstraction in the Busso Project

Now, look at the following code:

```
// 1
interface Presenter<V, VB : ViewBinder<V>> {
  // 2
  fun bind(viewBinder: VB)
  // 3
  fun unbind()
}
```

The interface is simple, but it has some important things to note:

1. It's a generic interface in the generic type variables `V` and `VB`. `V` is related to the **View** and `VB` to the **ViewBinder**, which has to be related to the same type `V`.
2. A `Presenter` is usually bound to the lifecycle of an Android standard component related to the View it manages. `bind()` is what binds the `ViewBinder` implementation. If you're familiar with RxJava, this is where you'd usually subscribe to an `Observable` to receive the updates.

3. `unbind()` is the symmetric function you invoke to **unbind** the `ViewBinder` from the **Presenter**. You also have the opportunity to release some resources here. In RxJava, this would be where you'd dispose of the subscriptions to some observables.

All the `Presenter` implementations have something in common so it's handy to have a simple base implementation. You'll cover that next.

Using a base Presenter implementation

Binding and unbinding the `ViewBinder` from the Presenter is very common. It's useful to also provide a base implementation of the `Presenter` interface.

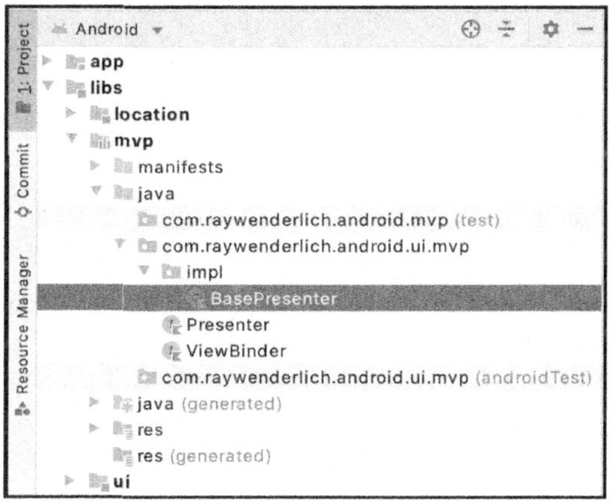

Figure 5.6 — The Presenter base implementation in the Busso Project

As shown in Figure 5.6, find **BasePresenter.kt** in the **libs/mvp** module. It's in a **impl** subpackage with the following code:

```
// 1
abstract class BasePresenter<V, VB : ViewBinder<V>> :
Presenter<V, VB> {
  // 2
  private var viewBinder: VB? = null
  // 3
  @CallSuper
  override fun bind(viewBinder: VB) {
    this.viewBinder = viewBinder
  }
  // 4
  @CallSuper
  override fun unbind() {
    viewBinder = null
  }
```

```
  // 5
  protected fun useViewBinder(consumer: VB.() -> Unit) {
    viewBinder?.run {
      consumer.invoke(this)
    }
  }
}
```

In this code, you:

1. Define the `BasePresenter` abstract class, which implements the `Presenter` `interface` using the same constraints for the generic-type parameters.
2. Create the private property, `viewBinder`, which references the `ViewBinder` implementation.
3. Implement the `bind()` operation, saving the reference to the `ViewBinder`, which you receive as a parameter, to the private `viewBinder` property. `@CallSuper` forces the realizations of the `BasePresenter` to call the same operation on `super` when overriding the `bind()` operation. This makes the initialization of the `viewBinder` property safe.
4. Implement `unbind()`, resetting `viewBinder` to `null`. `unbind()` also uses the `@CallSuper` annotation.
5. Create `useViewBinder()`, which is a Kotlin way of accessing the `ViewBinder` property through a function, as you'll see in the next paragraph.

Now, you have everything you need to implement the Presenter for the `BusStopFragment` class.

The BusStopListPresenter interface

Setting up the Presenter for `BusStopFragment` is simple. Create a new file named **BusStopListPresenter.kt** in **ui.view.bustop** and enter the following code:

```
// 1
interface BusStopListPresenter : Presenter<View,
BusStopListViewBinder>,
BusStopListViewBinder.BusStopItemSelectedListener  {
  // 2
  fun start()
  fun stop()
}
```

In these few lines of code, note that:

1. `BusStopListPresenter` is an interface extending the `Presenter` abstraction using the Android `View` and `BusStopListViewBinder` as actual values for the generic type variables `V` and `VB`.
2. You define two functions, `start()` and `stop()`, which allow you to bind the `BusStopListPresenter` to the lifecycle of an Android component. In this case, you bind it to the `BusStopFragment`.

Implementing `BusStopListPresenter` is also very simple.

The BusStopListPresenter implementation

Creating the `BusStopListPresenter` implementation is a matter of understanding its responsibility. Looking at the existing code in `BusStopFragment`, this class needs to:

1. Observe `Observable<LocationEvent>` and use the `Location` information to fetch the data from the server that uses `BussoEndpoint`.
2. Display the `BusStop` list on the screen using the `BusStopListViewBinder`.
3. React to the selection of a `BusStop` on the list and use the `Navigator` to get to the next screen with the list of arrival times.
4. In case of error, use the `BusStopListViewBinder` to notify the user and manage the `retry()` option.
5. Release all the resources when `Fragment` is no longer displayed.

From the previous list, you understand how `BusStopListPresenter` **depends on** the following components:

- Navigator
- Observable
- BussoEndpoint
- BusStopListViewBinder

This makes the code quite simple to understand.

Create a new file named **BusStopListPresenterImpl.kt** in the **ui.view.bustop** of `BusStopListPresenter` and enter the following code:

```
class BusStopListPresenterImpl(
  // 1
  private val navigator: Navigator,
  private val locationObservable: Observable<LocationEvent>,
  private val bussoEndpoint: BussoEndpoint
) : BasePresenter<View, BusStopListViewBinder>(),
BusStopListPresenter {

  private val disposables = CompositeDisposable()

  // 2
  override fun start() {
    disposables.add(
      locationObservable
        .filter(::isLocationEvent)
        .observeOn(AndroidSchedulers.mainThread())
        .subscribe(::handleLocationEvent, ::handleError)
    )
  }

  private fun handleLocationEvent(locationEvent: LocationEvent)
{
    when (locationEvent) {
      is LocationNotAvailable -> useViewBinder {
        displayErrorMessage("Location Not Available")
      }
      is LocationData -> useLocation(locationEvent.location)
    }
  }

  private fun useLocation(location: GeoLocation) {
    disposables.add(
      bussoEndpoint
        .findBusStopByLocation(location.latitude,
location.longitude, 500)
        .subscribeOn(Schedulers.io())
        .observeOn(AndroidSchedulers.mainThread())
        .map(::mapBusStop)
        .subscribe(::displayBusStopList, ::handleError)
    )
  }

  private fun displayBusStopList(busStopList:
List<BusStopViewModel>) {
    useViewBinder {
      displayBusStopList(busStopList)
    }
  }
```

```
  private fun handleError(throwable: Throwable) {
    useViewBinder {
      displayErrorMessage("Error: $
{throwable.localizedMessage}")
    }
  }

  // 3
  override fun stop() {
    disposables.clear()
  }

  private fun isLocationEvent(locationEvent: LocationEvent) =
    locationEvent !is LocationPermissionRequest && locationEvent
!is LocationPermissionGranted

  override fun onBusStopSelected(busStopViewModel:
BusStopViewModel) {
    navigator.navigateTo(
      FragmentFactoryDestination(
        fragmentFactory = { bundle ->
          BusArrivalFragment().apply {
            arguments = bundle
          }
        },
        anchorId = R.id.anchor_point,
        withBackStack = "BusArrival",
        bundle = bundleOf(
          BUS_STOP_ID to busStopViewModel.stopId
        )
      )
    )
  }

  override fun retry() {
    start()
  }
}
```

The main things to note here are:

1. The dependencies for `BusStopListPresenterImpl` are not all parameters of its primary constructor. You're using **constructor injection** to note that you'll pass the `BusStopListViewBinder` later, using the `bind()` operation you inherit from `BasePresenter`.

2. When the app invokes `start()`, you start observing the `Observable<LocationEvent>`, just as the `BusStopFragment` did in the starter project.

3. `stop()` releases the resources by invoking `clear()` on the `CompositeDisposable`, which is now a property of `BusStopListPresenterImpl`.

The remaining code is mostly the same as what you previously had in `BusStopFragment`, except for the access to the `BusStopListViewBinder`, which now uses `useViewBinder()`. The big difference is that now, the code is much simpler to test. You'll see that for yourself in the next step.

Testing BusStopPresenterImpl

Testing `BusStopPresenterImpl` is now much simpler. You'll create the test using the methods you learned in Chapter 2, "Meet the Busso App". To start, enter the following code:

```
@RunWith(RobolectricTestRunner::class)
@Config(sdk = [Build.VERSION_CODES.P])
class BusStopListPresenterImplTest {

  lateinit var presenter: BusStopListPresenter
  lateinit var navigator: Navigator
  lateinit var locationObservable: PublishSubject<LocationEvent>
  lateinit var bussoEndpoint: BussoEndpoint
  lateinit var busStopListViewBinder: BusStopListViewBinder

  @Before
  fun setUp() {
    navigator = mock(Navigator::class.java)
    locationObservable = PublishSubject.create();
    bussoEndpoint = mock(BussoEndpoint::class.java)
    busStopListViewBinder =
mock(BusStopListViewBinder::class.java)
    presenter = BusStopListPresenterImpl(
      navigator,
      locationObservable,
      bussoEndpoint,
    )
    presenter.bind(busStopListViewBinder)
  }

  @Test
  fun
start_whenLocationNotAvailable_displayErrorMessageInvoked() {
    presenter.start()
    locationObservable.onNext(LocationNotAvailable("Provider"))
    verify(busStopListViewBinder).displayErrorMessage("Location
Not Available")
  }
}
```

The test in this code allow you to verify that, when `Observable<LocationEvent>` emits a `LocationNotAvailable` event, `BusStopListPresenterImpl` sends a **Location Not Available** error message to the `BusStopListViewBinder`.

> **Note**: Complete testing coverage for `BusStopListPresenterImpl` requires knowledge of RxJava and RxKotlin. You can learn more about them by reading the Reactive Programming with Kotlin (https://www.raywenderlich.com/books/reactive-programming-with-kotlin) book.

> **Note**: Tests in this chapter use the Mockito Library (https://site.mockito.org/), which is outside the scope of this book.

Congratulations! You've implemented a **Model**, a **ViewBinder** and a **Presenter** for `BusStopFragment`. You're getting close to the end now.

Putting it all together

Now that you've implemented the Model, ViewBinder and Presenter for the `BusStopFragment`, you need to connect all the dots. Following what you've done in the previous chapters, you need to:

1. Create and manage the instances of `BusStopListPresenter` and `BusStopListViewBinder` implementations into the `ServiceLocator` for the proper scope.
2. Use `BusStopListPresenter` and `BusStopListViewBinder` in the `BusStopFragment`.
3. Implement the Injector for `BusStopFragment`.

Extending the FragmentServiceLocator

You now have two more objects to manage. Open **FragmentServiceLocator.kt** from the **di.locators** package for the **app** module, then add the following code without changing the existing `fragmentServiceLocatorFactory` definition:

```
const val BUSSTOP_LIST_PRESENTER = "BusStopListPresenter"
const val BUSSTOP_LIST_VIEWBINDER = "BusStopListViewBinder"

// ...

class FragmentServiceLocator(
  val fragment: Fragment
```

```
) : ServiceLocator {

  var activityServiceLocator: ServiceLocator? = null
  var busStopListPresenter: BusStopListPresenter? = null
  var busStopListViewBinder: BusStopListViewBinder? = null

  @Suppress("IMPLICIT_CAST_TO_ANY", "UNCHECKED_CAST")
  override fun <A : Any> lookUp(name: String): A = when (name) {
    BUSSTOP_LIST_PRESENTER -> {
      // 1
      if (busStopListPresenter == null) {
        // 2
        val navigator: Navigator =
activityServiceLocator!!.lookUp(NAVIGATOR)
        // 2
        val locationObservable: Observable<LocationEvent> =
activityServiceLocator!!.lookUp(
          LOCATION_OBSERVABLE
        )
        // 2
        val bussoEndpoint: BussoEndpoint =
activityServiceLocator!!.lookUp(BUSSO_ENDPOINT)
        busStopListPresenter = BusStopListPresenterImpl(
          navigator,
          locationObservable,
          bussoEndpoint
        )
      }
      busStopListPresenter
    }
    BUSSTOP_LIST_VIEWBINDER -> {
      // 1
      if (busStopListViewBinder == null) {
        // 2
        val busStopListPresenter: BusStopListPresenter =
lookUp(BUSSTOP_LIST_PRESENTER)
        busStopListViewBinder =
BusStopListViewBinderImpl(busStopListPresenter)
      }
      busStopListViewBinder
    }
    else -> activityServiceLocator?.lookUp<A>(name)
      ?: throw IllegalArgumentException("No component lookup for
the key: $name")
  } as A
}
```

Important to note is:

1. You create instances for the `BusStopListPresenter` and `BusStopListViewBinder` implementations in a lazy way and retain them with a scope bound to the `Fragment` lifecycle.

2. You use the `ServiceLocator` to look up the dependencies for the objects you're providing.

Now, it's time to use the `BusStopListPresenter` and `BusStopListViewBinder` in the `BusStopFragment`

Injecting BusStopListPresenter and BusStopListViewBinder into the BusStopFragment

Open **BusStopFragment.kt** and replace the existing code with the following:

```
class BusStopFragment : Fragment() {
  // 1
  lateinit var busStopListViewBinder: BusStopListViewBinder
  lateinit var busStopListPresenter: BusStopListPresenter

  override fun onAttach(context: Context) {
    // 2
    BusStopFragmentInjector.inject(this)
    super.onAttach(context)
  }

  override fun onCreateView(
    inflater: LayoutInflater,
    container: ViewGroup?,
    savedInstanceState: Bundle?
  ): View? = inflater.inflate(R.layout.fragment_busstop_layout,
container, false).apply {
    // 3
    busStopListViewBinder.init(this)
  }


  override fun onStart() {
    super.onStart()
    // 4
    with(busStopListPresenter) {
      bind(busStopListViewBinder)
      start()
    }
  }

  override fun onStop() {
    // 5
    with(busStopListPresenter) {
      stop()
      unbind()
```

```
    }
    super.onStop()
  }
}
```

If you compare this to `BusStopFragment`'s previous code, there's a great improvement. Now you:

1. Define just the property for `BusStopListViewBinder` and `BusStopListPresenter`.
2. Assign a value to the previous properties using `BusStopFragmentInjector` in `onAttach()`.
3. Invoke `init()` on the `BusStopListViewBinder` implementation in `onCreateView()`.
4. Bind `BusStopListViewBinder` to the `BusStopListPresenter` in `onStart()`. In the same method, you also invoke `start()` on the Presenter.
5. Invoke `stop()` and then `unbind()` on `onStop()`.

Great! Now there's just one more step to take.

Extending BusStopFragmentInjector

The very last step is to implement `BusStopFragmentInjector`. Open **BusStopFragmentInjector.kt** and replace the existing code with the following:

```
object BusStopFragmentInjector : Injector<BusStopFragment> {
  override fun inject(target: BusStopFragment) {
    val parentActivity = target.context as AppCompatActivity
    val activityServiceLocator =

parentActivity.lookUp<ServiceLocatorFactory<AppCompatActivity>>(
ACTIVITY_LOCATOR_FACTORY)
        .invoke(parentActivity)
    val fragmentServiceLocator =

activityServiceLocator.lookUp<ServiceLocatorFactory<Fragment>>(F
RAGMENT_LOCATOR_FACTORY)
        .invoke(target)
    with(target) {
      // HERE
      busStopListPresenter =
fragmentServiceLocator.lookUp(BUSSTOP_LIST_PRESENTER)
      busStopListViewBinder =
fragmentServiceLocator.lookUp(BUSSTOP_LIST_VIEWBINDER)
```

```
        }
    }
}
```

Here, you just use `fragmentServiceLocator` to look up the references to the `BusStopListViewBinder` and `BusStopListPresenter` implementations, assigning them to the corresponding `BusStopFragment` properties.

And that's it! Build and run the Busso App. Everything should work, and you'll see what's shown in Figure 5.7:

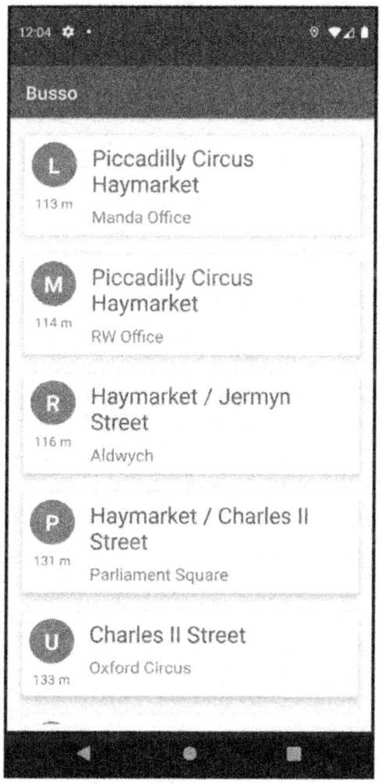

Figure 5.7 — The Presenter base implementation in the Busso Project

Great job!

Key points

- Using an architectural pattern like Model View Presenter is a fundamental step toward the creation of a professional app.
- Design Patterns and Architectural Patterns address different problems in different contexts.
- Model, View and Presenter allow the creation of classes that are easier to test.
- The **Model** is the **data layer**.
- The **View** is the **UI Layer**.
- Using a **ViewBinder** allows you to decouple the presentation logic from the specific Android component.
- The **Presenter** mediates between **View** and **Model**. It's often bound to the lifecycle of an Android standard component.

Congratulations! In this chapter, you've achieved a lot by applying an architectural pattern, Model View Controller, to the Busso App. The code for `BusStopFragment` is much cleaner now and you have good testing coverage.

You've now written a lot of code using only the information about the dependencies between the different components of the Busso App. But... do you really need to write all this code? Since you only needed the information about dependencies, would it be possible to somehow provide the same information and generate all the code you need?

Welcome on board, you're now ready to begin your journey to Dagger and Hilt!

Where to go from here?

If you want to learn more about Mockito, Roboelectric and testing in Android, read the Android Test-Driven Development by Tutorials (https://www.raywenderlich.com/books/android-test-driven-development-by-tutorials) book.

Section II: Introducing Dagger

In this section, you'll learn what Dagger is, how it works, and how it slashes the amount of code you need to write by hand when you implement dependency injection in your app.

You'll learn how to deal with constructor, field and method injection with Dagger, how to simplify the implementation of @Module by using @Binds in cases when you have abstraction and its implementation, and how to use @Singleton to solve a very common problem.

Chapter 6: Hello, Dagger

By Massimo Carli

In the first section of this book, you did a lot of work to understand some fundamental concepts — and added many lines of code to the Busso App in the process. You started with the concept of **dependency**. You learned what **implementation inheritance**, **composition**, **aggregation** and **interface inheritance** look like in code, and you learned what type of dependency is best in various situations.

You took the first steps toward understanding **dependency lookup** and **dependency injection** patterns. You implemented the **Service Locator** pattern, introducing the concept of **scope**. Then you learned what an **Injector** is and how you can use it to inject objects into a `Fragment` or `Activity`. Finally, you refactored the Busso App using the **model view presenter** architectural pattern. Now, Busso is much easier to test and simpler to change.

Yes. it's been a lot of work! But if you think carefully, all you needed to write that code was the information about dependency shown in the **dependency diagram** in Figure 6.1:

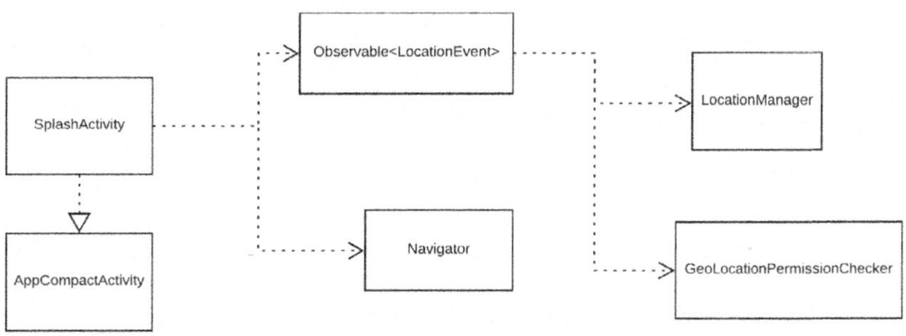

Figure 6.1 — Example of Dependency Diagram

You might wonder, then, if there's a way to generate all that code automatically. Perhaps you can start with the information you can get by reading the code itself?

Going back to an early example from Chapter 3, "Dependency Injection", consider this code:

```
class Server() {

  lateinit var repository: Repository

  fun receive(data: Date) {
    repository.save(date)
  }
}
```

Is there a way to generate all the code to inject an instance of the `Repository` implementation into the `Server`? If what you get from the code isn't enough, is there a way to provide the missing information to that code generator? The answer is yes: **Dagger**!

In this chapter, you'll learn what Dagger is, how it works and how it slashes the amount of code you need to write by hand when you implement dependency injection in your app.

What is Dagger?

Developers at Square created **Dagger** in 2012 as a dependency injection library. Dagger is a **code generation tool**.

> **Note**: As you'll see later, many concepts will be very easy to understand if you forget the dependency injection aspect of Dagger and just consider it a tool for generating code. Dagger is smart enough to get some information from the code itself. In other cases, it'll need your help.

Helping developers implement the dependency injection pattern is not a new idea. Before Dagger, tools like PicoContainer (http://picocontainer.com/) and Guice (https://github.com/google/guice/wiki/GettingStarted) were already available. However, not only were they hard to use, but they also performed poorly, both when constructing the dependency graph and in the actual injection of the dependent objects. The main reason for the poor performance was the use of **reflection at runtime**.

Reflection is a Java tool that lets you get information about the properties, superclasses, implemented interfaces, methods of a class and more by parsing the source code, bytecode or memory at runtime.

Reflection has a big problem: **performance**. Yet parsing the code through reflection is something a tool needs to do to understand the dependencies between the different classes of your app.

Square had the great idea of moving the code parsing before the compilation task by using an **annotation processor**. The goal of this code generation task is to create the code you execute to achieve dependency injection.

Understanding the build process

As you know, Java and Kotlin are both compiled languages. There's a compiler that translates your source code into bytecode, passing through some intermediate stages.

To understand what the build process is, do a simple experiment. Create a new Kotlin project with IntelliJ — or simply open the one you can find in the material code for this chapter named **Empty** — and select the **build task** from the Gradle window, as in Figure 6.2:

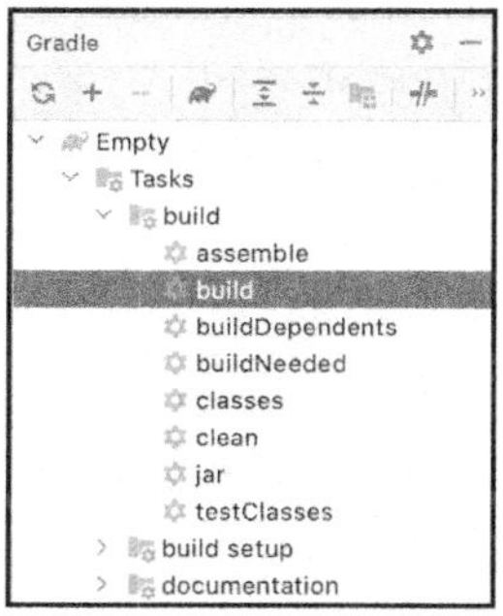

Figure 6.2 — The Build task in Gradle

When you double-click the build option, the **Build** window will display output like the following:

```
> Task :compileKotlin
> Task :compileJava
> Task :classes
> Task :jar
> Task :assemble
> Task :build
```

This is quite self-explanatory, and some of the tasks have been removed to save space. Without going into too many details, you initially **compile** the source code and create a **jar archive** with the **classes** files. Before you can generate source code automatically, you need to add some more tasks including adding an **annotation processor**.

Using an annotation processor

An **annotation processor** is a plug-in that lets you extend the build process of a project. adding some tasks for:

1. **Parsing the source code**: Searching for custom annotations with data that provides additional information about the code itself.
2. **Generating source files**: Using the information from the previous step to create source files that the compiler will add to the existing ones.

To see how this works, you'll create a very simple DI framework next.

Building the "RayDi" DI framework

To demonstrate how the annotation processor works, you'll create your own implementation of Dagger named **RayDi**. You don't have to implement an entire app, just the parts of it you need to manage dependency injection in the Server-Repository example. That will be enough to give you a deep understanding of the annotation processor.

> **Note**: The actual implementation of an annotation processor is outside the scope of this book. Therefore, you'll find the code for **RayDi** in the materials for this project.

For this example, the main things the framework needs to do are:

1. Identify the injection points.
2. Understand which object to inject.

Your framework may understand some of the information directly from the code, but it'll need you to give it some help by using **annotations**.

Your first step is to **mark** the `repository` property as an entry point for the `Server` by using the `@RayInject` annotation, like this:

```
@RayDi
class Server() {

  @RayInject
  lateinit var repository: Repository

  fun receive(data: Data) {
    repository.save(data)
  }
}
```

You also use the `@RayDi` annotation to tell **RayDi** that `Server` is a class you want to add to the dependency graph for the app.

There's a problem though: `Repository` is an interface and **RayDi** doesn't know which implementation to use. You can help it by using the `@RayBind` annotation, like this:

```
@RayBind(Repository::class)
class FakeRepository : Repository {

  var collection: MutableList<Data> = mutableListOf()

  override fun save(data: Data) {
    collection.add(data)
    println("Added $data")
  }
}
```

With this code, you tell the **RayDi** tool that whenever you want to inject an object of type `Repository`, you need to create an instance of `FakeRepository`. Now, the **RayDi** framework has all the information it needs to create the code for the injection.

Next, you'll learn how you can inject `FakeRepository` into `Server`'s `repository`.

Diving into the RayDi project

Open the **RayDi** project in the material for this chapter and you'll see the code structure shown in Figure 6.3:

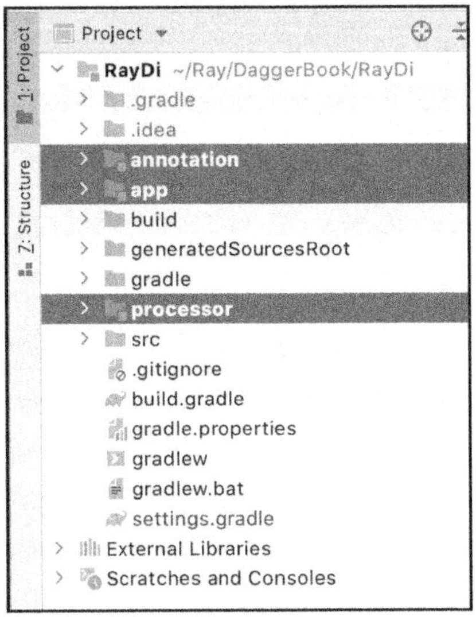

Figure 6.3 — The RayDi Project Structure

As you can see, RayDi contains the following modules:

1. annotation
2. processor
3. app

Before you continue, take a deeper look at each of these modules:

Annotation

The **annotation module** contains the definitions of `@RayDi`, `@RayInject` and `@RayBind`. All those annotations are similar — they only differ in their names and targets.

For example, in **RayBind.kt**, you'll see the following code:

```
// 1
@Retention(AnnotationRetention.SOURCE)
// 2
@Target(AnnotationTarget.CLASS)
```

```
// 3
annotation class RayBind(val interfaceClazz: KClass<*>)
```

Here you:

1. Use `@Retention` to tell the compiler that the information about this annotation should persist at the source code level so it can be removed at bytecode and runtime. That's because the compiler is the only one that will use the annotation.
2. Tell the compiler that it can only use `@RayBind` when it applies to a class. You can't apply that annotation to a field, property or any other construct. If you try, you'll get a compilation error.
3. Define `@RayBind` with a mandatory parameter named `interfaceClazz` and the type `KClass<*>`. This attribute sets the type of interface the annotated class implements.

The annotation module also contains the following interface:

```
interface RayDiObjectFactory<T> {
  fun create(): T
}
```

As you'll see later, RayDi will generate an implementation of `RayDiObjectFactory<T>` for every class that's part of the dependency graph.

Now, it's time to look at the second module: processor.

Processor

The **processor module** contains code to handle annotation processing when building the project.

> **Note**: The description of the code in this module is outside the scope of this chapter, but you can have a look if you're interested.

Take a deeper look at **build.gradle**, which contains the following definitions:

```
apply plugin: 'kotlin'
// 1
apply plugin: 'kotlin-kapt'

repositories {
  mavenCentral()
```

```
}
// 2
compileKotlin {
  kotlinOptions {
    jvmTarget = "1.8"
  }
}
compileTestKotlin {
  kotlinOptions {
    jvmTarget = "1.8"
  }
}

dependencies {
  implementation "org.jetbrains.kotlin:kotlin-stdlib-
jdk8:$kotlin_version"
  // 3
  implementation project(':annotation')
  // 4
  implementation "com.squareup:kotlinpoet:$kotlinpoet_version"
  // 5
  implementation "com.google.auto.service:auto-service:
$auto_service_version"
  kapt "com.google.auto.service:auto-service:
$auto_service_version"
}
```

In this file, you can see that:

1. You use the **kotlin-kapt** plugin, which lets you use the annotation processor in Kotlin to add all the required tasks.
2. The target JVM has version 1.8.
3. You add the dependency to the annotation module.
4. To generate the Kotlin code, you use Kotlin Poet. This is another framework from Square. It makes it simpler to generate Kotlin code.
5. You also use the **auto-service** annotation processor to simplify the installation of generic annotation processors, creating all the configuration files.

To see what happens when you have this configuration, double-click the **build task** for the **app** module shown in Figure 6.4:

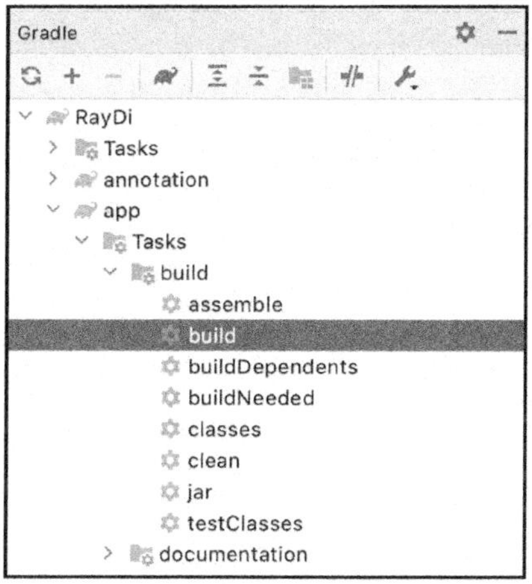

Figure 6.4 — The build task for the app module

Now, look at the output in the Build window of IntelliJ:

```
// 1
> Task :annotation:compileKotlin
> Task :annotation:compileJava
> Task :annotation:classes
> Task :annotation:jar
// 2
> Task :processor:kaptGenerateStubsKotlin
> Task :processor:kaptKotlin

> Task :processor:compileKotlin
> Task :processor:compileJava
> Task :processor:classes
> Task :processor:jar

// 3
> Task :app:kaptGenerateStubsKotlin
> Task :app:kaptKotlin
> Task :app:compileKotlin
> Task :app:compileJava
> Task :app:classes
> Task :app:jar
> Task :app:assemble
> Task :app:testClasses
> Task :app:build
```

Here are several interesting things to notice:

1. The build for the **annotation module** is exactly the same as the **Empty** project's was.
2. The **processor module** contains two additional tasks: kaptGenerateStubsKotlin and kaptKotlin. kaptGenerateStubsKotlin generates some stub classes to simplify the interoperability between Java and Kotlin. You need this because RayDi generates Kotlin code, but existing frameworks usually generate Java code. You can disable this feature with a specific kapt option, because it impacts your app's performance. The kaptKotlin task contains the actual logic to generate the code.
3. Gradle executes the kaptGenerateStubsKotlin and kaptKotlin tasks for the app module as well.

> **Note**: The code generation that the **processor module** executes is related to the auto-service kapt dependency. The annotation processor logic for RayDi is enabled in the **app module**, as you'll see soon.

App

The **app module** contains the code for the app. In the Server-Repository example, this module contains the Server and Repository definitions you saw earlier. Again, take a closer look at **build.gradle**'s contents:

```
apply plugin: 'kotlin'
// 1
apply plugin: 'kotlin-kapt'
// 2
kapt {
  generateStubs = false
}

kotlin {
  // 3
  sourceSets.getByName("main") {
    kotlin.srcDir("${buildDir.absolutePath}/generated/source/
kaptKotlin/")
  }
}

dependencies {
  implementation project(path: ':annotation')
  // 4
```

```
    kapt project(':processor')
}
```

There are some interesting things to note here:

1. You need `kotlin-kapt` to enable the **annotation processor**.
2. Here, you can see how to enable stub generation using `generateStubs`. The default value is `false` because, as mentioned earlier, it has performance implications.
3. Configure the destination for the generated code using **kotlin.srcDic**.
4. The main thing to note here is that you can use `kapt` to enable the RayDi annotation processing in the app module.

Next, you'll build the project and generate the code using the RayDi annotation processor — and see what happens.

Generating code

Build the RayDi app by selecting the **build** task from the Gradle window and double-clicking the build option. Open **build/generated/source/kaptKotlin/main**, as shown in Figure 6.5:

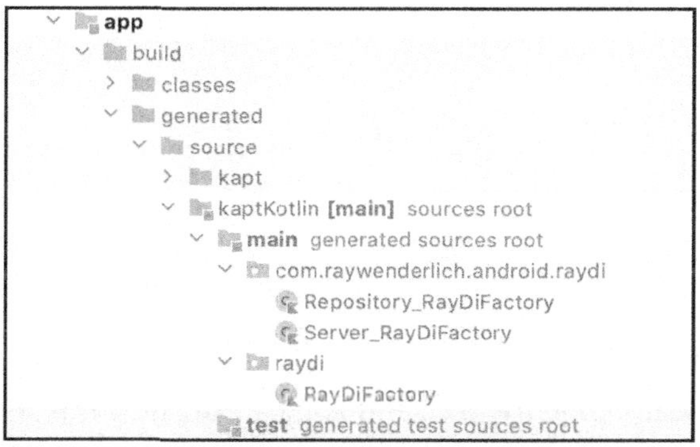

Figure 6.5 — The generated code structure

You can now verify that two classes were generated, named:

1. `Repository_RayDiFactory`
2. `Server_RayDiFactory`

These are the implementations of the `RayDiObjectFactory<T>` interface you saw earlier for each class annotated with `@RayDi` or `RayBind`.

Open the second one, **Server_RayDiFactory.kt**, and you'll see the following code:

```
class Server_RayDiFactory : RayDiObjectFactory<Server> {
  override fun create(): Server = Server()
}
```

You can see that the `Server_RayDiFactory` creates an instance of the `Server` class.

More interesting is what's inside **Repository_RayDiFactory.kt**:

```
class Repository_RayDiFactory : RayDiObjectFactory<Repository> {
  override fun create(): Repository = FakeRepository()
}
```

In this case, the return type is `Repository` but the actual object you return is an instance of `FakeRepository`. Using the `@RayBind` annotation you specified which implementation of the interface you want to use.

Even more interesting is the content of **RayDiFactory.kt**:

```
class RayDiFactory {
  @Suppress("UNCHECKED_CAST")
  fun <T> get(type: KClass<out Any>): T {
    val target = when (type) {
      Server::class -> Server_RayDiFactory().create()
          .apply {
            repository = Repository_RayDiFactory().create()
          } as T
      Repository::class -> Repository_RayDiFactory().create() as
T
      else -> throw IllegalStateException()
    }
    return target as T
  }
}
```

RayDiFactory.kt gets an instance for the provided type.

RayDi generated all this code for you, and you can see how it also managed the dependency of `Server` from the implementation of the `Repository` interface.

Now, have a look at **Main.kt** to check if the generated code works as expected:

```
fun main() {
  val server: Server = RayDiFactory()
      .get(Server::class)
  server.receive(Data("Hello"))
}
```

Build the app and run `main()` and you'll see the following output:

```
Added Data(name=Hello)
```

This proves that `Server` has a reference to the correct implementation of the `Repository` interface: `FakeRepository`.

> **Note**: You can do a simple exercise. Just create a new implementation for the `Repository` interface and use `@RayBind` to replace the actual instance the `Server` uses.

Great job! You learned how to use an annotation processor to generate code.

Of course, RayDi is very simple and limited. What happens, for instance, if the `Server` also has a dependency it declares using parameters in the primary constructor? What if `FakeRepository` has other dependencies? How can you detect cyclic dependencies? Handling these complications isn't a simple job, but Dagger's here to help!

Beginning with Dagger

At this point, you not only know how to start working with **Dagger**, but you also have a deep understanding of the type of code it's going to generate. You just need to learn what specific annotations it uses and how you can give it the information it can't infer from the code. It works exactly as you've seen in RayDi's annotation processor.

> **Note**: If you're wondering what happened to the Busso App, don't worry. You'll migrate it to Dagger very soon. You just need some examples of how Dagger works in simpler apps first.

To prove that, start by implementing the Server-Repository example from above in Dagger. In this case, you'll need to define:

1. The Dagger dependency in your project.
2. The entry point for the injection into `Server`.

3. How to create the `Repository` implementation to inject.
4. A way to get the reference to the `Server` instance.

You already did all these steps for RayDi!

DaggerServerRepository

Use IntelliJ to open the **DaggerServerRepository** project from the **starter** folder in the materials for this chapter. It's a very simple project with the file structure shown in Figure 6.6:

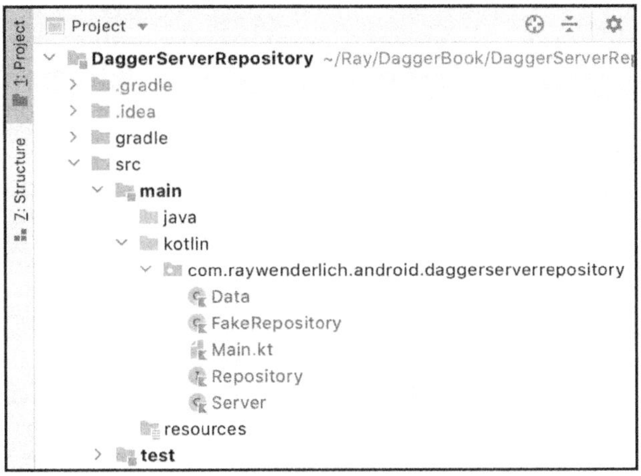

Figure 6.6 — DaggerServerRepository code structure

The initial code is actually a little different from the one in the **app** module of the RayDi example. Open **Server.kt**, where you'll see the following:

```
class Server() {

  lateinit var repository: FakeRepository // HERE

  fun receive(data: Data) {
    repository.save(data)
  }
}
```

At the moment, the `repository`'s property type is `FakeRepository` and not `Repository`. When you open **FakeRepository.kt**, you get this:

```
class FakeRepository : Repository {

  var collection: MutableList<Data> = mutableListOf()
```

```
  override fun save(data: Data) {
    collection.add(data)
    println("Added $data")
  }
}
```

This class has the same definition as the one in RayDi. You need to make `repository` property of the `Server` class of an interface type to be able to easily swap the implementations without changing the `Server` class. At the moment, `DaggerServerRepository` only has pseudo-code in **Main.kt**:

```
fun main() {
  // Get the reference to a Server instance
  // Invoke the receive() method
}
```

For your first step, you need to add the dependency to Dagger.

Installing Dagger

As you learned in the previous paragraphs, **Dagger is just a code generator tool** implemented as an annotation processor. Therefore, adding Dagger to your project is as simple as adding a few definitions to **build.gradle** for your project's module.

Start by opening **build.gradle** for the **DaggerServerRepository** project, as in Figure 6.7:

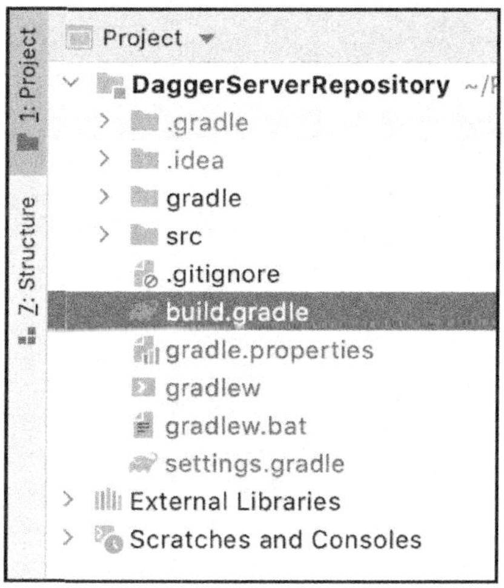

Figure 6.7 — build.gradle file for the DaggerServerRepository project

Now, change its contents to the following:

```
plugins {
  id 'org.jetbrains.kotlin.jvm' version '1.4.10'
  // 1
  id "org.jetbrains.kotlin.kapt" version "1.4.10"
}

group 'org.example'
version '1.0-SNAPSHOT'

repositories {
  mavenCentral()
}

dependencies {
  implementation "org.jetbrains.kotlin:kotlin-stdlib"
  // 2
  implementation "com.google.dagger:dagger:2.28"
  // 3
  kapt "com.google.dagger:dagger-compiler:2.28"
}
```

After your work with the RayDi project, this should look very familiar. In this code, you:

1. Install the **kotlin-kapt** plugin. The syntax might look different from the previous case, but it's simply another way to install a **gradle** plugin given its **ID** and **version**.
2. Add the dependency to the **dagger** library. The current version at the time of writing is 2.28, but that will most likely change.
3. Install the Dagger annotation processor using the **kapt** dependency handler.

Look for an icon like the one in Figure 6.8 in the top-right of the IDE:

Figure 6.8 — "Sync Project with Gradle" file button

When you select it, Gradle will download the missing files — and you're ready to use Dagger in your project.

@Component

In the Server-Repository example with RayDi, you generated `RayDiFactory` as the factory for all the components of the dependency graph. Dagger generates an equivalent class by defining a `@Component`.

> **Note**: In this book, you'll call any interface annotated with the `@Component` annotation **@Component**. The same will happen with other types of annotations.

For Dagger to be able to provide a reference to an instance of the `Server` class, you just need to create a simple interface. Do this by creating a new package named **di**. Inside, create a new file named **AppComponent.kt**. Finally, copy the following code into the new file:

```
// 1
@Component
// 2
interface AppComponent {
  // 3
  fun server(): Server
}
```

This is a very simple but important interface with many interesting things to note:

1. It must contain `@Component`, which you use to define classes with factory responsibility, just as you did with `RayDiFactory` in the RayDi example. In the following chapter, you'll learn more about this fundamental annotation.
2. When you create a `@Component`, you don't need to define any concrete class — an **interface** is enough. This is a way to tell Dagger that you just want to get an instance of a given type, along with all its dependencies, without knowing the details about how Dagger does its job.
3. The **return type** of the operation you define in the `@Component` interface is the **only thing** that really matters. The only reason the name of the operation is important is to make your code more readable.

Believe it or not, with this simple definition, you've started to talk to Dagger, telling it that you need an instance of a `Server`. But at this point, when you build the app, you'll get an error with the following message:

```
[Dagger/MissingBinding]
com.raywenderlich.android.daggerserverrepository.Server cannot
be provided without an @Inject constructor or an @Provides-
annotated method.
public abstract interface AppComponent {
```

Dagger is just a generator tool, remember? You asked it to create a `Server`, but it doesn't know how to. You need to give Dagger more information, and you'll find out how to do so next.

@Inject

In the previous paragraph, you learned how to use `@Component` to tell Dagger what you need. You asked for a `Server`, but Dagger doesn't know how to create one. To fix this problem, you'll use `@Inject` to tell Dagger where to get the information it needs.

Unlike `@Component`, `@Inject` isn't something Dagger created. Instead, it's part of **Java Specification Request 300**.

> **Note**: **JSR-300** is a document that proposes a way to standardize dependency injection in Java. It defines annotations in the **javax.inject** package. As you'll see later, `@Inject` is just one of the JSR-300 annotations Dagger supports.

In this case, you'll use `@Inject` to tell Dagger how to create an instance of `Server`. Start by opening **Server.kt** and annotating `Server`, as in the following code:

```
class Server @Inject constructor() { // HERE
  lateinit var repository: FakeRepository

  fun receive(data: Data) {
    repository.save(data)
  }
}
```

By using `@Inject` to annotate `Server`'s **primary constructor**, you're telling Dagger how to create an instance.

Now you can build the app and verify that the error disappeared and everything is successful. But what did Dagger generate? And how can you use it? You'll look at that next.

Looking at the generated code

Now, the build was successful and Dagger generated some code. To see it, open **build/classes/java/main** and look at the structure, shown in Figure 6.9:

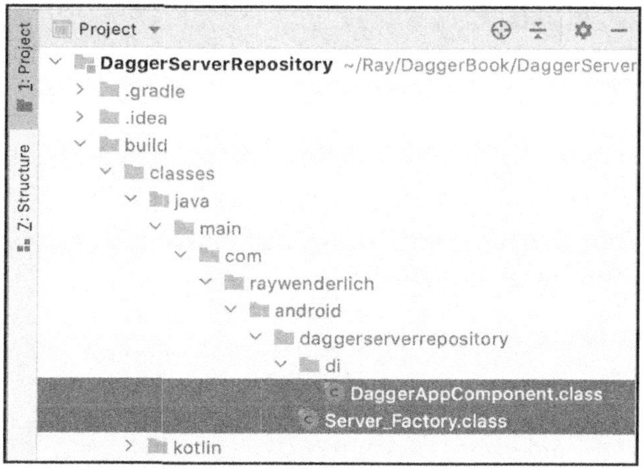

Figure 6.9 — Dagger-generated code

Here, you can see the following two files:

- Server_Factory.class
- DaggerAppComponent.class

It's important to note that these are both Java classes. `Server_Factory` is very similar to `RayDiObjectFactory` from the RayDi app. `DaggerAppComponent` is quite a lot like `RayDiFactory`.

In this case, it's also important to note how the name `DaggerAppComponent` is the concatenation of the prefix **Dagger** and the name of the `@Component` you created earlier.

Now that Dagger has created these classes, you just need to use them.

Using the @Component

In the previous paragraph, you learned how to define a `@Component` — but how do you use it? That's what you'll cover next.

Open **Main.kt** and replace the existing code with the following:

```
fun main() {
  // 1
  val server = DaggerAppComponent
      .create()
      .server()
  // 2
  server.receive(Data("Hello"))
}
```

In this code, you:

1. Invoke the `create()` static factory method on `DaggerAppComponent`, which Dagger generated for you, and then on the `server()` factory method. By doing this, you're asking Dagger to give you an instance of `Server`, which you then assign to the local variable `server`.
2. Use `server`, invoking its `receive()`.

That's easy, right? Now, build and run `main()`.

Oops! Unfortunately, something went wrong. You get this error:

```
Exception in thread "main"
kotlin.UninitializedPropertyAccessException: lateinit property
repository has not been initialized
  at
com.raywenderlich.android.daggerserverrepository.Server.receive(
Server.kt:42)
```

Of course! Nobody told Dagger to inject the `FakeRepository` into the `Server` instance it provides. How would it know?

You'll solve the problem using `@Inject`. Open **Server** and add `@Inject`, like this:

```
class Server @Inject constructor() {

  @Inject // HERE
  lateinit var repository: FakeRepository

  fun receive(data: Data) {
    repository.save(data)
```

```
    }
  }
```

Here, you simply use `@Inject` for `lateinit var repository`.

Is everything OK now? Of course not! So far you told Dagger that:

- You need a `Server`.
- To create an instance of `Server`, it needs to invoke its primary constructor.
- `Server` needs a `FakeRepository`.

But how can Dagger create the instance of `FakeRepository`? The answer is easy: Use `@Inject`.

Open **FakeRepository.kt** and annotate the primary constructor like this:

```
class FakeRepository @Inject constructor() : Repository {
  // ...
}
```

Now, you can finally build and run the app. You'll get the following output:

```
Added Data(name=Hello)
```

Congratulations! You just ran your first app using Dagger. There's still a lot to learn in the following chapters, but before that, there's still something you need to do.

Using @Module and @Provides

In the previous sections, you managed to get a `Server` that delegates the persistence of some `Data` to a `FakeRepository`. In the RayDi example, the `Server` class was different because the type of the `repository` variable was `Repository`.

Open **Server.kt** and replace it with this:

```
class Server @Inject constructor() {

  @Inject
  lateinit var repository: Repository // HERE

  fun receive(data: Data) {
    repository.save(data)
  }
}
```

Build now and you'll see the same error you got before:

```
error: [Dagger/MissingBinding]
com.raywenderlich.android.daggerserverrepository.Repository
cannot be provided without an @Provides-annotated method.
public abstract interface AppComponent {
```

Dagger is complaining because you asked to **provide** an instance of type `Repository`, but it doesn't know how to do that. It needs some more help from you, and the error message explains what help it needs.

In the following chapters, you'll see how to provide this information in many different ways. At the moment, the simplest way is to define a `@Module`.

Create a new file named **MainModule.kt** in the **di** module and enter the following code:

```
// 1
@Module
object MainModule {
  // 2
  @Provides
  fun provideRepository(): Repository = FakeRepository()
}
```

In this code. you:

1. Create an object annotated with **@Module**. A module is a way to give Dagger additional information about the dependency graph.
2. Define `provideRepository()` and annotate it with **@Provides**. In this case, the name of the function is important only for readability. The only thing that matters here is the return type. Here, you're telling Dagger that every time it needs to inject an object of type `Repository`, it should invoke this function to get one. This function **provides** the instance of type `Repository` Dagger needs.

Here, it's important to note that Dagger is no longer responsible for creating the instance of `FakeRepository`. You do that in the `provideRepository()` function implementation instead.

For this reason, you don't need `@Inject` in `FakeRepository` anymore. Open **FakeRepository.kt** and remove the annotation, getting the following code:

```
class FakeRepository : Repository { // HERE
  // ...
}
```

The simple definition of `@Module` is not enough. You still need to tell Dagger which `@Component` uses it.

Open **AppComponent.kt** and replace it with this:

```
@Component(modules = arrayOf(MainModule::class)) // HERE
interface AppComponent {

  fun server(): Server
}
```

`AppComponent` is the object that provides you the reference to the `Server` instance with all its dependencies. It needs to know how to create the object of type `Repository` to inject.

Using the **modules** attribute of `@Component`, you tell Dagger where to find the information it needs: `MainModule`.

Now, build the code and run `main()`. You'll get the following successful output:

```
Added Data(name=Hello)
```

Congratulations, you've now used Dagger to achieve the same result you got with the RayDi annotation processor. But this is just the beginning of what you can do with Dagger!

Key points

- **Dagger is just a code generation tool**, helping you implement the dependency injection pattern in your project.
- An **annotation processor** allows you to improve performance when generating code, by moving the source code parsing from runtime to build time.
- Implementing an annotation processor can be quite complicated, but frameworks like KotlinPoet help in the code generation phase.
- Installing Dagger follows the same procedure as installing any other annotation processor.
- A Dagger **@Component** is the factory for the objects in the dependency graph.
- You can use **@Inject** to tell Dagger how to create an instance of a class.
- **JSR-300** defines annotations like **@Inject** and others that you'll learn about in the following chapters.
- **@Inject** also lets you tell Dagger what property to inject.
- **@Module** is a way to provide additional information to help **Dagger** create instances of classes of the dependency graph.
- **@Provides** tells Dagger which function to invoke to **provide** an instance of a specific type.

Congratulations! In this chapter, you learned how Dagger works and what the main annotations to implement the dependency injection pattern in your app are. You also had the chance to learn how an annotation processor works and why it's a very powerful tool.

This is just the beginning — there's much more to learn. In the next chapter, you'll cover more details about how Dagger implements the different types of injections and get to know some utilities that help improve the performance of your app. See you there!

Chapter 7: More About Injection

By Massimo Carli

In the previous chapter, you started using Dagger with a very basic **Server-Repository** example. As you remember from the first chapter, the code you implemented uses a simple dependency between the `Server` and a `Repository` called **loosely coupled**. You represent this dependency with the UML diagram in Figure 7.1:

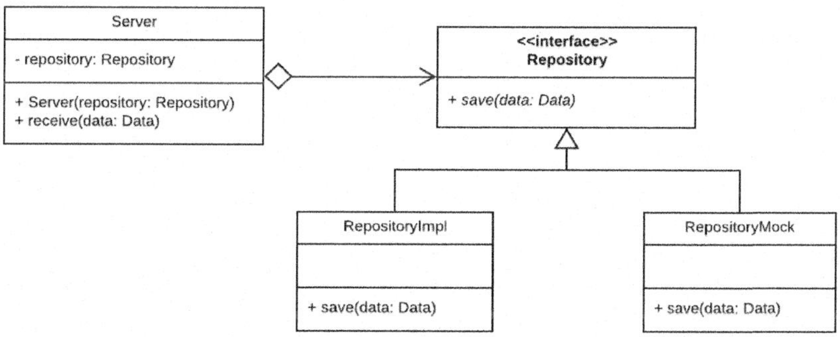

Figure 7.1 — Loosely coupled dependency

You learned how to tell Dagger how to generate the **factory** for the instances in the dependency graph using the **@Component** annotation. You then learned how to use the **@Inject** annotation to accomplish two different goals:

1. Tell Dagger what constructor to call to create an instance of a class.
2. Mark properties as targets for injection.

If the type of dependency is an abstraction, like an interface, Dagger needs some additional information. You provide this information by using a **@Module** containing some functions that you annotate with **@Provides**. This way, you tell Dagger which function to invoke to get an instance of a class for a specific type. Luckily, Dagger is a good listener. :]

You learned that the `@Inject`, `@Component`, `@Module` and `@Provides` annotations are all you need to implement dependency injection in your app with Dagger. The rest of the annotations let you improve performance when generating and executing the code.

In this chapter, you'll discover even more about dependency injection with Dagger. You'll learn how to:

- Deal with **constructor**, **field** and **method** injection with Dagger.
- Simplify the implementation of `@Module` by using `@Binds` in cases when you have an abstraction and its implementation. You saw how this works in the `Repository` and `FakeRepository` example.
- Use `@Singleton` for the first time to solve a very common problem.

There's still a lot to do. Prepare to have some more fun!

Getting started

In the previous chapter, you learned how to use some Dagger annotations in a Kotlin project in IntelliJ. In this chapter, you'll return to Android with the **RaySequence** app. This is a very simple app that allows you to display a numeric value of a sequence on the screen every time you press a `Button`.

To get started, use **Android Studio** to open the **RaySequence** project in the **starter** folder of the materials for this chapter. Build and run and you'll get the screen shown in Figure 7.2:

Figure 7.2 — Initial RaySequence app

> **Note**: Don't worry about the Busso App. In a few chapters, you'll migrate it to Dagger and everything will seem very easy to you.

At the moment, the app doesn't work: When you click the `Button`, nothing happens. Figure 7.3 shows the file structure of the app:

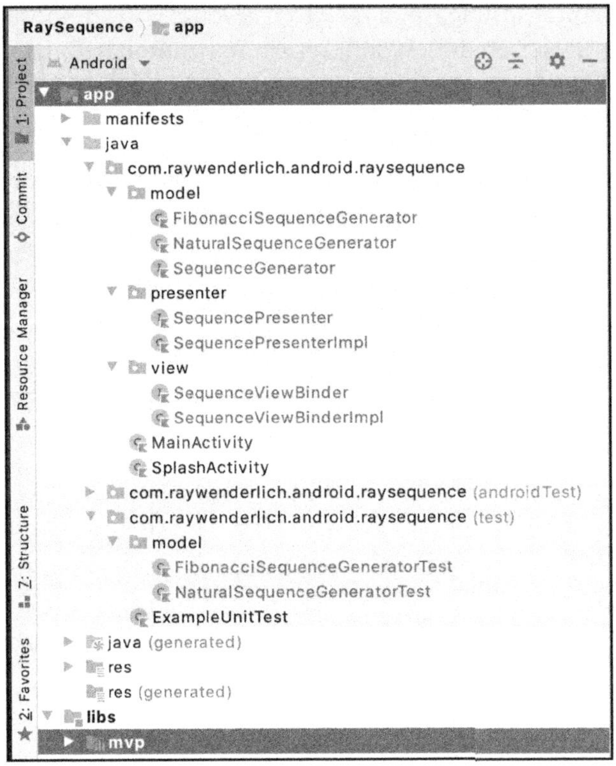

Figure 7.3 — RaySequence file structure

As you see, the app uses the same **mvp** library you saw in the previous chapters and the implementations for **Model**, **ViewBinder** and **Presenter** have already been done. However, you still need to connect the dots.

Before doing this, take a quick look at the model. Open **SequenceGenerator.kt** in the **model** package of the **app** module and look at the following code:

```
interface SequenceGenerator<T> {
    fun next(): T
}
```

`SequenceGenerator<T>` is a simple abstraction to let any object provide the next element of a sequence through its `next()` operation.

> **Note**: The Kotlin standard library already provides the Sequence<T> interface, which is similar to SequenceGenerator<T> and has some utility builders like the sequence() higher-order function. However, using Sequence<T> requires you to define an Interator<T>, which makes the code a bit more complex with no gain in the context of dependency injection.

In the same **model** package are two SequenceGenerator<T> implementations. **NaturalSequenceGenerator.kt** contains a simple way to generate natural numbers:

```
class NaturalSequenceGenerator(
    private var start: Int
) : SequenceGenerator<Int> {
    override fun next(): Int = start++
}
```

While **FibonacciSequenceGenerator.kt** contains a more interesting implementation for the **Fibonacci sequence**:

```
class FibonacciSequenceGenerator() : SequenceGenerator<Int> {
  private var pair = 0 to 1

  override fun next(): Int {
    val next = pair.first
    pair = pair.second to pair.first + pair.second
    return next
  }
}
```

You'll use this in the next chapter

In the code for the test build type, you'll also find some unit tests.

The **gradle.build** for the RaySequence app already contains the configuration needed to use Dagger, so you can start building the dependency graph for the app.

> **Note**: To save space, some of the code for this project isn't printed out. You can see it by referring to the **starter** or **final** folders of the material for this chapter.

Different injection types with Dagger

In this chapter, you'll have the opportunity to implement different types of injection with Dagger in an Android project. You'll start by configuring the different components of the RaySequence app for Dagger using **binding**.

Keep in mind that binding means: **connecting different components according to their dependencies**.

Then, you'll bind the following components:

- `SequenceViewBinder`
- `SequencePresenter`
- `MainActivity`

Finally, you'll provide all the information Dagger needs to make RaySequence work.

Ready to get started? Jump right in!

Binding the ViewBinder with constructor injection

Open **SequenceViewBinderImpl.kt** in the **view** package of the **app** module and look at the following code:

```
class SequenceViewBinderImpl(
    // HERE
    private val sequenceViewListener:
SequenceViewBinder.Listener
) : SequenceViewBinder {
  private lateinit var output: TextView

  override fun showNextValue(nextValue: Int) {
    output.text = "$nextValue"
  }

  override fun init(rootView: MainActivity) {
    output =
rootView.findViewById(R.id.sequence_output_textview)
    rootView.findViewById<Button>(R.id.next_value_button)
        .setOnClickListener {
            sequenceViewListener.onNextValuePressed()
        }
  }
}
```

As you see, `SequenceViewBinderImpl` depends on the implementation of `SequenceViewBinder.Listener` you pass as the primary constructor parameter. This is an example of **constructor injection**.

You also know that `SequenceViewBinderImpl` implements `SequenceViewBinder`. That's also the type you'll use to define the dependency. In this case, Dagger offers you two different options to create an instance of `SequenceViewBinderImpl`. You can:

1. **Invoke** the constructor directly.
2. **Delegate** the creation of the instance to Dagger.

Both solutions require you to define a `@Module` because you want to use `SequenceViewBinder` as the type of the instance in the dependency.

Whichever method you choose, the first step is the same: Create a new **di** package with a new file named **AppModule.kt** in it. What you put inside depends on the approach you decide to take.

Invoke the constructor directly

If you decide to invoke the constructor of `SequenceViewBinderImpl` directly, copy the following code into the newly created **AppModule.kt**:

```
// 1
@Module
object AppModule {
 // 2
  @Provides
  fun provideSequenceViewBinder(
      // 3
      viewBinderListener: SequenceViewBinder.Listener
      // 4
  ): SequenceViewBinder =
SequenceViewBinderImpl(viewBinderListener)
}
```

In these few lines of code, there are many interesting points:

1. You define a `@Module` to provide Dagger with some of the information it needs to build the dependency graph for the RaySequence app.
2. Using `@Provides`, you tell Dagger which function to invoke to provide the objects of type `SequenceViewBinder`. The **return type** of the function is what matters here.

3. `provideSequenceViewBinder()`, whose name is only important for readability, has a parameter of type `SequenceViewBinder.Listener`. `SequenceViewBinderImpl` requires this in its primary constructor.

4. You use the function parameter `viewBinderListener` to create the instance of `SequenceViewBinderImpl` to return. This is where you explicitly create the instance of `SequenceViewBinderImpl`.

In a configuration where an instance of type `SequenceViewBinder` is required, Dagger will invoke `provideSequenceViewBinder()`, passing the reference to an implementation of `SequenceViewBinder.Listener` — which you still need to configure. In this case, it's important to note that Dagger doesn't need to know anything about how to create the instance of `SequenceViewBinderImpl`.

Delegating the construction to Dagger using @Binds

On the other hand, you can make Dagger responsible for creating the instance of `SequenceViewBinderImpl` and its dependencies. In this case, you need to tell Dagger two things:

1. That `SequenceViewBinderImpl` is the class to use the implementation for a dependency of type `SequenceViewBinder`.

2. How to create an instance of `SequenceViewBinderImpl`.

To accomplish the first task, replace the contents of **AppModule.kt** with the following code:

```
// 1
@Module
object AppModule {
  // 2
  @Module
  interface Bindings {
    // 3
    @Binds
    fun bindSequenceViewBinder(impl: SequenceViewBinderImpl):
SequenceViewBinder
  }
}
```

As you can see, there's less code here than in the previous case. Here you:

1. Define a `@Module` to give Dagger some of the information it needs to build the dependency graph, as in the previous case.

2. Create a `Bindings` interface annotated as `@Module` that will contain all the binding definitions.

3. Use `@Binds` to **bind** the type of abstraction to the implementation to use. The type of the **abstraction** is the return type of the **binding function**. The type of the **implementation** is the type of the **unique parameter** for the same function. In this case, you're telling Dagger that whenever it needs an object of type `SequenceViewBinder`, it needs to return an instance of `SequenceViewBinderImpl`.

> **Note**: Using an internal interface for the definition of `@Binds` is just the convention this book uses. It's a simple way to keep the concrete `@Provides` functions in one concrete object and the abstract `@Binds` functions in another, but still in the same file. However, you'll see other conventions in your future work with Dagger.

When you ask Dagger to create an instance of `SequenceViewBinderImpl` for you, you need to tell it how to do so. As you learned in the previous chapter, you do that by using `@Inject`.

Open **SequenceViewBinderImpl.kt** and apply the following change:

```
class SequenceViewBinderImpl @Inject constructor( // HERE
    private val sequenceViewListener:
SequenceViewBinder.Listener
) : SequenceViewBinder {
  // ...
}
```

In both cases, Dagger knows what to do to provide an instance of `SequenceViewBinder`, but one piece of information is still missing: It doesn't know how to resolve the instance for the type `SequenceViewBinder.Listener`. It needs this as a parameter for `provideSequenceViewBinder()` in the first scenario, and as a constructor parameter for `SequenceViewBinderImpl` in the second. To solve this problem, you need to work on the `Presenter`.

It's interesting to note that, right now, you can build the app with no errors. That's because you don't have any `@Component` yet so Dagger doesn't have anything to do.

Binding the Presenter with field injection

In the previous example, you learned how to use **constructor injection** with Dagger for the `SequenceViewBinder` implementation. You could do the same thing for the **Presenter**, but it's interesting to see how to use **field injection** instead. To do this, open **SequencePresenterImpl.kt** in the **presenter** package and look at the following code:

```
class SequencePresenterImpl : BasePresenter<MainActivity,
    SequenceViewBinder>(),
    SequencePresenter {
  lateinit var sequenceModel: SequenceGenerator<Int> // HERE

  override fun displayNextValue() {
    useViewBinder {
      showNextValue(sequenceModel.next())
    }
  }

  override fun onNextValuePressed() {
    displayNextValue()
  }
}
```

This is the code for `SequencePresenterImpl`, which is the implementation for `SequencePresenter`. This is the **Presenter** for the `MainActivity` of the RaySequence app. In this code, you see how `SequencePresenterImpl` **depends on** an implementation of `SequenceGenerator<Int>`.

In theory, `SequencePresenterImpl` also depends on the `SequenceViewBinder` implementation. As you'll see in a few moments, however, this is something you can solve using the `bind()`/`unbind()` functions, which the class inherits from `BasePresenter`.

Inside **SequencePresenter.kt**, you'll find this code, which tells you that `SequencePresenter` IS-A `SequenceViewBinder.Listener`.

```
interface SequencePresenter :
    Presenter<MainActivity, SequenceViewBinder>,
    SequenceViewBinder.Listener { // HERE
  fun displayNextValue()
}
```

You can represent these relations using the UML diagram in Figure 7.4:

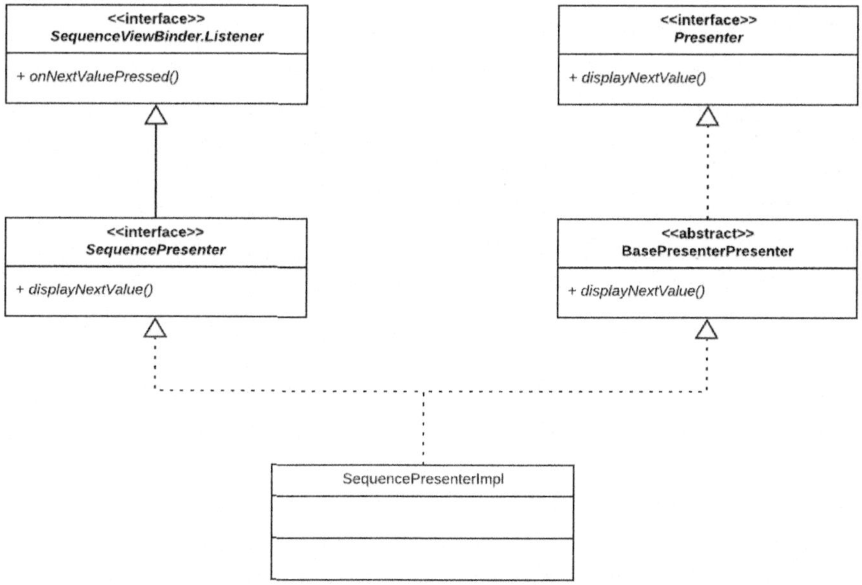

Figure 7.4 — UML Diagram for SequencePresenterImpl

Here, you need to tell Dagger to:

1. Use `SequencePresenterImpl` as an implementation for the `SequencePresenter` abstraction.
2. Inject the dependency to the `SequenceGenerator<Int>` implementation into `SequencePresenterImpl` in `sequenceModel`.
3. Create the instance of `SequenceGenerator<Int>` to use as a model.
4. Use the `SequencePresenter` implementation whenever it needs an object of type `SequenceViewBinder.Listener`.

You already know how to do all this. You'll put that knowledge to work next.

Using @Binds for the Presenter

To **bind** `SequencePresenterImpl` to `SequencePresenter`, you'll use `@Binds`. Open **AppModule.kt** and add the following definition, leaving the rest as it is:

```
@Module
object AppModule {
  @Module
  interface Bindings {
    // ...
    @Binds
    fun bindSequencePresenter(impl: SequencePresenterImpl):
SequencePresenter // HERE
  }
}
```

In this code, you're telling Dagger to create an instance of `SequencePresenterImpl` every time it needs an object of type `SequencePresenter`.

Using field injection for the Presenter

Now, you need to tell Dagger how to create the instance of `SequencePresenterImpl` with all its dependencies. Open **SequencePresenterImpl.kt** and change it to this:

```
// 1
class SequencePresenterImpl @Inject constructor(
) : BasePresenter<MainActivity,
    SequenceViewBinder>(),
    SequencePresenter {
  // 2
  @Inject
  lateinit var sequenceModel: SequenceGenerator<Int>
  // ...
}
```

In this code, you use `@Inject` for two different purposes:

1. Identifying the constructor to invoke to create the instance of type `SequencePresenterImpl`.
2. Marking `sequenceModel` as the target to be injected with an object of type `SequenceGenerator<Int>`, which is still an abstraction.

This is an example of **field injection** in Dagger.

Providing the SequenceGenerator implementation

`SequencePresenterImpl` needs an implementation of `SequenceGenerator<Int>`. You could use `@Binds` again, or you could directly provide the instance. In this case, you'll use the second option.

Open **AppModule.kt** and add the following definition to `AppModule`:

```
@Module
object AppModule {
  // ...
  @Provides
  fun provideSequenceGenerator(): SequenceGenerator<Int> =
      NaturalSequenceGenerator(0)
  // ...
}
```

In this case, you just define `provideSequenceGenerator()` for binding `NaturalSequenceGenerator` type to the `SequenceGenerator<Int>` abstraction and, at the same time, create the instance. Don't forget to annotate `provideSequenceGenerator()` with `@Provides`.

Handling the SequenceViewBinder.Listener implementation

Right now, the **ViewBinder** isn't complete because you still need to tell Dagger what to inject as the implementation for `SequenceViewBinder.Listener`

As you saw earlier, this is the Presenter and it must be **the same instance** of the `SequencePresenter` implementation that you defined in the previous paragraphs. Because you're binding a class to an abstraction, you can just add the following code to **AppModule.kt**:

```
@Module
object AppModule {
  // ...
  @Module
  interface Bindings {
    // ...
    // 1
    @Binds
    // 2
    fun bindViewBinderListener(impl: SequencePresenter):
        // 3
        SequenceViewBinder.Listener
  }
}
```

With that code, you:

1. Use `@Binds` to bind the implementation of `SequencePresenter` to the one Dagger has to return as an object of type `SequenceViewBinder.Listener`.
2. The parameter's type is abstract. That's possible because `SequencePresenter` extends `SequenceViewBinder.Listener`, as you saw in Figure 7.4. Again, the name of the function is only important for readability.
3. The return type is an abstraction: `SequenceViewBinder.Listener`.

Whenever Dagger needs an instance of `SequenceViewBinder.Listener`, it will return the implementation for `SequencePresenter` according to what's specified in the `AppModule`.

MainActivity

What you've done so far is really cool, but you still need to apply that work to RaySequence.

As you learned in the previous chapter, when you build the app, the annotation processor creates some code for you. So far, Dagger hasn't done anything — it can't until you create a `@Component` to use as the factory for the required instances. In RaySequence's case, you need a **Presenter** and a **ViewBinder**. You'll handle that next.

To start, open **MainActivity.kt** and change it like this:

```
class MainActivity : AppCompatActivity() {
  // 1
  lateinit var presenter: SequencePresenter
  // 2
  lateinit var viewBinder: SequenceViewBinder

  override fun onCreate(savedInstanceState: Bundle?) {
    super.onCreate(savedInstanceState)
    setContentView(R.layout.activity_main)
    // 3
    viewBinder.init(this)
  }

  // 4
  override fun onStart() {
    super.onStart()
    presenter.bind(viewBinder)
  }
```

```
    // 5
    override fun onStop() {
      presenter.unbind()
      super.onStop()
    }
  }
```

In this code, you:

1. Define the `presenter` property to be of type `SequencePresenter`.
2. Define the `viewBinder` property to have the type `SequenceViewBinder`.
3. Invoke `init()` on the `viewBinder` to initialize the UI into the `onCreate()` lifecycle method.
4. Bind the `viewBinder` to the `presenter` using `bind()`, inherited from `BasePresenter` in the `onStart()` lifecycle function.
5. Unbind the `viewBinder` from the `presenter` using the `unbind()` operation inherited from `BasePresenter` in the `onStop()` lifecycle function.

Build and run now... and it will crash. That's because nobody initialized the `lateinit vars`. To do this, you need a `@Component`.

Defining @Component

Dagger now has a lot of information, but it doesn't know how to use it. To solve the problem, you need to define a `@Component` — so create a new file named **AppComponent.kt** in the **di** package and copy the following code into it:

```
// 1
@Component(modules = [
  AppModule::class,
  AppModule.Bindings::class
])
interface AppComponent {
  // 2
  fun viewBinder(): SequenceViewBinder
  // 3
  fun presenter(): SequencePresenter
}
```

This code should already look familiar to you. It defines:

1. A `@Component` to use as a **factory** for the instances of the dependency graph. You use `AppModule` and `AppModule.Bindings` to get the binding information.

2. `viewBinder()` as a factory method to implement `SequenceViewBinder`.

3. `presenter()` as a factory method for `SequencePresenter`.

Once again, the **return type** of the operation you define is what's important for resolving the instances in the dependency graph.

Now, you can finally build the app and Dagger will generate some code for you. But how can you use that code in `MainActivity`? You'll see next

Injecting into MainActivity

In the previous sections, you've configured the dependencies for the RaySequence app's **ViewBinder** and **Presenter**. Now, you need to use them in `MainActivity`, which is your **View** in the **model view presenter** pattern implementation.

The simplest way of doing this is to open **MainActivity.kt** and change `onCreate()` to the following:

```
class MainActivity : AppCompatActivity() {
  lateinit var presenter: SequencePresenter
  lateinit var viewBinder: SequenceViewBinder

  override fun onCreate(savedInstanceState: Bundle?) {
    // 1
    DaggerAppComponent.create().apply {
      // 2
      presenter = presenter()
      viewBinder = viewBinder()
    }
    super.onCreate(savedInstanceState)
    setContentView(R.layout.activity_main)
    viewBinder.init(this)
  }
  // ...
}
```

In this code, you:

1. Invoke the `create()` static method on `DaggerAppComponent`, which Dagger generated for you, to create an instance of the `@Component` you defined using the `AppComponent` interface.

2. `DaggerAppComponent` is an implementation of the `AppComponent` interface you created. It provides implementations for the `presenter()` and `viewBinder()` operations, which you invoke to initialize `presenter` and `viewBinder`.

If you don't like how the injection happens here, don't worry, you'll improve the code soon.

Now you can build and run, but the app still doesn't work! It doesn't crash, but when you click on the button, nothing happens. Everything should be fine, so what's wrong?

As mentioned above, you didn't use the best way to initialize `presenter` and `viewBinder`, but that's not what's causing the problem.

Meet @Singleton

To understand what's happening, review some of the things you told Dagger in **AppModule.kt**. You told it to:

1. Create an instance of `SequencePresenterImpl`, invoking its primary constructor every time it needs an object of type `SequencePresenter`.

2. Do the same every time it needs an instance of an implementation of `SequenceViewBinder.Listener`.

However, this doesn't answer a simple question: Is the instance it returns in those two cases the same instance? Or does Dagger create a new instance every time it needs a reference to an object?

To answer this question, you'll make a simple change in the code to add some logs. Open **SequenceViewBinderImpl.kt** and add the following code to it:

```
class SequenceViewBinderImpl @Inject constructor(
    private val sequenceViewListener:
SequenceViewBinder.Listener
) : SequenceViewBinder {
  init {
    Log.d("DAGGER_LOG", "Listener: $sequenceViewListener") //
HERE
  }
  // ...
}
```

With that code, you simply print the reference to the `SequenceViewBinder.Listener` implementation you're using as listener of `SequenceViewBinder`.

Now, open **MainActivity.kt** and add the log:

```
class MainActivity : AppCompatActivity() {
```

```
  // ...
  override fun onCreate(savedInstanceState: Bundle?) {
    DaggerAppComponent.create().apply {
      presenter = presenter()
      Log.d("DAGGER_LOG", "Presenter: $presenter") // HERE
      viewBinder = viewBinder()
    }
    super.onCreate(savedInstanceState)
    setContentView(R.layout.activity_main)
    viewBinder.init(this)
  }
  // ...
}
```

This prints the reference to the instance of `SequencePresenter` that Dagger injects into `MainActivity`.

Now, build and run and use the filtering option in the **LogCat window** in Android Studio to see what's happening, as in Figure 7.5:

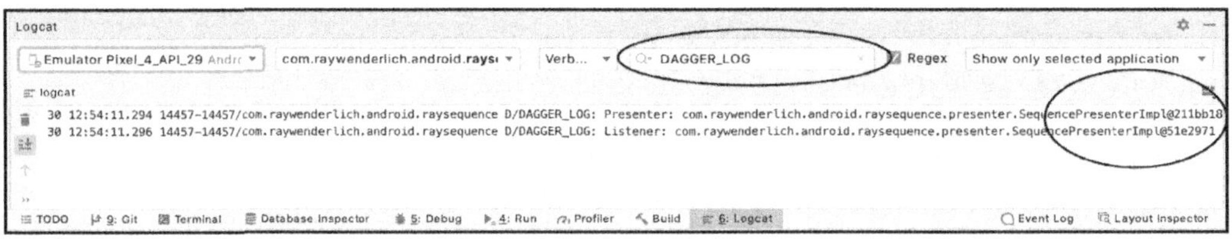

Figure 7.5 — Logging the instances Dagger has created

Once you remove the irrelevant information, you get the log shown below. It proves that the instance of `SequencePresenterImpl` Dagger provides to `MainActivity` is not the same one it injects into `SequenceViewBinderImpl` to notify it about events on the `Button`. Of course, your values will differ from those shown below since each execution will give a different result.

```
D/DAGGER_LOG: Presenter: com...SequencePresenterImpl@211bb18
D/DAGGER_LOG: Listener: com...SequencePresenterImpl@51e2971
```

This means that, as things now stand, Dagger creates a **new instance** of a class every time it needs a **reference to an object of the related type**. In most cases you don't need a new instance every time, you can use the same instance each time it's injected.

> **Note**: The **ServiceLocator** implementations you created in the first section of the book already took this into account. It didn't create unnecessary instances.

How can you fix that? This is a good opportunity to introduce the `@Singleton` annotation.

Using @Singleton

You already met the fundamental concept of **scope** in Chapter 4, "Dependency Injection & Scopes", and you'll learn a lot more in the following chapters. However, it's very important to say: `@Singleton` is nothing special.

Take careful note: **Any** annotation you use as a scope annotation is a way to bind the lifecycle of the objects handled by a specific `@Component` to the lifecycle of the `@Component` itself.

You'll read the previous statement many times in the following chapters because it's a fundamental concept you need to learn to master Dagger.

To see what this means, open **SequencePresenterImpl.kt** and replace the header of the class with this:

```
@Singleton // HERE
class SequencePresenterImpl @Inject constructor(
) : BasePresenter<MainActivity,
    SequenceViewBinder>(),
    SequencePresenter {
  // ...
}
```

Using `@Singleton`, you tell Dagger that a `@Component` should only create a single instance of `SequencePresenterImpl`.

Build the app now, however, and Dagger will complain with the following error:

```
AppComponent.java:7: error: [Dagger/IncompatiblyScopedBindings]
com.raywenderlich.android.raysequence.di.AppComponent
 (unscoped) may not reference scoped bindings:
public abstract interface AppComponent {
```

That's because you didn't tell Dagger everything! You told it to bind the instance of `SequencePresenterImpl` to the instance of a component, but you didn't tell which `@Component`.

To tell Dagger that the scope for `AppComponent` is `@Singleton`, open **AppComponent.kt** and apply the following change:

```
@Component(modules = [
  AppModule::class,
  AppModule.Bindings::class
])
@Singleton // HERE
interface AppComponent {

  fun viewBinder(): SequenceViewBinder

  fun presenter(): SequencePresenter
}
```

By annotating `AppComponent` with `@Singleton`, you're telling Dagger that the `@Component` is the factory for objects with or without a scope. If they have a scope, it *must* be the `@Singleton` scope.

For objects with no scope, like `SequenceViewBinder`, Dagger will create a new instance every time you need an object of that type. For objects annotated with `@Singleton`, `AppComponent` will always return the same instance.

> **Note**: You'll cover these concepts in detail in the following chapters. Remember that two different instances of `AppComponent` will always return different instances. Using `@Singleton` or another scope annotation won't change this.

Build and run and check the log again. Now, you'll see something like this:

```
D/DAGGER_LOG: Presenter: com...SequencePresenterImpl@211bb18
D/DAGGER_LOG: Listener: com...SequencePresenterImpl@211bb18
```

As you see, you always use the same `SequencePresenterImpl` now. More importantly, RaySequence works.

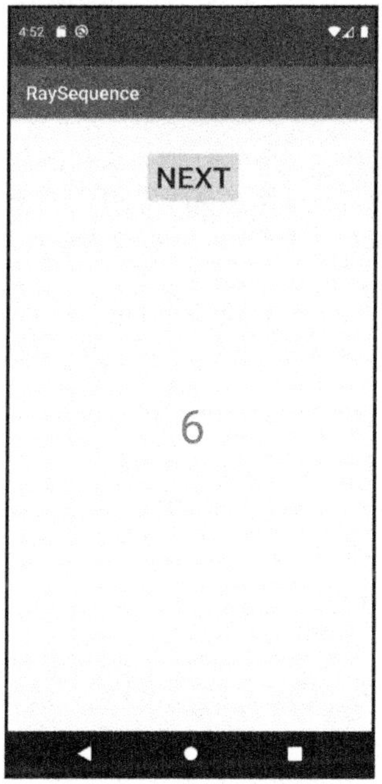

Figure 7.6 — A Working RaySequence App

Using method injection

For the sake of completeness, take a quick look at how you'd achieve the same goal with **method injection**. The change is simple.

Open **SequenceViewBinderImpl.kt** and replace the first part of the code with the following:

```
class SequenceViewBinderImpl @Inject constructor(
) : SequenceViewBinder {
  // 1
  private var sequenceViewListener: SequenceViewBinder.Listener?
= null

  init {
    Log.d("DAGGER_LOG", "Listener: $sequenceViewListener")
  }

  // 2
  @Inject
  fun configSequenceViewListener(listener:
```

```
  SequenceViewBinder.Listener) {
      sequenceViewListener = listener
    }
    // ...
  }
```

Now:

1. `sequenceViewListener` is not a primary constructor parameter, but rather a private property of optional type `SequenceViewBinder.Listener?`.
2. You define `configSequenceViewListener()` with a single parameter of type `SequenceViewBinder.Listener` and you annotate it with `@Inject`.

Build and run and you'll note that the app still works. You already learned when to use **method injection** and what the possible advantages are in Chapter 3, "Dependency Injection". However, it's useful to know that Dagger supports it, as well.

Cleaning up the injection for MainActivity

Earlier, you read that you'd use a better way to inject the **Presenter** and **ViewBinder** into the `MainActivity`. Good news — you're ready to do that now.

When you have a deeper understanding of how `@Components` work, you'll discover different approaches for the injection. But after reading this chapter, you already have all the information to implement something similar to the `Injector<T>` you saw in Chapter 4, "Dependency Injection & Scopes". You'll do that next.

Open **AppComponent.kt** and replace its contents with the following:

```
@Component(modules = [
  AppModule::class,
  AppModule.Bindings::class
])
@Singleton
interface AppComponent {
  // HERE
  fun inject(mainActivity: MainActivity)
}
```

With this code, you replaced the factory method for `SequenceViewBinder` and `SequencePresenter` with a function that accepts `MainActivity` as the single parameter.

> **Note**: Using the name `inject()` for these functions is a convention. However, nothing's stopping you from picking another name, if you prefer.

Now, you need to utilize the code Dagger generates. Open **MainActivity.kt** and replace the first part of the class with the following:

```
class MainActivity : AppCompatActivity() {
  // 1
  @Inject
  lateinit var presenter: SequencePresenter
  // 2
  @Inject
  lateinit var viewBinder: SequenceViewBinder

  override fun onCreate(savedInstanceState: Bundle?) {
    // 3
    DaggerAppComponent.create().inject(this)
    super.onCreate(savedInstanceState)
    setContentView(R.layout.activity_main)
    viewBinder.init(this)
  }
  // ...
}
```

Here, you:

1. Annotate the `presenter` with `@Inject`.
2. Do the same for `viewBinder`.
3. Create the `DaggerAppComponent` instance using `create()` and invoke `inject()` on it, passing the reference to the `MainActivity` itself.

In this case, it's important to note that what matters here is the **type of the parameter** of the `inject()` operation. This cannot be a generic type, but must be the explicit type of the object destination of the injection.

Build and run. Now, everything works as expected. You've seen that Dagger allows you to define, declaratively, how to generate an **Injector** for a given class. Cool, right? :]

Key points

- Dagger supports **constructor**, **method** and **field injection**.
- `@Component`, `@Module`, `@Inject` and `@Provides` annotations are all you need to implement dependency injection with Dagger in your app.
- `@Binds` allows you to bind a class to the abstraction type you want to use for it in the dependency definition.
- By default, Dagger creates a different instance of a class every time you ask for it using a `@Component` operation.
- `@Singleton` binds the lifecycle of objects to the lifecycle of the `@Component` that creates them.
- Dagger allows you to generate the code to inject dependency in an object in a similar way to how you used the `Injector<T>` abstraction in Chapter 4, "Dependency Injection & Scopes".

Where to go from here?

Congratulations! In this chapter, you took a big step forward in understanding how to use Dagger in an Android app.

Using the RaySequence app, you learned how to use the main Dagger annotations in a simple **model view presenter architecture**. You learned how the `@Module`, `@Component`, `@Provides` and `@Inject` annotations help you define the dependency graph. Finally, you met the `@Binds` and `@Singleton` annotations for the first time and used them to solve some very common problems.

There are many other scenarios that Dagger can help with, however. In the next chapter, you'll learn everything you need to know about the `@Module` annotation.

Chapter 8: Working With Modules

By Massimo Carli

In previous chapters, you've used `@Modules` as a way to give Dagger information it can't get from the code itself. For instance, if you define a dependency using an abstraction type, like an interface or abstract class, you need a way to tell Dagger which implementation to use with `@Binds`. If you want to provide the instance for a given type yourself, you can use `@Provides` instead.

But you can use `@Modules` for more than that. As the name implies, they're also a way to group definitions. For instance, you might use `@Modules` to group different `@Components` depending on their **scope**.

Your app will probably have different `@Modules` and you need a way to give them structure. `@Modules` can have **dependencies** as well.

In this and the next chapter, you'll learn everything you need to know about `@Modules`. In this chapter, you'll learn how to:

- Use **different** Dagger `@Modules` in the same app.
- **Optimize** start-up performances using Dagger's **`Lazy<T>`** interface.
- Avoid **cycled dependencies** using the **`Provider`** interface.
- Use **optional bindings**.

As you see, there's a lot to learn about @Modules.

> **Note**: In this chapter, you'll continue working on the RaySequence app. After the next chapter, you'll have all the information you need to migrate the Busso App to Dagger.

Throughout the chapter, you'll change configurations often. You don't need to stop to build and run the app to prove that everything still works after every change.

Why use modules?

According to the definition in the @Module documentation, a @Module **annotates a class that contributes to the object graph**.

> **Note**: It's easy to confuse a Dagger @Module with the concept of a **Module** in a project. You'll see a note like this when there's possible ambiguity.

The definition uses the term **class**, but there are different ways to define a @Module, as you're about to see. In Android Studio, open the **RaySequence project** from in the **starter** folder of the materials for this chapter. Now, open **AppModule.kt** in the **di** package and look at the following code:

```
@Module
object AppModule {

  @Provides
  fun provideSequenceGenerator(): SequenceGenerator<Int> =
      NaturalSequenceGenerator(0)

  @Module
  interface Bindings {

    @Binds
    fun bindSequenceViewBinder(impl: SequenceViewBinderImpl):
SequenceViewBinder

    @Binds
    fun bindSequencePresenter(impl: SequencePresenterImpl):
SequencePresenter

    @Binds
```

```
    fun bindViewBinderListener(impl: SequencePresenter):
        SequenceViewBinder.Listener
  }
}
```

As mentioned in the previous chapter, this is just a way to define some `@Binds` and `@Provides` functions in the same file. These are actually two different modules. You can prove this by opening **AppComponent.kt** in the same **di** package:

```
@Component(
    modules = [
      AppModule::class,
      AppModule.Bindings::class
    ]
)
@Singleton
interface AppComponent {

  fun inject(mainActivity: MainActivity)
}
```

The **modules** attribute for the `@Component` annotation accepts an `array` of `KClass<*>`. In the previous code, `AppModule` and `AppModule.Bindings` are related, giving you a simple way to improve the code. In **AppModule.kt**, replace `AppModule`'s header with this:

```
@Module(includes = [AppModule.Bindings::class]) // HERE
object AppModule {
  // ...
}
```

`@Module` has an `includes` attribute that allows you to do what the name says: Including `AppModule.Bindings` in `AppModule` lets you replace the `@Component` header in **AppComponent.kt** with this:

```
@Component(modules = [AppModule::class]) // HERE
@Singleton
interface AppComponent {
 // ...
}
```

This is a small step that helps organize the code in your project.

Using multiple @Modules

To make your code easier to read, split the definitions in **AppModule.kt** into two. Create a new file named **AppBindings.kt** in the **di** package and add the following code:

```
@Module
interface AppBindings {

  @Binds
  fun bindSequenceViewBinder(impl: SequenceViewBinderImpl):
SequenceViewBinder

  @Binds
  fun bindSequencePresenter(impl: SequencePresenterImpl):
SequencePresenter

  @Binds
  fun bindViewBinderListener(impl: SequencePresenter):
      SequenceViewBinder.Listener
}
```

Now, open **AppModule.kt** and replace its code with the following:

```
@Module(includes = [AppBindings::class]) // HERE
object AppModule {

  @Provides
  fun provideSequenceGenerator(): SequenceGenerator<Int> =
      NaturalSequenceGenerator(0)
}
```

Here, you removed the internal `Bindings` and updated the value for `includes`. This isn't a big deal, but it allows you to explore other ways of defining a `@Module`.

Using an abstract class

AppBindings.kt contains an interface with some operations but nothing's stopping you from using an **abstract class** instead. To do so, change the `AppBindings` code like this:

```
@Module
abstract class AppBindings {

  @Binds
  abstract fun bindSequenceViewBinder(impl:
SequenceViewBinderImpl): SequenceViewBinder
```

```
  @Binds
  abstract fun bindSequencePresenter(impl:
SequencePresenterImpl): SequencePresenter

  @Binds
  abstract fun bindViewBinderListener(impl: SequencePresenter):
      SequenceViewBinder.Listener
}
```

Now the class is abstract, like `@Binds` are. So what influence does that have on the code Dagger generates? None at all.

It's easy to see that the code is the same. Just check what's in **build/generated/source/kapt/debug** in the **app** module for the two cases:

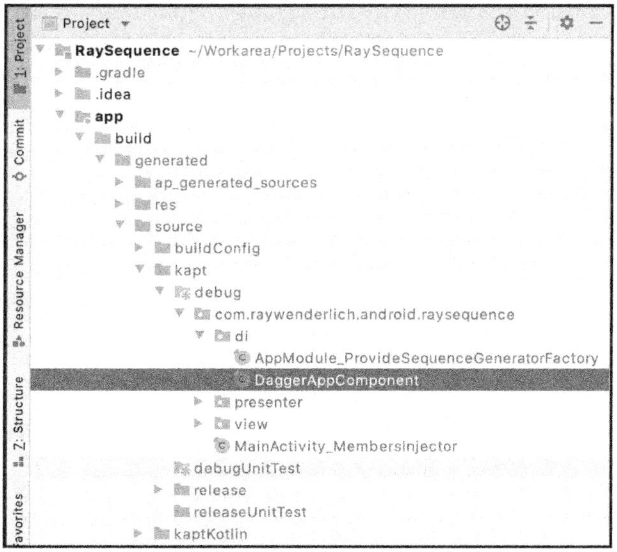

Figure 8.1 — Location for the code Dagger generates

Here, you can see how the generated code hasn't changed. That's because you've just used two different ways of telling Dagger the same thing.

Using a concrete class

What about `AppModule`? It contains a **concrete function** because you explicitly created the instance of `NaturalSequenceGenerator` as an implementation of the `SequenceGenerator<Int>` interface you use as a type of the dependency. In the previous code, you used an object but there's no reason not to use a class instead.

Open **AppModule.kt** and replace `object` with `class`, like this:

```
@Module(includes = [AppBindings::class])
class AppModule { // HERE

  @Provides
  fun provideSequenceGenerator(): SequenceGenerator<Int> =
      NaturalSequenceGenerator(0)
}
```

Build and run to see that everything's fine but, this time, the code Dagger generated is different. Remember that, at the moment, Dagger works in a Java environment so what really matters is the Java equivalent of the code you write in Kotlin. Look at **build/generated/source/kapt/debug** in the **app** module again, and you'll see that Dagger generates a file for each `@Provides` in the `@Module`.

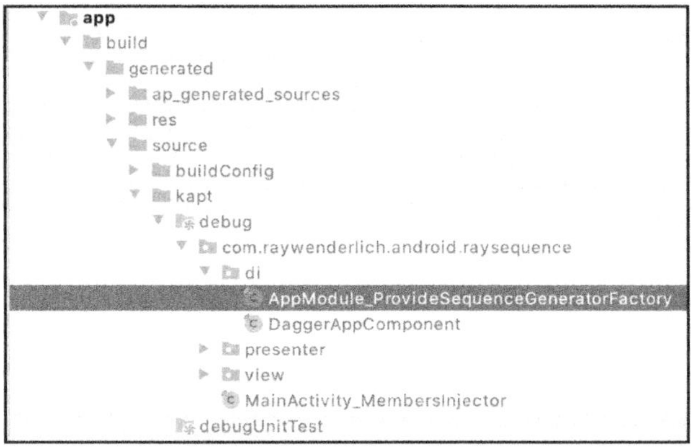

Figure 8.2 — Generated code for the AppModule

In this case, you only needed to provide `provideSequenceGenerator()` for Dagger to generate **AppModule_ProvideSequenceGeneratorFactory.kt**. The content of this file changes depending on whether you define the `@Module` with a class or with an `object`.

The difference is that the object is basically a singleton: You already have one single instance. With the class, you need to create at least one instance — but you could create many.

Open **AppModule.kt** with Android Studio and select **Tools ▸ Kotlin ▸ Show Kotlin Bytecode**, as in Figure 8.3:

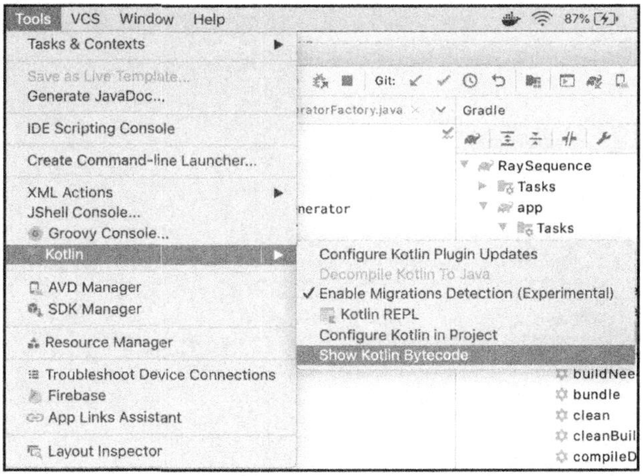

Figure 8.3 — Show Kotlin Bytecode option in Android Studio

A window like the one in Figure 8.4 will appear on the right side of Android Studio.

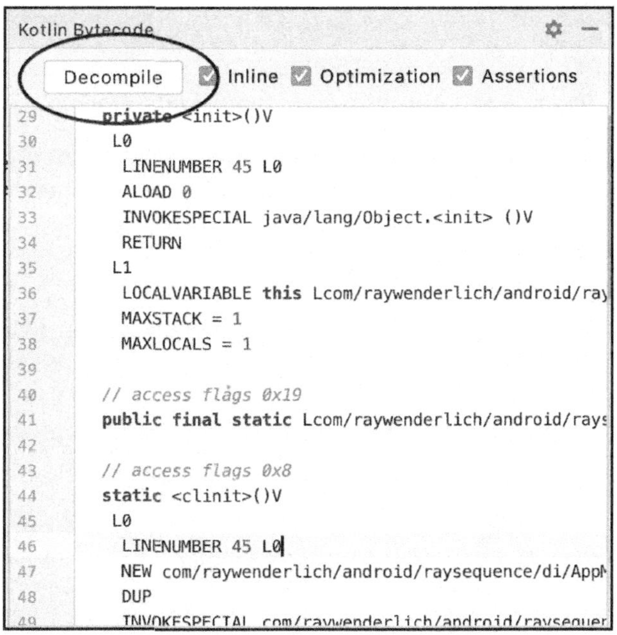

Figure 8.4 — Kotlin Bytecode Window

You can ignore that bytecode and just select the **Decompile** button and you'll get a new source tag similar to the one in Figure 8.5:

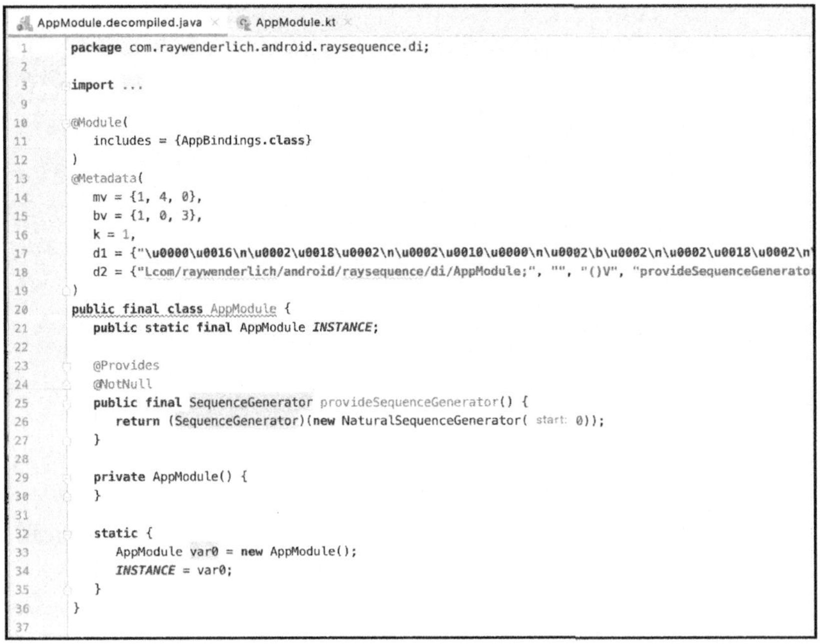

Figure 8.5 — Kotlin code decompiled into Java code

This is not code you can actually compile but it helps you get an idea of what's happening. When you define the `AppModule` as a **class**, you get code like this:

```
public final class AppModule {
  @Provides
  @NotNull
  public final SequenceGenerator provideSequenceGenerator() {
    return (SequenceGenerator)(new NaturalSequenceGenerator(0));
  }
}
```

When you use an **object** instead, `AppModule`'s code looks like this:

```
public final class AppModule {
  public static final AppModule INSTANCE;

  @Provides
  @NotNull
  public final SequenceGenerator provideSequenceGenerator() {
    return (SequenceGenerator)(new NaturalSequenceGenerator(0));
  }
```

```
  private AppModule() {
  }

  static {
    AppModule var0 = new AppModule();
    INSTANCE = var0;
  }
}
```

In this code, you can recognize the implementation of the **Singleton pattern**. This is the code Dagger processes to generate code. If you use a class, Dagger will **create an instance** of `AppModule` to delegate the creation of the `SequenceGenerator<T>` implementation. If you use an **object**, Dagger **doesn't create an instance**, but uses the existing one instead.

You can easily compare how Dagger generates the code in these two cases by looking at the **build** folder.

In theory, you could make `AppModule` abstract. Try it out by changing the code of **AppModule.kt**, like this:

```
@Module(includes = [AppBindings::class])
abstract class AppModule { // HERE

  @Provides
  fun provideSequenceGenerator(): SequenceGenerator<Int> =
      NaturalSequenceGenerator(0)
}
```

Building the app now results in an error with the following message:

```
AppComponent.java:8: error:
com.raywenderlich.android.raysequence.di.AppModule is abstract
and has instance @Provides methods. Consider making the methods
static or including a non-abstract subclass of the module
instead.
```

Dagger is complaining that `provideSequenceGenerator()` is **not static**. That's because Dagger needs an instance of `AppModule`, but it's abstract — and you can't create an instance of abstract classes. It's also true that `AppModule` doesn't have any state. `provideSequenceGenerator()` could be **static**, though. How can you do that in Kotlin? You'll see in the next step.

Using a companion object

Earlier, you tried to define a `@Module` using an abstract class and you got an error saying that you could only do that using a static function. To fix the problem, you need a **companion object**. Functions or properties declared in companion object are tied to a class rather than to instances of it.

Open **AppModule.kt** and add the following:

```
@Module(includes = [AppBindings::class])
abstract class AppModule { // 1
  // 2
  companion object {
    // 3
    @Provides
    // 4
    @JvmStatic
    fun provideSequenceGenerator(): SequenceGenerator<Int> =
        NaturalSequenceGenerator(0)
  }
}
```

As you can see, in that code you:

1. Define the `AppModule` as an abstract class.
2. Use a `companion object`.
3. Use `@Provides` to annotate `provideSequenceGenerator()`, which is now a function of the companion object.
4. Use the Kotlin `@JvmStatic` annotation to tell the compiler that it should generate static `provideSequenceGenerator` function in the enclosing `AppModule` class.

Build and run to confirm that Dagger's happy now and everything works.

Using Dagger's Lazy interface

In the previous paragraphs, you saw that `@Module` contains information about *how* to create an instance of an object in the dependency graph. Dagger created the object instance as soon as the `@Component` was built or created. However, this operation can impact the **cold start time** of the app.

The cold start time is how long the app takes to start from scratch. This includes the time used to load and launch the app, display a starting window, create the process for the app, launch the main thread, create the main `Activity`, inflate the views, lay out the screen and perform the initial draw. The cold start time should always be less than two seconds.

> **Note**: The following example is just a way to show how the `Lazy<T>` interface works in Dagger. The best way to improve the cold start time is to run the heavy code off the main thread, which is outside the scope of this book.

Suppose you want to simulate creating an object of the graph for the RaySequence app that is expensive in terms of taking a lot of time to load. Open **NaturalSequenceGenerator.kt** and add the `init` block with the following code:

```
class NaturalSequenceGenerator(private var start: Int) :
SequenceGenerator<Int> {
  init {
    sleep(3000) // HERE
  }

  override fun next(): Int = start++
}
```

Here, you added an `init()` block with a three-second `sleep` to simulate the lag from creating an expensive object. Build and run and you'll notice some delay, but it would be better to have an objective measure of how long it takes.

How can you measure the cold start time for the RaySequence app? Since Android 4.4, this information is easy to get. Just look at the LogCat window in the bottom part of Android Studio and filter the log using the text **"Displayed"**. Also, select the **No Filter** option in the combo on the right, as in Figure 8.6

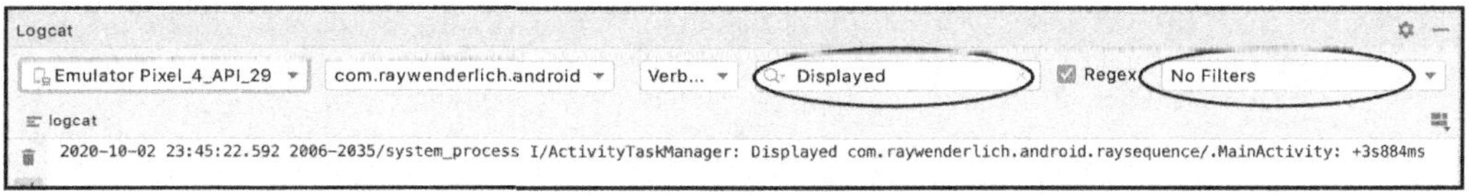

Figure 8.6 — Use LogCat to filter the Startup time for the app

You can't build and run the app yet, however, because the `Activity` for the `LAUNCH` is `SplashActivity`, which doesn't contain `@Component`'s initialization. To help with this, there's already a **build type** named `coldstart` in the project.

`coldstart` uses a different **AndroidManifest.xml**, which configures `MainActivity` as the one to launch when you start the app.

Now, open the **Build Variant Window** on the left side of Android Studio and select **coldstart** for the **app** and **mvp** modules, as in Figure 8.7:

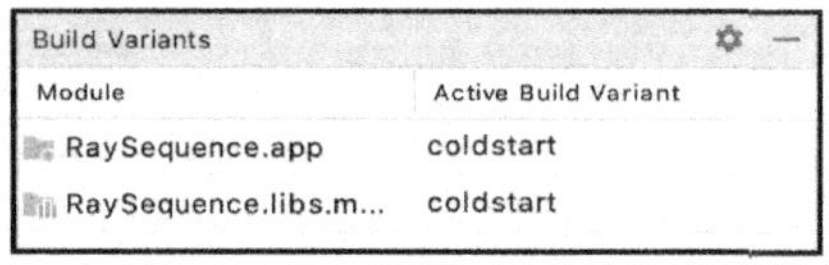

Figure 8.7 — Select the coldstart build variant

Now, you can finally build and run, then check the value you get in the LogCat window. You should see this output:

```
system_process I/ActivityTaskManager: Displayed
com.raywenderlich.android.raysequence/.MainActivity: +3s884ms
```

In this case, the cold start time is **3 seconds and 884 ms**. Of course, this is due to the `sleep(3000)` you introduced in the `init` block of `NaturalSequenceGenerator`.

So the model is slowing the app down at start time — but you don't need that model until you press the button on the screen. This means you could create `NaturalSequenceGenerator` later, making the app start more quickly. Dagger allows you to use the `Lazy<T>` interface to delay the creation of an object.

> **Note**: It's important to distinguish Dagger's **`dagger.Lazy<T>`** interface from Kotlin's similarly named **`kotlin.Lazy<T>`**.

To see how it works, open **SequencePresenterImpl.kt** and apply the following:

```
@Singleton
class SequencePresenterImpl @Inject constructor() :
    BasePresenter<MainActivity, SequenceViewBinder>(),
    SequencePresenter {

  @Inject
  lateinit var sequenceModel:
dagger.Lazy<SequenceGenerator<Int>> // 1

  override fun displayNextValue() {
    useViewBinder {
      showNextValue(sequenceModel.get().next()) // 2
    }
  }
```

```
    // ...
}
```

Here, you can see two very important things:

1. The type for the dependency is now `dagger.Lazy<SequenceGenerator<Int>>`.
2. Now that the `sequenceModel` is of type `Lazy<SequenceGenerator<Int>>`, you need to invoke `get()` to get the reference to the specific `SequenceGenerator<Int>>` implementation.

Build and run and you'll get a cold start time similar to the following:

```
system_process I/ActivityTaskManager: Displayed
com.raywenderlich.android.raysequence/.MainActivity: +799ms
```

Now, the cold start time is **799ms**, much smaller than the previous start time. Of course, you pay a price for this when you need the `SequenceGenerator<Int>` implementation. The **first time** you click the button, you'll notice the delay when the model creation takes a while.

Finally, it's important to note that:

1. If you define a dependency type with `Lazy<T>`, you get a faster startup time for free. You just need to provide the object of type **T**. Dagger applies the laziness automatically.
2. You create the object the first time you invoke `get()` and, after that, you'll get always the same instance. However, `Lazy<T>` is **not** like `@Singleton`. The former is an optimization, the latter is a matter of scope. You'll learn more about this later.

`Lazy<T>` is a good tool, but it's not the solution to every problem.

Before you move on, remember to restore the current build type to **debug** and to remove `delay(3000)` from `NaturalSequenceGenerator`.

Resolving cycled dependencies

RaySequence uses the small **mvp** library you already saw in the previous chapters. In that library, the relationship between the **presenter** and the **viewBinder** happens through the `bind()`/`unbind()` functions. This is how you pass the reference of the `SequenceViewBinder` implementation to the implementation of `SequencePresenter` into `MainActivity`, as you see in this code:

```
class MainActivity : AppCompatActivity() {
  @Inject
  lateinit var presenter: SequencePresenter
  @Inject
  lateinit var viewBinder: SequenceViewBinder

  override fun onStart() {
    super.onStart()
    presenter.bind(viewBinder) // HERE
  }

  override fun onStop() {
    presenter.unbind() // HERE
    super.onStop()
  }
  // ...
}
```

This is fine, but what if you want to manage the dependency between the **presenter** and the **viewBinder** using Dagger? You'll see how to do that next.

Adding a new implementation

Create a new file named **CycledSequencePresenter.kt** in RaySequence's **presenter** and add the following code:

```
@Singleton
class CycledSequencePresenter @Inject constructor(
    private val viewBinder: SequenceViewBinder // 1
) : SequencePresenter { // 2

  @Inject
  lateinit var sequenceModel: SequenceGenerator<Int>

  override fun displayNextValue() {
    viewBinder.showNextValue(sequenceModel.next())
  }
  // 3
  override fun bind(viewBinder: SequenceViewBinder) {}
```

```
  override fun unbind() {}

  override fun onNextValuePressed() {
    displayNextValue()
  }
}
```

This is just another implementation of the `SequencePresenter` interface that:

1. Receives the reference to the `SequenceViewBinder` as a primary constructor parameter.
2. Doesn't extend the `BasePresenter` utility class.
3. Has empty implementation for the `bind()` and `unbind()` operations.

Telling Dagger to use the new implementation

Now, you need to tell Dagger to use this implementation instead of `SequencePresenterImpl`. Open **AppBindings.kt** and replace `@Binds` in the `SequencePresenter` interface with this:

```
@Module
abstract class AppBindings {
  // ...
  @Binds
  abstract fun bindSequencePresenter(impl:
CycledSequencePresenter): SequencePresenter
}
```

Now you're telling Dagger to use an instance of `CycledSequencePresenter` every time it needs an implementation of the `SequencePresenter` interface.

Encountering a cycled dependency error

You can now build the app — but something's wrong. Dagger is complaining, giving you this error:

```
error: [Dagger/DependencyCycle] Found a dependency cycle:
```

Injecting the `SequenceViewBinder` in the `SequencePresenter` has created a **cycled dependency**. The name **Dagger** comes from **Direct Acyclic Graph**, which means it doesn't like cycle dependencies. But what is the cycle?

You can read the stack trace in the error message or look at the UML diagram in Figure 8.8 to find out:

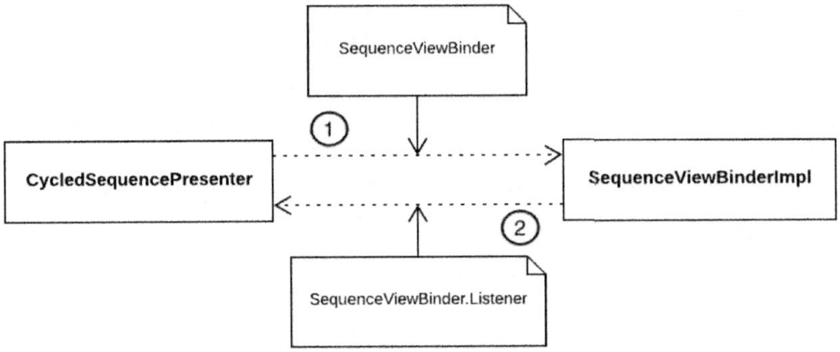

Figure 8.8 — Cycle dependency

In this diagram, you can see that:

1. `CycleSequencePresenter` depends on `SequenceViewBinderImpl` through the `SequenceViewBinder`.
2. `SequenceViewBinderImpl` depends on `CycleSequencePresenter` through the `SequenceViewBinder.Listener`.

You **need** to break this cycle. But how can you do that? `Lazy<T>` comes to the rescue.

Resolving the problem with Lazy

Open **CycledSequencePresenter.kt** and change it like this:

```
@Singleton
class CycledSequencePresenter @Inject constructor(
    private val viewBinder: dagger.Lazy<SequenceViewBinder> // 1
) : SequencePresenter {
  override fun displayNextValue() {
    viewBinder.get().showNextValue(sequenceModel.next()) // 2
  }
  // ...
}
```

In this code, you:

1. Change the type of the viewBinderprimary constructor parameter to Lazy<SequenceViewBinder>.
2. Use get() to get the reference to the actual SequenceViewBinder implementation.

Now, you'll be able to successfully build the project. When you try to run, however, you get an error that you've already met before, in SequenceViewBinderImpl:

```
lateinit property output has not been initialized
```

That's because, when you press the button on the screen, Dagger creates the first instance of the lazy SequenceViewBinder implementation — which is different from the one it already injected into MainActivity.

Now, you might think that using Lazy<SequenceViewBinder> everywhere would be a solution. Unfortunately, this isn't true. **Lazy is not a scope**. The laziness of viewBinder in CycledSequencePresenter is local to that injection.

To verify this, open **MainActivity.kt** and change it to this:

```
class MainActivity : AppCompatActivity() {

  @Inject
  lateinit var presenter: SequencePresenter

  @Inject
  lateinit var viewBinder: dagger.Lazy<SequenceViewBinder>

  override fun onCreate(savedInstanceState: Bundle?) {
    DaggerAppComponent.create().inject(this)
    super.onCreate(savedInstanceState)
    setContentView(R.layout.activity_main)
    viewBinder.get().init(this)
  }
}
```

In this case, the Lazy you define in the MainActivity differs from the one in CycledSequencePresenter. In short, Dagger will create two distinct instances: one for the MainActivity and one for the CycledSequencePresenter.

Before continuing, build and run to check that the app still crashes with the same error.

A **possible solution** to the previous problem is to annotate `SequenceViewBinderImpl` with `@Singleton`, like this:

```
@Singleton // HERE
class SequenceViewBinderImpl @Inject constructor(
    private var sequenceViewListener:
SequenceViewBinder.Listener,
    private val context: Context
) : SequenceViewBinder {
  // ...
}
```

Now you can build and run successfully — but there's a *but*! You just used the `Lazy` type to solve a problem that had nothing to do with performance. You needed to break a cycle and not to defer the creation of an object. But there could be a better solution: `Provider<T>`.

Solving the dependency problem with Provider

In the previous paragraph, you broke a cycle dependency using `Lazy<T>`. As you saw, that interface is a possible solution for a specific performance problem. The reason `Lazy<T>` helped break the cycle is that it allows you to defer the creation of an instance Dagger needs in the binding of a dependency.

If you just need to defer something without the caching feature `Lazy<T>` provides, `Provider<T>` is the interface for you.

Open **CycledSequencePresenter.kt** and replace `Lazy<T>` with `Provider<T>`, like so:

```
@Singleton
class CycledSequencePresenter @Inject constructor(
    private val viewBinder: Provider<SequenceViewBinder> // 1
) : SequencePresenter {

  override fun displayNextValue() {
    viewBinder.get().showNextValue(sequenceModel.next()) // 2
  }
  // ...
}
```

In this code, you:

1. Replaced `dagger.Lazy<T>` with `javax.inject.Provider<T>`.
2. Didn't change the way you get the reference to the provided instance. You still use `get()`.

It's worth mentioning that Provider<T> isn't a Dagger interface. Like @Inject, it's part of **Java Specification Request 330**.

Now, when you build and run, everything works fine. But there's something important to mention. Open **CycledSequencePresenter.kt** and change displayNextValue() like this:

```
@Singleton
class CycledSequencePresenter @Inject constructor(
    private val viewBinder: Provider<SequenceViewBinder>
) : SequencePresenter {
  override fun displayNextValue() {
    val binder = viewBinder.get() // 1
    Log.d("DAGGER_LOG", "Binder: $binder") // 2
    binder.showNextValue(sequenceModel.next())
  }
  // ...
}
```

Here you:

1. Invoke get() on the Provider<SequenceViewBinder> every time you click the button.
2. Log out the reference of the binder.

Build and run the app, then click the Button and use ***DAGGER_LOG** as the filter. You'll get a log like this:

```
D/DAGGER_LOG: Binder: com...SequenceViewBinderImpl@f4f3efa
D/DAGGER_LOG: Binder: com...SequenceViewBinderImpl@f4f3efa
D/DAGGER_LOG: Binder: com...SequenceViewBinderImpl@f4f3efa
// ...
```

The object you get from Provider<T> is always the same — but this isn't because of Provider<T> itself, but because of the @Singleton annotation you used on CycledSequencePresenter.

When you invoke get() on a Provider, Dagger resolves the object for the related type. Take a quick moment to prove this. Create a new file named **RandomModule.kt** in the **di** package and add the following code:

```
@Module
class RandomModule {

  @Provides
  fun provideRandomInt(): Int = Random.nextInt()
}
```

Now, add this module to the ones in `AppComponent` in **AppComponent.kt**, as in this code:

```
@Component(modules = [
  AppModule::class,
  RandomModule::class  // HERE
])
@Singleton
interface AppComponent {
  // ...
}
```

Finally, change `CycledSequencePresenter` to this:

```
@Singleton
class CycledSequencePresenter @Inject constructor(
    private val viewBinder: Provider<SequenceViewBinder>,
    private val randomProvider: Provider<Int> // HERE
) : SequencePresenter {
  override fun displayNextValue() {
    val binder = viewBinder.get()
    Log.d("DAGGER_LOG", "Binder: $binder $
{randomProvider.get()}")  // HERE
    binder.showNextValue(sequenceModel.next())
  }
  // ...
}
```

Here you:

1. Inject a `Provider<Int>` with the `randomProvider` primary constructor parameter.
2. Invoke `get()` on the `randomProvider` every time you print a log message.

Now, build and run and click the **Next** button a few times. You'll get an output similar to this:

```
D/DAGGER_LOG: Binder: com...SequenceViewBinderImpl@f4f3efa
1771794424
D/DAGGER_LOG: Binder: com...SequenceViewBinderImpl@f4f3efa
-323421530
// ...
```

As you see, `randomProvider` provides a different value every time you invoke `get()`.

As a good exercise, check what happens if you inject a `Lazy<Int>` instead. Moreover, check what happens if you inject two different `Lazy<Int>`s. Enjoy!

Key points

- A `@Module` can include other modules by using the `includes` attribute.
- When you define a `@Module` with an **interface** or an **abstract class**, it doesn't change the code Dagger generates.
- Dagger parses the Java equivalent of your Kotlin to generate its code.
- Don't confuse the Kotlin `Lazy<T>` with Dagger's `dagger.Lazy<T>`.
- `dagger.Lazy<T>` lets you defer creating an object of the dependency graph.
- `dagger.Lazy<T>` is not a scope.
- You can break cycle dependencies using the `Provider<T>` interface.

In this chapter, you've learned more about Dagger `@Modules`. You saw how to structure different `@Modules` and how to use `dagger.Lazy<T>` and `Provider<T>`, depending on the problem you want to solve. In the next chapter, you'll dig in even deeper and learn more about Dagger `@Modules`.

Chapter 9: More About Modules

By Massimo Carli

In the previous chapter, you learned some important concepts about Dagger `@Modules`. You saw how to split the bindings for your app into multiple files using **abstract classes**, **objects**, **companion objects** and **interfaces**. You learned when and how to use the **`dagger.Lazy<T>`** interface to improve performance. And you used the **`Provider<T>`** interface to break cycled dependencies.

In this chapter you'll learn :

- The benefits of using the **`@Binds`** annotation in a `@Module`.
- How to provide **existing objects**. The Android `Context` is a classical example.
- When **optional bindings** can help.
- How to provide different implementations of the same abstraction using **qualifiers** with the **`@Named`** annotation.
- When to create **custom qualifiers** to make the code easier to read and less error-prone.
- How Android Studio can help you navigate the dependency tree.

As you can see, there's still a lot to learn about `@Modules`.

> **Note**: In this chapter, you'll continue working on the RaySequence app but by the next one, you'll have all the information you need to migrate the Busso App to Dagger.

More about the @Binds annotation

You've already learned how to use `@Binds` to bind an abstract type to the implementation class Dagger considers fit for that type. But `@Binds` has other benefits, as well. You'll see proof of that next.

Open **AppModule.kt** and replace the existing code with the following:

```
@Module(includes = [AppBindings::class])
class AppModule {

  @Provides
  fun provideSequenceGenerator(): SequenceGenerator<Int> =
      FibonacciSequenceGenerator()
}
```

Here, you're using `FibonacciSequenceGenerator` because it has a default constructor. You'll see how to deal with the `NaturalSequenceGenerator` in a `@Binds` scenario later in the chapter.

Now,look at the **di** package in **build/generated/source/kapt/debug**, as shown in Figure 9.1:

Figure 9.1 — Generated code with @Provides in @Module

As you see, there are two different files:

- **AppModule_ProvideSequenceGeneratorFactory.kt**, with 29 lines of code.
- **DaggerAppComponent.kt**, with 73 lines of code.

You also know that you can provide an instance of the `SequenceGenerator<Int>` implementation using `@Binds`. Replace the previous code with the following:

```
@Module(includes = [AppBindings::class])
interface AppModule {

  @Binds
  fun bindsSequenceGenerator(impl: FibonacciSequenceGenerator):
      SequenceGenerator<Int>
}
```

Because you're now delegating the creation of `FibonacciSequenceGenerator` to Dagger, you also need to change **FibonacciSequenceGenerator.kt** by adding the `@Inject` annotation, like so:

```
class FibonacciSequenceGenerator @Inject constructor() :
SequenceGenerator<Int> {
  // ...
}
```

Now, you can build again and check what's in **build/generated/source/kapt/debug**, as shown in Figure 9.2:

Figure 9.2 — Generated code with @Binds in @Module

As you can see, you now have just one file:

- **DaggerAppComponent.kt** with 62 lines of code.

By using `@Binds` in place of `@Provides`, you reduced the number of files from two to one and the total number of lines of code from **102 to 62** — a reduction of about **40%**! This has a great impact on your work: Fewer classes and lines of code mean faster building time.

`@Binds` was added in Dagger 2.12 specifically to improve performance. So you might wonder, why not always use `@Binds`? In theory, they're the best choice, but:

- In practice, you **don't always have an abstraction** for a specific class.
- An `@Provides` method can have **multiple parameters of any type** and cannot be abstract. A `@Binds` function must be abstract and can only have **one parameter** that must be a **realization of its return type.**
- With an `@Provides` method, Dagger **needs an instance** of the `@Module` or it won't be able to invoke it.
- On the other hand, a `@Provider` can have some logic that decides which implementation to use based on some parameter values.

These are all aspects you need to consider before choosing the best option for you.

Providing existing objects

As you've learned, the `@Component` implementation is the **Factory** for the objects of the dependency graph. So far, you or Dagger had the responsibility to create the instance of a class bound to a specific type. But what happens if the object you want to provide already exists? A practical example can help.

Open **SequenceViewBinderImpl.kt** in the **view** package and apply the following changes:

```
class SequenceViewBinderImpl @Inject constructor(
    private var sequenceViewListener:
SequenceViewBinder.Listener,
    // 1
    private val context: Context
) : SequenceViewBinder {
  // ...
  override fun showNextValue(nextValue: Int) {
    // 2
    output.text =
context.getString(R.string.value_output_format, nextValue)
  }
  // ...
}
```

In this code, you:

1. Add a second parameter to the primary constructor. This is the reference to the Android `Context` you use in `showNextValue()`.
2. Use the `context` to get access to a resource to format the output on the screen.

If you build the project now, you'll get an error. This is expected because you're delegating the creation of the instance of `SequenceViewBinderImpl` to Dagger, but you didn't tell it how to create the `Context`. How can you do that? One option is to use `@Module`. But all your modules are interfaces now, and you need something more concrete.

Create a new file named **ContextModule.kt** in the **di** package and enter the following code:

```
@Module
class ContextModule(val context: Context) { // HERE

  @Provides
  fun provideContext(): Context = context
}
```

`ContextModule` is a class with a primary constructor that accepts a parameter with type `Context`. The object you pass into the primary constructor is the one you provide though `provideContext()`, annotated with `@Provides`. To use this `@Module`, you need to add it to the `@Component` module's attribute values.

To do that, open **AppComponent.kt** and change it like this:

```
@Component(modules = [
  AppModule::class,
  ContextModule::class // HERE
])
@Singleton
interface AppComponent {

  fun inject(mainActivity: MainActivity)
}
```

Build the app now and you'll get the compilation error in Figure 9.3:

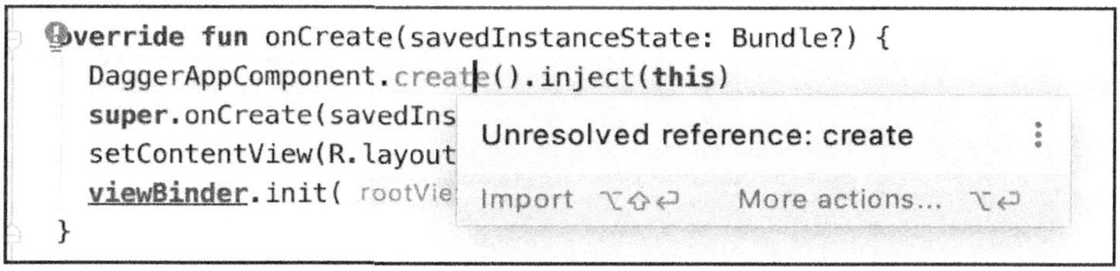

Figure 9.3 — The DaggerAppComponent doesn't compile

This happens because Dagger is smart enough to understand that it needs a `Context` to create the dependency graph. The code Dagger generates now is different.

To fix this, open **MainActivity.kt** and change the implementation of `onCreate()` like this:

```
class MainActivity : AppCompatActivity() {
  // ...
  override fun onCreate(savedInstanceState: Bundle?) {
    DaggerAppComponent
        .builder() // 1
        .contextModule(ContextModule(this)) // 2
        .build() // 3
        .inject(this)
    super.onCreate(savedInstanceState)
    setContentView(R.layout.activity_main)
    viewBinder.init(this)
  }
  // ...
}
```

Now, Dagger creates a `DaggerAppComponent` that contains a:

1. `builder()`, to get access to an implementation of the **Builder Pattern** for the `AppComponent` implementation.
2. `contextModule()` that has `ContextModule` as a parameter type. Here, you create the instance of `ContextModule` and pass the reference to `MainActivity`, which is the `Context` implementation you need.
3. `build()`, which is the one that the **Builder Pattern** defines to create the `AppComponent` implementation instance.

Now, you can build and run and check that everything works as expected. You've added a small label before the current value for the sequence, as shown in Figure 9.4:

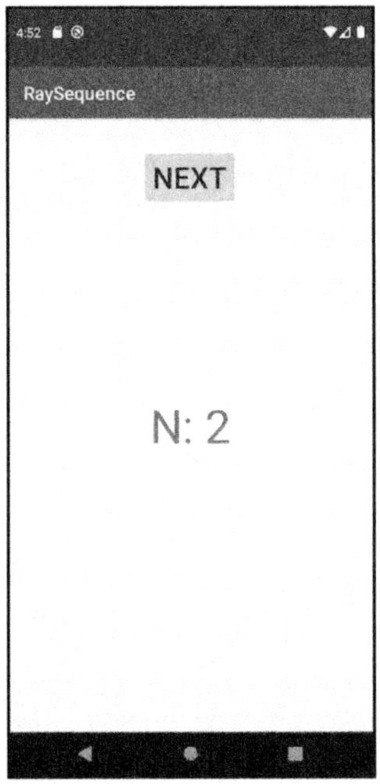

Figure 9.4 — RaySequence in execution

> **Note**: In the next chapter, you'll learn another way to do the same thing, by working on the `@Component` definition.

Adding `Context` this way is a common Android use case, but you could do the same with any other object.

Using optional bindings

What happens if a binding isn't present? So far, you get a compilation error, but sometimes you need to make a binding optional.

Open **SequenceViewBinderImpl.kt** and apply the following changes:

```
@Singleton
class SequenceViewBinderImpl @Inject constructor(
    // 1
    private val context: Context
) : SequenceViewBinder {

  // 1
  @Inject
  var sequenceViewListener: SequenceViewBinder.Listener? = null

  override fun init(rootView: MainActivity) {
    output =
rootView.findViewById(R.id.sequence_output_textview)

rootView.findViewById<Button>(R.id.next_value_button).setOnClick
Listener {
      sequenceViewListener?.onNextValuePressed() // 2
    }
  }
  // ...
}
```

In this code, you:

1. Move `sequenceViewListener` from being a primary constructor parameter to a normal **optional** property. Basically, you use **field injection** instead of **constructor injection**.
2. Because `sequenceViewListener` is now optional, you use the **safe call operator**: ?.

Now, build and run. Hey, what's happening? You're getting an error like this:

```
error: [Dagger/InjectBinding] Dagger does not support injection
into private fields
```

You already learned in the first section of the book that it isn't possible to inject objects into private fields, but isn't `sequenceViewListener` public by default?

Well, the **property** is, but the **field** is not. Dagger is a Java tool, remember? Look at the Java code for `SequenceViewBinderImpl` and you'll see something like this:

```
public final class SequenceViewBinderImpl implements
SequenceViewBinder {
   @Inject
   @Nullable
   private Listener sequenceViewListener; // HERE
   @Nullable
   public final Listener getSequenceViewListener() {
      return this.sequenceViewListener;
   }

   public final void setSequenceViewListener(@Nullable Listener
var1) {
      this.sequenceViewListener = var1;
   }
  // ...
}
```

The `sequenceViewListener` instance variable is **private**. The property is **public** because of `getSequenceViewListener()` and `setSequenceViewListener()`.

Fortunately, the Kotlin language gives you a helping hand. Just change the definition of `sequenceViewListener` in **SequenceViewBinderImpl.kt**, like this:

```
@Singleton
class SequenceViewBinderImpl @Inject constructor(
    private val context: Context
) : SequenceViewBinder {

  @set:Inject // HERE
  var sequenceViewListener: SequenceViewBinder.Listener? = null
  // ...
}
```

By using the **set:** prefix, you're telling the compiler to annotate the setter function of the property. The Java code for this is:

```
public final class SequenceViewBinderImpl implements
SequenceViewBinder {
   @Nullable
   private Listener sequenceViewListener;
   @Nullable
   public final Listener getSequenceViewListener() {
      return this.sequenceViewListener;
   }

   @Inject // HERE
   public final void setSequenceViewListener(@Nullable Listener
```

```
var1) {
        this.sequenceViewListener = var1;
    }
}
```

After the change, `@Inject` is on `setSequenceViewListener()`. In theory, this isn't **field injection**, right? It looks more like **method injection**. But whatever it is, you can successfully build and run now.

Could you use the **optional type**, instead? Give it a try. Open **AppBindings.kt** and comment out — or simply remove — the binding for the `SequenceViewBinder.Listener` type like this:

```
@Module
abstract class AppBindings {
  // ...
  /*
  @Binds
  abstract fun bindViewBinderListener(impl: SequencePresenter):
      SequenceViewBinder.Listener
  */
}
```

Build again and Dagger complains that:

```
SequenceViewBinder.Listener cannot be provided without an
@Provides-annotated method.
```

The optional doesn't work. The reason is still that Dagger is a Java tool, but there's a solution: the `Optional<T>` type.

> **Note**: Dagger supports the `Optional<T>` type in the package `java.util` in Android, but only from the **API Level 24**. The RaySequence app supports API Level 19, so you use the `Optional<T>` in the **com.google.common.base** package of https://github.com/google/guava, which you can already see in the dependencies in the **build.gradle** for the project.

Using @BindsOptionalOf

Open **SequenceViewBinderImpl.kt** and change the property definition like this:

```
@Singleton
class SequenceViewBinderImpl @Inject constructor(
    private val context: Context
```

```
) : SequenceViewBinder {

  @set:Inject
  var sequenceViewListener:
Optional<SequenceViewBinder.Listener> = Optional.absent() // 1

  override fun init(rootView: MainActivity) {
    output =
rootView.findViewById(R.id.sequence_output_textview)

rootView.findViewById<Button>(R.id.next_value_button).setOnClick
Listener {
      // 2
      if (sequenceViewListener.isPresent) {
        sequenceViewListener.get().onNextValuePressed()
      }
    }
  }
  // ...
}
```

In this code, you:

1. Change the type of `sequenceViewListener` to `Optional<SequenceViewBinder.Listener>` with an initial value of `Optional.absent()`.
2. Check if the value is present using `isPresent`. If `true`, you get its reference using `get()`.

Build the app now, and Dagger will complain again! That's because it has no idea how to deal with `Optional<T>`. The problem is that `Optional<T>` is not a standard type, like the others. And that's exactly why `@BindsOptionalOf` exists.

Open **AppBindings.kt** and add the following definition:

```
@Module
abstract class AppBindings {
  @BindsOptionalOf // HERE
  abstract fun provideSequenceViewBinderListener():
SequenceViewBinder.Listener
  // ...
}
```

With the previous code, you're telling Dagger that it might find an `Optional<SequenceViewBinder.Listener>` and that it shouldn't complain if there isn't a binding for it.

Now you can successfully build the app — but when you press the button, nothing happens. That's because `Optional<SequenceViewBinder.Listener>`'s property `sequenceViewListener` has no bindings, so it's `Optional.absent()`.

To make the app work again, open **AppBindings.kt** and restore the following definition:

```
@Module
abstract class AppBindings {
  // ...
  @Binds
  abstract fun bindViewBinderListener(impl: SequencePresenter):
      SequenceViewBinder.Listener
}
```

Build and run now and everything works as expected. `Optional<SequenceViewBinder.Listener>` now has a value.

Using qualifiers

RaySequence contains two different model implementations of `SequenceGenerator<T>`:

- `NaturalSequenceGenerator`
- `FibonacciSequenceGenerator`

You bound each of these in **AppModule.kt** in different examples. For instance, you moved from the `NaturalSequenceGenerator` to the `FibonacciSequenceGenerator` because of the primary constructor parameter. It would be nice to have both implementations at the same time and to make it easier to change which one you use. However, if you just use both, Dagger will complain.

Open **AppModule.kt** and change it like this:

```
@Module(includes = [AppBindings::class])
interface AppModule {

  @Binds
  fun bindsNaturalSequenceGenerator(impl:
NaturalSequenceGenerator): SequenceGenerator<Int>

  @Binds
  fun bindsFibonacciSequenceGenerator(impl:
FibonacciSequenceGenerator):
      SequenceGenerator<Int>
}
```

Build the app and you'll get the following error:

```
error: [Dagger/DuplicateBindings]
com...SequenceGenerator<java.lang.Integer> is bound multiple
times:
```

Of course! You get this error because you have multiple bindings for the same abstraction. Dagger allows you to solve this problem with the concept of **qualifiers**.

Using the @Named annotation

The easiest way to solve the previous problem is by using the **@Named** annotation. To do that, just open **AppModule.kt** and add the following code:

```
// 1
const val NATURAL = "NaturalSequence"
const val FIBONACCI = "FibonacciSequence"

@Module(includes = [AppBindings::class])
interface AppModule {

  @Binds
  @Named(NATURAL) // 2
  fun bindsNaturalSequenceGenerator(impl:
NaturalSequenceGenerator): SequenceGenerator<Int>

  @Binds
  @Named(FIBONACCI) // 3
  fun bindsFibonacciSequenceGenerator(impl:
FibonacciSequenceGenerator):
      SequenceGenerator<Int>
}
```

In this code, you:

1. Define the `NATURAL` and `FIBONACCI` constants you'll use to identify the two different `SequenceGenerator<Int>` implementations.
2. Use the `@Named` annotation with the `NATURAL` constant as its parameter to identify the `NaturalSequenceGenerator` implementation.
3. Do the same for the `FibonacciSequenceGenerator` implementation using the `@Named` annotation and the `FIBONACCI` parameter value.

Build now, but Dagger keeps complaining. Now it doesn't know which one to use in `SequencePresenterImpl`.

Fix this by opening **SequencePresenterImpl.kt** and applying the following change:

```
@Singleton
class SequencePresenterImpl @Inject constructor(
) : BasePresenter<MainActivity,
    SequenceViewBinder>(),
    SequencePresenter {

  @Inject
  @Named(NATURAL) // HERE
  lateinit var sequenceModel: SequenceGenerator<Int>
  // ...
}
```

Using `@Named`, you're telling Dagger that the instance you want to inject is the one with the `NATURAL` constant as the parameter of `@Named`. But now that you're delegating creating the instance of `NaturalSequenceGenerator` to Dagger, it needs some small changes. Open **NaturalSequenceGenerator.kt** and add `@Inject` to the primary constructor, like this:

```
class NaturalSequenceGenerator @Inject constructor( // HERE
    private var start: Int
) : SequenceGenerator<Int> {

  override fun next(): Int = start++
}
```

But you're not quite finished yet. Build the app now, and you'll get the following error:

```
error: [Dagger/MissingBinding] java.lang.Integer cannot be
provided without an @Inject constructor or an @Provides-
annotated method.
```

Of course! Dagger doesn't know what to pass as the value to the constructor parameter of type `Int`. But you already know how to fix this. Open **AppModule.kt** and add the following definitions:

```
const val NATURAL = "NaturalSequence"
const val FIBONACCI = "FibonacciSequence"
const val START_VALUE = "StartValue" // 1

@Module(includes = [AppBindings::class])
interface AppModule {
  // 2
  companion object {
    @Provides
    @JvmStatic
    @Named(START_VALUE) // 3
    fun provideStartValue(): Int = 0
  }
}
```

In this code, you:

1. Add a new `START_VALUE` constant.
2. Create a companion object, because Dagger doesn't like to have concrete functions in an interface.
3. Annotate `provideStartValue()` with `@Named` using `START_VALUE`.

Now, you can finally edit **NaturalSequenceGenerator.kt**, adding `@Named` as a qualifier of the parameter you want to use for the primary constructor.

```
class NaturalSequenceGenerator @Inject constructor(
    @Named(START_VALUE) private var start: Int
) : SequenceGenerator<Int> {

  override fun next(): Int = start++
}
```

Now, you can finally successfully build and run and verify everything's working as expected.

Providing values for basic types

Providing a value for common types like `Int` or `String` with no qualifier can be dangerous. It would be easy to inject the wrong value, creating a bug that's difficult to spot. Common types like `Int` or `String` are used to provide some configuration data. In that case **encapsulation** can help.

> **Note**: In Kotlin, there's no concept of **primitive types** like in Java. In Kotlin, you have the concept of the following **basic types**: `Byte`, `Short`, `Int`, `Long`, `Float`, `Double`, `Char` and `Boolean`. For the integers, you also have the `Unsigned` counterparts: `UByte`, `UShort`, `UInt` and `ULong`. Although a `String` is not a **primitive Java type**, you can consider a `String` a **Kotlin basic type**.

Create a new package named **conf**, add a new file named **Config.kt** to it and add the following code:

```
data class Config(
    val startValue: Int
)
```

Then, change the code in **AppModule.kt** like this:

```
@Module(includes = [AppBindings::class])
interface AppModule {
  // ...
  companion object {
    @Provides
    @JvmStatic
    fun provideConf(): Config = Config(0) // HERE
  }
}
```

Here, you basically replace `provideStartValue()` with `provideConf()`, returning an instance of `Config` encapsulating all the configuration values you need. This allows you to remove `@Named` as well.

To complete the process, open **NaturalSequenceGenerator.kt** and apply the following changes:

```
class NaturalSequenceGenerator @Inject constructor(
    config: Config // 1
) : SequenceGenerator<Int> {

  private var start = config.startValue // 2

  override fun next(): Int = start++
}
```

In this code, you:

1. Inject the `Config` instance as the primary constructor parameter.
2. Initialize the `start` variable with `Config.startValue`.

You changed `NaturalSequenceGenerator`, so you need to update the tests accordingly. Open **NaturalSequenceGeneratorTest.kt** in the **test** build type and change it like this:

```
class NaturalSequenceGeneratorTest {

  @Test
  fun `test natural sequence value`() {
    val naturalSequenceIterator =
NaturalSequenceGenerator(Config(0)) // HERE
    listOf(0, 1, 2, 3, 4, 5, 6, 7, 8, 9, 10).forEach {
      assertEquals(it, naturalSequenceIterator.next())
    }
  }

  @Test
  fun `test natural sequence value starting in diffenet value`()
{
    val naturalSequenceIterator =
NaturalSequenceGenerator(Config(10)) // HERE
    listOf(10, 11, 12, 13, 14, 15, 16, 17, 18, 19, 20).forEach {
      assertEquals(it, naturalSequenceIterator.next())
    }
  }
}
```

Now, you can successfully build and run!

Using custom qualifiers

In the previous section, you learned how to bind different definitions to the same type using `@Named`. To do this, you had to define some `String` constants to use in your code. Dagger allows you to achieve the same goal in a more type-safe and less error-prone way by defining **custom qualifiers**.

Create a new file named **NaturalSequence.kt** in the **di** package and add the following code:

```
@Qualifier // 1
@MustBeDocumented // 2
@Retention(AnnotationRetention.BINARY) // 3
annotation class NaturalSequence //4
```

These few lines of code are very important — they allow you to define an annotation named `NaturalSequence`.

In this code, you:

1. Use `@Qualifier` to identify this annotation as a way to qualify a specific binding, just like you did with `@Named`. `@Qualifier` isn't a Dagger annotation, but rather another definition in the **javax.inject** package of the JSR-330.
2. Tag this annotation as something that's part of a public API for a feature. Because of this, it needs a Javadoc.
3. Set the retention of the annotation to `BINARY`. This means that the annotation is stored in binary output, but invisible for reflection.
4. Finally, define `NaturalSequence`, which has no attributes.

Next, create a new file in the **di** package named **FibonacciSequence.kt** and add the following code:

```
@Qualifier
@MustBeDocumented
@Retention(AnnotationRetention.BINARY)
annotation class FibonacciSequence
```

The names are the only difference between `@FibonacciSequence` and `@NaturalSequence`.

Now, open **AppModule.kt** and change its content to the following:

```
@Module(includes = [AppBindings::class])
interface AppModule {
  // ...
  @Binds
  @NaturalSequence // 1
  fun bindsNaturalSequenceGenerator(impl:
NaturalSequenceGenerator): SequenceGenerator<Int>

  @Binds
  @FibonacciSequence // 2
  fun bindsFibonacciSequenceGenerator(impl:
FibonacciSequenceGenerator):
      SequenceGenerator<Int>
}
```

Here, you removed the `NATURAL` and `FIBONACCI` constants and replaced `@Named` with:

1. `@NaturalSequence`
2. `@FibonacciSequence`

Next, open **SequencePresenterImpl.kt** and change the code like this:

```
@Singleton
class SequencePresenterImpl @Inject constructor(
) : BasePresenter<MainActivity,
    SequenceViewBinder>(),
    SequencePresenter {

  @Inject
  @NaturalSequence // HERE
  lateinit var sequenceModel: SequenceGenerator<Int>
  // ...
}
```

With this code, you also replaced `@Named` with your custom `@NaturalSequence`.

Now, you can build and run and check that everything works.

So what do custom qualifiers cost in terms of the code Dagger generates for you? Very little. Aside from the definitions and compilation of the source code for the annotations themselves, Dagger doesn't generate any additional code. It just uses custom qualifiers to choose which specific implementation to inject. Nice job, Dagger!

Modules, bindings & Android Studio

While you were developing the example, you might have noticed some new icons in Android Studio, like the ones you see when you open **AppModule.kt**:

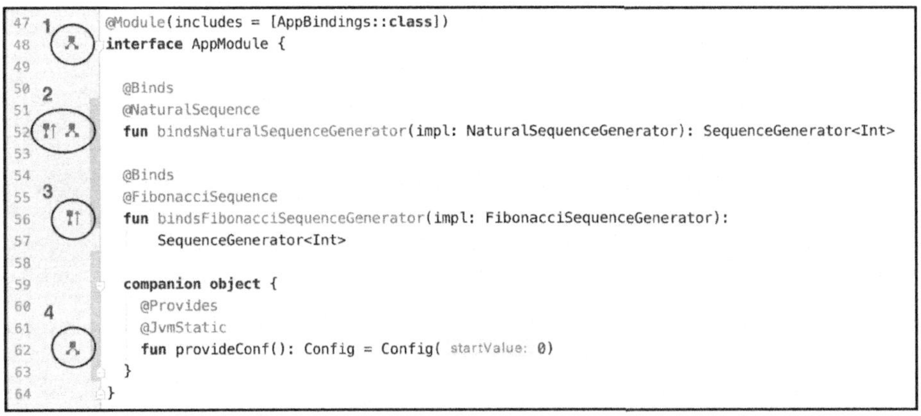

Figure 9.5 — Android Studio support for Dagger

Since Android Studio 4.2, you can navigate the Dagger bindings directly from the code. There are two different icons that, when you click on them, tell you where you:

- Define the binding for the type.
- Use the type as a dependency.

It's easy to see how this works.

Finding a type's binding

You can find the source of a binding for a specific type by clicking the icon in Figure 9.6:

Figure 9.6 — Find Bindings icon

Try it on the icon numbered **3** — you end up in **FibonacciSequenceGenerator.kt**, which is the type bound to `SequenceGenerator<Int>`, which `@Binds` defines in **AppModule.kt**.

In Figure 9.7, you see that the second icon allows you to find where Dagger binds type.

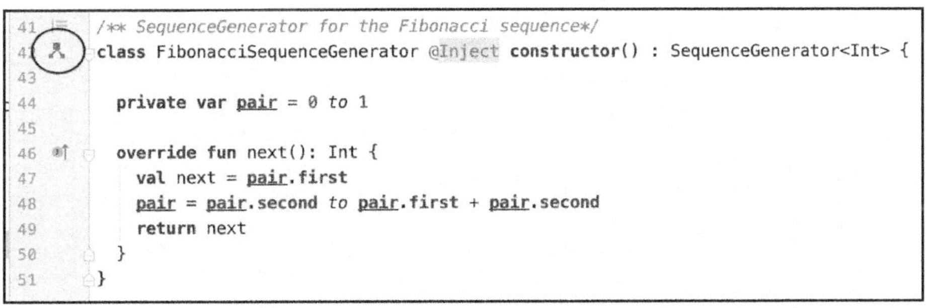

```
/** SequenceGenerator for the Fibonacci sequence*/
class FibonacciSequenceGenerator @Inject constructor() : SequenceGenerator<Int> {

  private var pair = 0 to 1

  override fun next(): Int {
    val next = pair.first
    pair = pair.second to pair.first + pair.second
    return next
  }
}
```

Figure 9.7 — Source of the binding definition

Finding a type's usage

In Figure 9.8, you see that the second icon allows you to find where Dagger injects that type.

Figure 9.8 — Find injection for a type

Click on the icon in Figure 9.6 and you'll return to **AppModule.kt**.

More interesting is what happens when you click the icon in Figure 9.8 in the `@Component` definition in **AppComponent.kt**: Android Studio shows what's in Figure 9.9:

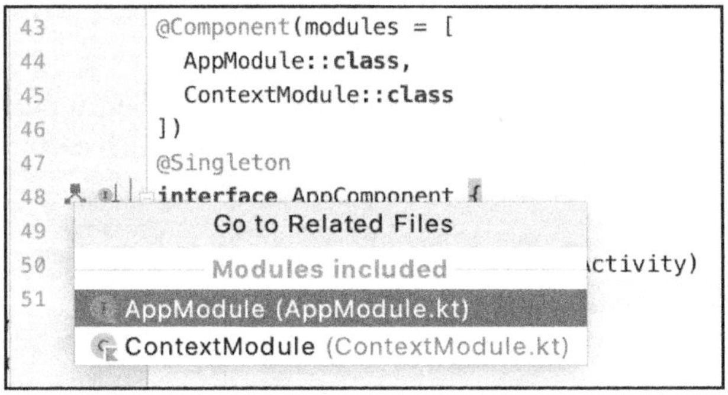

Figure 9.9 — Modules for a Components

As a rule of thumb, you can use the icon in Figure 9.6 to go **down** in the dependency tree and the one in Figure 9.8 to go **up**.

Key points

- By using @Binds, Dagger generates fewer and shorter files, making the build more efficient.
- Dagger @Modules allow you to provide existing objects, but you need to pass an instance of them to the @Component builder that Dagger generates for you.
- @BindsOptionalOf allows you to have optional bindings.
- You can provide different implementations for the same type by using @Named.
- Custom qualifiers allow you to provide different implementations for the same type in a type-safe way.
- From Android Studio 4.1, you can easily navigate the dependency graph from the editor.

Great job! With this chapter, you've completed Section Two of the book. You learned everything you need to know about Dagger @Modules and you experimented with using different fundamental annotations like @Binds, @Provides and BindsOptionalOf as well as useful interfaces like dagger.Lazy<T> and Provider<T>.

You also learned what qualifiers are, how to implement them with @Named and how to use custom @Qualifiers.

Now, it's time to learn everything you need about @Components. See you in the next chapter!

Section III: Components & Scope Management

In this section, you'll migrate the Busso App from the homemade framework to Dagger. In the process, you'll learn how to migrate the existing ServiceLocators and Injectors to the equivalent Dagger @Modules and @Components, how to provide existing objects with a customized Builder for the @Component using @Component.Builder, and how to use @Component.Factory as a valid alternative to @Component.Builder.

The first migration will not be optimal — there will still be some fundamental aspects you will improve.

Chapter 10: Understanding Components

By Massimo Carli

In the previous chapters, you learned how to deal with `@Modules` in Dagger. You learned how a **`@Module`** helps you structure the code of your app and how you can use them to control the way Dagger creates instances of the objects in the dependency graph.

You also had the opportunity to meet the most important concept in Dagger: the **`@Component`**. You learned that a `@Component` defines the factory methods for the objects in your app's dependency graph. When you get a reference to an object using a `@Component`'s factory method, you're confident that Dagger has resolved all its dependencies. You saw this in both the simple `Server-Repository` example and in the more complex RaySequence app.

In this chapter, you'll go back to working on the Busso App. You'll learn how to:

- Migrate the existing `ServiceLocators` and `Injectors` to Dagger's equivalent `@Modules` and `@Components`.
- Provide existing objects with a customized **Builder** for the `@Component` using `@Component.Builder`.
- Use `@Component.Factory` as a valid alternative to `@Component.Builder`.

These are fundamental concepts you must understand to master Dagger. They're also a prerequisite for the next chapter, where you'll learn all about scopes. So get ready to dive in!

Migrating Busso to Dagger

As mentioned earlier, `@Components` are one of the most important concepts in Dagger. As you saw in the previous examples, a `@Component`:

- Is the **factory** for all the objects in the dependency graph.
- Allows you to implement the object you referred to as an `Injector` in the first section of the book.

Don't worry if you don't remember everything. With Busso's help, you'll review all the concepts over the course of this chapter. In particular, you'll see how to:

- Remove the `Injector` implementations, delegating the actual injection of the dependent objects to the code Dagger generates for you from a `@Component`.
- Replace the `ServiceLocator` implementations with `@Modules`.

To start, use Android Studio to open the Busso App from the **starter** folder in the downloaded materials for this chapter. As you see in the code, the app uses the **model view presenter** and has `ServiceLocator` and `Injector` implementations for all the `Activity` and `Fragment` definitions.

In Figure 10.1, you can see the project structure of the **di** package, which you'll switch over to Dagger first.

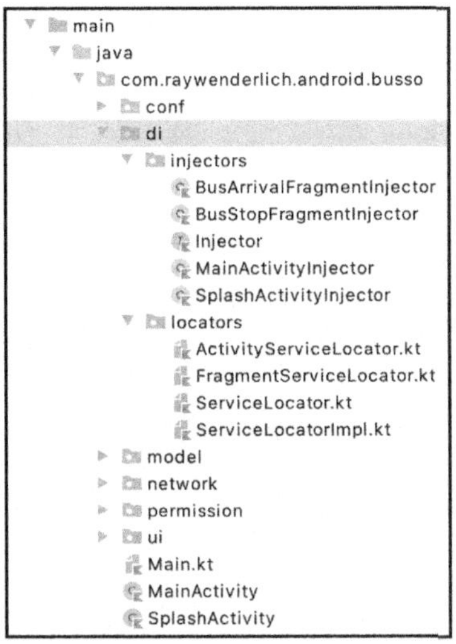

Figure 10.1 — Starting project structure of the Busso app

It's always nice to delete code in a project and make it simpler. So let the fun begin!

Installing Dagger

The first thing you need to do is to install the dependencies Dagger needs for the project. Open **build.gradle** from the **app** module and apply the following changes:

```
plugins {
  id 'com.android.application'
  id 'kotlin-android'
  id 'kotlin-android-extensions'
  id 'kotlin-kapt' // 1
}
apply from: '../versions.gradle'

// ...

dependencies {
  // ...
  // 2
  // Dagger dependencies
  implementation "com.google.dagger:dagger:$dagger_version"
  kapt "com.google.dagger:dagger-compiler:$dagger_version"
}
```

As you learned in the previous chapters, you add Dagger support to the Busso App by:

1. Enabling the **annotation processor plugin**, `kotlin-kapt`.
2. Adding dependencies to the Dagger library. The library's version is already included in **versions.gradle** in the root folder of the project.

Select **File ▸ Sync Project with Gradle Files** to update the Gradle configuration in Android Studio. You can also select the icon shown in Figure 10.2, which appears as soon as you update some Gradle files:

Figure 10.2 — Sync Gradle file icon

Now, you're ready to migrate Busso to Dagger.

Studying the dependency graph

In the previous examples, you learned that a:

- `@Component` describes which objects in the dependency graph you can inject, along with all their dependencies.
- `@Module` tells Dagger how to create the objects in the dependency graph.

With these definitions in mind, you know that you need to migrate the existing `Injectors` to `@Components` and `ServiceLocators` to `@Modules`. Start the migration from the `SplashActivity` using the **dependency graph**, as shown in Figure 10.3:

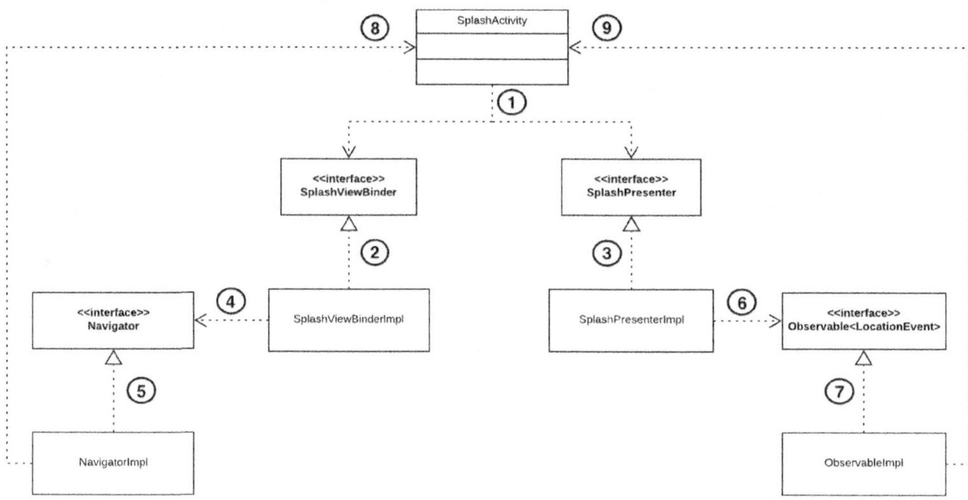

Figure 10.3 — SplashActivity dependency graph

The dependency diagram in Figure 10.3 shows that:

1. `SplashActivity` depends on `SplashViewBinder` and `SplashPresenter`.
2. `SplashViewBinderImpl` is the class to create when you need an object of type `SplashViewBinder`.
3. For the `SplashPresenter` type, you use `SplashPresenterImpl`.
4. `SplashViewBinderImpl` depends on a `Navigator`.
5. `NavigatorImpl` is the class to use for the `Navigator` type.
6. `SplashPresenterImpl` depends on an `Observable<LocationEvent>` implementation.

7. In the diagram, `ObservableImpl` just represents the `Observable<LocationEvent>` implementation you'll get from `provideRxLocationObservable()`.
8. `NavigatorImpl` depends on the `Activity`.
9. Also, the `Observable<LocationEvent>` implementation needs an `Activity`.

To migrate the Busso App to Dagger, you need to describe the dependency diagram in Figure 10.3 using Dagger annotations.

Removing the injectors

Start by opening **SplashActivityInjector.kt** from **di.injectors** and looking at the current implementation:

```
object SplashActivityInjector : Injector<SplashActivity> {
  // 1
  override fun inject(target: SplashActivity) {
    // 2
    val activityServiceLocator =

target.lookUp<ServiceLocatorFactory<AppCompatActivity>>(ACTIVITY
_LOCATOR_FACTORY)
            .invoke(target)
    // 3
    target.splashPresenter =
activityServiceLocator.lookUp(SPLASH_PRESENTER)
    target.splashViewBinder =
activityServiceLocator.lookUp(SPLASH_VIEWBINDER)
  }
}
```

This code is familiar by now. Think about what it does and what the responsibilities of `@Components` and `@Modules` are. You can see that:

1. The `SplashActivityInjector` defines `inject()` with a parameter of type `SplashActivity`, which is the target of the injection. Note that a Dagger `@Component` can do the same thing.
2. Now, you get a reference to the `ActivityServiceLocator`, which is the object that knows how to get the instances of the `SplashViewBinder` and `SplashPresenter` implementations. A `@Module` has this responsibility in Dagger.
3. Here, you assign `SplashPresenter`'s and `SplashViewBinder`'s references to the related properties in the `SplashActivity`.

This tells you that to migrate the `SplashActivityInjector` class to Dagger, you need to:

1. Define a `@Module` that tells Dagger how to get the `SplashViewBinder` and `SplashPresenter` implementations.
2. Define a `@Component` using the previous `@Module`, which defines `inject()` for `SplashActivity`.
3. Use the `@Component` in `SplashActivity`.

It's time to put this theory into code.

Creating the @Module

Create a new file named **AppModule.kt** in the **di** package and add the following code:

```
// 1
@Module(includes = [AppModule.Bindings::class])
class AppModule {
  // 2
  @Module
  interface Bindings {
    // 3
    @Binds
    fun bindSplashPresenter(impl: SplashPresenterImpl):
SplashPresenter
    // 4
    @Binds
    fun bindSplashViewBinder(impl: SplashViewBinderImpl):
SplashViewBinder
  }
}
```

This code should be quite familiar. In it, you:

1. Create a new module named **AppModule** as a class. You'll understand very soon why it's a class. Here, you also include the `Bindings` module that's defined in the same file. You've seen this pattern in previous chapters.
2. Define the `Bindings` interface, because you need some abstract functions that aren't possible in a concrete class.
3. Use `@Binds` to bind `SplashPresenterImpl` to `SplashPresenter`.
4. Do the same for `SplashViewBinder` and its implementation, `SplashViewBinderImpl`.

Creating SplashPresenter and SplashViewBinde

Now, Dagger knows which classes to use when you need an object of type `SplashPresenter` or `SplashViewBinder`. It doesn't know how to create them, though. To start solving that problem, open **SplashPresenterImpl.kt** from **ui.splash** and look at its header:

```
class SplashPresenterImpl constructor( // HERE
    private val locationObservable: Observable<LocationEvent>
) : BasePresenter<SplashActivity, SplashViewBinder>(),
SplashPresenter {
  // ...
}
```

`SplashPresenterImpl` uses **constructor injection** and needs a reference to an implementation of `Observable<LocationEvent>`. Here, you just need to use `@Inject` like this:

```
class SplashPresenterImpl @Inject constructor( // HERE
    private val locationObservable: Observable<LocationEvent>
) : BasePresenter<SplashActivity, SplashViewBinder>(),
SplashPresenter {
```

Dagger now knows that when you need an object of type `SplashPresenter`, it has to create an instance of `SplashPresenterImpl` using the primary constructor, and that constructor needs an object of type `Observable<LocationEvent>`. How can you tell Dagger how to get what it needs? Simple, just add that information in the `@Module`.

Go back to **AppModule.kt** and apply the following changes to tell Dagger how to get a reference to an object of type `Observable<LocationEvent>`:

```
@Module(includes = [AppModule.Bindings::class])
class AppModule(
    // 1
    private val activity: Activity
) {
  // ...
  // 2
  @Provides
  fun provideLocationObservable(): Observable<LocationEvent> {
    // 3
    val locationManager =
activity.getSystemService(Context.LOCATION_SERVICE) as
LocationManager
    // 4
```

```
    val geoLocationPermissionChecker =
GeoLocationPermissionCheckerImpl(activity)
    // 5
    return provideRxLocationObservable(locationManager,
geoLocationPermissionChecker)
  }
}
```

In this code, you:

1. Add a constructor parameter of type `Activity`. You already learned why you need that constructor in the last chapter, where you treated `Context` the same way.
2. Define `provideLocationObservable()` , which is a `@Provides` method responsible for providing the `Observable<LocationEvent>` implementation.
3. Use the `activity` you got from the `AppModule` primary constructor as a parameter to get the reference to `LocationManager`.
4. Use `activity` again to create an instance of `GeoLocationPermissionCheckerImpl`.
5. Use the `LocationManager` and `GeoLocationPermissionCheckerImpl` to invoke `provideRxLocationObservable()`.

Now, Dagger has all the information it needs to create an instance of `SplashPresenterImpl`. But you still need to deal with `SplashViewBinderImpl`.

Handling SplashViewBinderImpl

Open **SplashViewBinderImpl.kt** from **ui.splash** and look at the class' header:

```
class SplashViewBinderImpl( // HERE
    private val navigator: Navigator
) : SplashViewBinder {
  // ...
}
```

In this case, you need to do two things:

1. Annotate the primary constructor with `@Inject`.
2. Tell Dagger how to get an object of type `Navigator`.

Start by adding @Inject to the SplashViewBinderImpl primary constructor, like this:

```
class SplashViewBinderImpl @Inject constructor( // HERE
    private val navigator: Navigator
) : SplashViewBinder {
  // ...
}
```

Then, open **AppModule.kt** and add the following definition:

```
@Module(includes = [AppModule.Bindings::class])
class AppModule(
    private val activity: Activity
) {
  // ...
  @Provides
  fun provideNavigator(): Navigator = NavigatorImpl(activity) //
HERE
}
```

Here, you create an instance of NavigatorImpl using the Activity you got from the primary constructor.

Great! It's been a long journey, but Dagger now has all the information about the objects it needs to implement SplashActivity. It's time to implement the @Component and get rid of SplashInjector.

Creating & using the @Component

Now that you've created AppModule, Dagger knows everything it needs to bind the objects for the SplashActivity implementation. Now, you need a way to access all those objects — which means it's time to implement the @Component.

Create a new file named **AppComponent.kt** in the **di** package and add the following content:

```
// 1
@Component(modules = [AppModule::class])
interface AppComponent {
  // 2
  fun inject(activity: SplashActivity)
}
```

Again, this should look familiar. In this code, you define:

1. An `AppComponent` interface annotated with `@Component`. It's important to note that you're using `AppModule` as a value for the `modules` attribute. This tells Dagger to use what's in `AppModule` to create the objects it needs.
2. `inject()` as the function that injects all the dependencies `SplashActivity` needs.

This `@Component` contains the same information you previously had in `SplashActivityInjector`.

Now, open **SplashActivity.kt** and apply the following changes:

```
class SplashActivity : AppCompatActivity() {

  @Inject // 1
  lateinit var splashViewBinder: SplashViewBinder

  @Inject // 2
  lateinit var splashPresenter: SplashPresenter

  override fun onCreate(savedInstanceState: Bundle?) {
    super.onCreate(savedInstanceState)
    makeFullScreen()
    setContentView(R.layout.activity_splash)
    DaggerAppComponent.builder() // 3
        .appModule(AppModule(this)) // 4
        .build() // 5
        .inject(this)  // 6
    splashViewBinder.init(this)
  }
  // ...
}
```

Note: Dagger generates `DaggerAppComponent` when you build the app. This happens even if the configuration isn't complete, unless some big mistake prevents it. If you don't see `DaggerAppComponent`, try to build the app first.

In the previous code, you:

1. Use `@Inject` to tell Dagger that `SplashActivity` needs a reference to an object of type `SplashViewBinder` in the `splashViewBinder` property.
2. Do the same for the object of type `SplashPresenter` for the `splashPresenter` property.

3. Use `builder()` to get the reference to the **Builder** Dagger has created for you, for the implementation of the `AppComponent` interface.
4. Pass an instance of `AppModule` to the `AppComponent` Builder implementation. It needs this to create the `Navigator` and `Observable<LocationEvent>` implementations.
5. Create the `AppComponent` implementation instance, invoking `build()` on the Builder.
6. Invoke `inject()` on the `SplashActivity` for the actual injection.

Before continuing, you need to:

- Note that you removed the existing `inject()` invocation on the `onCreate()` in `SplashActivity`.
- Completely delete **SplashActivityInjector.kt** from the **di.injectos** package. You don't need it anymore!

Congrats! You completed the first step in migrating Busso to Dagger: making `SplashActivity` use `AppComponent` to inject all its dependencies. Build and run now, and everything works as expected:

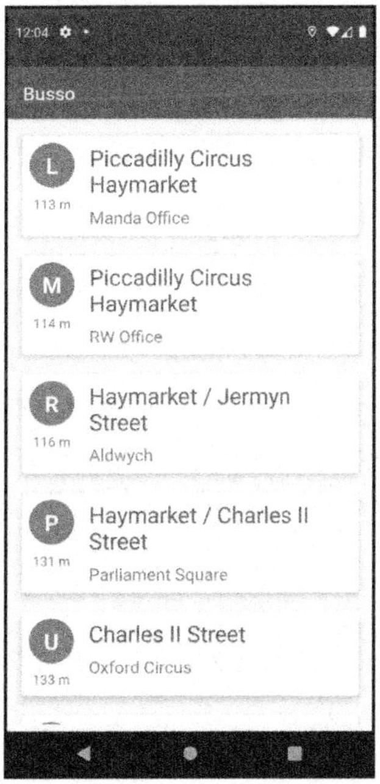

Figure 10.4 — The Busso App

In a real app, you'd need to repeat the same process for `MainActivity`, `BusStopFragment` and `BusArrivalFragment`, getting rid of all the `Injector` and `ServiceLocator` implementations.

For this chapter, however, you have two options. You can code along and complete the migration of Busso to Dagger, giving you some valuable practice, or you can simply check the project in the **final** folder from the downloaded materials for this chapter. In that folder, all the work has been done for you.

If you want to take the second option, jump ahead to the **Customizing @Component creation** section. In that case, see you there. Otherwise, continue on.

Completing the migration

If you're reading this, you decided to complete Busso's migration to Dagger. Great choice! Now that `SplashActivity` is done, it's time to continue the migration for the other components. You'll notice this is really simple.

The classes you need to migrate are:

- `MainActivity`
- `BusStopFragment`
- `BusArrivalFragment`

You're about to delete a load of code. Buckle up!

> **Note**: It's important to note that the following migration is not the best. You still need to manage different `@Components` for different `@Scopes`, which isn't ideal. Don't worry, you'll fix this in the next chapter.

Migrating MainActivity

Open **MainActivityInjector.kt** from **di.injectors** and look at the following code:

```
object MainActivityInjector : Injector<MainActivity> {
  override fun inject(target: MainActivity) {
    val activityServiceLocator =

target.lookUp<ServiceLocatorFactory<AppCompatActivity>>(ACTIVITY
_LOCATOR_FACTORY)
            .invoke(target)
```

```
    target.mainPresenter =
activityServiceLocator.lookUp(MAIN_PRESENTER) // HERE
  }
}
```

> **Note**: It's curious how the `MainActivity` has a `Presenter` but no `ViewBinder`. All it needs to do is to display a `Fragment`, while the navigation responsibility is something you usually assign to the `Presenter`.

This code tells you that `MainActivity` depends on the `MainPresenter` abstraction. This is just one thing you can see from the complete dependency graph in Figure 10.5:

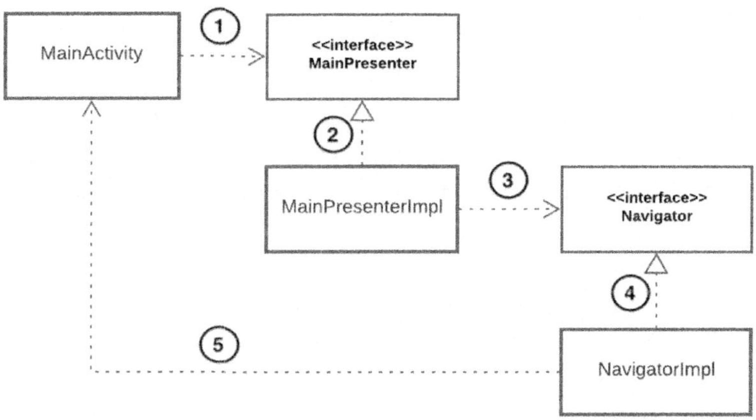

Figure 10.5 — MainActivity dependency graph

The dependency diagram above contains all the information Dagger needs to define the dependency graph. This diagram tells you that:

1. `MainActivity` depends on the `MainPresenter` abstraction.
2. `MainPresenterImpl` is the class to instantiate for the `MainPresenter` type.
3. `MainPresenterImpl` depends on the `Navigation` abstraction.
4. `NavigatorImpl` is the class to use as the `Navigator` implementation.
5. `NavigatorImpl` depends on `Activity`.

Note that Dagger knows some of this information already, like how to bind `NavigatorImpl` to `Navigator`. What Dagger *doesn't* know is how to bind `MainPresenterImpl` to `MainPresenter`.

Open **AppModule.kt** and add the following definition to the `Bindings` interface:

```
@Module(includes = [AppModule.Bindings::class])
class AppModule(
    private val activity: Activity
) {

  @Module
  interface Bindings {
    // ...
    @Binds
    fun bindMainPresenter(impl: MainPresenterImpl):
MainPresenter // HERE
  }
  // ...
}
```

Here, you use `@Binds` to bind `MainPresenterImpl` to `MainPresenter`. Now, you need to tell Dagger how to create the instance of `MainPresenterImpl`. Open **MainPresenterImpl.kt** from **ui.view.main** and apply the following, now obvious, change:

```
class MainPresenterImpl @Inject constructor( // HERE
    private val navigator: Navigator
) : MainPresenter {
  override fun goToBusStopList() {
    navigator.navigateTo(FragmentDestination(BusStopFragment(),
R.id.anchor_point))
  }
}
```

You use `@Inject` to tell Dagger that it needs to invoke the primary constructor to create an instance of `MainPresenterImpl`. It already knows how to provide a `Navigator` implementation.

Now, you need to define `inject()` for the `MainActivity` in the `AppComponent`. Open **AppComponent.kt** from **di** and add the following definition:

```
@Component(modules = [AppModule::class])
interface AppComponent {
  // ...
  fun inject(activity: MainActivity) // HERE
}
```

It's very important to note that **the parameter type matters**. The parameter must match the target's type for the injections. In short, you can't use a parameter of type `Activity`, which would include both `MainActivity` and `SplashActivity`. Remember that you're giving Dagger information, you're not writing actual code; Dagger creates the code for you. Again, `inject()`'s name doesn't matter, it's just a convention.

For your last step, open **MainActivity.kt** from **ui.view.main** and apply the following changes:

```
class MainActivity : AppCompatActivity() {

  @Inject // 1
  lateinit var mainPresenter: MainPresenter

  override fun onCreate(savedInstanceState: Bundle?) {
    super.onCreate(savedInstanceState)
    setContentView(R.layout.activity_main)
    // 2
    DaggerAppComponent
        .builder()
        .appModule(AppModule(this))
        .build()
        .inject(this) // 3
    if (savedInstanceState == null) {
      mainPresenter.goToBusStopList()
    }
  }
}
```

As you did for `SplashActivity`, you:

1. Use `@Inject` to tell Dagger you want the reference to the `MainPresenter` implementation in the `mainPresenter` property.
2. Create the `AppComponent` implementation using the **Builder** Dagger generated for you.
3. Invoke `inject()` to run the actual injection on the `MainActivity`.

Now, build and run and check that everything works. Then, delete **MainActivityInjector.kt**, since you don't it need anymore.

Migrating Busso's fragments

Migrating `BusStopFragment` and `BusArrivalFragment` to Dagger is easy now. There's just one small thing to consider: They both extend `Fragment` but they need access to the `AppComponent` implementation you created in `MainActivity`. That's because they use classes that depend on:

- `BussoEndpoint`
- `Observable<LocationEvent>`

These are objects you manage at the `Activity` level. At this point, you need to:

- Make the `AppComponent` available to the `Fragments`.
- Fix the missing dependency by creating a `@Module` for the `BussoEndpoint`.
- Inject the dependencies you need into the `Fragments`.

You'll start by exposing `AppComponent`.

Exposing AppComponent to the fragments

Here, you need to make the `AppComponent` available to the app's `Fragments`. You'll learn how Dagger solves this problem in the following chapters. At the moment, the easiest way is to add a simple utility method.

Open **MainActivity.kt** and apply the following changes:

```
class MainActivity : AppCompatActivity() {
  // ...
  lateinit var comp: AppComponent // 1

  override fun onCreate(savedInstanceState: Bundle?) {
    super.onCreate(savedInstanceState)
    setContentView(R.layout.activity_main)
    // 2
    comp = DaggerAppComponent
        .builder()
        .appModule(AppModule(this))
        .build().apply {
          inject(this@MainActivity)
        }
    if (savedInstanceState == null) {
      mainPresenter.goToBusStopList()
    }
  }
}
// 3
```

```
val Context.comp: AppComponent?
  get() = if (this is MainActivity) comp else null
```

In this code, you:

1. Add the `comp` property of type `AppComponent`. This is the reference to the `AppComponent` instance you create for `MainActivity`.
2. Create the `AppComponent` implementation using the **Builder** Dagger generated for you, then save its reference in the `comp` property.
3. Define `comp` as an extension property for the `Context` type. If the `Context` receiver IS-A `MainActivity`, it's the reference to the `AppComponent` instance. Otherwise, it's `null`.

Now, you just need to tell Dagger how to create an implementation for the `BussoEndpoint` type and then migrate the two `Fragments`.

Adding the NetworkModule

You're now going to create a `@Module` to tell Dagger how to get an implementation of `BussoEndpoint` to add to the dependency graph. Create a new file named **NetworkModule.kt** in the **network** package for the app and add this content:

```
private val CACHE_SIZE = 100 * 1024L // 100K

@Module
class NetworkModule(val context: Context) { // HERE

  @Provides
  fun provideBussoEndPoint(): BussoEndpoint {
    val cache = Cache(context.cacheDir, CACHE_SIZE)
    val okHttpClient = OkHttpClient.Builder()
        .cache(cache)
        .build()
    val retrofit: Retrofit = Retrofit.Builder()
        .baseUrl(BUSSO_SERVER_BASE_URL)
        .addCallAdapterFactory(RxJava2CallAdapterFactory.create(
))
        .addConverterFactory(
            GsonConverterFactory.create(
                GsonBuilder().setDateFormat("yyyy-MM-
dd'T'HH:mm:ssZ").create()
            )
        )
        .client(okHttpClient)
        .build()
    return retrofit.create(BussoEndpoint::class.java)
```

```
  }
}
```

This code is very similar to the one in **BussoEndpoint.kt** in the same package. In that case, the signature has `Context` as a parameter.

```
fun provideBussoEndPoint(context: Context): BussoEndpoint {
  // ...
}
```

In **NetworkModule.kt**, the same function has no parameter because it uses the `Context` the `NetworkModule` receives in its primary constructor.

```
@Module
class NetworkModule(val context: Context) { // HERE

  @Provides
  fun provideBussoEndPoint(): BussoEndpoint {
    // ...
  }
}
```

You can now remove `provideBussoEndPoint()` from **BussoEndpoint.kt**. Then add `NetworkModule` to the values for `modules` `@Component` attribute. Open **AppComponent.kt** and apply the following:

```
@Component(modules = [AppModule::class,
NetworkModule::class]) // HERE
interface AppComponent {
  // ...
}
```

This last change has some consequences. You're telling Dagger that the `AppComponent` implementation needs a `NetworkModule`. This means that Dagger will generate a function in the builder for it.

Creating the NetworkModule instance

Next, open **MainActivity** and add the following:

```
class MainActivity : AppCompatActivity() {
  // ...
  override fun onCreate(savedInstanceState: Bundle?) {
    super.onCreate(savedInstanceState)
    setContentView(R.layout.activity_main)
    comp = DaggerAppComponent
        .builder()
```

```
          .appModule(AppModule(this))
          .networkModule(NetworkModule(this)) // HERE
          .build().apply {
            inject(this@MainActivity)
          }
      if (savedInstanceState == null) {
        mainPresenter.goToBusStopList()
      }
    }
  }
  // ...
```

> **Note**: Remember to build the app if `networkModule()` is not available. Dagger needs to generate it from the previous configuration.

Here, you create an instance of `NetworkModule`, passing a reference to the `MainActivity` that IS-A `Context`. The bad news is that you have to do the same in **SplashActivity.kt**, which should then look like this:

```
class SplashActivity : AppCompatActivity() {
  // ...
  override fun onCreate(savedInstanceState: Bundle?) {
    super.onCreate(savedInstanceState)
    makeFullScreen()
    setContentView(R.layout.activity_splash)
    DaggerAppComponent.builder()
        .appModule(AppModule(this))
        .networkModule(NetworkModule(this)) // HERE
        .build()
        .inject(this)
    splashViewBinder.init(this)
  }
  // ...
}
```

> **Note**: Yeah. There's a lot of repetition here. Don't worry, you'll get rid of all of this very soon.

At this point, the `BussoEndpoint` implementation is part of the dependency graph and you have everything you need to quickly complete the migration.

Handling deprecated @Modules

Before proceeding, it's worth mentioning that the editor might display something like you see in Figure 10.6:

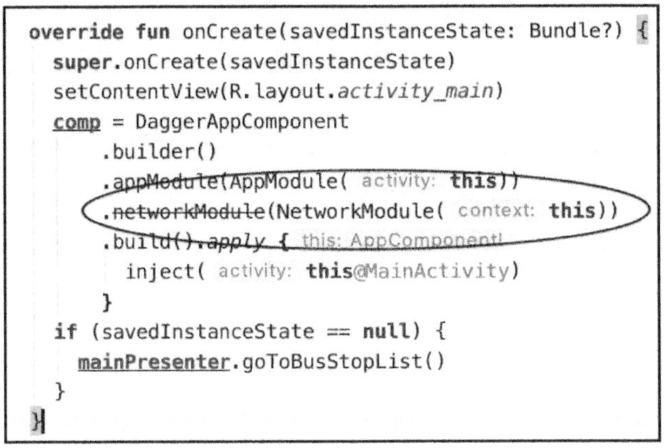

Figure 10.6 — A deprecated @Module

Here, Android Studio marks `networkModule()` as **deprecated**. That's because you're not using the bindings in the `NetworkModule` — because you haven't yet completed the migration for the `Fragments`. You can just ignore this warning for now.

Migrating BusStopFragment

Your next step is to quickly migrate the `BusStopFragment` following the same process you used above. Open **AppModule.kt** and add the following bindings:

```
@Module(includes = [AppModule.Bindings::class])
class AppModule(
    private val activity: Activity
) {

  @Module
  interface Bindings {
    // ...
    @Binds
    fun bindBusStopListViewBinder(impl:
BusStopListViewBinderImpl): BusStopListViewBinder

    @Binds
    fun bindBusStopListPresenter(impl:
BusStopListPresenterImpl): BusStopListPresenter
```

```
    @Binds
    fun bindBusStopListViewBinderListener(impl:
BusStopListPresenterImpl):
BusStopListViewBinder.BusStopItemSelectedListener
  }
  // ...
}
```

It's important to note that you're not only binding `BusStopListPresenterImpl`to the `BusStopListPresenter` type, but also to `BusStopListViewBinder.BusStopItemSelectedListener`. You have to be careful that Dagger uses the same instance for the two bindings.

> **Note**: You had the same problem with the RaySequence app, but you solved it using `@Singleton`.

Now, you need to use `@Inject` the primary constructor for `BusStopListPresenterImpl` and `BusStopListViewBinderImpl`.

Open **BusStopListPresenterImpl.kt** and add the following:

```
@Singleton // 1
class BusStopListPresenterImpl @Inject constructor( // 2
    private val navigator: Navigator,
    private val locationObservable: Observable<LocationEvent>,
    private val bussoEndpoint: BussoEndpoint
) : BasePresenter<View, BusStopListViewBinder>(),
    BusStopListPresenter {
  // ...
}
```

Note that Dagger knows all about the primary constructor parameter types. Remember to use `@Singleton` to ensure you're using the same instance of `BusStopListPresenterImpl` for `BusStopListPresenter` and for `BusStopListViewBinder.BusStopItemSelectedListener`.

Finally, do the same in **BusStopListViewBinderImpl.kt**:

```
class BusStopListViewBinderImpl @Inject constructor( // HERE
    private val busStopItemSelectedListener:
BusStopListViewBinder.BusStopItemSelectedListener
) : BusStopListViewBinder {
  // ...
}
```

Using AppComponent in BusStopFragment

Your last step is to use AppComponent in BusStopFragment. First, open **AppComponent.kt** and add the following definitions:

```
@Component(modules = [AppModule::class, NetworkModule::class])
@Singleton // 1
interface AppComponent {
  // ...
  fun inject(fragment: BusStopFragment) // 2
}
```

Here, you're:

1. Using @Singleton because of BusStopListPresenterImpl. As you read earlier, you need this to bind the lifecycle of BusStopListPresenterImpl to AppComponent's lifecycle.
2. Adding inject() for the BusStopFragment.

Then, open **BusStopFragment.kt** and apply the following changes:

```
class BusStopFragment : Fragment() {

  @Inject // 1
  lateinit var busStopListViewBinder: BusStopListViewBinder

  @Inject // 1
  lateinit var busStopListPresenter: BusStopListPresenter

  override fun onAttach(context: Context) {
    context.comp?.inject(this) // 2
    super.onAttach(context)
  }
  // ...
}
```

Here, you use:

1. @Inject for the busStopListViewBinder and busStopListPresenter properties.
2. The extended property, comp, to access the AppComponent implementation in the MainActivity and then to invoke the inject().

Now, repeat the same process for BusArrivalFragment.

Migrating BusArrivalFragment

You're very close to completing the migration of Busso to Dagger. Open **AppModule.kt** and add the following bindings:

```
@Module(includes = [AppModule.Bindings::class])
class AppModule(
    private val activity: Activity
) {

  @Module
  interface Bindings {
    // ...
    @Binds
    fun bindBusArrivalPresenter(impl: BusArrivalPresenterImpl):
BusArrivalPresenter

    @Binds
    fun bindBusArrivalViewBinder(impl:
BusArrivalViewBinderImpl): BusArrivalViewBinder
  }
  // ...
}
```

Now, open **BusArrivalPresenterImpl.kt** and add `@Inject`, like this:

```
class BusArrivalPresenterImpl @Inject constructor( // HERE
    private val bussoEndpoint: BussoEndpoint
) : BasePresenter<View, BusArrivalViewBinder>(),
    BusArrivalPresenter {
  // ...
}
```

Do the same for **BusArrivalViewBinderImpl.kt**, like this:

```
class BusArrivalViewBinderImpl @Inject constructor() :
BusArrivalViewBinder { // HERE
  // ...
}
```

Again, open **AppComponent.kt** and add the following definition:

```
@Component(modules = [AppModule::class, NetworkModule::class])
interface AppComponent {
  // ...
  fun inject(fragment: BusArrivalFragment) // HERE
}
```

Finally, open **BusArrivalFragment** and apply the following changes:

```
class BusArrivalFragment : Fragment() {
  // ...
  @Inject // 1
  lateinit var busArrivalViewBinder: BusArrivalViewBinder

  @Inject // 1
  lateinit var busArrivalPresenter: BusArrivalPresenter

  override fun onAttach(context: Context) {
    context.comp?.inject(this) // 2
    super.onAttach(context)
  }
  // ...
}
```

Here, you follow the same approach you used for `BusStopFragment`. Build the project now. You'll see some compilation errors, but only because you need some clean-up. :]

Cleaning up the code

The errors you see after building the app are due to the existing `ServiceLocator` and `Injector` implementations. To fix them, you just have to delete the:

- **injectors** package
- **locators** package
- **Main.kt** file in the app's main package and its reference in **AndroidManifest.xml**
- `ServiceLocatorImplTest` in the **di.locators** package in the `test` build type

After this, the directory structure for the project will match Figure 10.7.

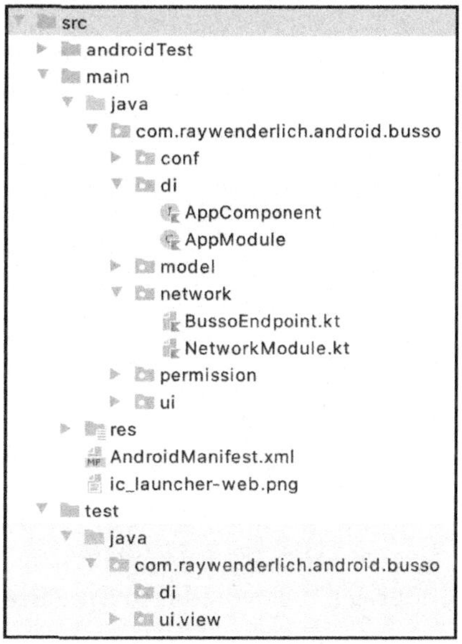

Figure 10.7 — File structure after Dagger migration

Now, you can finally build and run — and the app will work as expected.

Great job! You've completely migrated Busso to Dagger.

Customizing @Component creation

As you saw in the previous code, providing the reference to existing objects like `Context` or `Activity` isn't uncommon. In your case, you just provided an `activity` as a parameter for the primary constructor of the `@Module`, as in **AppModule.kt**:

```
@Module(includes = [AppModule.Bindings::class])
class AppModule(
    private val activity: Activity // HERE
) {
  // ...
}
```

This method lets you use the existing object — `activity`, in this case — in any `@Provides` function in the same **AppModule.kt**. That's because `activity` acts like a normal property of `AppModule`.

Then, you need to explicitly create the `@Module` instance and use it during the building process for the `@Component`, as you did in **SplashActivity.kt**:

```
class SplashActivity : AppCompatActivity() {
  // ...
  override fun onCreate(savedInstanceState: Bundle?) {
    super.onCreate(savedInstanceState)
    makeFullScreen()
    setContentView(R.layout.activity_splash)
    DaggerAppComponent.builder()
        .appModule(AppModule(this)) // HERE
        .networkModule(NetworkModule(this)) // HERE
        .build()
        .inject(this)
    splashViewBinder.init(this)
  }
  // ...
}
```

Here, you also had to create the `NetworkModule` for the same purpose: to provide an implementation of `Context`. It would be nice if you could pass the reference to an existing object to `@Component` by adding it directly to the dependency graph. That would make the provided object accessible to any other objects that depend on it. Fortunately, you can actually do that by using `@Component.Builder` and `@Component.Factory`.

Using @Component.Builder

Open **AppComponent.kt** and add the following code:

```
@Component(modules = [AppModule::class, NetworkModule::class])
interface AppComponent {
  // ...
  // 1
  @Component.Builder
  interface Builder {

    @BindsInstance // 2
    fun activity(activity: Activity): Builder

    fun build(): AppComponent // 3
  }
}
```

These few lines of code are very important. In the `AppComponent` interface, you:

1. Add `Builder` as an internal interface annotated with `@Component.Builder`. That tells Dagger you want to customize the code it'll generate as `Builder` of the `AppComponent` implementation.
2. Define a function that accepts **a unique parameter** of the type you want to provide. In this case, you define `activity()` with a parameter of type `Activity`. This function **must return** the same **Builder** because it's going to generate one of the methods you must invoke to pass the existing object to the `@Component`. To make that object available to the dependency graph, you must annotate the function with `@BindsInstance`. In short, here you tell Dagger that your `AppComponent` needs an `Activity` and that you're providing its reference by invoking `activity()` on the `Builder` implementation Dagger generates for you.
3. Must have a unique function with no parameters, returning a reference to the `AppComponent`. The name of the function doesn't matter.

If you don't use the `@BindsInstance` annotation, you'll get the not-so-clear message: `error: @Component.Builder has setters for modules or components that aren't required.`

Build the app now and you'll get some compilation errors. This happens because you told Dagger that you want to provide a custom `Builder` for the `AppComponent` implementation that ignores `AppModule` and `NetworkModule`.

One solution is to implement the exact same `Builder` Dagger would. Just replace the previous `Builder` implementation with the following:

```
@Component(modules = [AppModule::class, NetworkModule::class])
interface AppComponent {
  // ...
  @Component.Builder
  interface Builder {

    fun appModule(appModule: AppModule): Builder

    fun networkModule(networkModule: NetworkModule): Builder

    fun build(): AppComponent
  }
}
```

Now, you can successfully build and run because the custom `Builder` implementation you configured is exactly the same as the one Dagger would have created without the `@Component.Builder`. The `appModule()` and `networkModule` functions have the same name.

> **Note**: It's important to know that it's not mutually exclusive to pass the reference to both a `@Module` and an existing object. You could have both in your Builder. Also note that, in this case, you don't need to use `@BindsInstance`.

Of course this isn't what you want. Restore the previous version of `Builder` in **AppComponent.kt** and apply the following changes to **AppModule.kt**:

```
@Module(includes = [AppModule.Bindings::class])
class AppModule { // 1
  // ...
  @Provides // 2
  fun provideNavigator(activity: Activity): Navigator =
NavigatorImpl(activity)

  @Provides // 3
  fun provideLocationObservable(activity: Activity):
Observable<LocationEvent> {
    val locationManager =
activity.getSystemService(Context.LOCATION_SERVICE) as
LocationManager
    val geoLocationPermissionChecker =
GeoLocationPermissionCheckerImpl(activity)
    return provideRxLocationObservable(locationManager,
```

```
geoLocationPermissionChecker)
  }
}
```

In this code, you:

1. Remove the `activity` constructor parameter of the `AppModule` class.
2. Pass the `Activity` as the parameter for `provideNavigator()`.
3. Do the same for `provideLocationObservable()`.

You basically treat the `Activity` type as something that's already part of the dependency graph for the `@Component`.

Now, open **NetworkModule.kt** and make the same change, like this:

```
@Module
class NetworkModule { // 1

  @Provides // 2
  fun provideBussoEndPoint(activity: Activity): BussoEndpoint {
    val cache = Cache(activity.cacheDir, CACHE_SIZE)
    // ...
  }
}
```

In this code, you:

1. Remove the constructor parameter of type `Context`.
2. Use a parameter of type `Activity` in `provideBussoEndPoint()`.

Build the app now, and you'll still get some compilation errors because the Builder implementation for the `AppComponent` has changed. To fix this, open **MainActivity.kt** and apply the following changes:

```
class MainActivity : AppCompatActivity() {
  // ...
  override fun onCreate(savedInstanceState: Bundle?) {
    super.onCreate(savedInstanceState)
    setContentView(R.layout.activity_main)
    comp = DaggerAppComponent
        .builder()
        .activity(this) // HERE
        .build().apply {
          inject(this@MainActivity)
        }
    if (savedInstanceState == null) {
      mainPresenter.goToBusStopList()
```

```
        }
      }
    }
    // ...
```

In the code above, you simply use `activity()` to pass the reference to the existing object to the dependency graph. Because of this, `NetworkModule` also gets the reference to the same object.

Before you build and run, you also need to apply the same change to **SplashActivity.kt**, like this:

```
class SplashActivity : AppCompatActivity() {
  // ...
  override fun onCreate(savedInstanceState: Bundle?) {
    super.onCreate(savedInstanceState)
    makeFullScreen()
    setContentView(R.layout.activity_splash)
    DaggerAppComponent.builder()
        .activity(this) // HERE
        .build()
        .inject(this)
    splashViewBinder.init(this)
  }
  // ...
}
```

Now you can finally build and run the app successfully.

Using @Component.Factory

Using `@Component.Builder`, you learned how to customize the **Builder** implementation for the `@Component` Dagger creates for you. Usually, you get the reference to the `Builder` implementation, then you invoke some `setter` methods that pass the parameter you need and finally, you invoke `build()` to create the final object.

Dagger also allows you to implement a **factory** as a way to generate a **factory method**. You can use this to create an instance of the `@Component` that invokes a simple function to pass all the parameters at the same time.

Open **AppComponent.kt** and replace the `@Component.Builder` definition with the following:

```
@Component(modules = [AppModule::class, NetworkModule::class])
interface AppComponent {
```

```
  // ...
  @Component.Factory // 1
  interface Factory {
    // 2
    fun create(@BindsInstance activity: Activity): AppComponent
  }
}
```

In this case, you define:

1. The `Factory` interface and annotate it with `@Component.Factory`.
2. A `create()` function with a parameter of type `Activity`. `create()` can have any parameters you need, but it must return an object with the same type as the `@Component`. In this case, the return type is `AppComponent`. `@BindsInstance` here has the same meaning you learned in the previous paragraph: If you use it for a parameter, the provided value becomes part of the dependency graph and is available for injection.

Build and run the project and you'll get some compilation errors. That's because Dagger generates different code now. To fix this, open **SplashActivity.kt** and apply the following changes:

```
class SplashActivity : AppCompatActivity() {
  // ...
  override fun onCreate(savedInstanceState: Bundle?) {
    super.onCreate(savedInstanceState)
    makeFullScreen()
    setContentView(R.layout.activity_splash)
    DaggerAppComponent
        .factory() // 1
        .create(this) // 2
        .inject(this) // 3
    splashViewBinder.init(this)
  }
  // ...
}
```

In this code, you invoke:

1. `factory()` to get the reference to the **Factory** for the `AppComponent` implementation.
2. `create()`, passing the `Activity` it needs to create the `AppComponent` implementation.
3. `inject()` for the actual injection.

Of course, you need to do the same for **MainActivity** as well, applying the same changes:

```
class MainActivity : AppCompatActivity() {
  // ...
  override fun onCreate(savedInstanceState: Bundle?) {
    super.onCreate(savedInstanceState)
    setContentView(R.layout.activity_main)
    comp = DaggerAppComponent
        .factory() // HERE
        .create(this).apply {
          inject(this@MainActivity)
        }
    if (savedInstanceState == null) {
      mainPresenter.goToBusStopList()
    }
  }
}
// ...
```

Note that `@Component.Builder` and `@Component.Factory` are basically two different ways of doing the same thing. A rule of thumb about which one to use involves the number of objects you need to provide for the actual construction of the `@Component` implementation.

In both cases, you can pass one of these objects as optional by using `@Nullable` as its parameter. `@Component.Factory` allows you to write less code, passing all the parameters in one call, while `@Component.Builder` is a little bit more verbose.

Great job! In this chapter, you finally migrated the Busso App from your homemade framework to Dagger. This long, and occasionally repetitive process reduced the number of lines of code in your project. Well, at least the lines of code you wrote.

The Dagger configuration you used in this chapter is still not optimal, however. To use your resources more efficiently, some components should have different lifecycles than others. While the `BussoEndpoint` should live as long as the app, the `Navigator` lifecycle should be bound to the `Activity` lifecycle.

In the next chapter, you'll make more important changes. See you there!

Key points

- The most important concept to understand in Dagger is the `@Component`, which works as the **factory** for the objects in the dependency graph.
- You migrated `Injectors` to Dagger `@Components` and `ServiceLocators` to Dagger `@Modules`.
- A **dependency diagram** helps you migrate an existing app to Dagger.
- `@Component.Builder` lets you customize the **Builder** implementation that Dagger creates for your `@Component`.
- With `@Component.Factory`, you ask Dagger to create a **factory method** to create your `@Component` implementation.

Chapter 11: Components & Scopes

By Massimo Carli

In the previous chapter, you migrated the Busso App from a homemade framework with `ServiceLocator`s and `Injector`s to Dagger. You converted `Injector`s into `@Component`s and `ServiceLocator`s into `@Module`s, according to their responsibilities. You learned how to manage existing objects with types like `Context` or `Activity` by using a `@Component.Builder` or `@Component.Factory`.

However, the migration from the previous chapter isn't optimal — there are still some fundamental aspects you need to improve. For instance, in the current code, you:

- Create a **new instance** of `BussoEndpoint` every time you need a reference to an object of type `BusStopListPresenter` or a `BusArrivalPresenter` that depends on it. Instead, you should have just one instance of the endpoint, which lives as long as the app does.
- Use the `@Singleton` annotation to solve the problem of multiple instances of `BusStopListPresenterImpl` that are bound to the `BusStopListPresenter` and `BusStopListViewBinder.BusStopItemSelectedListener` abstractions. However, `@Singleton` isn't always a good solution, and you should understand when to use it and when not to.
- Get the reference to `LocationManager` from an `Activity`, but it should have a broader lifecycle, like the app does, and it should also depend on the app `Context`.

These are just some of the problems you'll fix in this chapter. You'll also learn:

- The definition of a **component** and how it relates to **containers**.
- What a **lifecycle** is, why it's important and what its relationship to **scope** is.
- More about **@Singletons**.
- What a **@Scope** is and how it improves your app's performance.

It's going to be a very interesting and important chapter, so get ready to dive in!

Components and Containers

It's important to understand the concept behind **components**. When you ask what a component is in an interview, you usually get different answers. In the Java context, one of the most common answers is, "A component is a class with getters and setters." However, even though a component's implementations in Java might have getters and setters, the answer is incorrect.

> **Note**: The getter and setter thing is probably a consequence of the JavaBean specification that Sun Microsystems released way back in 1997. A JavaBean is a Java component that's reusable and that **a visual IDE can edit**. The last property is the important one. An IDE that wants to edit a JavaBean needs to know what the component's properties, events and methods are. In other words, the component needs to describe itself to the container, either explicitly — by using `BeanInfo` — or implicitly. To use the implicit method, you need to follow some conventions, one of which is that a component has the property `prop` of type `T` if it has two methods — `getProp(): T` and `setProp(T)`. Because of this, a JavaBean can have getters and setters — but even when a class has getters and setters, it's not necessarily a JavaBean.

The truth is that **there's no component without a container**. In the relationship between the components and their container:

1. The container is **responsible for the lifecycle** of the components it contains.
2. There is always a way to **describe the component to the container**.
3. Implementing a component means defining **what do to when its state changes** according to its lifecycle.

A related interview question in Android is, "What are the standard components of the Android platform?" The correct answer is:

- `Activity`
- `Service`
- `ContentProvider`
- `BroadcastReceiver`

In this case, the following applies to the components:

1. The Android environment is the container that manages the lifecycle of standard components according to the available system resources and user actions.
2. You describe these components to the Android Environment using **AndroidManifest.xml**.
3. When you define an Android component, you provide implementations for some callback functions, including `onCreate()`, `onStart()`, `onStop()` and so on. The container invokes these to send a notification that there's a transition to a different state in the lifecycle.

> **Note**: Is a `Fragment` a standard component? In theory, no, because the Android Environment doesn't know about it. It's a component that has a lifecycle bound to the lifecycle of the `Activity` that contains it. From this perspective, it's just a class with a lifecycle, like any other class. But because it's an important part of any Android app, as you'll see, it has the dignity of a specific scope.

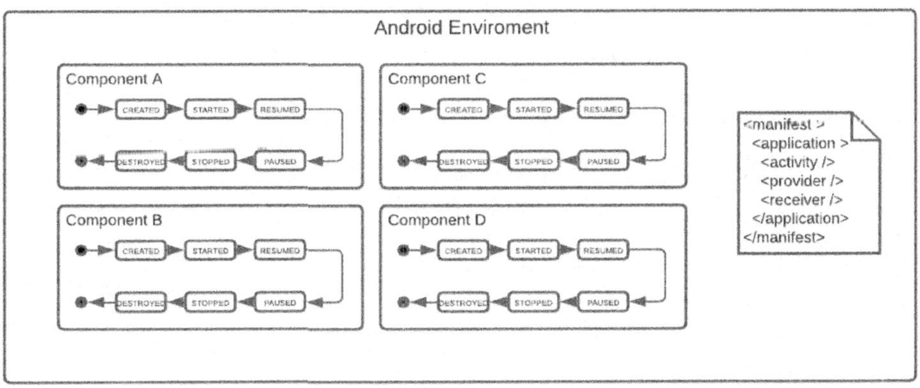

Figure 11.1 — The Android Environment as Container

But why, then, do you need to delegate the lifecycle of those components to the container — in this case, the Android environment? Because it's the system's responsibility to know which resources are available and to decide what can live and what should die. This is true for all the Android standard components and `Fragments`. But all these components have dependencies.

In the Busso App, you've seen how an `Activity` or `Fragment` depends on other objects, which have a **presenter**, **model** or **viewBinder** role. If a component has a lifecycle, its dependencies do, too. Some objects need to live as long as the app and others only need to exist when a specific `Fragment` or `Activity` is visible.

As you can see, you still have work to do to improve the Busso App.

Fixing the Busso App

Open the Busso project from the **starter** folder in this chapter's materials. The file structure for the project that is of interest right now is the one in Figure 11.2:

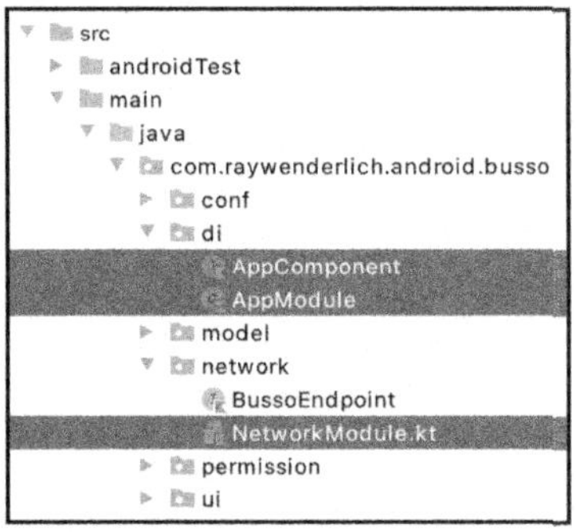

Figure 11.2 — Busso initial project structure

You can see that this structure has:

- A single `@Component` in **AppComponent.kt** under the **di** package.
- Two different `@Modules`, one in **AppModule.kt** in that **di** package with the `@Component` and the other in **NetworkModule.kt** in the **network** package.

Open **AppComponent.kt** and look at the current implementation:

```
@Singleton
@Component(modules = [AppModule::class, NetworkModule::class])
interface AppComponent {

  fun inject(activity: SplashActivity)
```

```
  fun inject(activity: MainActivity)

  fun inject(fragment: BusStopFragment)

  fun inject(fragment: BusArrivalFragment)

  @Component.Factory
  interface Factory {

    fun create(@BindsInstance activity: Activity): AppComponent
  }
}
```

The `AppComponent` interface is responsible for the entire app's dependency graph. You have `inject()` overloads for all the `Fragment` and `Activity` components and you're using all the `@Modules`. That means all the app's objects are part of the same graph. This has important implications for scope.

So far, you learned that:

- By default, Dagger creates a new instance of the class that's bound to a specific abstraction type every time an injection of that type occurs.
- Using `@Singleton`, you can only bind the lifecycle of an instance to the lifecycle of the `@Component` you use to get its reference.

In other words, a `@Singleton` **IS NOT** a Singleton!

Using `@Singleton` doesn't give you a unique instance of a class across the entire app. It just means that each instance of a `@Component` always returns the same instance for an object of a given type. **Different** `@Component` instances will return different instances for the same type, even if you use `@Singleton`.

As you'll see later, if you want an instance of an object that lives as long as the app does, you need a `@Component` that matches the app's lifespan.

> **Note**: Singleton is a foundational Gang Of Four Design Pattern that describes a way to have **one and only one instance** of a class, which you can access from any part of the app's code. Many developers consider it an **anti-pattern** because of the concurrency issues that can arise, especially in a distributed environment.

To better understand this concept, your next step will be to fix the `BussoEndpoint` in the Busso app.

Fixing BussoEndpoint

The `BussoEndpoint` implementation is a good place to start optimizing the Busso App. It's a typical example of a component that needs to be unique across the entire app. To recap, `BussoEndpoint` is an interface which abstracts the endpoint for the application.

Understanding the problem

Before you dive into the fix, take a moment to prove that, at the moment, Dagger creates a new instance every time it needs to inject an object with the `BussoEndpoint` type. Using the Android Studio feature in Figure 11.3, you see that two classes depend on `BussoEndpoint`:

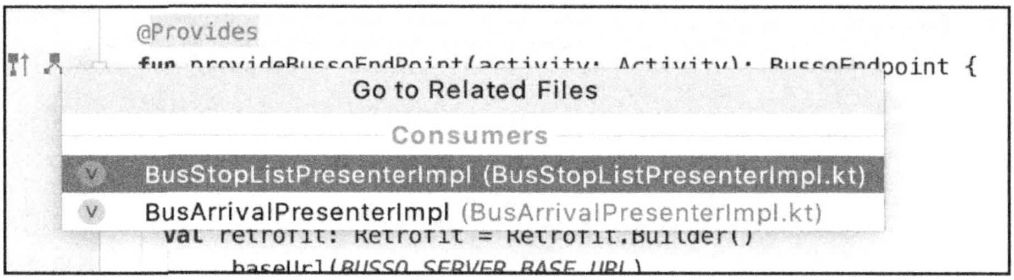

Figure 11.3 — Find BussoEndpoint injections

Those are:

- `BusStopListPresenterImpl`
- `BusArrivalPresenterImpl`

Open **BusStopListPresenterImpl.kt** in **ui.view.busstop** and add the following `init` block:

```
@Singleton
class BusStopListPresenterImpl @Inject constructor(
    private val navigator: Navigator,
    private val locationObservable: Observable<LocationEvent>,
    private val bussoEndpoint: BussoEndpoint
) : BasePresenter<View, BusStopListViewBinder>(),
    BusStopListPresenter {
  // HERE
  init {
    Log.d("BUSSOENDPOINT", "StopList: $bussoEndpoint")
  }
  // ...
}
```

Now, open **BusArrivalPresenterImpl.kt** in **ui.view.busarrival** and do the same thing:

```
class BusArrivalPresenterImpl @Inject constructor(
    private val bussoEndpoint: BussoEndpoint
) : BasePresenter<View, BusArrivalViewBinder>(),
    BusArrivalPresenter {
  // HERE
  init {
    Log.d("BUSSOENDPOINT", "Arrival: $bussoEndpoint")
  }
  // ...
}
```

That just added some logs that print information about the specific `BussoEndpoint` instance. Build and run, then navigate back and forth a few times in the arrivals fragment, and you'll get a log like this:

```
D/BUSSOENDPOINT: StopList: retrofit2.Retrofit$1@68c7c92
D/BUSSOENDPOINT: Arrival: retrofit2.Retrofit$1@cb74e1b
D/BUSSOENDPOINT: Arrival: retrofit2.Retrofit$1@542346a
D/BUSSOENDPOINT: Arrival: retrofit2.Retrofit$1@dfeaf68
```

Now, you can clearly see that the `BusStopListPresenterImpl` and `BusArrivalPresenterImpl` objects are all using different instances for the `BussoEndpoint` type. It's important to note that all the `Fragments` are using the **same** `AppComponent` instance through the `comp` extended property you defined in **MainActivity.kt**. You already know what to do to ensure that `@Component` always returns the same instance for the `BussoEndpoint`: Use `@Singleton`.

Using @Singleton

As you've learned, using `@Singleton` is the first solution to the multiple instances problem. In this specific case, however, something's different: You can't access the code of the class that's bound to the `BussoEndpoint` interface because the **Retrofit framework** created it for you.

However, using Dagger gives you a way to get around this problem. Open **NetworkModule.kt** in the **network** and apply the following change:

```
@Module
class NetworkModule {

  @Provides
  @Singleton // HERE
  fun provideBussoEndPoint(activity: Activity): BussoEndpoint {
```

```
        // ...
    }
}
```

Using `@Singleton` in `provideBussoEndPoint()` achieves the same goal. You're asking Dagger to create a single instance of the `BussoEndpoint` implementation. If you repeat the previous experiment with this new code, you'll get the following output:

```
D/BUSSOENDPOINT: StopList: retrofit2.Retrofit$1@dc70bea
D/BUSSOENDPOINT: Arrival: retrofit2.Retrofit$1@dc70bea
D/BUSSOENDPOINT: Arrival: retrofit2.Retrofit$1@dc70bea
D/BUSSOENDPOINT: Arrival: retrofit2.Retrofit$1@dc70bea
```

Now, the instance for the `BussoEndpoint` type is always the same. Everything seems to work, but this isn't a good solution for the reason mentioned above. Using `@Singleton` didn't give you a single instance for the `BussoEndpoint` implementation for the entire app.

With this configuration, you're creating an instance for `BussoEndpoint` for each instance of `AppComponent` — but you have one `AppComponent` per `Activity`. In the app, you have two of them.

To create a single `BussoEndpoint` instance across the entire app, you need to define a `@Component` with the same lifespan. This is called an **application scope**. You'll learn how to define and use application scopes next.

Defining an application scope

When objects live as long as the app does, they have an application scope.

You already know what to do to make Dagger provide a single instance for a given type across the entire app. You need to define a:

1. `@Module` that encapsulates the information about how to create the objects.
2. `@Component` as a factory for those objects.
3. Way to make the `@Component` live as long the app, and make it accessible from any other point in the code.

Look at Busso's code and you'll see that there are three types of objects that have an application scope:

- `BussoEndpoint`
- `LocationManager`
- `GeoLocationPermissionChecker`

You'll start by defining the `@Module`.

> **Note**: As you know, the `Observable<LocationEvent>` depends on the `LocationManager` and `GeoLocationPermissionChecker`, but it's a good practice to create a new instance every time. You could create a single instance of `Observable<LocationEvent>` to keep alive as long as the app, but you'd need to create a `shareable` version of it. To learn more about `RxJava` or `RxKotlin`, check out the book, Reactive Programming with Kotlin.

> **Note**: As you improve the Dagger configuration, you won't be able to successfully build and run after each step — you need to complete the refactoring for the app to run properly. But don't worry, just code along and everything will be fine. :]

Defining ApplicationModule

This `@Module` tells Dagger how to create the objects it needs for the application scope. You have an opportunity to improve the structure of your code by putting your new Dagger knowledge to work.

You don't want to have all the definitions in a single place, so your first step is to improve some of the existing files. Open **NetworkModule.kt** in the **network** and add the following:

```
@Module
class NetworkModule {
  // 1
  @Provides
  @Singleton
  fun provideCache(application: Application): Cache =
      Cache(application.cacheDir, 100 * 1024L)// 100K
  // 2
  @Provides
  @Singleton
```

```
  fun provideHttpClient(cache: Cache): OkHttpClient =
      Builder()
          .cache(cache)
          .build()
  // 3
  @Provides
  @Singleton
  fun provideBussoEndPoint(httpClient: OkHttpClient):
BussoEndpoint {
    val retrofit: Retrofit = Retrofit.Builder()
        .baseUrl(BUSSO_SERVER_BASE_URL)
        .addCallAdapterFactory(RxJava2CallAdapterFactory.create(
))
        .addConverterFactory(
            GsonConverterFactory.create(
                GsonBuilder().setDateFormat("yyyy-MM-
dd'T'HH:mm:ssZ").create()
            )
        )
        .client(httpClient)
        .build()
    return retrofit.create(BussoEndpoint::class.java)
  }
}
```

This code gives you a better definition of the dependencies. In particular, you define:

1. `provideCache()`, which returns the reference to the `Cache` implementation. It's important to note that it has the same scope as the `@Component` annotated with the `@Singleton` that uses it. Another fundamental change is the input parameter for `proviitsdeCache()`: It's now **Application**.

2. `provideHttpClient()`, which returns the `OkHttpClient` that receives the `Cache` implementation as its parameter. You use `@Singleton` again here.

3. `provideBussoEndPoint()`, which returns the **Retrofit** `BussoEndpoint` implementation from the `OkHttpClient` it receives as a parameter. You want this to be a `@Singleton` as well.

> **Note**: You might wonder if `Cache` and `OkHttpClient` actually need to be `@Singleton`s or not. In the app, you're just consuming the `BussoEndpoint` object, which is the only one that needs to be `@Singleton`, so you could avoid the annotation on its dependencies. On the other hand, you should only have one `Cache` and one `OkHttpClient` in the app. Therefore, it's preferable to use `@Singleton` on them as well.

Now, create a new file named **LocationModule.kt** in **di** and add the following code:

```
@Module
class LocationModule {
  // 1
  @Singleton
  @Provides
  fun provideLocationManager(application: Application):
LocationManager =
      application.getSystemService(Context.LOCATION_SERVICE) as
LocationManager
  // 2
  @Singleton
  @Provides
  fun providePermissionChecker(application: Application):
GeoLocationPermissionChecker =
      GeoLocationPermissionCheckerImpl(application)
  // 3
  @Provides
  fun provideLocationObservable(
      locationManager: LocationManager,
      permissionChecker: GeoLocationPermissionChecker
  ): Observable<LocationEvent> =
provideRxLocationObservable(locationManager, permissionChecker)
}
```

This refactoring is similar to the one you did before, but it's a bit more important. In this code, you define:

1. `provideLocationManager()`, which returns the `LocationManager` from the `Application` you pass as a parameter. You only need a single `LocationManager`, so you use `@Singleton`.
2. `providePermissionChecker()`, which returns the implementation for `GeoLocationPermissionChecker` using the `Application` you get as a parameter. You only need one, so you use `@Singleton` again.
3. `provideLocationObservable()`, which returns the `Observable<LocationEvent>` implementation using the `LocationManager` and `GeoLocationPermissionChecker` you get as parameters. Because of the previous `@Provides` functions, Dagger will create a new `Observable<LocationEvent>` implementation from the same `LocationManager` and `GeoLocationPermissionChecker` objects it gets as input parameters.

Note that in `LocationManager`'s case, you don't actually know if you need `@Singleton` or not. That's because the `LocationManager` you get from the `Context` using `getSystemService()` might already be a **Singleton** in the **Design Pattern** sense.

Finally, you'll merge the two modules into one as a convenience. Create a new file named **ApplicationModule.kt** in **di** and enter the following code:

```
@Module(includes = [
  LocationModule::class,
  NetworkModule::class
])
object ApplicationModule
```

This lets you keep all the `@Modules` for the application scope objects in the same place.

> **Note**: Before implementing the `@Component`, remember to delete the `provideLocationObservable()` definition from **AppModule.kt** in **di**.

Defining ApplicationComponent

Now, you need to define the `@Component` for the objects with **application scope**. The main thing to note here is that `NetworkModule` and `LocationModule` need an `Application`, which is an object you don't have to **create**. You **provide** it instead.

You already know how to do that. Create a new file named **ApplicationComponent.kt** in **di** and enter the following code:

```
@Component(modules = [ApplicationModule::class]) // 1
@Singleton // 2
interface ApplicationComponent {

  @Component.Factory
  interface Builder {

    fun create(@BindsInstance application: Application):
ApplicationComponent // 3
  }
}
```

This is a very simple but important definition. Here, you:

1. Require the information from `ApplicationModule`.
2. Use `@Singleton` because you have bindings that should have the same lifespan as the `ApplicationComponent`.

3. Define a `@Component.Factory` that generates a factory method, which you'll use to create the `ApplicationComponent` instance from the existing `Application` object.

You don't have any `inject()` functions in this code because you won't use the `ApplicationComponent` directly. As you'll see shortly, you just need a way to make these objects available to other `@Components` with different `@Scopes`.

For instance, both `SplashActivity` and `BusStopListPresenterImpl` need `Observable<LocationEvent>`, and they definitely don't have **application scope**.

> **Note**: You'll learn all about **@Component dependency** in the next chapter. Here, you'll use the **dependencies** attribute of the `@Component` annotation, which is also the approach originally implemented in Dagger.

To get the reference to an object in the dependency graph from a `@Component`, Dagger requires you to be **explicit**. Using `inject()`s, you ask Dagger to create the code to inject dependencies into a target object — but you don't have direct access to the objects it injects.

To do that, Dagger asks you to provide **factory methods** for the objects you want to expose. To access `Observable<LocationEvent>` and `BussoEndpoint` directly from the `ApplicationComponent`, you need to add the following code to the `@Component` definition in **ApplicationComponent.kt**.

```
@Component(modules = [ApplicationModule::class])
@Singleton
interface ApplicationComponent {
  // 1
  fun locationObservable(): Observable<LocationEvent>
  // 2
  fun bussoEndpoint(): BussoEndpoint

  @Component.Factory
  interface Builder {

    fun create(@BindsInstance application: Application):
ApplicationComponent
  }
}
```

Once you get the reference to ApplicationComponent's instance, you just need to invoke:

1. locationObservable() to get a reference to the Observable<LocationEvent> implementation.

2. bussoEndpoint() to get the reference to the BussoEndpoint.

These functions also make the Observable<LocationEvent> and BussoEndpoint available to other dependent @Components, as you'll see shortly.

Now, you need to create a unique instance of ApplicationComponent and make it available across the entire app. In later chapters, you'll learn another way for sharing objects between different @Components with different @Scopes called @Subcomponents. For now, you'll use Main.

The Main component

As you learned in the first section of this book, Main is the object that kicks off the creation of the dependency graph. In this case, it must be an object where you create the instance of ApplicationComponent, which keeps it alive as long as the app is. In Android, this is easy because you just need to:

1. Create a class that extends Android's Application.

2. Create the ApplicationComponent instance and make it available from any point in the Busso app's code.

3. Register this class in **AndroidManifest.xml**.

Start by creating a new file named **Main.kt** in the main package of the app with the following code:

```
// 1
class Main : Application() {
  // 2
  lateinit var appComponent: ApplicationComponent

  override fun onCreate() {
    super.onCreate()
    // 3
    appComponent = DaggerApplicationComponent
        .factory()
        .create(this)
  }
}
// 4
val Context.appComp: ApplicationComponent
```

```
    get() = (applicationContext as Main).appComponent
```

Here, you:

1. Create Main, which extends the Android Application.
2. Define lateinit appComponent, which will contain a reference to ApplicationComponent.
3. Invoke create() on the **Factory** you get from the static factory method, factory(). This passes the reference to the Application itself and saves the ApplicationComponent instance in the appComponent property.
4. Define the appComp extension property for the Context type. If you try to access this property from a Context that's not using Main as its ApplicationContext, you'll get a crash. This is good because it lets you catch errors early in development.

To access DaggerApplicationComponent, you need to build the app. Don't worry if the build fails, Dagger will be able to generate the code for the ApplicationComponent, anyway.

Now, open **AndroidManifest.xml** and apply the following change, adding the android:name attribute for the application element:

```
<?xml version="1.0" encoding="utf-8"?>
<manifest xmlns:android="http://schemas.android.com/apk/res/
android"
  xmlns:tools="http://schemas.android.com/tools"
  package="com.raywenderlich.android.busso">

  <application ...
    android:name=".Main"> // HERE
    // ...
  </application>
</manifest>
```

You've now set up everything you need to manage objects with application scope. But how can you actually use them?

Check out SplashActivity and you see that it needs the reference to the SplashPresenter and SplashViewBinder implementations. SplashPresenterImpl needs the reference to Observable<LocationEvent>, but SplashViewBinderImpl needs a Navigator that depends on the Activity — and that's not available at the Application level. That means you need another scope.

Creating a custom @Scope

In the previous section, you implemented all the code you need to manage objects with **application scope**. These are objects that need to live as long as the app does. You managed them with a `@Component` that you created by using the `Application` you got from `Main`.

You also realized that there are other objects, like `Navigator`, that need an `Activity`, instead. You need to bind the lifecycle of these objects to the lifecycle of the `Activity` they depend upon. Based on what you've learned so far, you should just follow these steps:

1. Create the `@Modules` for the objects that depend on the `Activity`.
2. Define a `@Component` that uses those `@Modules` and has a `@Component.Builder` or `@Component.Factory` that accepts the reference to the `Activity` they need.
3. Use `@Singleton` for the objects you want to bind to the `Activity` lifecycle.
4. Create the instance of this `@Component` in the `onCreate()` of the specific `Activity` implementation, as you did for the existing `AppComponent`.

This is exactly what you're going to do, but with a small but very important difference: You're going to create and use a new `@Scope` named **@ActivityScope**.

Creating @ActivityScope

As you read in the previous chapters, `@Singleton` is nothing special. It doesn't say that an object is a **Singleton**, it just tells Dagger to bind the lifecycle of the object to the lifestyle of a `@Component`. For this reason, it's a good practice to define a custom scope using the `@Scope` annotation.

To do this, create a new file named **ActivityScope.kt** in a new **di.scopes** package and add the following code:

```
@Scope // 1
@MustBeDocumented // 2
@Retention(RUNTIME) // 3
annotation class ActivityScope // 4
```

You already defined a custom annotation when you learned about custom qualifiers. This isn't much different. Here, you:

1. Use `@Scope` to mark this annotation as a way to define a scope. Like `@Singleton`, `@Scope` is part of Java Specification Request 330. In `@Singleton`'s source code, you can see it has the same `@Scope` annotation.
2. Use `@MustBeDocumented` to mark that a Java doc should be generated for this annotation.
3. Apply `RUNTIME` as a retention value. This means that you store the annotation in binary output where it's visible for reflection.
4. Create a simple **annotation class** named `ActivityScope`.

Now, you're ready to use the `@ActivityScope` in the same way you used `@Singleton`. The only difference is the name.

Creating the ActivityModule

Now, you need to define a `@Module` for the objects with an `@ActivityScope`. In this case, those objects are implementation for:

- `Navigator`
- `SplashPresenter`
- `SplashViewBinder`
- `MainPresenter`

To do this, create a new file named **ActivityModule.kt** in **di** and enter the following code:

```
@Module(includes = [ActivityModule.Bindings::class])
class ActivityModule {

  @Module
  interface Bindings {
    @Binds
    fun bindSplashPresenter(impl: SplashPresenterImpl):
SplashPresenter

    @Binds
    fun bindSplashViewBinder(impl: SplashViewBinderImpl):
SplashViewBinder

    @Binds
    fun bindMainPresenter(impl: MainPresenterImpl):
MainPresenter
```

```
  }

  @Provides
  @ActivityScope
  fun provideNavigator(activity: Activity): Navigator =
NavigatorImpl(activity)
}
```

It's important to note that you use `@ActivityScope` to tell Dagger it should always return the same instance of the `Navigator` implementation if you get the reference through a `@Component` that has `@ActivityScope` as one of the scopes it supports. At the moment, you don't have any `@Components` like that — so it's time to create one.

Remember to delete the same definitions from the existing **AppModule.kt** file.

Creating the ActivityComponent

Create a new file named **ActivityComponent.kt** in **di** and add the following code:

```
@Component(
    modules = [ActivityModule::class] // 1
)
@ActivityScope // 2
interface ActivityComponent {

  fun inject(activity: SplashActivity) // 3

  fun inject(activity: MainActivity) // 3

  fun navigator(): Navigator // 4

  @Component.Factory
  interface Factory {
    // 5
    fun create(@BindsInstance activity: Activity):
ActivityComponent
  }
}
```

This code should be familiar. Here, you:

1. Create a `@Component` with a reference to the `@Modules` it needs to create the objects for its dependency graph.
2. Use `@ActivityScope` to tell Dagger that the objects that use the same annotation have a lifecycle bound to an `ActivityComponent`.
3. Define `inject()` for `SplashActivity` and `MainActivity`.

4. Define `navigator()` as the factory method for `Navigator`. This is also necessary to make `Navigator` visible to its dependent `@Component`.

5. Use `@Component.Factory` to ask Dagger to generate a factory method that creates an `ActivityComponent` from an `Activity`.

Now, take a quick look at the dependencies in Figure 11.4:

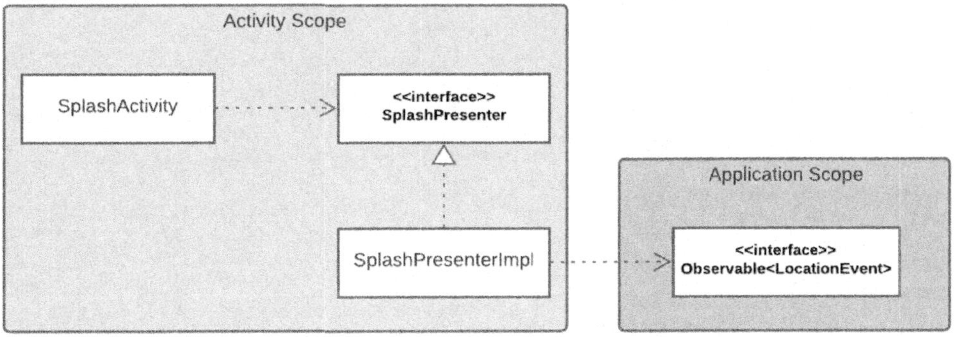

Figure 11.4 — SplashActivity dependencies

In this class diagram, you can see that `SplashActivity` depends on the `SplashPresenter` abstraction whose implementation is `SplashPresenterImpl`. This class depends on `Observable<LocationEvent>`. The problem is that `SplashActivity` has an **activity scope** while `Observable<LocationEvent>` has an **application scope**.

You need a way for `ActivityComponent` to access the object of the `ApplicationComponent` graph. You'll tackle that problem next.

Managing @Component dependencies

The problem now is finding a way to share the objects in the `ApplicationComponent` dependency graph with the ones in `ActivityComponent`. Is this a problem similar to the one you saw with existing objects? What if you think of the `Observable<LocationEvent>` and `BussoEndpoint` as objects that already exist and that you can get from an `ApplicationComponent`? That's exactly what you're going to do now. Using this method, you just need to:

1. Tell Dagger that you need the objects from another `@Component`.

2. Create a `@Component.Builder` or `@Component.Factory` that allows you to pass the reference of the dependent `@Component`.

Open **ActivityComponent.kt**, which you just created in **di**, and make the following changes:

```
@Component(
    modules = [ActivityModule::class],
    dependencies = [ApplicationComponent::class] // 1
)
@ActivityScope
interface ActivityComponent {

  fun inject(activity: SplashActivity)

  fun inject(activity: MainActivity)

  fun navigator(): Navigator

  @Component.Factory
  interface Factory {
    fun create(
        @BindsInstance activity: Activity,
        applicationComponent: ApplicationComponent // 2
    ): ActivityComponent
  }
}
```

In this code, you:

1. Use the dependencies' `@Component` attribute to tell Dagger which **dependent `@Components`** it needs to build its dependency graph.
2. Add a new `applicationComponent` parameter of type `ApplicationComponent` to the **static factory method** for the `ActivityComponent`. Note that you're not using `@BindsInstance`. As you recall, you can accomplish this by using `@Modules` as parameters.

This is going to change the code Dagger generates for you. To see how, you'll use this component in `SplashActivity` and `MainActivity`.

Using the ActivityComponent

In the previous paragraph, you changed the `@Component.Factory` definition for the `ActivityComponent`. Now, you need to change how to use it in Busso's activities.

Start by opening **SplashActivity.kt** and applying the following changes:

```
class SplashActivity : AppCompatActivity() {
  // ...
  override fun onCreate(savedInstanceState: Bundle?) {
    super.onCreate(savedInstanceState)
```

```
    makeFullScreen()
    setContentView(R.layout.activity_splash)
    DaggerActivityComponent.factory() // 1
        .create(this, this.application.appComp) // 2
        .inject(this) // 3
    splashViewBinder.init(this)
  }
  // ...
}
```

In this code, you:

1. Use `factory()` to get the **Factory** implementation that Dagger created for you.
2. Invoke `create()`, passing the reference to the current `Activity` as the first parameter. As the second parameter, you pass the reference to the `ApplicationComponent` that you get by using the `appComp` extended property you defined in **Main.kt**. It's fundamental to understand that you only have one instance of `appComp` across the entire app.
3. Inject the dependent objects using `inject()` as usual.

Now, you can do the same for `MainActivity`. Open **MainActivity.kt** in the **ui.view.main** and apply the following changes:

```
class MainActivity : AppCompatActivity() {

  @Inject
  lateinit var mainPresenter: MainPresenter

  lateinit var comp: ActivityComponent // 1

  override fun onCreate(savedInstanceState: Bundle?) {
    super.onCreate(savedInstanceState)
    setContentView(R.layout.activity_main)
    comp = DaggerActivityComponent // 2
        .factory()
        .create(this, this.application.appComp)
        .apply {
          inject(this@MainActivity)
        }
    if (savedInstanceState == null) {
      mainPresenter.goToBusStopList()
    }
  }
}

val Context.activityComp: ActivityComponent // 3
  get() = (this as MainActivity).comp
```

In this code, you can see that:

1. The `@Component` type you want to retain is `ActivityComponent`.
2. You create the instance of `DaggerActivityComponent` as you did before — by saving `ActivityComponent`'s reference in the `comp` property.
3. You implement the `activityComp` extension property to access the `ActivityComponent` from the `Fragment` the `MainActivity` will contain.

At this point, you're using:

- `@Singleton` in a `@Component` for the objects with **application scope**.
- `@ActivityScope` in a `@Component` for the objects with **activity scope**.

What about the `Fragments`? Well, at this point, you should know exactly what to do — create another custom scope.

Creating the @FragmentScope

Not all of Busso's objects will have an application or activity scope. Most of them live as long as a `Fragment`, so they need a new scope: the **FragmentScope**. Knowing that, you just repeat the same process you followed for `@Singleton` and `@ActivityScope`.

Create a new file named **FragmentScope.kt** in **di.scopes** with the following code:

```
@Scope
@MustBeDocumented
@Retention(RUNTIME)
annotation class FragmentScope
```

This defines the new `@FragmentScope`. The only way this code differs from `@Singleton` and `@ActivityScope` is in its name.

Now, create a new file named **FragmentModule.kt** in the **di** folder and add the following code:

```
@Module
interface FragmentModule {

  @Binds
  fun bindBusStopListViewBinder(impl:
BusStopListViewBinderImpl): BusStopListViewBinder

  @Binds
  fun bindBusStopListPresenter(impl: BusStopListPresenterImpl):
BusStopListPresenter
```

```
  @Binds
  fun bindBusStopListViewBinderListener(impl:
BusStopListPresenterImpl):
BusStopListViewBinder.BusStopItemSelectedListener

  @Binds
  fun bindBusArrivalPresenter(impl: BusArrivalPresenterImpl):
BusArrivalPresenter

  @Binds
  fun bindBusArrivalViewBinder(impl: BusArrivalViewBinderImpl):
BusArrivalViewBinder
}
```

This is nothing new — you just define the bindings for the components you need in the `Fragments` of the Busso App. Note that this code contains the remaining definitions you had in **AppModule.kt**, so **delete** that file now.

Then, create a new file named **FragmentComponent.kt** in **di** with the following code:

```
@Component(
    modules = [FragmentModule::class],
    dependencies = [ActivityComponent::class,
ApplicationComponent::class] // 1
)
@FragmentScope // 2
interface FragmentComponent {

  fun inject(fragment: BusStopFragment) // 3

  fun inject(fragment: BusArrivalFragment) // 3

  @Component.Factory
  interface Factory {
    // 4
    fun create(
        applicationComponent: ApplicationComponent,
        activityComponent: ActivityComponent
    ): FragmentComponent
  }
}
```

This code just contains the:

1. Definition of the dependencies on the `ActivityComponent` and `ApplicationComponent` `@Components`. It's important to note here that these dependencies are not transitive, so the dependency on `ApplicationComponent` must be explicit.

2. `@FragmentScope` annotation, because some bindings need to have a lifecycle bound to this `@Component`.
3. Definition of the `inject()` methods for the actual injection of the dependencies in `BusStopFragment` and `BusArrivalFragment`.
4. The `@Component.Factory` interface that asks Dagger to generate a **factory method** that creates a `FragmentComponent` from the existing `ApplicationComponent` and `ActivityComponent`.

This allows you to finally **delete AppComponent.kt** in the **di** package.

Now, it's time to use the `FragmentComponent` in Busso's `Fragments`.

Using the FragmentScope

In the previous paragraph, you added a new `@Component.Builder` that asks Dagger to generate a custom **factory method** for you. You now need to create the `FragmentComponent` instances in `BusStopFragment` and `BusArrivalFragment`. Before doing that, it's important to open **BusStopListPresenterImpl.kt** in the **ui.view.busstop** package and apply the following change:

```
@FragmentScope // HERE
class BusStopListPresenterImpl @Inject constructor(
    private val navigator: Navigator,
    private val locationObservable: Observable<LocationEvent>,
    private val bussoEndpoint: BussoEndpoint
) : BasePresenter<View, BusStopListViewBinder>(),
    BusStopListPresenter {
  // ...
}
```

This binds the lifecycle of `BusStopListPresenterImpl` to `FragmentComponent` with the scope `@FragmentScope` — which means you have to replace `@Singleton` with it. Otherwise, you'd prevent Dagger from generating `DaggerFragmentComponent`, which you'll use in your `Fragments`.

Next, open **BusStopFragment.kt** in **ui.view.busstop** and apply the following change:

```
class BusStopFragment : Fragment() {
  // ...
  override fun onAttach(context: Context) {
    with(context) {
      DaggerFragmentComponent.factory()
          .create(applicationContext.appComp, activityComp) //
HERE
```

```
          .inject(this@BusStopFragment)
    }
    super.onAttach(context)
  }
  // ...
}
```

The only thing to mention here is that you use the references to `ApplicationComponent` and `ActivityComponent` as parameters of the factory method for the `FragmentComponent`.

Now, open **BusStopFragment.kt** in **ui.view.busstop** and apply the same change:

```
class BusArrivalFragment : Fragment() {
  // ...
  override fun onAttach(context: Context) {
    with(context) {
      DaggerFragmentComponent.factory()
          .create(applicationContext.appComp, activityComp) //
HERE
          .inject(this@BusArrivalFragment)
    }
    super.onAttach(context)
  }
  // ...
}
```

Now, you can finally build and run Busso and check that everything works as expected.

Key points

- There's no **component** without a **container** that's responsible for its lifecycle.
- The **Android environment** is the container for the **Android standard components** and manages their lifecycle according to the resources available.
- `Fragments` are not standard components, but they have a lifecycle.
- Android components have dependencies with lifecycles.
- `@Scopes` let you bind the lifecycle of an object to the lifecycle of a `@Component`.
- `@Singleton` is a `@Scope` like any other.
- A `@Singleton` is not a **Singleton**.
- You can implement `@Component` dependencies by using the **dependencies** `@Component` attribute and providing explicit factory methods for the object you want to export to other `@Components`.

Great job! This was another important chapter, and you managed to implement different `@Scopes` for Busso's components. But you're far from done! Dagger is evolving and there are many other important concepts to learn. See you in the next chapter.

Chapter 12: Components Dependencies

By Massimo Carli

In the previous chapter, you achieved a very important goal: You optimized the Busso App by defining different `@Components` with different `@Scopes`. Using the existing `@Singleton` as well as custom `@ActivityScopes` and `@FragmentScopes`, you gave each object the right lifecycle, optimizing the app's resources. In the process, you had the opportunity to experience what **component dependency** means.

In this chapter, you'll learn even more about `@Components` and dependencies. In particular, you'll learn:

- Why `@Singleton` isn't so different from the other `@Scopes`.
- Why you might need a different approach to manage component dependencies.
- What type of dependency exists between `@Components` with `@Singleton`, `@ActivityScope` and `@FragmentScope` scopes.
- How to use `@Subcomponent.Builder` and `@Subcomponent.Factory` and why you might need them.
- When and how to use the `@Reusable` annotation.

You still have a lot to learn.

Comparing @Singleton to other scopes

So, is `@Singleton` really something special? As you saw in the previous chapter, `@Singleton` is like any other `@Scope`. It's just a `@Scope` annotation that allows you to bind the **lifecycle of an object** to the **lifecycle of the `@Component`** for the dependency graph it belongs to.

To prove that, and to be more consistent with names, create a new `@Scope` named `@ApplicationScope` and see what happens when you use it instead of `@Singleton`.

Create a new file named **ApplicationScope.kt** in the **di.scopes** package and add the following code:

```
@Scope
@MustBeDocumented
@Retention(RUNTIME)
annotation class ApplicationScope
```

The only difference between `@ActivityScope` and `@FragmentScope` is the name.

Now, open **ApplicationComponent.kt** in **di** and replace `@Singleton` with `@ApplicationScope`:

```
@Component(modules = [ApplicationModule::class])
@ApplicationScope // HERE
interface ApplicationComponent {
  // ...
}
```

Now, you have to do the same in **LocationModule.kt** in **di**:

```
@Module
class LocationModule {
  @ApplicationScope // HERE
  @Provides
  fun provideLocationManager(application: Application):
LocationManager =
      application.getSystemService(Context.LOCATION_SERVICE) as
LocationManager

  @ApplicationScope // HERE
  @Provides
  fun providePermissionChecker(application: Application):
GeoLocationPermissionChecker =
      GeoLocationPermissionCheckerImpl(application)
  // ...
}
```

Finally, apply the same changes in **NetworkModule.kt** in **network**:

```
@Module
class NetworkModule {
  @Provides
  @ApplicationScope // HERE
  fun provideCache(application: Application): Cache =
      Cache(application.cacheDir, 100 * 1024L)// 100K

  @Provides
  @ApplicationScope // HERE
  fun provideHttpClient(cache: Cache): OkHttpClient =
      Builder()
          .cache(cache)
          .build()

  @Provides
  @ApplicationScope // HERE
  fun provideBussoEndPoint(httpClient: OkHttpClient):
BussoEndpoint {
    //...
  }
}
```

Now, you can build and run Busso to prove that nothing's changed, other than using more consistent naming in the app's @Scopes.

> **Note**: Umm... If creating a custom @Scope is so easy, there's a chance that every team or project will follow its own conventions. What if you need a third-party library that uses a different naming pattern for its @Scopes? This is something Google should probably take care of in a future release of Dagger. :]

Component dependencies

Using the **dependencies** attribute of `@Component` lets you add objects from one dependency graph to the objects of another. It's a kind of **graph composition**. If `@Component` **A** needs some objects that are part of the dependency graph of `@Component` **B**, you just add **B** as one of the **dependencies** for **A**.

To do this, the objects of **B** need to be **explicitly exposed** using **factory methods**. You can see this in Figure 12.1, where `@Component` **B** exposes the green objects to the other `@Components`. This is also why you had to add `ApplicationComponent` as a dependency of `FragmentComponent`.

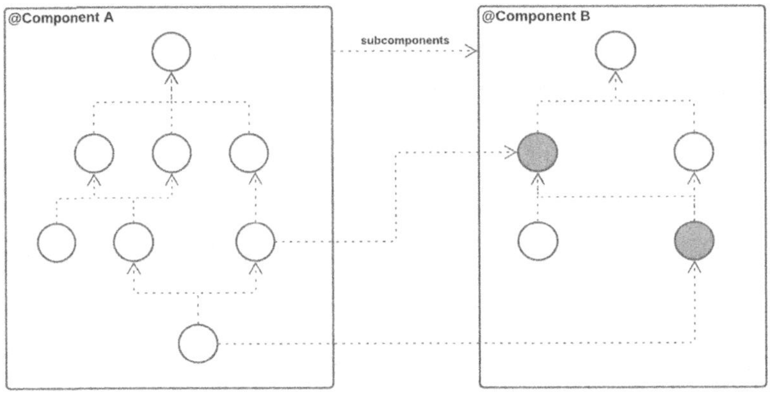

Figure 12.1 — @Component dependencies

While this is good to know, you might wonder if it's possible to implement something similar to an **inheritance** relationship between different `@Components`.

Something that allows you to say that **`@Component` A IS-A `@Component` B**, and so inherits all the objects in its dependency graph, as shown in Figure 12.2.

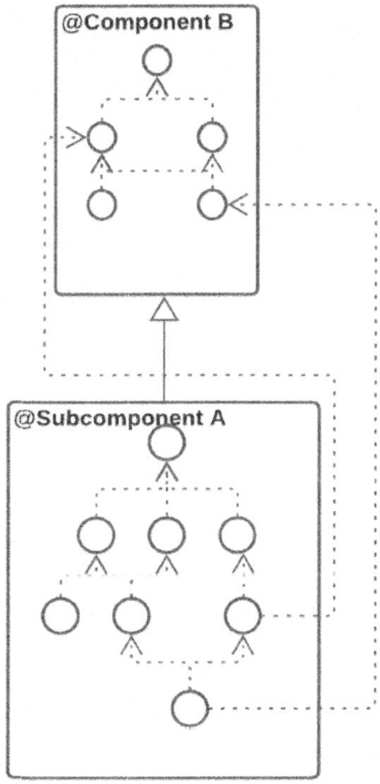

Figure 12.2 — @Subcomponent dependencies

That's where `@Subcomponents` come in. Soon, you'll learn all about what a `@Subcomponent` is and how it differs from a `@Component`. Before you dive into that, however, it's important to quickly recap what you have in Busso.

Your scoped Busso App

As mentioned in the introduction, you achieved a very important goal in the previous chapter: Giving each object of the Busso App a proper @Scope. You implemented this by creating three different @Components:

- ApplicationComponent
- ActivityComponent
- FragmentComponent

for three different @Scopes:

- @ApplicationScope
- @ActivityScope
- @FragmentScope

That was quite straightforward. The most interesting part is the way objects from different components depend on each other. Objects with @ApplicationScope should be available to objects with @ActivityScope and @FragmentScope, while objects with @ActivityScope should be also accessible from objects with @FragmentScope.

You can represent the relationship between objects with @ApplicationScope and @ActivityScope, as shown in Figure 12.3:

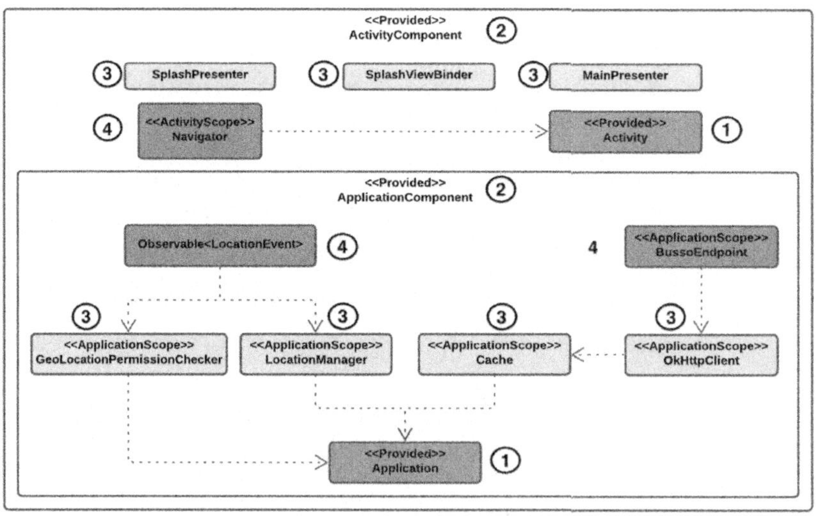

Figure 12.3 — @ApplicationComponent and @ActivityComponent dependencies

This diagram shows two different `@Components`:

- `ActivityComponent`
- `ApplicationComponent`

It also tells you many interesting things:

1. The **«Provided»** stereotype tells you which objects you need to **explicitly provide** when you create an instance of a `@Component`. For instance, you need to provide an `Application` when you create an `@ApplicationComponent` and an `Activity` when you create an `ActivityComponent`.
2. When you create the `ActivityComponent` instance, you have to provide the instance of the `ApplicationComponent` it depends on. That's why `ApplicationComponent` has the `Provided` stereotype. The same is true for the `ActivityComponent` that you need to provide to the `FragmentComponent` — although, to keep the diagram clean and clear, that isn't shown above.
3. Objects with a **gray background** are private to the `@Component`. This means that these objects aren't directly visible to other `@Components` using the **dependencies** attribute. This is important because you can only access objects you explicitly expose using factory methods, as you did in **ApplicationComponent.kt**:

```
@Component(modules = [ApplicationModule::class])
@ApplicationScope
interface ApplicationComponent {

  fun locationObservable(): Observable<LocationEvent> // HERE

  fun bussoEndpoint(): BussoEndpoint // HERE

  @Component.Factory
  interface Builder {

    fun create(@BindsInstance application: Application):
ApplicationComponent
  }
}
```

Here, you can see:

1. Objects with a green background are **public**. `@Component` **explicitly exposes** them to dependent `@Components` using **factory methods**. This is why `Observable<LocationEvent>` and `BussoEndpoint` are part of the dependency graph for `ActivityComponent` and `FragmentComponent`. For the same reason, objects in `FragmentComponent` can inject a `Navigator` implementation.

If you consider only the **provided** and **public** objects, Figure 12.4 shows what happens for the `FragmentComponent`:

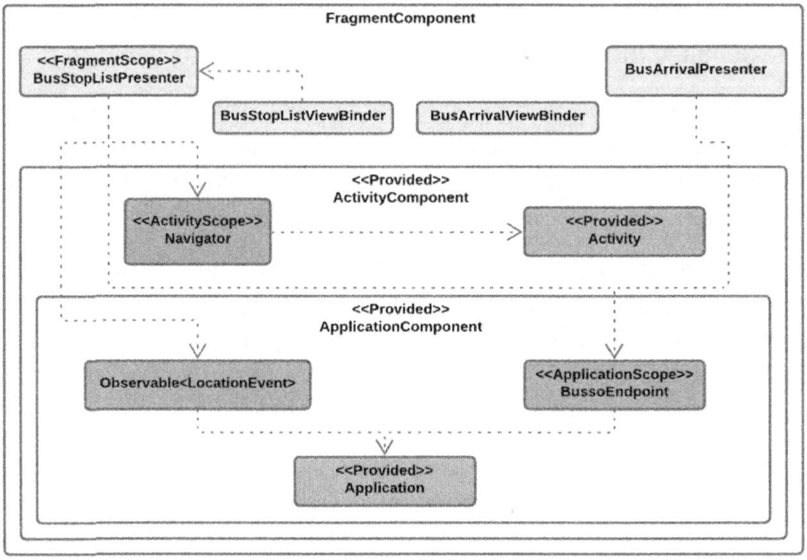

Figure 12.4 — @FragmentComponent dependencies

This diagram shows how:

1. The implementation for `BusStopListPresenter` depends on objects with different scopes. Specifically: `Navigator`, which has `@ActivityScope` and `Observable<LocationEvent>` and `BussoEndpoint`, which both have `@ApplicationScope`.

2. All of `FragmentComponent`'s objects are private to the `@Component` because no other `@Components` depend on it.

This is all well and good, but Dagger allows you to implement the same thing using `@Subcomponents`, creating a sort of **inheritance relationship** among dependency graphs with different `@Scopes`.

Using @Subcomponents

So, you've just learned in detail how the objects of different `@Components` of the Busso App depend on one other. You also learned that Busso requires some kind of inheritance relationship between the `@Components` because you want to use the objects from the `ApplicationComponent` in the `ActivityComponent` and in the `FragmentComponent`. You also want to use the objects of the `ActivityComponent` in the `FragmentComponent`.

To do all this, you need an **inheritance relationship** like the one in Figure 12.5:

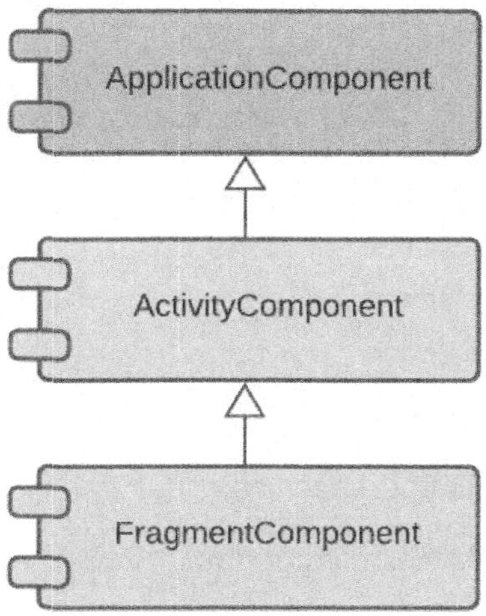

Figure 12.5 — @Component inheritance

Dagger allows you to implement that relationship using `@Subcomponents`, but doing so requires some important changes in Busso. You need to:

1. Change the dependent `@Components` to `@Subcomponents` to tell Dagger that an inheritance relationship is taking place.
2. You need to create the dependency and use it to tell Dagger which `@Component` or `@Subcomponent` you're inheriting from. As you'll see very soon, you do this using a tool you've used before: **factory methods**.
3. Use `@Subcomponent.Builder` or `@Subcomponent.Factory` in the `@Subcomponents` when you need to provide an existing object.
4. Update the way you create the `@Components` for the different `@Scopes`.

> **Note**: As often happens, you won't be able to successfully build the app until the end of the migration. Just code along and everything will be fine.

For your next step, you'll start identifying which `@Components` should be `@Subcomponents`.

Migrating @Components to @Subcomponents

Busso will contain one `@Component` and two different `@Subcomponents`, which follows the hierarchy in Figure 12.5. Open **ActivityComponent.kt** from **di** and apply the following change:

```
// 1
@Subcomponent(
    modules = [ActivityModule::class]
    // 2
)
@ActivityScope
interface ActivityComponent {
  // ...
}
```

It's very important to note that you need to:

1. Replace `@Component` with `@Subcomponent`.
2. Delete the **dependencies** attribute since `@Subcomponent` doesn't support it.

Now, open **FragmentComponent.kt** in **di** and apply the same change:

```
// 1
@Subcomponent(
    modules = [FragmentModule::class]
    // 2
)
@FragmentScope
interface FragmentComponent {
  // ...
}
```

Here you do exactly the same thing:

1. Replace `@Component` with `@Subcomponent`.
2. Delete the **dependencies** attribute.

So far, you're just telling Dagger that `ActivityComponent` and `FragmentComponent` are `@Subcomponents`, but you haven't told Dagger anything about their parents. In the next step, you'll create that relationship by adding a factory method for the `@Subcomponent` to the parent `@Components`.

Creating the @Subcomponent relationship

For your next step, you need to tell Dagger that:

- `ActivityComponent` is a `@Subcomponent` of `ApplicationComponent`.
- `FragmentComponent` is a `@SubComponent` of `ActivityComponent`.

Usually, you'd just need to provide a factory method for the `@Subcomponent`. For `ApplicationComponent`, you'd add something like this:

```
@Component(modules = [ApplicationModule::class])
@ApplicationScope
interface ApplicationComponent {

  fun activityComponent(): ActivityComponent // HERE

  // ...
}
```

Unfortunately, in Busso's case, you need a bit more because `ActivityComponent` needs an `Activity`. So what if, instead of creating a method that returns the `ActivityComponent`, you define a method to get the `Factory` or the `Builder` for it? This is what you can use to **create** or **build** the `ActivityComponent` given an `Activity`.

This is actually how Dagger works. Open **ApplicationComponent.kt** in **di** and add the following definition:

```
@Component(modules = [ApplicationModule::class])
@ApplicationScope
interface ApplicationComponent {

  fun activityComponentFactory(): ActivityComponent.Factory //
HERE
  // ...
}
```

It might be a little weird to have a factory method that returns a factory, but that's exactly what the code above does. :]

You now need to do the same for `ActivityComponent` but, in this case, the `FragmentComponent` doesn't need any existing objects other than the one it inherits from the other `@Components`.

Open **ActivityComponent** in **di** and add the following definition:

```
@Subcomponent(
    modules = [ActivityModule::class]
)
@ActivityScope
interface ActivityComponent {
  // ...
  fun fragmentComponent(): FragmentComponent // HERE
}
```

Now, you've created the `@Subcomponent` relationship between `ApplicationComponent` and `ActivityComponent` and the same relationship between `ActivityComponent` and `FragmentComponent`. Because `ActivityComponent` needs an `Activity`, you've defined a factory method for its **Factory**.

`FragmentComponent` doesn't need anything specific, so you just define a factory method for it.

Because of this change in the way you create the `@Components`, you now need to make some changes to the `Factory` and `Builder`.

Using @Subcomponent.Builder & @Subcomponent.Factory`

Dagger now understands the relationship between Busso's `@Components`. Before you go any farther, however, you need to do some clean-up. Start by opening **FragmentComponent.kt** in **di** and change it like this:

```
@Subcomponent(
    modules = [FragmentModule::class]
)
@FragmentScope
interface FragmentComponent {

  fun inject(fragment: BusStopFragment)

  fun inject(fragment: BusArrivalFragment)
}
```

This completely deletes the definition of `@Component.Factory`. You can do that because, according to the `@Subcomponent` relationship, `FragmentComponent` already inherits what it needs from its parent, `ActivityComponent`.

The same isn't true for `ActivityComponent`, because it needs an `Activity` that it doesn't inherit from its parent, `ApplicationComponent`. To handle this, open **ActivityComponent.kt** in **di** and apply the following change:

```
@Subcomponent(
    modules = [ActivityModule::class]
)
@ActivityScope
interface ActivityComponent {
  // ...
  @Subcomponent.Factory // 1
  interface Factory {
    fun create(
        @BindsInstance activity: Activity
        // 2
    ): ActivityComponent
  }
}
```

You can assume that `ActivityComponent` already received the objects from its parent, `ApplicationComponent`, so the **Factory**'s `create()` only needs one parameter. Because it's a `@Subcomponent`, Dagger asks you to use either `@Subcomponent.Factory` or the dual `@Subcomponent.Builder`. Therefore, in the code above, you:

1. Replace `@Component.Factory` with `@Subcomponent.Factory`.
2. Remove the existing parameter of type `ApplicationComponent`, because you'll **implicitly inherit** all its objects.

> **Note**: Another option would be to use `@Subcomponent.Builder` instead. You'll see how this works later in the chapter.

Very good! Now Dagger knows how Busso's `@Components` and `@Subcomponents` relate to one another.

Keep in mind that if you build the app now, you'll get some errors. That's because Dagger generates something different than you had before, and you need to update the way you create the different `@Components` and `@Subcomponents`.

Using @Subcomponent's generated code

Dagger should now be able to happily generate all the code to create:

- `ApplicationComponent`
- `ActivityComponent`
- `FragmentComponent`

Of course, the build still fails because you need to update your code accordingly.

Updating how you use ApplicationComponent

The first place you need to check is **Main.kt** in the app's main package. This is where you create the `ApplicationComponent` instance.

Open the file and you'll see the following code:

```
class Main : Application() {

  lateinit var appComponent: ApplicationComponent

  override fun onCreate() {
    super.onCreate()

    appComponent = DaggerApplicationComponent
        .factory()
        .create(this)
  }
}

val Context.appComp: ApplicationComponent
  get() = (applicationContext as Main).appComponent
```

It's good to see that in this case, you don't have to do anything. :] That's because you didn't change the way you create `ApplicationComponent`. Just like before, you need to create an instance of `ApplicationComponent` to save in the `appComponent` property you expose using the `appComp` extension property.

Now, you need to check how you create the instance of the `ActivityComponent`.

Updating how you use ActivityComponent

You create a new instance of the `ActivityComponent` in the following places:

- `SplashActivity`
- `MainActivity`

Open **SplashActivity.kt** from the **ui.view.splash** package and apply the following change:

```
class SplashActivity : AppCompatActivity() {
  // ...
  override fun onCreate(savedInstanceState: Bundle?) {
    super.onCreate(savedInstanceState)
    makeFullScreen()
    setContentView(R.layout.activity_splash)
    application.appComp // 1
        .activityComponentFactory() // 2
        .create(this) // 3
        .inject(this) // 4
    splashViewBinder.init(this)
  }
  // ...
}
```

In this code, you now:

1. Use `application` to access `appComp`.
2. `appComp` is the reference to the `ApplicationComponent` that now exposes `activityComponentFactory()` to get the **Factory** for the `ActivityComponent`.
3. Invoke `create()` on the `activityComponentFactory()`, passing the reference of the `Activity` and creating the `ActivityComponent` instance.
4. Use `inject()` to execute the actual injection.

> **Note**: During this migration, you'll need to delete the missing imports, which Android Studio displays in red.

Now, you need to do the same for `MainActivity`. Open **MainActivity.kt** from **ui.view.main** and apply the following:

```
class MainActivity : AppCompatActivity() {
  // ...
  override fun onCreate(savedInstanceState: Bundle?) {
    super.onCreate(savedInstanceState)
    setContentView(R.layout.activity_main)
    comp = application.appComp // HERE
        .activityComponentFactory()
        .create(this)
        .apply {
          inject(this@MainActivity)
        }
    if (savedInstanceState == null) {
      mainPresenter.goToBusStopList()
    }
  }
}
```

In this case, remember that you also save the `ActivityComponent` reference in the `comp` extended variable.

Now, it's time to update the code for `FragmentComponent`.

Updating how you use FragmentComponent

The two places you create `FragmentComponents` are:

- `BusStopFragment`
- `BusArrivalFragment`

The change you need to make is basically the same as what you did for `ActivityComponent` above. Open **BusStopFragment.kt** in **ui.view.busstop** and apply the following change:

```
class BusStopFragment : Fragment() {
  // ...
  override fun onAttach(context: Context) {
    context.activityComp // 1
        .fragmentComponent() // 2
        .inject(this) // 3
    super.onAttach(context)
  }
  // ...
}
```

In this code, you:

1. Access the `activityComp` extended property of the `Context` you receive as a parameter of `onAttach()`.
2. Invoke `fragmentComponent()` to get the reference to the new `FragmentComponent` instance.
3. Use `inject()` for the actual injection.

This is exactly what you have to do in **BusArrivalFragment.kt** in **ui.view.busarrival**:

```
class BusArrivalFragment : Fragment() {
  // ...
  override fun onAttach(context: Context) {
    context.activityComp // HERE
        .fragmentComponent()
        .inject(this)
    super.onAttach(context)
  }
  // ...
}
```

Now, you can finally build and run the app and see something similar to Figure 12.6:

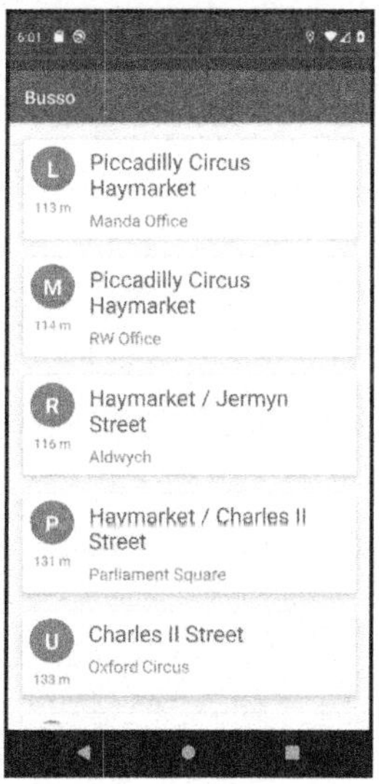

Figure 12.6 — The Busso App

Great job, but there's still one small thing to do: some clean-up!

Cleaning up the factory methods

Using `@Subcomponents`, you discovered a new way to implement a `@Component` dependency. Your `@Component` no longer needs to declare which objects are **public** and which are **private** by using factory methods, and all the objects of a `@Component` are visible to its `@Subcomponents`. This allows you to remove the factory methods from:

- `ApplicationComponent`
- `ActivityComponent`

Open **ApplicationComponent.kt** in **di** and remove `locationObservable()` and `bussoEndpoint()`. The content of this file becomes:

```
@Component(modules = [ApplicationModule::class])
@ApplicationScope
interface ApplicationComponent {

  fun activityComponentBuilder(): ActivityComponent.Builder

  @Component.Factory
  interface Builder {

    fun create(@BindsInstance application: Application):
ApplicationComponent
  }
}
```

Next, open **ActivityComponent.kt** in **di** and remove `navigator()`. That file should now look like this:

```
@Subcomponent(
    modules = [ActivityModule::class]
)
@ActivityScope
interface ActivityComponent {

  fun inject(activity: SplashActivity)

  fun inject(activity: MainActivity)

  fun fragmentComponent(): FragmentComponent

  @Subcomponent.Factory
  interface Factory {
    fun create(
        @BindsInstance activity: Activity
    ): ActivityComponent
```

```
    }
}
```

Build and run the app to check that everything still works as expected. This proves that those factory methods are no longer necessary.

Using @Subcomponent.Builder

In the previous example's `ActivityComponent`, you used `@Subcomponent.Factory`, but you could have used `@Subcomponent.Builder`, instead. To prove this, open **ActivityComponent.kt** from **di** and apply the following change:

```
@Subcomponent(
    modules = [ActivityModule::class]
)
@ActivityScope
interface ActivityComponent {
  // ...
  @Subcomponent.Builder // 1
  interface Builder {
    // 2
    fun activity(
        @BindsInstance activity: Activity
    ): Builder
    // 3
    fun build(): ActivityComponent
  }
}
```

Here you:

1. Replace `@Subcomponent.Factory` with `@Subcomponent.Builder`.
2. Add `activity()` to provide the reference to the `Activity` you need. This function must return the reference to the `Builder` itself.
3. Define the `build()` method the `Builder` needs to create `ActivityComponent`.

Because you're now using a **Builder** instead of a **Factory**, you also need to update `ApplicationComponent`. Open **ApplicationComponent.kt** in **di** and replace the existing `activityComponentFactory()` with the following:

```
@Component(modules = [ApplicationModule::class])
@ApplicationScope
interface ApplicationComponent {
  // ...
  fun activityComponentBuilder(): ActivityComponent.Builder //
HERE
```

```
  // ...
}
```

This tells Dagger that you need a `Builder` to create `ActivityComponent` from `ApplicationComponent`.

Finally, you need to update the code when you create `ActivityComponent`. Open **SplashActivity.kt** in **ui.view.splash** and change the following code:

```
class SplashActivity : AppCompatActivity() {
  // ...
  override fun onCreate(savedInstanceState: Bundle?) {
    super.onCreate(savedInstanceState)
    makeFullScreen()
    setContentView(R.layout.activity_splash)
    application.appComp
        .activityComponentBuilder() // 1
        .activity(this) // 2
        .build() // 3
        .inject(this)
    splashViewBinder.init(this)
  }
  // ...
}
```

In this code, you now:

1. Use `activityComponentBuilder()` to access the `Builder` Dagger generates for you.
2. Invoke `activity()` to pass the reference of the `Activity` you need.
3. Use `build()` to actually create `ActivityComponent`.

In `MainActivity`, you need to do the same. Open **MainActivity.kt** in **ui.view.main** and apply the following change:

```
class MainActivity : AppCompatActivity() {
  // ...
  override fun onCreate(savedInstanceState: Bundle?) {
    super.onCreate(savedInstanceState)
    setContentView(R.layout.activity_main)
    comp = application.appComp
        .activityComponentBuilder() // HERE
        .activity(this)
        .build()
        .apply {
          inject(this@MainActivity)
        }
    if (savedInstanceState == null) {
```

```
        mainPresenter.goToBusStopList()
      }
    }
  }
```

Now, build and run Busso and make sure that everything works as expected.

How do you know when to use a `@Subcomponent.Factory` or a `@Subcomponent.Builder`? You use the same criteria as you learned to decide between `@Component.Factory` and `@Component.Builder`.

@Subcomponents versus @Component dependencies attribute

In the last two chapters, you learned how to use `@Components` with different `@Scopes`. You also learned two different ways of managing dependencies between objects with different `@Scopes` using:

1. The **dependencies** attribute of the `@Component` annotation
2. `@Subcomponents`

But which one is the best? As always, there's no answer that works in every case. Each solution has its pros and cons.

If you use **@Component dependencies**:

- You need to use **factory methods** to explicitly publish the objects that a `@Component` wants to share with others.
- The **dependent `@Component`** must list the dependency `@Components` as values of its **dependencies** attribute.
- In this case, the dependency **is not transitive**. If `@Component` **A** depends on **B** and **B** depends on **C**, that doesn't mean **A** depends on **C**. If you need that relationship, the dependency must be explicit and you need to list all the dependent `@Components` in the **dependencies** attribute.
- When you have existing objects, you can use `@Component.Builder` and `@Component.Factory`.
- As you'll see in the next chapter, **multibinding doesn't work** when you manage `@Component` dependencies using the **dependencies** attribute.

If you use **@Subcomponents**:

- Each `@Subcomponent` inherits **all the objects** of the parent `@Components` or `@Subcomponents`. You don't need to explicitly publish any of them.
- In this case, the dependency between `@Subcomponents` **is transitive**. If `@Subcomponent` **A** inherits from **B** and **B** inherits from **C**, then **A** inherits from **C**.
- You create `@Subcomponent` instances using **factory methods** you define in the parent `@Component` or `@Subcomponent`.
- When you have existing objects, you can use `@Subcomponent.Builder` and `@Subcomponent.Factory`. The parent will define **factory methods** for them.
- As you'll see in the next chapter, **multibinding** works with `@Subcomponents`.

In the following chapters, you can use either solution unless limitations are in place.

Using @Reusable

In this and the previous chapters, you learned a lot about the concepts of `@Component` and `@Scope`. In particular, you learned how to create a custom `@Scope` that's not much different than the existing `@Singleton`.

`@Scope` allows you to control the number of instances Dagger creates for the injection of a specific type. You can create a new instance for a specific type any time you need to inject it or you can ask Dagger to create only one that is bound to the `@Component` it belongs to. As you've read many times now, the lifespan of a scoped object is bound to the lifespan of the `@Component` with the same scope.

Sometimes, for performance reasons, you might need to limit the number of instances for a given type *without* binding those instances to the lifespan of a specific `@Component`. If you want Dagger to check if a **convenient** instance of an object already exists before creating a new one, you can use **@Reusable**.

`@Reusable`'s source code looks like this:

```
@Documented
@Beta
@Retention(RUNTIME)
@Scope
public @interface Reusable {}
```

As you can see, `@Reusable` is a `@Scope` that Dagger treats in a particular and privileged way. You don't need to use any objects with `@Reusable` scope for Busso, but it's interesting to note how Dagger manages them.

> **Note**: As you can see in the previous code, `@Reusable` is in `@Beta`, so the logic Dagger uses for it might change in future releases.

To give an example, suppose you define a `@Component` hierarchy as in Figure 12.7:

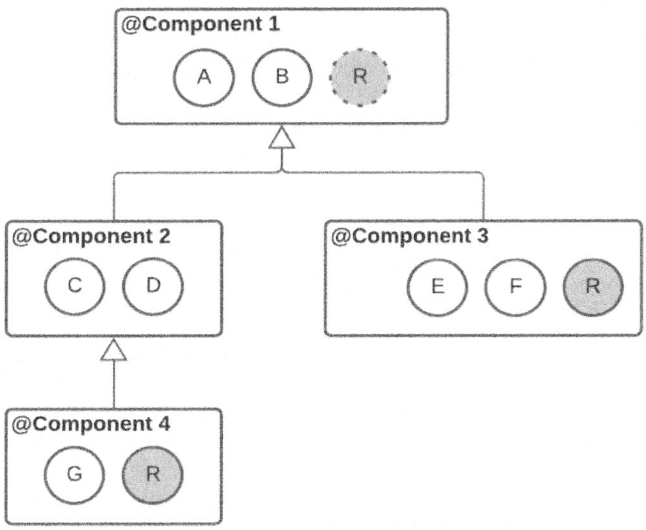

Figure 12.7 — Using @Reusable scope

Here you have four `@Components`, where:

- `@Component1` defines the binding between two objects with types **A** and **B**.
- `@Component2` does the same for two objects with types **C** and **D**.
- `@Component3` handles binding the two objects with types **E**, **F** and **R**
- `@Component4` defines a binding between two objects with types **G** and **R**.

`@Component4` and `@Component3` define the bindings for objects of the same type **R**, but the objects are bound to different `@Scopes`.

At this point, you'd consider whether you can reuse the objects of type **R**. If so, you can bind them to the `@Reusable` scope and Dagger will treat them as if they were bound to the scope for `@Component1`. This is the scope of the **least common ancestor** `@Component`.

In this case, you'd consider the pros and cons of `@Reusable` scopes. For a modern JVM implementation running on a desktop or server, creating and destroying objects isn't a big issue. On mobile, things are different because the Garbage Collector can impact an app's performance. `@Reusable` is an interesting tool you should always consider, but it isn't the best choice in every situation.

Wow! This has been another dense and important chapter. In it, you learned one of the most difficult topics in Dagger: how to implement `@Component` dependencies using `@Subcomponents`. This chapter also concludes Section Three of this book. Congratulations!

Key points

- `@Component` dependencies are a fundamental concept you should master when using Dagger.
- Using the `@Component` dependencies attribute requires you to explicitly expose the objects you want to share using **factory methods**. The dependency is **not transitive**.
- `@Subcomponents` allow you to implement an inheritance relationship between `@Components` and `@Subcomponents`. In this case, you don't need to use a factory method. Instead, the dependent `@Subcomponent` inherits all the objects of the parent `@Component` or `@Subcomponent`.
- To provide existing objects to a `@Subcomponent`, use `@Subcomponent.Factory` or `@Subcomponent.Builder`.
- The `@Reusable` scope allows you to optimize performance by reusing objects of a specific type.

In the next chapter, you'll learn all about a very important and useful Dagger feature: **multibindings**.

Section IV: Advanced Dagger

In this section, you'll dive deeper into the advanced features of Dagger like multi-binding. Multibinding is a very interesting feature of Dagger because it simplifies the integration of new features using a plugin pattern you'll learn in this section.

You'll implement a simple framework that allows you to integrate new services in the Busso app in a very simple and declarative way. You'll learn all you need to know about multi-binding with Set and Map.

Chapter 13: Multibinding

By Massimo Carli

In the previous sections, you learned how Dagger works by migrating the Busso app from a homemade injection framework based on the **ServiceLocator pattern** to a **fully scoped Dagger app**. Great job!

Now, it's time to use what you've learned to add a new feature to the Busso App, which will display messages from different endpoints at the top of the BusStop screen. For instance, you can display information about the weather and any traffic problems at your destination.

You also want to let the user add or remove new endpoints in a simple and declarative way. To do this, you'll implement a small framework called an **information plugin framework**. Its high-level architecture looks like this:

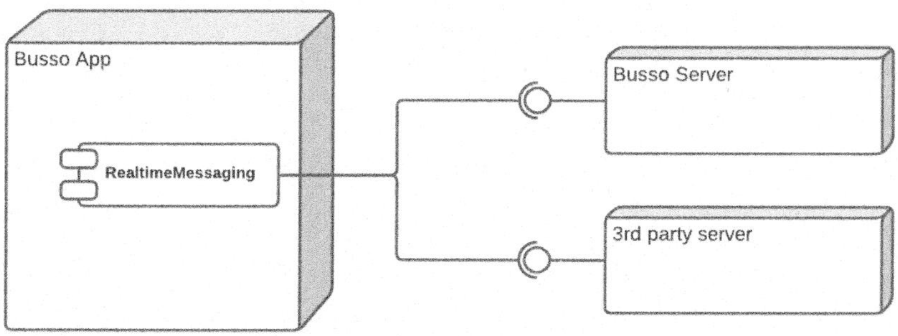

Figure 13.1 — Information from a server

Busso connects to different endpoints, gets some information and displays the messages at the top of the BusStop screen. This is a very simple use case that allows you to learn what **Dagger multibinding** is.

In this chapter's **starter project**, you'll find a version of Busso that already contains the first implementation of the information plugin framework.

In this chapter, you'll examine the existing code, learning:

- What multibinding is.
- How to use multibinding with `Set`.

Multibinding is a very interesting Dagger feature because it simplifies how you integrate new features by using a plugin pattern, which you'll learn all about in this chapter.

The information plugin framework

As you read in the introduction, Busso already contains a small framework that lets you fetch information to display at the top of the BusStop `Fragment`.

You can already see this very simple feature at work. Right now, it displays the coordinates of your current location:

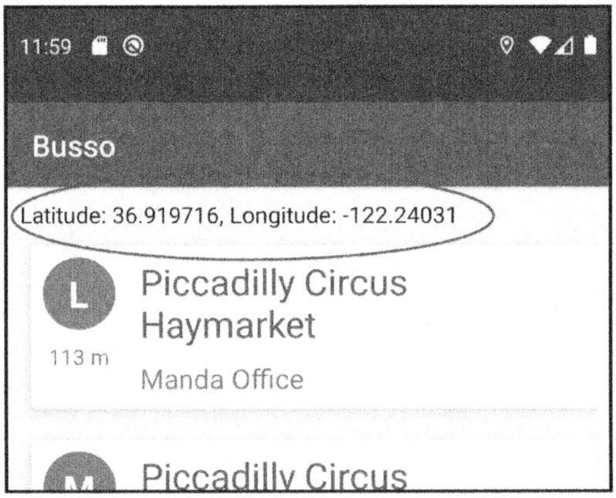

Figure 13.2 — The WhereAmI information

> **Note**: If the architecture of the information plugin framework is already clear to you, just skip to the **Introducing Dagger Multibinding** section ahead.

When you open the **Busso** project with Android Studio, you'll see the source directory structure in Figure 13.3:

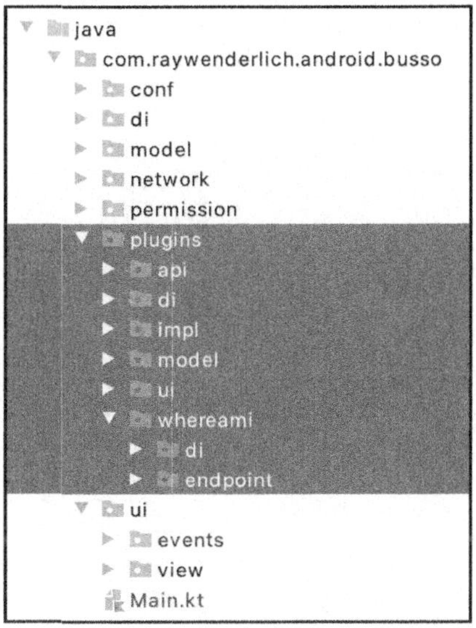

Figure 13.3 — The initial source directory structure

In particular, you'll see a new **plugins** package. Here are its sub-packages and what they contain:

- **api**: The main abstraction of the framework.
- **di**: Dagger definitions.
- **impl**: Implementation of the main abstraction.
- **model**: A very simple class that models the information you'll receive from the server.
- **ui**: The **presenter** and **viewbinder** of the framework.
- **whereami**: The classes you'll need to implement the feature that displays the coordinates of your current location, as shown in Figure 13.3. This is the first feature that uses the information plugin framework.

An in-depth description of all the code would take too much space and time, so in this chapter, you'll focus on the aspects related to dependency injection and, of course, Dagger.

Dagger configuration

The main aspect of this framework is the Dagger configuration you find in the **plugins.di** package. Open **InformationPluginModule.kt** in **plugins.di** and look at its code:

```
interface InformationPluginModule { // 1

  @Module
  interface ApplicationBindings { // 1
    @Binds
    fun bindInformationPluginRegistry(
        impl: InformationPluginRegistryImpl // 2
    ): InformationPluginRegistry
  }

  @Module
  interface FragmentBindings { // 1
    @Binds
    fun bindInformationPluginPresenter(
        impl: InformationPluginPresenterImpl // 3
    ): InformationPluginPresenter

    @Binds
    fun bindInformationPluginViewBinder(
        impl: InformationPluginViewBinderImpl // 3
    ): InformationPluginViewBinder
  }
}
```

This is the code of a `@Module` that contains all the bindings for the information plugin framework. These definitions give you insight into many important aspects of the framework. In particular:

1. You define the `InformationPluginModule` using a simple interface that encapsulates all the bindings in a single place. In particular, `ApplicationBindings` acts as the `@Module` for the binding with `@ApplicationScope`. Similarly, `FragmentBindings` is the `@Module` for the objects with `@FragmentScope`.

2. The framework has just one object that has `@ApplicationScope`: The `InformationPluginRegistry`, which contains the definitions for the plugins you want to use in the app. As you'll see, this will need a way to describe the plugin to the framework and to register it.

3. The bindings with `@FragmentScope` are related to **presenter** and **view binder**, which you can see directly in the source code in the project.

If you're wondering why you need an `InformationPluginRegistry` at all, you'll find out next.

InformationPluginRegistry

When it comes to working with plugins, frameworks, including the information plugin framework, have some important characteristics in common. They all need to:

1. Describe the plugin to the framework.
2. Register the plugin.

That's why you need an abstraction to handle the registry responsibilities. In your case, this is `InformationPluginRegistry`, whose contents you can see in **InformationPluginRegistry.kt** in **plugins.api**:

```
interface InformationPluginRegistry {

  fun register(spec: InformationPluginSpec) // 1

  fun plugins(): List<InformationPluginSpec> // 2
}
```

A **registry** allows you to:

1. Register the description of a plugin.
2. Access the collection of existing plugins.

In the same interface, you can also see that you describe each plugin instance using an `InformationPluginSpec`. Open **InformationPluginSpec.kt** in **plugins.api** and look at its code:

```
interface InformationPluginSpec {

  val informationEndpoint: InformationEndpoint // 1

  val serviceName: String // 2
}
```

An `InformationPluginSpec` describes a specific **information plugin** in terms of:

1. The endpoint to invoke.
2. A name.

Now, look at the current implementation of `InformationPluginRegistry` by opening **InformationPluginRegistryImpl.kt** in **plugins.impl** and looking at the code:

```
@ApplicationScope
class InformationPluginRegistryImpl @Inject constructor() :
InformationPluginRegistry {

  private val plugins = mutableListOf<InformationPluginSpec>()

  override fun register(spec: InformationPluginSpec) {
    plugins.add(spec)
  }

  override fun plugins(): List<InformationPluginSpec> = plugins
}
```

This is a very simple implementation that stores the `InformationPluginSpec` instances you register in a simple `MutableList<InformationPluginSpec>`.

Next, you'll look at how Busso uses `InformationPluginSpec` and `InformationPluginRegistry`.

The WhereAmI information plugin

To implement an information plugin, you need to follow these steps:

1. Create an endpoint.
2. Define a `@Module` to tell Dagger how to create the endpoint.
3. Create an `InformationPluginSpec` for the **information plugin**.
4. Add the `@Module` to `ApplicationComponent`, enhancing its dependency graph.
5. Register the `InformationPluginSpec` to the `InformationPluginRegistry`.
6. Build and run the app.

Look in the starter project in the material for this chapter to find the WhereAmI information plugin and you'll see that it has each of these steps already completed for you. Here's a closer look at how they work for the **WhereAmI** feature.

Creating an endpoint

Assuming that you have an actual endpoint to call, your first step is to define an implementation of `InformationEndpoint`, which you find in **plugins.api**.

Open **InformationEndpoint.kt** in **plugins.api** and you'll see that `InformationEndpoint` is a very simple interface with a single operation. It allows you to fetch some information given a `GeoLocation`, which is simply a model with the `longitude` and `latitude` properties you already used for the bus stops.

```
interface InformationEndpoint {

  fun fetchInformation(location: GeoLocation):
Single<InfoMessage>
}
```

The specific `InformationEndpoint` for the **WhereAmI** information plugin is in **WhereAmIEndpoint.kt** in **plugins.whereami.endpoint**:

```
interface WhereAmIEndpoint : InformationEndpoint
```

Find its implementation in **WhereAmIEndpointImpl.kt** in **plugins.whereami.endpoint**. Open it and you'll see it contains the following code:

```
class WhereAmIEndpointImpl @Inject constructor(
    private val myLocationEndpoint: MyLocationEndpoint // 1
) : WhereAmIEndpoint {
  override fun fetchInformation(location: GeoLocation):
Single<InfoMessage> =
      myLocationEndpoint.whereAmIInformation(location.latitude,
location.longitude) // 2
}
```

In this class, you:

1. Receive `MyLocationEndpoint` as the primary constructor parameter.
2. Delegate `MyLocationEndpoint` to execute `fetchInformation()`.

But what's `MyLocationEndpoint`? Opening **MyLocationEndpoint.kt** in **plugins.whereami.endpoint** shows you that it's simply the interface you define using Retrofit:

```
interface MyLocationEndpoint {
  @GET("${BUSSO_SERVER_BASE_URL}myLocation/{lat}/{lng}")
  fun whereAmIInformation(
      @Path("lat") latitude: Double,
      @Path("lng") longitude: Double
  ): Single<InfoMessage>
}
```

> **Note**: The **WhereAmI** information plugin uses an existing endpoint in the **Busso Server** on Heroku. It simply returns a formatted string for the location that the server receives as a `@Path` of a **GET** request.

The UML diagram in Figure 13.4 gives you a better idea of the relationship between the different endpoint abstractions:

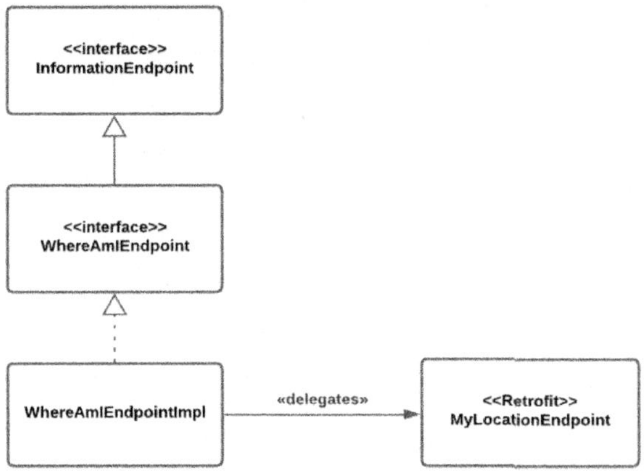

Figure 13.4 — The InformationEndpoint diagram

Your next step is to create the `@Module`.

Defining a @Module and creating InformationPluginSpec

Now, you need to tell Dagger how to create the objects it needs for WhereAmI. Open **WhereAmIModule.kt** in **plugins.whereami.di** and look at the code:

```
@Module(includes = [WhereAmIModule.Bindings::class])
object WhereAmIModule {

  @Provides
  @ApplicationScope // 1
  fun provideMyLocationEndpoint(retrofit: Retrofit):
MyLocationEndpoint {
    return retrofit.create(MyLocationEndpoint::class.java)
  }

  @Provides
  @ApplicationScope // 2
  fun provideWhereAmISpec(endpoint: WhereAmIEndpointImpl):
InformationPluginSpec = object : InformationPluginSpec {
    override val informationEndpoint: InformationEndpoint
```

```
      get() = endpoint
    override val serviceName: String
      get() = "WhereAmI"
  }

  @Module
  interface Bindings { // 3

    @Binds
    fun bindWhereAmIEndpoint(
        impl: WhereAmIEndpointImpl
    ): WhereAmIEndpoint
  }
}
```

This code should be familiar to you. Here, you basically:

1. Provide the `MyLocationEndpoint` implementation using Retrofit.
2. Create and provide `InformationPluginSpec` for the `WhereAmI` plugin.
3. Bind `WhereAmIEndpoint` to `WhereAmIEndpointImpl`.

The most important thing here is that you create `InformationPluginSpec` for the **WhereAmI** plugin, which completes the third step in the previous TODO list.

Now, you can also see how `WhereAmIModule` is one of the modules that `ApplicationComponent` uses for the bindings. Inside **ApplicationComponent.kt** in **di**, you'll see:

```
@Component(modules = [
  ApplicationModule::class,
  InformationPluginModule.ApplicationBindings::class,
  WhereAmIModule::class // HERE
])
@ApplicationScope
interface ApplicationComponent {
  // ...
}
```

Now, it's finally time to register the `InformationPluginSpec` to the `InformationPluginRegistry`.

Registering InformationPluginSpec

This is the last and most important step in the process. Once you define `InformationPluginSpec`, you need to register it to `InformationPluginRegistry` to make it available to the framework. At the moment, you do this in **Main.kt**, which looks like this:

```
class Main : Application() {

  lateinit var appComponent: ApplicationComponent

  @Inject
  lateinit var informationPluginRegistry:
InformationPluginRegistry // 1

  @Inject
  lateinit var whereAmISpec: InformationPluginSpec // 2

  override fun onCreate() {
    super.onCreate()
    // 3
    appComponent = DaggerApplicationComponent
        .factory()
        .create(this).apply {
          inject(this@Main) // 3
        }
    informationPluginRegistry.register(whereAmISpec) // 4
  }
}
```

In this code, you:

1. Define `informationPluginRegistry`, which contains the reference to `InformationPluginRegistry`.
2. Add `whereAmISpec`, which contains the reference to `InformationPluginSpec` for the plugin.
3. Invoke `inject()` on `ApplicationComponent` for the injection. This, of course, requires that you define `inject()` with a parameter of type `Main` in `ApplicationComponent`.
4. Register `whereAmISpec` to `InformationPluginRegistry`, invoking `register()`.

Now you can finally build and run, getting what's in Figure 13.5:

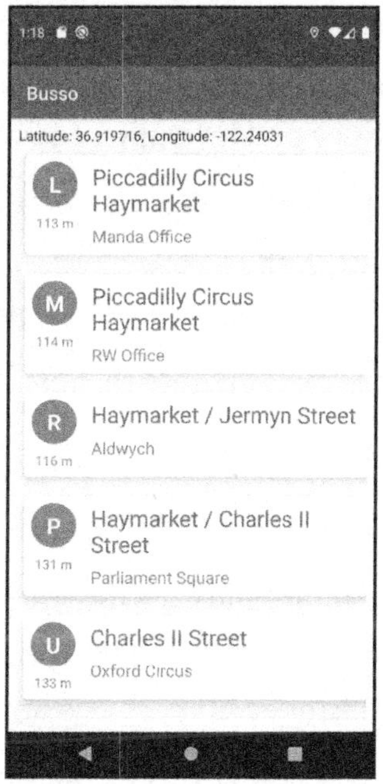

Figure 13.5 — The WhereAmI information

This is cool, but can you make the process easier and more declarative? That's where Dagger's **multibinding** feature comes in.

Introducing Dagger multibinding

To understand how **multibinding** helps implement the information plugin framework, take a moment to go over what you've done so far. You basically defined:

1. The main abstractions that the different **information plugins** need to implement to be able to integrate into the framework.
2. How to describe an information plugin to the framework.
3. A registry containing all the information plugin definitions.

Every time you implement a location plugin, you need to:

1. Describe the plugin using an `InformationPluginSpec`.
2. Register the plugin to the framework.

In the current project, you explicitly did this in **Main.kt** by:

1. Creating an instance of the `InformationPluginSpec` implementation.
2. Registering that `InformationPluginSpec` implementation instance to the `InformationPluginRegistry` and invoking `register()`.

But is all this scaffolding really necessary? The answer is, obviously, *no*.

Dagger multibinding solves this problem very simply, by letting you create a `Set` or a `Map` from some Dagger bindings in a **declarative** and **pluggable** way.

To see multibindings in action, you'll migrate the information plugin framework to use them.

Using multibinding with Set

Your first step is to use Dagger multibinding with `Set` to implement the information plugin registration mechanism. This allows you to:

1. Adapt the `InformationPluginRegistry` to use `Set<InformationPluginSpec>`.
2. Dynamically and declaratively add `InformationPluginSpec` to `Set<InformationPluginSpec>` from Dagger binding definitions.

That's all! In your next step, you'll make a small refactor that will have a big impact.

Refactoring InformationPluginRegistry

You want all the `InformationPluginSpecs` you register to be in a `Set<LocationPluginInfo>`, so you need to change `InformationPluginRegistry` accordingly. To do this, open **InformationPluginRegistryImpl.kt** in **plugins.impl** and apply the following changes:

```
@ApplicationScope
class InformationPluginRegistryImpl @Inject constructor(
    private val informationPlugins:
Set<InformationPluginSpec> // 1
) : InformationPluginRegistry {

  // 2
  override fun plugins(): List<InformationPluginSpec> =
informationPlugins.toList() // 3
}
```

In this code, you:

1. Add `informationPlugins` as the primary constructor parameter with a type of `Set<InformationPluginSpec>`. This means that Dagger will inject a proper value when it resolves the bindings.
2. You no longer need `register()` because you're asking Dagger to register the plugins for you. Dagger will do this by putting your plugin spec into `Set<InformationPluginSpec>` directly. For the same reason, you don't need `plugins` anymore, so you delete them both.
3. Return `informationPlugins` from `plugins()` as a `List<InformationPluginSpec>`.

The second point means you should also delete `register()` from the interface. Open **InformationPluginRegistry.kt** in **plugins.api** and change it to the following:

```
interface InformationPluginRegistry {

  fun plugins(): List<InformationPluginSpec>
}
```

Now, `InformationPluginRegistry` uses `Set<InformationPluginSpec>`, which you provide through Dagger.

Next, it's time to register the **WhereIAm** plugin.

Registering WhereIAm

This is the most interesting part: How can you register your plugin declaratively? Open **WhereAmIModule.kt** in **plugins.whereami.di** and you'll see that you're already telling Dagger how get an `InformationPluginSpec` for the `WhereAmI` plugin:

```
@Module(includes = [WhereAmIModule.Bindings::class])
object WhereAmIModule {
  // ...
  @Provides
  @ApplicationScope
  fun provideWhereAmISpec(endpoint: WhereAmIEndpointImpl):
InformationPluginSpec = object : InformationPluginSpec {
    override val informationEndpoint: InformationEndpoint
      get() = endpoint
    override val serviceName: String
      get() = "WhereAmI"

  }
  // ...
}
```

What you're not doing is telling Dagger to put that object into a Set<InformationPluginSpec>. Changing this is as simple as adding **@IntoSet** to the previous @Provides declaration, as in the following code:

```
@Module(includes = [WhereAmIModule.Bindings::class])
object WhereAmIModule {
  // ...
  @Provides // 1
  @ApplicationScope // 2
  @IntoSet // 3 HERE
  fun provideWhereAmISpec(endpoint: WhereAmIEndpointImpl):
InformationPluginSpec = object : InformationPluginSpec { // 4
    override val informationEndpoint: InformationEndpoint
      get() = endpoint
    override val serviceName: String
      get() = "WhereAmI"

  }
  // ...
}
```

You won't believe it, but this is all you have to do to configure multibinding.

Note: Spoiler alert! This isn't completely true. :] There's one thing you need to fix first, and you'll see what that is soon.

With this code, you use:

1. @Provides to provide the implementation of InformationPluginSpec that you want to put into Set<InformationPluginSpec>.
2. @ApplicationScope to tell Dagger that you want to bind just one instance of InformationPluginSpec to the ApplicationComponent lifecycle.
3. @IntoSet to tell Dagger that you want Set<InformationPluginSpec> to be available in the dependency graph, and that the instance you're providing should be one of the objects in that graph.
4. Finally, you return an object of type InformationPluginSpec. You're not returning a Set<InformationPluginSpec>, but just one of the elements you want.

Before building and running the app, you need to clean up a few things.

Cleaning up your code

Open **Main.kt** and remove the excess code so it looks like this:

```
class Main : Application() {

  lateinit var appComponent: ApplicationComponent

  override fun onCreate() {
    super.onCreate()
    appComponent = DaggerApplicationComponent
        .factory()
        .create(this)
  }
}

val Context.appComp: ApplicationComponent
  get() = (applicationContext as Main).appComponent
```

Here, you removed the:

1. `informationPluginRegistry` property of type `InformationPluginRegistry`.
2. `inject()` invocation on `ApplicationComponent`.
3. `register()` invocation on `informationPluginRegistry`.

Of course, you don't need `inject()` in the `Main` parameter of `ApplicationComponent` anymore because you don't need to inject anything into `Main`.

Now, you can build and run. Oops! Something went wrong.

Using @JvmSuppressWildcards

When you build now, you get the following error:

```
ApplicationComponent.java:8: error: [Dagger/MissingBinding]
java.util.Set<? extends
com.raywenderlich.android.busso.plugins.api
.InformationPluginSpec> cannot be provided without an @Provides-
annotated method.
```

What's going on? It looks like Dagger can't find the object to inject into `InformationPluginRegistry`.

But Dagger should provide a `Set<InformationPluginSpec>` because of the following declaration in **WhereAmI.kt** in **plugins.whereami.di**:

```
  @Provides
  @ApplicationScope
  @IntoSet
  fun provideWhereAmISpec(endpoint: WhereAmIEndpointImpl):
InformationPluginSpec = object : InformationPluginSpec {
    override val informationEndpoint: InformationEndpoint
      get() = endpoint
    override val serviceName: String
      get() = "WhereAmI"

  }
```

If you look carefully at the error message, however, you see that Dagger is looking for something other than **`Set<InformationPluginSpec>`**. It's looking for a binding with a type of **`Set<? extends InformationPluginSpec>`**.

In binding declarations, types are very important to Dagger. The **IS-A** relationship doesn't work unless it's explicit. That means that if you define a binding for the type **MyType**, Dagger will look for an object of type **MyType** and not for a type that **IS-A MyType**.

You've seen this many times. If you define a binding for a type `InformationPluginRegistry`, Dagger won't use an implementation like `InformationPluginRegistryImpl` unless you **explicitly** define it using `@Binds` or `@Provides`.

But why is Dagger looking for `Set<? extends InformationPluginSpec>` when you specified `Set<InformationPluginSpec>` as `InformationPluginRegistryImpl`'s primary constructor parameter type? Well, that's Kotlin's fault. :]

Kotlin converts any generic type into a Java generic with **wildcards**. That turns `Set<InformationPluginSpec>` into `Set<? extends InformationPluginSpec>` because `Set<A>` is **covariant**. If it would be contra-variant, a type `MyType<in A>` would become `MyType<? super A>`.

> **Note**: **Variance** is a fundamental concept in Kotlin and other languages. If you want to learn more, read the book, **Kotlin Apprentice** (https://www.raywenderlich.com/books/kotlin-apprentice/).

Kotlin is the problem here, but it also offers a solution: **`@JvmSuppressWildcards`**. Using this annotation, you can tell Kotlin to ignore the wildcards and, in this case, to consider `Set<InformationPluginSpec>` to be, ahem, `Set<InformationPluginSpec>`. :]

Implementing @JvmSuppressWildcard

To implement this, open **InformationPluginRegistryImpl.kt** in **plugins.impl** and apply this change:

```
@ApplicationScope
class InformationPluginRegistryImpl @Inject constructor(
    private val informationPlugins: @JvmSuppressWildcards
Set<InformationPluginSpec> // HERE
) : InformationPluginRegistry {

  override fun plugins(): List<InformationPluginSpec> =
informationPlugins.toList()
}
```

You could also use this as the annotation for the specific **generic type parameter**, if you needed to control each type parameter independently, like this:

```
@ApplicationScope
class InformationPluginRegistryImpl @Inject constructor(
    private val informationPlugins: Set<@JvmSuppressWildcards
InformationPluginSpec> // HERE
) : InformationPluginRegistry {

  override fun plugins(): List<InformationPluginSpec> =
informationPlugins.toList()
}
```

Now, you can finally build and run the app successfully. Just like before, you'll see something like this:

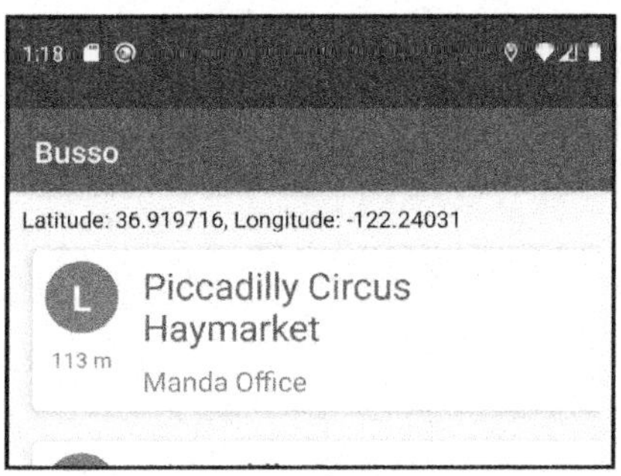

Figure 13.6 — The WhereIAm location plugin feature

Congratulations! You implemented the **Location Plugin Framework** using multibinding. Just by using `@IntoSet`, you've made an object available to a registry without any specific `registry()` invocation. Everything's now **declarative**.

Adding a new information service plugin

As you learned in the first chapter of this book, it's not important how fast you implement a feature but how fast you can change or extend it. To appreciate Dagger's multibinding capabilities, you're now going to add a new information plugin.

In this example, you'll use a simple service from the Busso Server that lets you print a random weather condition message. At this point, it's a simple text, but of course, you can extend the feature as you want.

As you learned earlier, you need to:

1. Define an endpoint for the weather information feature.
2. Define a `@Module` for the new information plugin that exposes `InformationEndpoint` and `InformationPluginSpec`.
3. Add the `@Module` to the ones in `ApplicationComponent`.
4. Build, run and enjoy your app.

It's time to write some code.

Defining an endpoint

Create a new package, **plugins.weather.endpoint**, then add a new file named **WeatherEndpoint.kt** to it with the following code:

```
interface WeatherEndpoint {

  @GET("${BUSSO_SERVER_BASE_URL}weather/{lat}/{lng}")
  fun fetchWeatherCondition(
      @Path("lat") latitude: Double,
      @Path("lng") longitude: Double
  ): Single<InfoMessage>
}
```

Next, you need an implementation of `WeatherInformationEndpoint`.

Create a new file named **WeatherInformationEndpoint.kt** in **plugins.wether.endpoint** with the following code:

```
interface WeatherInformationEndpoint : InformationEndpoint
```

Now, create a new file named **WeatherInformationEndpointImpl.kt** in the same package and enter the following code:

```
class WeatherInformationEndpointImpl @Inject constructor(
    private val weatherEndpoint: WeatherEndpoint
) : WeatherInformationEndpoint {
  override fun fetchInformation(location: GeoLocation):
Single<InfoMessage> =
      weatherEndpoint.fetchWeatherCondition(location.latitude,
location.longitude)
}
```

Your next step is to create the `@Module`.

Creating the weather information @Module

Now, you need to create a `@Module` to tell Dagger about the `InformationEndpoint` you just created. Create a new package, **plugins.weather.di**, add a new file named **WeatherModule.kt**, then give it this code:

```
@Module(includes = [WeatherModule.Bindings::class])
object WeatherModule {

  @Provides
  @ApplicationScope
  fun provideWeatherEndpoint(retrofit: Retrofit):
WeatherEndpoint {
    return retrofit.create(WeatherEndpoint::class.java)
  }

  @Provides
  @IntoSet // HERE
  @ApplicationScope
  fun provideWeatherSpec(endpoint: WeatherInformationEndpoint):
InformationPluginSpec = object : InformationPluginSpec {
    override val informationEndpoint: InformationEndpoint
      get() = endpoint
    override val serviceName: String
      get() = "Weather"

  }

  @Module
  interface Bindings {
```

```
    @Binds
    fun bindWeatherInformationEndpoint(
        impl: WeatherInformationEndpointImpl
    ): WeatherInformationEndpoint
  }
}
```

This follows the same structure as the `WhereAmIModule` you saw for the `WhereAmI` information plugin. The important part is that you use `@IntoSet` for `provideWeatherSpec()`.

Now, you need to make the plugin available to the framework.

Adding a weather plugin

To add the `WeatherModule` to the modules in `ApplicationComponent`, open **ApplicationComponent.kt** in **di** and apply the following change:

```
@Component(modules = [
  ApplicationModule::class,
  InformationPluginModule.ApplicationBindings::class,
  WhereAmIModule::class,
  WeatherModule::class // HERE
])
@ApplicationScope
interface ApplicationComponent {
  // ...
}
```

Great, you're ready to use the new plugin.

Checking your work

Now, build and run your app and you'll see something like Figure 13.7:

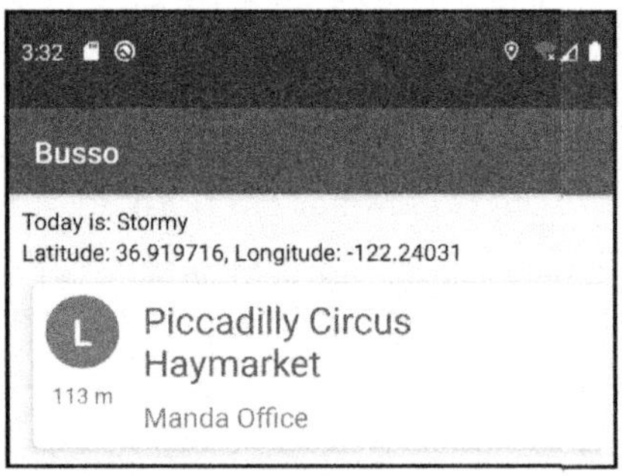

Figure 13.7 — The Weather location plugin feature

This shows the top part of the screen only, to save space.

This is cool, right? But there's a problem... in addition to the stormy weather here in London now. If you launch the app another time or you force `BusStopFragment` to reload, you might see the following output:

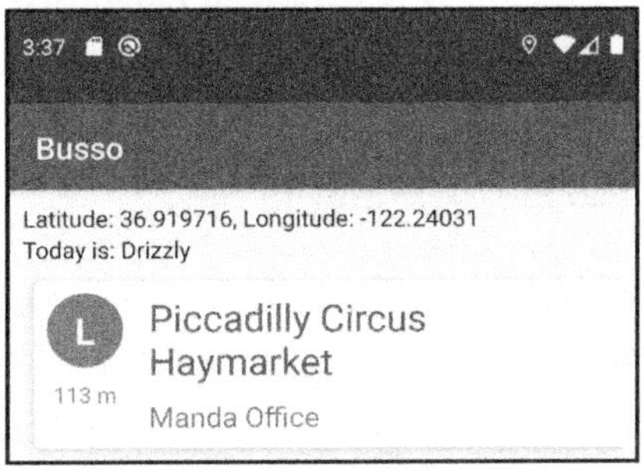

Figure 13.8 — The Weather location plugin feature

What's the problem? In Figure 13.7, the `WhereAmI` information displays *after* the `Weather` information but in Figure 13.8, the location information is above the weather. That's because a `Set` doesn't contain duplicates, but it also doesn't have any set order.

Of course, you could add a property to `InformationPluginSpec` and use it to sort how the data in the output displays.

However, this wouldn't actually be simple, because all the requests to the different endpoints are asynchronous. Just because you sort how you send the requests doesn't mean you'll receive the responses in the same order.

Adding specific information to the `InformationPluginSpec` to fix a problem of the framework isn't a good choice in terms of encapsulation and separation of concerns, either. As you'll see later, Dagger multibinding allows you to add some information to the actual binding using **multibinding with Map** and a custom **key**.

You can use what you'll learn in the following paragraphs to solve the ordering problem as an exercise.

More about Multibinding with Set: @ElementsIntoSet

In the previous example, you learned how to use `@IntoSet` to add a specific binding to a `Set` that Dagger creates for you and makes available to the dependency graph of the app.

It's worth mentioning that the `Set` Dagger creates is immutable. Dagger defines the content of the `Set` when it creates the dependency graph and you can't change it later. But nobody's preventing you from using a `Set<Provider<A>>` or `Set<Lazy<A>>` if you don't want to create everything when the app starts.

In the previous examples, you created a different definition for each `InformationPluginSpec`. In this case, each information plugin had to add this definition to the related `@Module`.

You have another option, though: defining all the `InformationPluginSpec` in the same place. Try this by creating a new file named **InformationSpecsModule.kt** in **plugins.di** and add the following code:

```
@Module(
    includes = [
      WhereAmIModule::class,
      WeatherModule::class
    ]
)
object InformationSpecsModule {

  @Provides
  @ElementsIntoSet // 1
  @ApplicationScope
  fun provideWeatherSpec(
      @Named(WHEREAMI_INFO_NAME) whereAmISpec:
InformationPluginSpec, // 2
      @Named(WEATHER_INFO_NAME) weatherSpec:
InformationPluginSpec // 2
  ): Set<InformationPluginSpec> { // 3
    return mutableSetOf<InformationPluginSpec>().apply {
      add(whereAmISpec)
      add(weatherSpec)
    }
  }
}
```

In this code, you can see that you use:

1. `@ElementsIntoSet` to add more than one element to the `Set<InformationPluginSpec>` at once.
2. `@Named(WHEREAMI_INFO_NAME)` and `@Named(WEATHER_INFO_NAME)` to identify the two different implementations of `InformationPluginSpec`. Without `@Named`, Dagger would be confused about which to use.
3. `Set<InformationPluginSpec>` as the return value's type.

Of course, you need to update the definition in **WhereAmIModule.kt**, like this:

```
const val WHEREAMI_INFO_NAME = "WhereAmI" // 1

@Module(includes = [WhereAmIModule.Bindings::class])
object WhereAmIModule {
  // ...
  @Provides
  @ApplicationScope
  // 2
  @Named(WHEREAMI_INFO_NAME) // 3
  fun provideWhereAmISpec(endpoint: WhereAmIEndpointImpl):
InformationPluginSpec = object : InformationPluginSpec {
    override val informationEndpoint: InformationEndpoint
      get() = endpoint
    override val serviceName: String
      get() = WHEREAMI_INFO_NAME
  }
}
```

Note that you:

1. Have a `WHEREAMI_INFO_NAME` constant for the name of the plugin.
2. Removed `@IntoSet`.
3. Added `@Named(WHEREAMI_INFO_NAME)` as a qualifier of the binding.

You need to do the same in **WeatherModule.kt**:

```
const val WEATHER_INFO_NAME = "Weather"

@Module(includes = [WeatherModule.Bindings::class])
object WeatherModule {
  // ...
  @Provides
  @Named(WEATHER_INFO_NAME)
  @ApplicationScope
  fun provideWeatherSpec(endpoint: WeatherInformationEndpoint):
      InformationPluginSpec = object : InformationPluginSpec {
    override val informationEndpoint: InformationEndpoint
      get() = endpoint
    override val serviceName: String
      get() = WEATHER_INFO_NAME
  }
}
```

For your last step, you need to update **ApplicationComponent.kt** to include `InformationSpecsModule::class` and to remove `WhereAmIModule::class` and `WeatherModule::class`.

Here's the result:

```
@Component(modules = [
  ApplicationModule::class,
  InformationPluginModule.ApplicationBindings::class,
  InformationSpecsModule::class
])
@ApplicationScope
interface ApplicationComponent {

  fun activityComponentBuilder(): ActivityComponent.Builder

  @Component.Factory
  interface Builder {

    fun create(@BindsInstance application: Application):
ApplicationComponent
  }
}
```

Now, just build and run and check that everything works as expected.

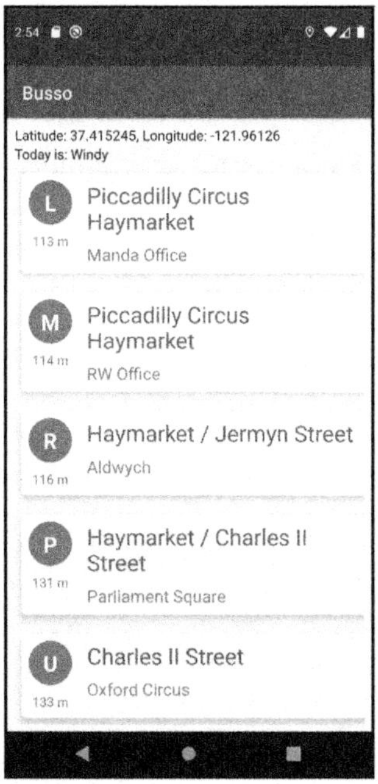

Figure 13.9 — The information plugins in the Busso app

`@ElementsIntoSet` is useful when you need to provide a set of objects as part of, for instance, an initial setup for the framework or a set of predefined objects.

Wow! This has been a very dense chapter. You learned a lot about multibinding and you managed to implement a simple framework that allows you to integrate new services in Busso in a simple and declarative way. Multibinding uses more than just `Set`.

In the next chapter, you'll learn everything you need to know about multibinding with `Map`.

Key points

- Dagger multibinding allows you to add functionality to your app in an easy and declarative way.
- You can use multibinding with both `Set` and `Map`.
- `@IntoSet` allows you to populate a `Set` when you initialize the dependency graph.
- Types are fundamental to Dagger. Use `@JvmSuppressWildcards` to fix a variance problem that occurs when Dagger resolves the objects to inject.
- `@ElementsIntoSet` allows you to put more than one object into a multibinding `Set`.

Chapter 14: Multibinding With Maps

By Massimo Carli

In the previous chapter, you learned how to use **multibinding with Set** by implementing a simple framework to integrate information from remote endpoints into the Busso App. By refactoring the **Information Plugin Framework**, you saw how to dynamically add features to Busso in a simple and declarative way.

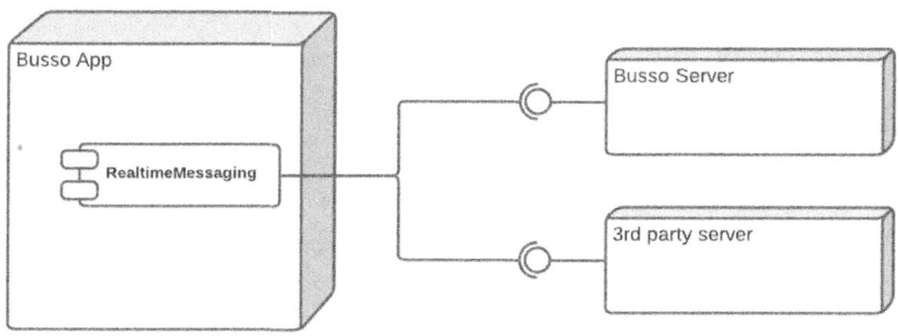

Figure 14.1 - Information Plugin Framework

In this chapter, you'll learn how to use multibinding with `Map`. In particular, you'll learn how to:

- Configure multibinding with `Map`.
- Use fundamental type keys with `@StringKey`, `@ClassKey`, `@IntKey` and `@LongKey`.
- Create a simple custom key.
- Use `@KeyMap` to build complex custom keys.

This is an opportunity to see how Dagger multibinding simplifies the architecture of the **Information Plugin Framework**.

Using multibinding with Map

In the previous chapter, you learned how to use multibinding with Sets. Set is an unordered data structure that lets you avoid duplicates. This is great but sometimes you might need something different. For instance, in the case of the **Information Plugin Framework**, a Set doesn't allow you to decide the order of the information to display on the screen.

In any case, Dagger offers you another option: multibinding with Map. Map is a data structure that allows you map a value to a key.

> **Note**: If you want to know more about data structures in Kotlin and crack interviews for getting your dream job, have a look at Data Structures & Algorithms in Kotlin (https://www.raywenderlich.com/books/data-structures-algorithms-in-kotlin).

In the following paragraph, you'll see how to use multibinding with **Map<K, V>** where the key, **K**, is one of the following:

- String,Int and Long
- Class<T>
- Custom type

Using a String is the simplest case, so you'll start with that.

Using @StringKey

For your first example, suppose you want to simplify InformationPluginSpec by removing the property name and giving the plugin a name when you add it to the registry.

To do this, open **InformationPluginSpec.kt** in **plugins.api** and remove serviceName, so it looks like this:

```
interface InformationPluginSpec {

  val informationEndpoint: InformationEndpoint
}
```

Now, open **InformationPluginRegistryImpl.kt** in **plugins.di** and change it like this:

```
@ApplicationScope
class InformationPluginRegistryImpl @Inject constructor(
    private val informationPlugins: @JvmSuppressWildcards
Map<String, InformationPluginSpec> /// 1
) : InformationPluginRegistry {

  override fun plugins(): List<InformationPluginSpec> =
      informationPlugins.values.toList() // 2
}
```

In this code, you:

1. Replaced `Set<InformationPluginSpec>` with `Map<String, InformationPluginSpec>`.
2. Returned `List<InformationPluginSpec>` from the values in `Map<String, InformationPluginSpec>`.

Now, you've set everything up and just need to register `InformationPluginSpec` in `InformationPluginRegistry`. After the changes you made above, you need to remove the definition in **InformationSpecsModule.kt** in **plugins.di**. So open that file and change it like this:

```
@Module(
    includes = [
      WhereAmIModule::class,
      WeatherModule::class
    ]
)
object InformationSpecsModule
```

Note: You could also delete it and restore the state of the app before **More about Multibinding with Set: @ElementsIntoSet**. However, simply deleting the previous definition is fine.

Next, open **WeatherModule.kt** in **plugins.weather.di** and apply the following change:

```
const val WEATHER_INFO_NAME = "Weather"
@Module(includes = [WeatherModule.Bindings::class])
object WeatherModule {
  @Provides
```

```
    @ApplicationScope
    @IntoMap // 1
    @StringKey(WEATHER_INFO_NAME) // 2
    fun provideWeatherSpec(endpoint: WeatherInformationEndpoint):
InformationPluginSpec = object : InformationPluginSpec {
      override val informationEndpoint: InformationEndpoint
        get() = endpoint
    }
    // ...
}
```

As you can see in this code, you use:

1. `@IntoMap` to tell Dagger that the object you `@Provides` is part of a multibinding definition with a `Map`.
2. `@StringKey(WEATHER_INFO_NAME)` to tell Dagger that the key of the object you `@Provides` is a `String` and, in this case, its value matches `WEATHER_INFO_NAME`.

Now, open **WhereAmIModule.kt** in **plugins.whereami.di** and replace the code with:

```
const val WHEREAMI_INFO_NAME = "WhereAmI"
@Module(includes = [WhereAmIModule.Bindings::class])
object WhereAmIModule {
    // ...
    @Provides
    @ApplicationScope
    @IntoMap
    @StringKey(WHEREAMI_INFO_NAME)
    fun provideWhereAmISpec(endpoint: WhereAmIEndpointImpl):
InformationPluginSpec = object : InformationPluginSpec {
      override val informationEndpoint: InformationEndpoint
        get() = endpoint
    }
}
```

You can now successfully build and run as usual.

> **Note**: Dagger also allows keys of type `Int` and `Long`. You can easily try them out on your own by using `@IntKey` and `@LongKey` and repeating what you just did for `@StringKey`.

Using `@StringKey`, you just set the name of the information plugin as the key of the `Map` you're using to multibind. In this case, you're not actually using that information, but you'll see how to use key information in a more complex example next.

Using @ClassKey

Another type of key Dagger gives you is `Class<T>`. You can use it the same way you used `String`, but for your next step, you'll try something more ambitious, instead.

You'll use code that's similar to the information plugins you implemented earlier. The main difference is in `InformationEndpoint` — the rest is just scaffolding.

To do this you basically need to:

1. Simplify the `InformationPluginSpec` interface
2. Update `InformationPluginRegistry` with its implementation
3. Use `InformationEndpoint` as abstraction for the information plugin endpoints
4. Configure multibindings for WhereAmI and Weather
5. Migrate `InformationPluginPresenterImpl` to the new abstractions
6. Clean up the unused code
7. Build and run the Busso app

Simplifying the InformationPluginSpec interface

Your first step will be to simplify the `InformationPluginSpec` interface. Open **InformationPluginSpec.kt** in **plugins.api** and change its content like this:

```
interface InformationPluginSpec {
  val serviceName: String
}
```

Basically, `InformationPluginSpec` is just a name now.

Update InformationPluginRegistry with its implementation

Next, open **InformationPluginRegistry** in **plugins.api** and change it to:

```
interface InformationPluginRegistry {
  fun plugins(): List<InformationEndpoint>
}
```

Here, you're just trying to get a list of `InformationEndpoints`, and that's what `InformationPluginRegistry` provides. The magic is in its implementation.

Now, open **InformationPluginRegistryImpl.kt** in **plugins.impl** and change it like this:

```
@ApplicationScope
class InformationPluginRegistryImpl @Inject constructor(
    private val retrofit: Retrofit, // 1
    informationPlugins: @JvmSuppressWildcards Map<Class<*>,
InformationPluginSpec> // 2
) : InformationPluginRegistry {

  val endpoints = informationPlugins.keys.map { clazz ->
    retrofit.create(clazz) // 3
  }.map { endpoint ->
    endpoint as InformationEndpoint
  }.toList()

  override fun plugins(): List<InformationEndpoint> =
endpoints // 4
}
```

In this code, you:

1. Add `Retrofit` as the primary constructor parameter. This is the object you need to create the actual `InformationEndpoint`.
2. Receive a `Map<Class<*>, InformationPluginSpec>` from Dagger. You'll see how this works very soon.
3. Initialize an `endpoints` variable of the type `InformationEndpoint` using `Retrofit` and the information about the multibinding that Dagger provides.
4. Return `endpoints` as `List<InformationEndpoint>`.

Because of **4** you need all the endpoint be an implementation of the `InformationEndpoint` interface.

Use InformationEndpoint as abstraction for the information plugin endpoints

Look at `MyLocationEndpoint` and `WeatherEndpoint` and notice there's a problem — they don't share any abstraction. The implementations `Retrofit` creates for you aren't `InformationEndpoint` implementations, and they all define operations with different names and parameters.

To fix this, open **InformationEndpoint.kt** in **plugins.api** and change it like this:

```
interface InformationEndpoint {

  fun fetchInformation(latitude: Double, longitude: Double):
Single<InfoMessage>
}
```

This gives you two parameters that are consistent with the specific Retrofit interfaces.

Now, change **MyLocationEndpoint.kt** in **plugins.whereami.endpoint** like this:

```
interface MyLocationEndpoint : InformationEndpoint { // 1
  @GET("${BUSSO_SERVER_BASE_URL}myLocation/{lat}/{lng}")
  override fun fetchInformation( // 2
      @Path("lat") latitude: Double,
      @Path("lng") longitude: Double
  ): Single<InfoMessage>
}
```

Here you:

1. Added the explicit implementation of the `InformationEndpoint` interface.
2. Renamed `whereAmIInformation()` in `fetchInformation()` to be consistent with `InformationEndpoint` and added the `override` keyword.

Now, open **WeatherEndpoint.kt** in **plugins.weather.endpoint** and do the same, getting the following code:

```
interface WeatherEndpoint : InformationEndpoint {

  @GET("${BUSSO_SERVER_BASE_URL}weather/{lat}/{lng}")
  override fun fetchInformation(
      @Path("lat") latitude: Double,
      @Path("lng") longitude: Double
  ): Single<InfoMessage>
}
```

You have the `InformationEndpoint` implementations for `MyLocationEndpoint` and `WeatherEndpoint` now. You can finally configure multibinding.

Configure multibindings for WhereAmI and Weather

Now it's time to configure multibinding with `Map` for the information plugins. Open **WhereAmIModule.kt** in **plugins.whereami.di** and change it to this:

```
const val WHEREAMI_INFO_NAME = "WhereAmI"
@Module
object WhereAmIModule {
  @Provides
  @ApplicationScope
  @IntoMap // 1
  @ClassKey(MyLocationEndpoint::class) // 2
  fun provideWhereAmISpec():
      InformationPluginSpec = object : InformationPluginSpec
{ // 3
    override val serviceName: String
      get() = WHEREAMI_INFO_NAME
```

```
  }
}
```

Here, you:

1. Use @IntoMap to tell Dagger to put the object you @Provide in a Map with values of type InformationPluginSpec.
2. Use @ClassKey(MyLocationEndpoint::class) to tell Dagger that the key is a Class<T>, where T is MyLocationEndpoint.
3. Remove endpoint, which you don't need anymore because the same information is in the @ClassKey attribute.

More importantly, WhereAmIModule contains just one definition. The others are no longer necessary because the registry now creates the endpoints.

Next, switch to **WeatherModule.kt** in **plugins.weather.di** and change it to the following:

```
const val WEATHER_INFO_NAME = "Weather"
@Module
object WeatherModule {
  @Provides
  @ApplicationScope
  @IntoMap // 1
  @ClassKey(WeatherEndpoint::class) // 2
  fun provideWeatherSpec():
      InformationPluginSpec = object : InformationPluginSpec
{ // 3
    override val serviceName: String
      get() = WEATHER_INFO_NAME
  }
}
```

As done in the case of WhereAmIModule you here:

1. Use @IntoMap to tell Dagger to put the object you @Provide in a Map with values of type InformationPluginSpec.
2. Use @ClassKey(WeatherEndpoint::class) to tell Dagger that the key is a Class<T>, where T is WeatherEndpoint.
3. Remove endpoint, which you don't need anymore because the same information is in the @ClassKey attribute.

Now you're ready to use the new configurations.

Migrate InformationPluginPresenterImpl to the new abstractions

You changed something in the abstraction for the framework, so you also need to change **InformationPluginPresenterImpl.kt** in **plugins.ui**. Just replace the `start()` implementation with the following:

```
    override fun start() {
      disposables.add(
          locationObservable.filter(::isLocationEvent)
              .map { locationEvent ->
                locationEvent as LocationData
              }
              .firstElement()
              .map { locationData ->
                val res = informationPluginRegistry.plugins().map
  { endpoint ->
                  val location = locationData.location
                  endpoint.fetchInformation(location.latitude,
  location.longitude) // HERE
                      .toFlowable()
                }
                Flowable
                    .merge(res)
                    .collectInto(mutableListOf<String>()) { acc,
  item ->
                      acc.add(item.message)
                    }
              }
              .subscribe(::manageResult, ::handleError)
      )
    }
```

What you get from the `InformationPluginRegistry` and the way you invoke the `InformationEndpoint` are now different.

Clean up the unused code

Before building and running, you have some cleanup to do. Delete the following files you don't need anymore:

- `WeatherInformationEndpoint`
- `WeatherInformationEndpointImpl`
- `WhereAmIEndpoint`
- `WhereAmIEndpointImpl`

Now you're ready to test the Busso app.

Build and run the Busso app

Now you can finally build and run the app and get the expected result in Figure 14.2:

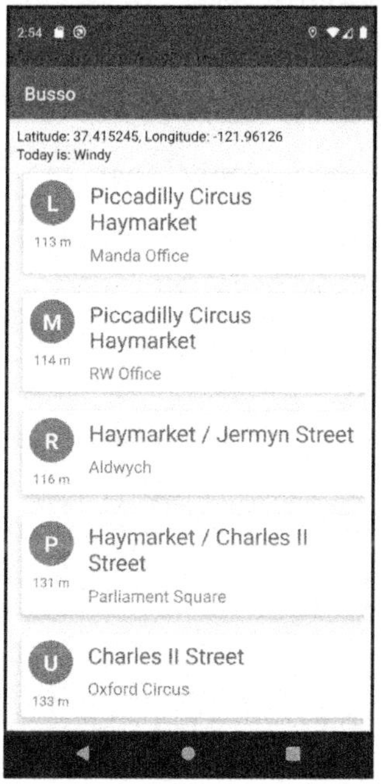

Figure 14.2 — The Busso App works as intended

The code is now much simpler, and you've removed most of the classes and interfaces from the first implementation of the framework.

The question now is: Can you do even better? You'll make more improvements in the next section.

Using multibinding with a custom Key

You can usually cover all the use cases you encounter by using `@StringKey` and `@ClassKey`. But just in case you need something special, Dagger offers multibinding with `Map` and a custom type for the key.

This is useful when you want to give Dagger additional information when you implement the multibindings, as you'll see also when you'll learn how Dagger works with **Google Architecture Components**. In this scenario, Dagger provides the following `@MapKey` annotation:

```
@Documented
@Target(ANNOTATION_TYPE) // 1
```

```
@Retention(RUNTIME)
public @interface MapKey {

  boolean unwrapValue() default true; // 2
}
```

There are some important things to understand here:

1. `@MapKey` is **an annotation for annotations**. This is the annotation you'll use to mark the type you'll use as the key for the multibinding.
2. It has an attribute, `unwrapValue`, that has a default value of `true`. You'll learn more about it soon, but in short, it tells Dagger whether or not the key is complex.

A code example will help you to better understand how all this works.

Using a simple custom @MapKey

As you read above, `@MapKey` annotates the class you use as the key when multibinding with `Map`.

As an example, suppose you want to do what you did with `@KeyClass` — provide `Class<InformationEndpoint>` for the endpoint of an information plugin. But this time, you want to use a custom type as the key.

The first step is to create a new file named **SimpleInfoKey.kt** in **plugins.api** with the following code:

```
@MapKey // 1
annotation class SimpleInfoKey(
    val endpointClass: KClass<*> // 2
)
```

In this very simple code, you:

1. Use `@MapKey` to annotate the custom `@SimpleInfoKey` annotation.
2. Define `endpointClass` as the only property of type `KClass<*>`.

Next, you need to replace the current `@ClassKey` with the custom annotation `@SimpleInfoKey`. Open **WeatherModule.kt** in **plugins.weather.di** and apply the following change:

```
@Module
object WeatherModule {
```

```
    @Provides
    @ApplicationScope
    @IntoMap
    @SimpleInfoKey(WeatherEndpoint::class) // HERE
    fun provideWeatherSpec(): InformationPluginSpec = object :
  InformationPluginSpec {
      override val serviceName: String
        get() = WEATHER_INFO_NAME
    }
  }
```

You just replaced `@ClassKey` with `@SimpleInfoKey`, keeping the same `WeatherEndpoint::class` value for the attribute.

Now, open **WhereAmIModule.kt** in **plugins.whereami.di** and do the same thing:

```
  @Module
  object WhereAmIModule {

    @Provides
    @ApplicationScope
    @IntoMap
    @SimpleInfoKey(MyLocationEndpoint::class) // HERE
    fun provideWhereAmISpec(): InformationPluginSpec = object :
  InformationPluginSpec {
      override val serviceName: String
        get() = WHEREAMI_INFO_NAME
    }
  }
```

And that's it. You don't have to do anything except build and run the app and it will work as expected.

When you use `@MapKey` to define a custom key that lets you use multibinding with `Map`, and `unwrapValue()` has a default value of `true`, it means that:

- Your key can only have a single property. In the previous example, it was `endpointClass`.
- The type for the key is same as the type for that single property — in this case, `KClass<*>`. That's why you didn't have to change `InformationPluginRegistryImpl`.

For your final task, you'll create a more complex key.

Using a complex custom @MapKey

Your final step is to make the `InformationPluginSpec` definition redundant and instead, put all the information you need in a custom key to use with multibinding and `Map`.

Start by creating a new file named **ComplexInfoKey.kt** in **plugins.api** and adding:

```
@MapKey(unwrapValue = false) // 1
annotation class ComplexInfoKey(
    val endpointClass: @JvmSuppressWildcards KClass<out
InformationEndpoint>, // 2
    val name: String // 2
)
```

This code has some interesting parts. Here, you:

1. Use `@MapKey` to pass `false` as the value for `unwrapValue`.
2. Define two different properties with the types `KClass<out InformationEndpoint>` and `String`.

In this case, the annotation has `false` as `unwrapValue`'s value, which means that the type for the key is now the **annotation itself**.

It's important to say that, if you want to use a complex `@MapKey` with `false` for the `unwrapValue` attribute, Dagger requires an additional dependency.

Add it by opening **build.gradle** for the main **app** module and adding the following definitions in the `dependencies` block:

```
    implementation "com.google.auto.value:auto-value-annotations:
$autovalue_annotation_version"
    kapt "com.google.auto.value:auto-value:$autovalue_version"
```

In this code you:

1. Add the dependency to the `auto-value-annotations` library
2. Configure the annotation processor the **auto value** library needs for the code generation.

> **Note**: The values for the version parameters are already available in **versions.gradle** in the root of the project.

Now, open **WeatherModule.kt** in **plugins.weather.di** and apply the following change:

```
@Module
object WeatherModule {

  @Provides
  @ApplicationScope
  @IntoMap
  @ComplexInfoKey( // 1
      WeatherEndpoint::class,
      WEATHER_INFO_NAME
  )
  fun provideWeatherSpec(): InformationPluginSpec =
InformationPluginSpec
}
```

In this code, you:

1. Use `@ComplexInfoKey` as the key, passing it `InformationEndpoint`'s information and the name of the plugin.
2. Return `InformationPluginSpec` — which you're only using now to put something into the `Map` for this exercise.

For this reason, you now need to open **InformationPluginSpec.kt** in **plugins.api** and make the following changes:

```
object InformationPluginSpec
```

Now, open **WhereAmIModule.kt** in **plugins.whereami.di** and apply the same change:

```
@Module
object WhereAmIModule {

  @Provides
  @ApplicationScope
  @IntoMap
  @ComplexInfoKey(
      MyLocationEndpoint::class,
      WHEREAMI_INFO_NAME
  )
  fun provideWhereAmISpec(): InformationPluginSpec =
InformationPluginSpec
}
```

When you use a complex key like this, you also need to change `Map`'s type, which now becomes the annotation type.

Do this by opening **InformationPluginRegistryImpl.kt** in **plugins.impl** and applying the following changes:

```
@ApplicationScope
class InformationPluginRegistryImpl @Inject constructor(
    private val retrofit: Retrofit,
    informationPlugins: @JvmSuppressWildcards
Map<ComplexInfoKey, InformationPluginSpec> // 1
) : InformationPluginRegistry {

  val endpoints = informationPlugins.keys.map { complexKey ->
    retrofit.create(complexKey.endpointClass.java as
Class<*>) // 2
  }.map { endpoint ->
    endpoint as InformationEndpoint
  }.toList()

  override fun plugins(): List<InformationEndpoint> = endpoints
}
```

In this code, you:

1. Make `ComplexInfoKey` the type for the key in the `Map` you inject as the primary constructor parameter.
2. Use `ComplexInfoKey`'s `endpointClass`, which you have as a key.

Now you can finally build and successfully run the Busso App.

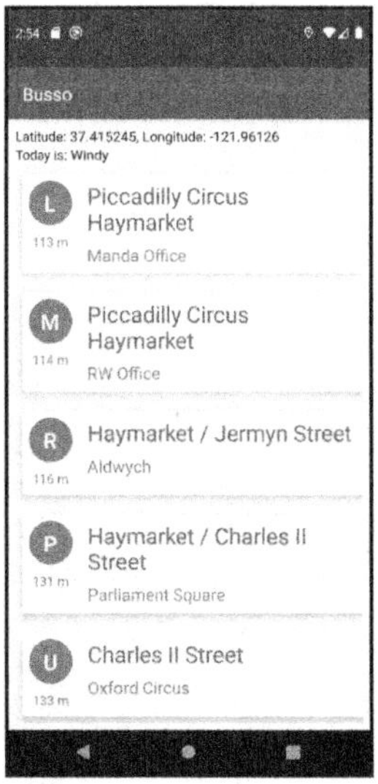

Figure 14.3 — The Busso App works as intended

Key points

- Dagger allows you to use multibinding with a `Map`.
- When you use a `Map` for multibinding, you can use keys of the following types: `String`, `Int`, `Long` and `KClass`.
- If you need more informative keys, `@KeyMap` allows you to create custom types, which you can use in a simple or complex way.
- If you use `@KeyMap` and an `unwrapValue` attribute with a default value of `true`, the type of the key is the type of the unique property of your custom key.
- A `@KeyMap` is complex if the value for the `unwrapValue` attribute is `false`. In this case, you need to add an auto-value as a dependency in your project.
- You must use a complex `@KeyMap` for the key of the `Map` you use in multibinding.

Wow! It's been a very interesting chapter. Using multibinding with `Map`, you managed to improve the **Information Plugin Framework** architecture even further.

But, what if you want a more structured and organized set of modules? In the next chapter, you'll learn how Dagger can help you.

Chapter 15: Dagger & Modularization

By Massimo Carli

In the previous chapters, you learned about multibinding with `Sets` and `Maps` to improve the architecture of the Information Plugin Framework. With that information, you can add new features to the Busso App in an easy, pluggable and declarative way.

You've vastly improved Busso's architecture, but there's still room to make it even better. For instance, all the code is currently in the main **app** module. It would be nice to split that code into different modules to reduce the building time of your app while increasing its reusability and extensibility. But how can you do that with Dagger? Is it even possible?

The answer, of course, is yes! In this chapter, you'll refactor the Busso App by moving some of the code from the main **app** module to other modules and changing the Dagger configuration accordingly.

> **Note**: In this chapter, you'll read the name **module** many times, referring to either the **Gradle Module** or the **Dagger Module**. To make everything clear, this chapter will refer to **Gradle Modules** as **modules** and **Dagger Modules** as **@Modules**.

What is modularization?

Modularization is the process of splitting the code and resources of your app into separate, smaller **modules** — in this case, Gradle modules. You can think of a **Gradle module** as a way to encapsulate code and resources. This makes it simpler to create a single library that you either use locally or publish in a repository like **Artifactory** to share with other developers.

A module might depend on other modules that you declare in the **dependencies** block of its **build.gradle**.

> **Note**: You'll use **Gradle modules** in this chapter, but the same concepts are valid with other systems, like Apache Maven or Apache Ivy.

Whether there's a big advantage to using different modules in your app depends on how big and complex that app is. In general, using different modules gives you the following benefits:

- Better organization and encapsulation of the code.
- Shorter building time.
- The opportunity to create libraries that make the code more reusable.
- Better ownership management.

This chapter will cover each point in more detail, giving you the chance to improve Busso along the way.

Start by opening the Busso App from the **starter** folder of the materials for this chapter in Android Studio.

You'll get an initial source folder structure, as Figure 15.1 shows:

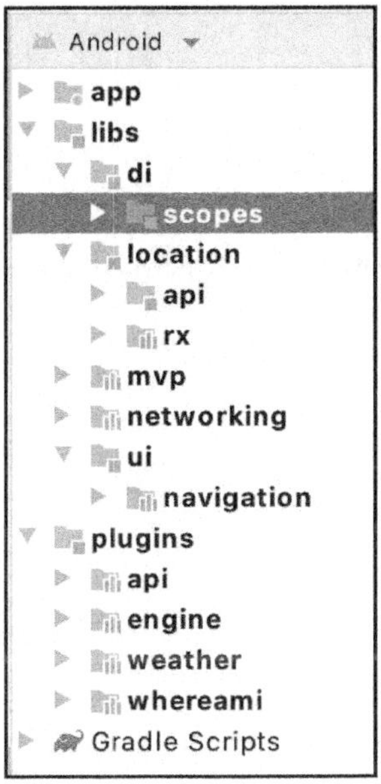

Figure 15.1 — Initial Busso App source folders structure

As you see, there are a few new modules, one of which is **libs.di.scopes**.

At the moment, the new modules are all empty. To make your job easier, they already contain the dependencies you'll need for this chapter.

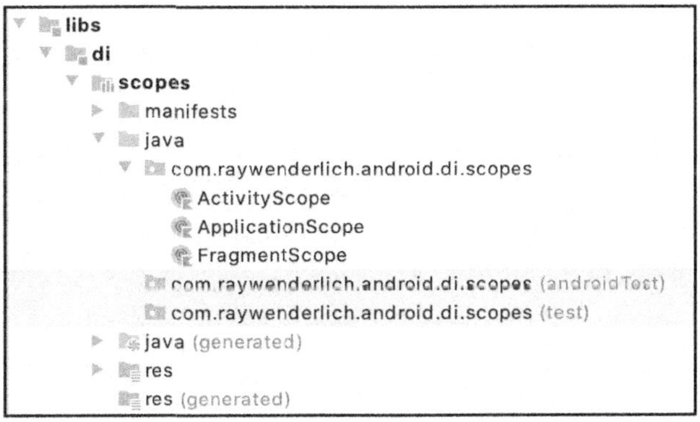

Figure 15.2 — The Scopes module source files

Speaking of reusability, this module already contains the definition of the different `@Scopes` you created in the previous chapters. As you see in Figure 15.2, you have:

- `ApplicationScope`
- `ActivityScope`
- `FragmentScope`

This module is very simple. It only depends on the **javax.inject** library, as you see by opening its **build.gradle**:

```
plugins {
  id 'kotlin'
}
apply from: '../../../versions.gradle'

dependencies {
  api "javax.inject:javax.inject:$javax_annotation_version"
  implementation "org.jetbrains.kotlin:kotlin-stdlib:
$kotlin_version"
}
```

You'll learn all about the other modules later.

Better organization and encapsulation of the code

As you know, **encapsulation** is one of the fundamental concepts in object-oriented programming, but it's also a principle to use in higher-level contexts like a library or a full architecture.

Encapsulating also means **hiding** the implementation details and exposing only the main abstractions that form what you call **public APIs**. This is part of what you learned in the very first chapter of this book: Encapsulation, or hiding details, is a way to reduce or avoid dependency.

ui.navigation is a simple example of the application of this principle. It's also a good starting point to modularize Busso.

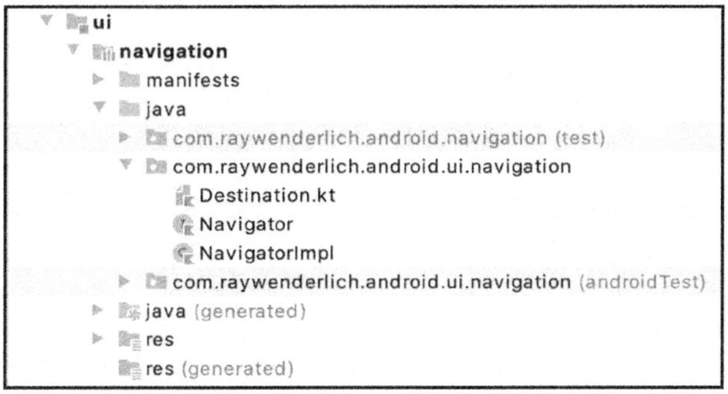

Figure 15.3 — The Navigation module source files

Look at the source files of **libs.ui.navigation** in Figure 15.3 and you'll find a:

- **Destination.kt** file.
- `Navigator` interface.
- `NavigatorImpl` class.

In **Destination.kt**, you just have the `Destination` **sealed class** with its implementations. These should stay public because they're just **data classes** that encapsulate values, not behavior.

`Navigator` is an interface that's public by definition. You should hide `NavigatorImpl`, instead.

Open **NavigatorImpl.kt** in **libs.ui.navigation** and make it **internal**, as in the following code:

```
// HERE
internal class NavigatorImpl(private val activity: Activity) :
Navigator {
  override fun navigateTo(destination: Destination, params:
Bundle?) {
    // ...
  }
}
```

Build the app now and you'll get the following error:

```
Cannot access 'NavigatorImpl': it is internal in
'com.raywenderlich.android.ui.navigation'
```

That's because you're trying to access `NavigatorImpl` from **ActivityModule.kt** in **app**.

```
@Module(includes = [ActivityModule.Bindings::class])
class ActivityModule {
  // ...
  @Provides
  @ActivityScope
  fun provideNavigator(activity: Activity): Navigator =
NavigatorImpl(activity) // HERE
}
```

But `NavigatorImpl` is now `internal` and, therefore, only visible to **libs.ui.navigation**. Next, you'll see how to fix this problem.

Defining an external @Module

As you know, you use `@Module` to tell Dagger how to create the objects that are part of a dependency graph. In this case, you tell Dagger which object to create to implement the `Navigator` interface. You do this in **ActivityModule.kt**, which is in the main **app**.

Create a new **di** package in **libs.ui.navigation** and add a new **NavigationModule.kt** with the following code:

```
@Module
object NavigationModule {

  @Provides
  @ActivityScope
  fun provideNavigator(activity: Activity): Navigator =
NavigatorImpl(activity)
}
```

Here, you moved the `@Provides` definition for `Navigator` from **ActivityModule.kt** in the **app** module to **NavigationModule.kt** in **libs.ui.navigation**. Now, you can access `NavigatorImpl` from a place where it's visible.

The `NavigationModule` definition needs the dependencies from the Dagger libraries. You also need to install the `kapt` plugin in **build.gradle** for the module. These dependencies have been already set up for you in the starter project.

Of course, you need to remove the same `@Provides` definition from **ActivityModule.kt**, where you add `NavigationModule` as value of the `includes` attribute. Because `ActivityModule` contains only `@Binds` definitions, you can make it an interface like this:

```
@Module(
  includes = [
    NavigationModule::class // 1
  ]
)
interface ActivityModule { // 2

  @Binds
  fun bindSplashPresenter(impl: SplashPresenterImpl):
SplashPresenter

  @Binds
  fun bindSplashViewBinder(impl: SplashViewBinderImpl):
SplashViewBinder

  @Binds
  fun bindMainPresenter(impl: MainPresenterImpl): MainPresenter
}
```

Here, you just:

1. Add `NavigationModule` as a value of the `includes` attribute.
2. Convert the existing class into an interface containing all the existing `@Binds` definitions.

Now, you can successfully build and run the app.

In **libs.ui.navigation**, you see your first, simple example of how to hide implementation details in a module and how this works with `@Modules`. In this case, you:

1. Reduced `NavigatorImpl`'s visibility by using the `internal` modifier. As a result, you've hidden `NavigatorImpl` from the main **app** and removed the dependency on it.
2. Created a new `@Module` in **ui.navigation**, which includes `@Provides` for the `Navigator` implementation. Of course, this means you have to fix the dependencies on the Dagger libraries and `kapt` plugin in **build.gradle** for the **navigation** module.
3. Added `NavigationModule` to the ones you **include** in `ActivityModule`.

This means you can eventually use a different `Navigator` implementation without a single change in the main app.

Later in this chapter, you'll see more complex use cases.

Reducing build time

In large, professional apps, you usually have thousands of source and resource files. As you learned above, a Gradle module is basically **a compilation unit**. It's what you need to compile so you can build the **archive** you include as a dependency in other modules and apps, or upload the code to a repository.

If you have small modules, you also have small compilation units, which means shorter building times. For example, suppose you have a monolithic app that contains 100 classes you can usually build in 100 seconds. If you change a class, you need to rebuild 100 classes and their related resources, which will take about the same time: 100 secs.

Gradle is smart enough to avoid repeating some of the tasks in the building process. Nevertheless, some of the tasks, like **compile** and **assemble**, need to be done.

Suppose now that you have 100 classes, but split them into five modules with 20 classes each. If you change a class in one module, you only need to compile that module and its 20 classes.

The building time won't be 1/5 of the original, because using modules introduces some overhead, but large apps will show noticeable improvement.

Now, in the previous **libs.ui.navigation** example, you won't need to build the module anymore unless you change some of the files in it.

Creating libraries

Right now, the **libs.ui.navigation** module is in the same Busso project. However, you could also publish it to an external repository and just leave a dependency to it in the **build.gradle** of the main **app**. In that case, it would be like any other external library you use, including Retrofit or Dagger itself. Having all classes and resources in the same **app** module increases build times and makes code harder to manage.

Publishing a library is a good solution when you:

- Don't change the code frequently.
- Want to make the library open source and allow other people to contribute.
- Need the same module in different apps.

A public library isn't a good option if you:

- Need to change the code very frequently.
- You can't or don't want to share the code.

As with many decisions, it isn't always black or white. For instance, if you publish your library to a private repository and need to change the code frequently, you can just depend on the `SNAPSHOT` of the library. Or you might use it as a local module at an early stage of your project, then open-source it after publishing it to an external repository.

In any case, you should consider this question during your development process.

Ownership management

Suppose you contribute to an app with many features, and each feature has a different team responsible for developing and maintaining its code. Then, imagine if all the code was in the main **app** module.

The developers from the different teams would all work on the same codebase. This is possible, but you could end up with severe problems because, in big companies, you have hundreds of developers working on the same app. For instance, you'll likely have a lot of conflicts in your pull requests because there are no formal boundaries between the code of the different features.

One solution is to split the work on a package basis, but this only works well in small apps. For a big project, it wouldn't make any difference.

Giving ownership of one or more modules to each team is a better way to manage the code and its lifecycle, avoiding conflicts and creating physical boundaries in the codebase.

Busso App modularization

Now that you know the main reasons to modularize, and you've seen the example of the **libs.ui.navigation** module, it's time to continue refactoring the Busso App.

Some modules are already available in the **starter** project and you'll add code to them, following along with the progression. You'll work on different modules, in particular on:

- **networking**
- **location**
- **plugins**

In each case, you'll learn what to do in situations with increasing complexity.

The networking module

In the starter project, the **network** package in the **app** module contains all the code you need for Busso's networking layer. Look at this code and you'll see that some of the definitions are:

- Generic, and can be reused in other projects.
- Specific to Busso.

As a rule, you should keep anything that depends on the specific application in the app and move what you can reuse to a different module.

In **NetworkModule.kt**, you'll see this:

```
@Module
class NetworkModule {
  @Provides
  @ApplicationScope
  fun provideCache(application: Application): Cache = // 1
    Cache(application.cacheDir, 100 * 1024L)// 100K

  @Provides
  @ApplicationScope
  fun provideHttpClient(cache: Cache): OkHttpClient = // 2
   // ...

  @Provides
  @ApplicationScope
  fun provideRetrofit(httpClient: OkHttpClient): Retrofit = // 3
```

```
    // ...

  @Provides
  @ApplicationScope
  fun provideBussoEndPoint(retrofit: Retrofit): BussoEndpoint
{ // 4
    return retrofit.create(BussoEndpoint::class.java)
  }
}
```

In this code, you provide implementations for:

1. `Cache`
2. `OkHttpClient`
3. `Retrofit`
4. `BussoEndpoint`

Points **1**, **2** and **3** relate to reusable objects and **4** is specific to Busso. You'd like to make the reusable code configurable from the main app. How can you do that?

In the starter project, you already have an empty **libs.networking** module available that includes **build.gradle** with all the dependencies you need.

> **Note**: In the code for the Busso App, you'll see some **.keep** files that are there to force Git to keep the empty folders in the repository. You can delete these files when the related folder is no longer empty.

What you need to do is:

1. Find a way to abstract any configuration parameters the networking module requires.
2. Create `NetworkingModule` with the bindings you can reuse.
3. Add the dependency to the **networking** module in the **build.gradle** of the main **app** module.
4. Implement the configuration parameters for the abstraction.
5. Change `ApplicationComponent` so it can provide the configuration object.
6. Update **NetworkModule.kt** in the **app** module.

These are a bunch of steps, but they're easy enough to code along with.

Defining the networking configuration abstraction

The components you want to put in the **libs.networking** module might need some configuration values. To understand how this works, create a new file, **NetworkingConfiguration.kt** in the **libs.networking** module and add the following code:

```
interface NetworkingConfiguration {
  val cacheSize: Long // 1
  val serverBaseUrl: String // 2
  val dateFormat: String // 3
}
```

Here, you define an interface that requires you to implement properties referring to the:

1. Size of the `Cache`.
2. Base URL for the connection.
3. Format to use for unmarshalling the dates.

The module doesn't know this information yet; the main **app** module should provide it. You also need to use this information in the new `@Module`, which you'll create in the next step.

Creating the NetworkingModule

Now, you need to create a `@Module` to tell Dagger how to create the object you need to connect Busso to the server using the configuration data the main **app** module provides.

Create a new **di** package in **libs.networking** and add a new file, **NetworkingModule.kt**, with the following code:

```
@Module
object NetworkingModule {

  @Provides
  @ApplicationScope
  fun provideCache(
    networkingConfiguration: NetworkingConfiguration, // 1
    application: Application
  ): Cache =
    Cache(
      application.cacheDir,
      networkingConfiguration.cacheSize // 1
    )
```

```
    @Provides
    @ApplicationScope
    fun provideHttpClient(cache: Cache): OkHttpClient =
      OkHttpClient.Builder()
        .cache(cache)
        .build()

    @Provides
    @ApplicationScope
    fun provideRetrofit(
      networkingConfiguration: NetworkingConfiguration, // 2
      httpClient: OkHttpClient
    ): Retrofit =
      Retrofit.Builder()
        .baseUrl(networkingConfiguration.serverBaseUrl) // 2
        .addCallAdapterFactory(RxJava2CallAdapterFactory.create())
        .addConverterFactory(
          GsonConverterFactory.create(
            GsonBuilder()
              .setDateFormat(networkingConfiguration.dateFormat) /
/ 2
              .create()
          )
        )
        .client(httpClient)
        .build()
}
```

In this code, you assume that an implementation of `NetworkingConfiguration` will eventually be available at runtime as part of the dependency graph for `@ApplicationScope`. Because of this, you:

1. Add `NetworkingConfiguration` as a parameter for `provideCache()` and use its `cacheSize` property in the `Cache` constructor.
2. Do the same for `provideRetrofit()`, using the `serverBaseUrl` and `dateFormat` properties to initialize the `Retrofit` implementation instance.

So far in this module, you haven't provided the implementation of `BussoEndpoint` that's specific to Busso. The next step is to make this module available to the main app.

Adding the dependency to the networking module

This step is very simple. Open **build.gradle** for the main **app** module and apply the following changes:

```
// ...
dependencies {
```

```
  // ...
  // Network Apis  TO_BE_REMOVED // 1
  // implementation "com.squareup.retrofit2:retrofit:
$retrofit_version"
  // implementation "com.squareup.retrofit2:converter-gson:
$retrofit_gson_converter_version"
  // implementation "com.squareup.retrofit2:adapter-
rxjava2:$retrofit_rx2_adapter_version"

  // Networking library
  implementation project(path: ':libs:networking') // 2
  // ...
}
```

Here, you:

1. Remove the existing dependencies on the libraries for `Retrofit`.
2. Add the dependency to the **networking** module, which will also provide the dependencies you removed previously as transitive dependencies.

You've now completed the **networking** module — it's time to work on the app.

Adding NetworkingConfiguration to the app

libs.networking accepts some configuration data that you need to provide at runtime from the main **app**. Open **Configuration.kt** in the **conf** package and change it like this:

```
const val BUSSO_SERVER_BASE_URL = "https://busso-
server.herokuapp.com/api/v1/"

object BussoConfiguration : NetworkingConfiguration { // 1
  override val cacheSize: Long
    get() = 100 * 1024L // 100K // 2
  override val serverBaseUrl: String
    get() = BUSSO_SERVER_BASE_URL // 3
  override val dateFormat: String
    get() = "yyyy-MM-dd'T'HH:mm:ssZ" // 4
}
```

In this code, you:

1. Create `BussoConfiguration` as the implementation of the `NetworkingConfiguration` interface.
2. Provide a value for `cacheSize`.

3. Do the same for `serverBaseUrl` using the existing `BUSSO_SERVER_BASE_URL` constant, which you'll also need in other places.
4. Provide the `dateFormat`.

But how do you tell Dagger to use this object as the implementation of `NetworkingConfiguration` to add to the dependency graph for the `@ApplicationScope`? You'll do that in the next step.

Adding NetworkingConfiguration to @ApplicationComponent's dependency graph

Now, you need to tell Dagger that you want to use `BussoConfiguration` as the `NetworkingConfiguration` implementation to add to the dependency graph for `@ApplicationScope`. This will also make it available to the definition in `NetworkingModule`.

It's important to note that `NetworkingConfiguration` is **a normal Kotlin interface** and not a Dagger `@Component`. The good news is that this doesn't stop you from using any implementation — `BussoConfiguration`, in this case — as an actual `@Component` that you can create a dependency on.

Open **ApplicationComponent.kt** in the **di** package of the **app** module and apply the following changes:

```
@Component(
  dependencies = [NetworkingConfiguration::class], // 1
  modules = [
    ApplicationModule::class,
    InformationPluginModule.ApplicationBindings::class,
    InformationSpecsModule::class
  ]
)
@ApplicationScope
interface ApplicationComponent {
  // ...
  @Component.Factory
  interface Factory {

    fun create(
      @BindsInstance application: Application,
      networkingConfiguration: NetworkingConfiguration // 2
    ): ApplicationComponent
  }
}
```

In this code, you:

1. Add `NetworkingConfiguration::class` as a value for the **dependencies** attribute of the `@Component` annotation. This tells Dagger that your `ApplicationComponent` depends on the object you'll provide through an implementation of `NetworkingConfiguration`.
2. Tell Dagger that you're going to provide the `NetworkingConfiguration` implementation as a parameter of the `Factory` Dagger will generate for you.

Changing `Factory` means you need to make a change when you create the instance of `ApplicationComponent`. To do this, open **Main.kt** in the main package of the **app** module and apply the following change:

```
class Main : Application() {
  // ...
  override fun onCreate() {
    super.onCreate()
    appComponent = DaggerApplicationComponent
      .factory()
      .create(this, BussoConfiguration) // HERE
  }
}
```

With this code, you pass `BussoConfiguration` as a second parameter of `create()`.

You're almost there! Now, you just need to remove the code you no longer need from **NetworkModule.kt**.

Updating NetworkModule.kt

Open **NetworkModule.kt** in the **network** package of the **app** module and change it to this:

```
@Module(
  includes = [
    NetworkingModule::class // HERE
  ]
)
object NetworkModule {

  @Provides
  @ApplicationScope
  fun provideBussoEndPoint(retrofit: Retrofit): BussoEndpoint {
    return retrofit.create(BussoEndpoint::class.java)
  }
}
```

Here, you only add the `NetworkingModule` in **includes** and remove the `@Provides` definitions that are now in the **networking** module. This `@Module` is now an **object** and not a simple **class**.

Now, you can finally build and successfully run the app!

What you achieved

With the help of the UML diagram in Figure 15.4, you can not get an overview of what you've achieved so far.

Following the modularization process for the Busso App, you wanted to move the reusable code for networking into a different **networking module**. In particular, you wanted to move the code that defines `Cache`, `HttpClient` and `Retrofit`. You created `NetworkingModule` to hold this code.

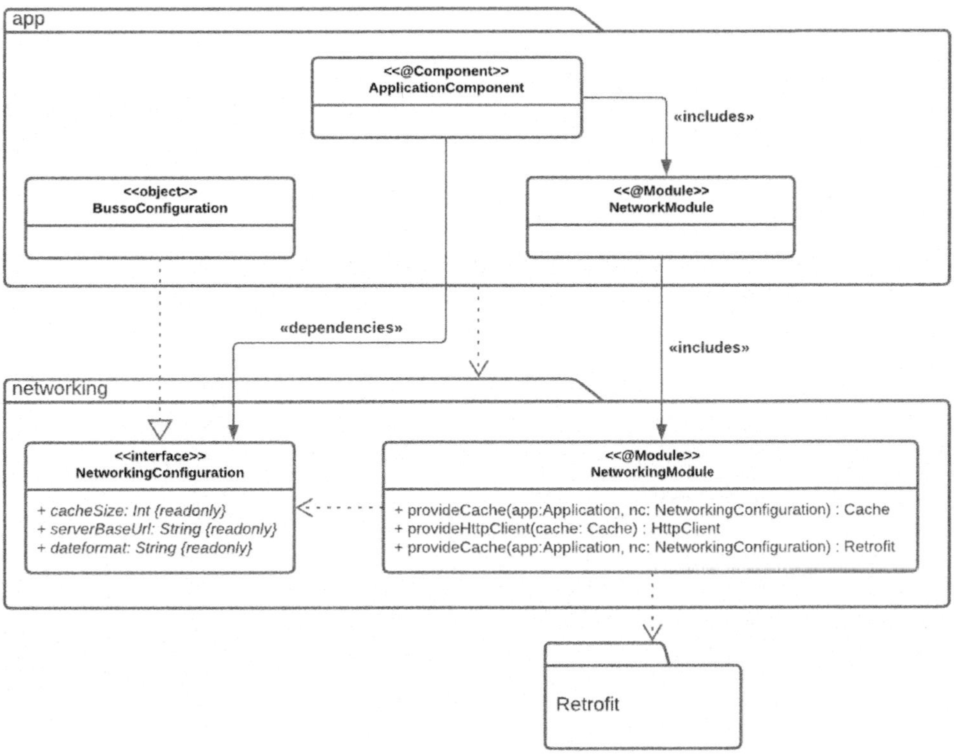

Figure 15.4 — The networking module UML diagram

The problem was that these objects require information that's specific to a particular app, like the base URL of the connection or the format to use when parsing dates.

The **networking module** cannot depend on the **app** module. The latter already depends on the former, so it would give you a circular dependency, as shown in Figure 15.5.

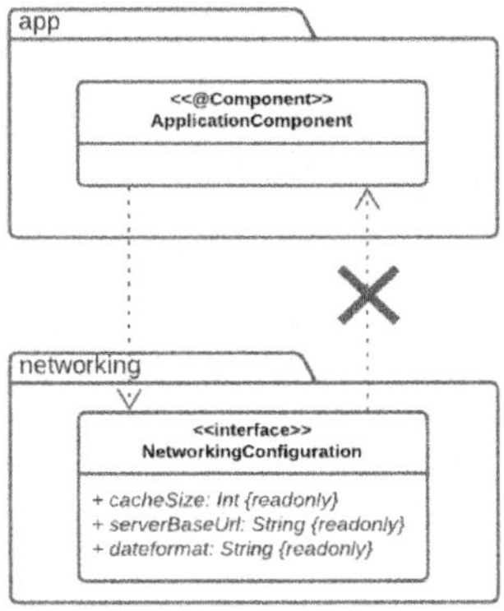

Figure 15.5 — Circular dependencies

`NetworkingConfiguration` is the solution. `NetworkingModule` accesses the configuration data it needs through an implementation of `NetworkingConfiguration` that the main **app** provides. But how?

The magic happens because the **app** and the **networking** modules both contribute to the dependency graph for `@ApplicationScope`, which you define with `ApplicationComponent`.

So, using the **dependencies** attribute of `@Component`, you added a `NetworkingConfiguration` implementation to the dependency graph for `ApplicationComponent`. Using a new parameter in the `@Component.Factory` for `ApplicationComponent`, you added `BussoConfiguration` as the `NetworkingConfiguration` implementation to use.

Now, all the objects that both the **app** and the **networking** modules need are in the dependency graph for `@ApplicationScope`.

The location module

To modularize the **location** module, you need to make a few changes similar to the ones you already made for the **networking** module. In this case, you need to:

1. Move the `LocationModule` definition into the **di** package in the **libs.location.rx** module.
2. Move `GeoLocationPermissionCheckerImpl` into the **permission** package in the **libs.location.rx** module.
3. Encapsulate `GeoLocationPermissionCheckerImpl` as a `GeoLocationPermissionChecker` implementation, making it `internal`.
4. Fix the imports in the **app** module due to some changes in the destination package. This should happen in **ApplicationModule.kt** in the **app** module.

After you've done these steps, the **libs.location.rx** source structure should look like the one in Figure 15.6:

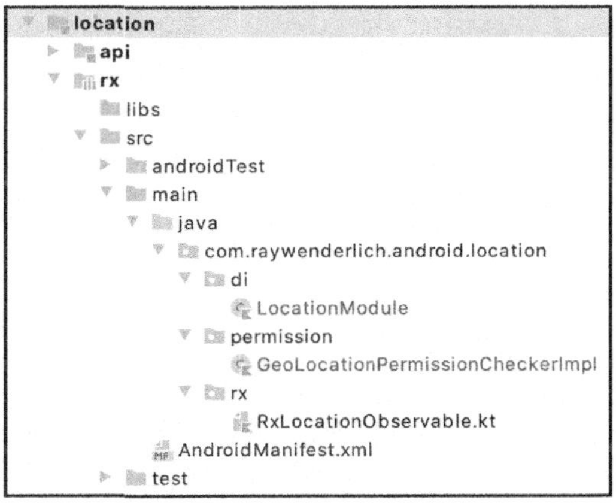

Figure 15.6 — The Location Rx Module

Now, `LocationModule` is the only thing you need if you want to use `Observable<LocationEvent>` in the main **app** module.

The plugins module

Refactoring the Information Plugin Framework is the most complex example of modularization in the Busso App.

> **Note**: A step-by-step description of the modularization process for the Information Plugin Framework would require too much space. You could do this yourself as an interesting and challenging exercise, or simply open the Busso App project in the **final** folder of the material for this chapter and look at the new structure.

To understand the new structure, look at the dependency diagram in Figure 15.7:

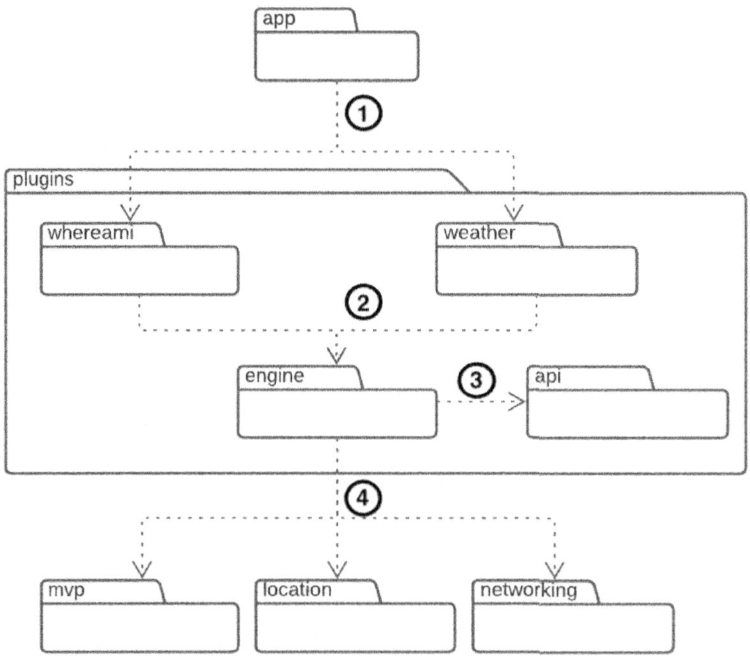

Figure 15.7 — Information Plugin Framework dependencies

In this diagram, you see that:

1. The main **app** module depends on the **weather** and **whereami** modules. You install the different plugins by adding their module in **InformationSpecsModule.kt** in the **plugins** package of the **app** module.
2. Each plugin module depends on **plugins.engine**, which contains the main implementations of the **api** of the framework.
3. Again, **plugins.engine** contains the implementation of the Information Plugin Framework's APIs.
4. The **engine** depends on other modules, like **mpv**, **location** and **networking**.

The **weather** and **whereami** modules are an example of how external modules contribute to `Set` or `Map` when using **multibinding**.

After looking at the code available in the **final** project for this chapter, you can successfully build and run the modularized version of the Busso App, getting what you see in Figure 15.8:

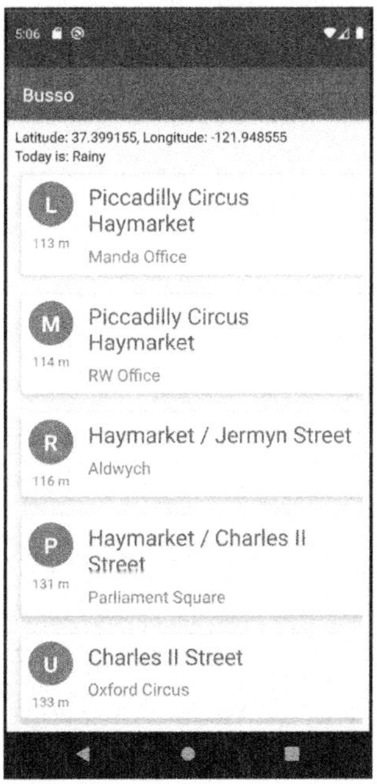

Figure 15.8 — The Busso App

Key points

- Modularization is a fundamental step in the development process of a project.
- Splitting your code into external modules can improve the build time of your app and make your code more reusable.
- Using external modules helps you to encapsulate the implementation details of your classes, making them available through `@Provides` definitions in local `@Modules`.
- You set a simple Kotlin interface as the dependency for a `@Component` and use it to pass information from the main app to a dependent module.

Congratulations! You've now created a modularized version of Busso, thereby completing the third section of this book. In the next section, you'll learn everything you need to know about using Dagger in an Android app.

Section V: Introducing Hilt

In the last section, you'll learn everything you need to know about Hilt. Hilt is a dependency injection library for Android that reduces the boilerplate of doing manual dependency injection in your project.

Hilt is built on top of the DI library Dagger to benefit from the compile-time correctness, runtime performance, scalability, and Android Studio support that Dagger provides.

Chapter 16: Dagger & Android

By Massimo Carli

In the previous chapters of this book, you became a Dagger guru. You learned many new concepts, in particular:

- How Dagger works and how it helps you implement the main principles of object-oriented programming in your app.
- The different types of injection, how to know which one to use for a specific use case and how to implement them with Dagger.
- How to use custom `@Scopes` to optimize the way your app uses resources.
- When to use `@Components` or `@Subcomponents` to manage dependencies between objects with different `@Scopes`.
- How to implement architecture based on the concept of plugins by using multibinding with `Sets` or `Maps`.
- How to create a structure for your app's code by splitting it into different modules, resulting in improved build times, reusability and extensibility.

You've done a great job. Dependency injection is a tough topic and Google is working to make it easier, improving the learning curve that, before this book, was very steep. The result of Google's effort is **Hilt**.

You'll learn about Hilt in the remaining chapters of this book. Before you get to that, though, take a moment to consider the legacy code you might need to maintain. To handle that, you'll learn about **Dagger Android** in this chapter.

There's still a lot of code out there that uses Dagger Android, which is a library that Google created with the goal of simplifying Dagger in Android apps. Unfortunately, the result was not very successful and the solution is sometimes more complicated than the problem it was supposed to solve.

For this reason, Google stopped developing new features for the Dagger Android library in favor of Hilt. As you'll learn in this chapter, Dagger Android helps reduce the lines of code you need to write to configure Dagger, but it also has some important limitations. You'll get to know about these limitations as you continue to refactor the Busso App.

In this chapter, you'll learn:

- Why you need a special tool to use Dagger in an Android app.
- How Android Dagger works under the hood.
- How to inject an `Activity` and a `Fragment`.
- Which utility classes Android Dagger provides.
- How to use `@ContributesAndroidInjector`.

Why Android is different for Dagger

In the previous chapters of this book, you converted Busso, which is an Android app, to Dagger. So if that worked, you might wonder why you'd need a specific Dagger Android library.

As you know, Android is a container that manages the lifecycle of its standard components, like `Activitys`, `Services`, `ContentProviders` and `BroadcastReceivers`. Because of that, Dagger can't create an instance of a standard component like, for example, an `Activity`. That falls under the Android environment's responsibilities.

You *cannot* use constructor injection in Android. Instead, you must write code like what you implemented in **BusStopFragment.kt** in the **ui.view.busstop** package of the **app** module:

```
class BusStopFragment : Fragment() {
  // ...
  override fun onAttach(context: Context) {
    context.activityComp
        .fragmentComponent()
```

```
        .inject(this)
      super.onAttach(context)
    }
    // ...
  }
```

You had to write this code in all the `Activitys` and `Fragments` of the app. You did this exactly four times in Busso, and a larger project could need it even more often.

Sometimes, the code you need to write becomes very verbose, like what you have in **SplashActivity.kt** in the **ui.view.splash** package in **app**.

```
class SplashActivity : AppCompatActivity() {
  // ...
  override fun onCreate(savedInstanceState: Bundle?) {
    super.onCreate(savedInstanceState)
    makeFullScreen()
    setContentView(R.layout.activity_splash)
    this.application.appComp
      .activityComponentBuilder()
      .activity(this)
      .build()
      .inject(this)
    splashViewBinder.init(this)
  }
  // ...
}
```

In a perfect world, injection should happen from the outside. In the previous example, `SplashActivity` should know nothing about the `ApplicationComponent` you use for the actual injection and it shouldn't have any code with `inject()`.

But, can you completely remove all that code? The answer is: no. What you can do is to make that code easier to write or, even better, ask Dagger to write it for you. That's exactly what **Dagger Android** does.

Dagger Android gives you a way to generate the code that, in the first part of this book, you put in **Injector** implementations. To do this, you need some libraries and, of course, an annotation processor. That's Dagger Android!

Installing Dagger Android dependencies

The first step toward using Dagger Android is to install its dependencies in the **app** module's **build.gradle** by adding the following to it:

```
  // Dagger Android
  implementation "com.google.dagger:dagger-android:
```

```
$dagger_version" // 1
  implementation "com.google.dagger:dagger-android-support:
$dagger_version" // 2
  kapt "com.google.dagger:dagger-android-processor:
$dagger_version" // 3
```

These definitions tell you some interesting things:

1. The **Dagger Android** library differs from the Dagger library you've used so far, meaning you need to add new dependencies to the app.
2. If your app uses the Android support library, Dagger Android needs some more classes, which you find in **dagger-android-support**.
3. You also need an **annotation processor**. This tells you that **Dagger Android** will generate some code for you.

Note that the Dagger Android library's version is the same as Dagger's version. That's because, when Google releases a new version of Dagger, it also releases a new version of the Android library as part of the same codebase.

As an example of how to use the Dagger Android library, you'll refactor the Busso App. In particular, you'll migrate:

1. `SplashActivity`
2. `MainActivity`
3. `BusStopFragment`
4. `BusArrivalFragment`

Throughout this chapter, you'll refer to the specific standard components or `Fragments` as the **injection target**.

During the refactoring process, you'll realize that Dagger Android has some advantages — but at the cost of less freedom in how you structure the code.

How Dagger Android works

To illustrate how Dagger Android works, you'll migrate Busso's `MainActivity` and `SplashActivity` injection targets following these steps:

1. Define an abstraction for the **injector**s.
2. Generate an **injector** for each injection target.

3. Simplify the code you use in the injection targets for the actual injection.
4. Set up your `Application` for Dagger Android.
5. Bind the injector to the specific injection target type.
6. If necessary, work around some Android Dagger limitations.
7. Build the app and enjoy. :]

Don't worry if these tasks look complicated — everything will be clearer when you code along. Executing each of these steps in order will help you understand how Dagger Android works.

In this chapter, you'll need to be very patient — the app won't build successfully until you've finished refactoring. As you learned in the previous chapters, it's good to try to build the app after each step anyway, to let Dagger generate whatever code it can.

Define an abstraction for the injectors

In Chapter 4, "Dependency Injection & Scopes", you created the `Injector<A>` interface as the abstraction for any component with the responsibility of injecting objects into an injection target of type `A`. The interface looked like this:

```
interface Injector<A> {

  fun inject(target: A)

}
```

Dagger Android does a similar thing with the definition of this interface in **dagger.android**:

```
interface AndroidInjector<T> { // 1

  fun inject(T instance) // 2

  // 3
  interface Factory<T> {
    // 4
    fun create(@BindsInstance instance: T): AndroidInjector<T>
  }
}
```

> **Note**: The Dagger Android library is in Java, but you see the Kotlin equivalent here.

There are some important things to note here, including:

1. The name of the interface is different because Google preferred to use `AndroidInjector<T>`.
2. `inject()`'s signature is the same as the one you had in `Injector<A>`.
3. The library also provides an inner `AndroidInjector.Factory<T>` interface for `AndroidInjector<T>` itself.
4. `AndroidInjector.Factory<T>` defines `create()` with **a single parameter** that must be of type `T`.

The last point is the reason for one of Dagger Android's limitations. If you want to create an `AndroidInjector<T>` through `AndroidInjector.Factory<T>`, you can only pass a single object that must be of the same type as the injection target.

> **Note**: Actually, `AndroidInjector<T>` also provides an `AndroidInjector.Builder<T>` interface that would solve the previous limitation. Unfortunately, this is now **deprecated**.

OK, but what's responsible for creating the `AndroidInjector<T>` for your injection target? In Busso, for instance, what generates the `AndroidInjector<MainActivity>` and `AndroidInjector<Splashctivity>` implementations?

Dagger Android, of course! But you need to tell it how to do so.

Generating an injector for each injection target

In the previous step, you learned that Dagger Android provides an `AndroidInjector<T>` interface that all injectors need to implement to resolve the dependencies of an object of type `T`, which you called the injection target.

Dagger Android also provides the `AndroidInjector.Factory<T>` interface with the factory method `create()`, which accepts an object of type `T`. What you need to do now is to tell Dagger which specific `AndroidInjector<T>` to create — and, so, which specific injection target to address.

In your case, you need to do this for `MainActivity` and `SplashActivity`. But how? Well, you just need to remember what you already did without the Android Dagger library — specifically, where you put the `inject()` functions earlier.

Refactoring MainActivity

Open **ActivityComponent.kt** in the **di** package of **app** and you'll see the following:

```
@Subcomponent(
  modules = [ActivityModule::class]
)
@ActivityScope
interface ActivityComponent {

  fun inject(activity: SplashActivity) // HERE

  fun inject(activity: MainActivity) // HERE

  fun fragmentComponent(): FragmentComponent

  @Subcomponent.Builder
  interface Builder {
    fun activity(
      @BindsInstance activity: Activity // HERE
    ): Builder

    fun build(): ActivityComponent
  }
}
```

This tells you that `AndroidInjector<T>` must be either a `@Component` or a `@Subcomponent`. In the same code, you can also see how the existing `Builder` is similar to `AndroidInjector.Factory<T>`.

Of course, one is a `Builder<T>` and the other a `Factory<T>`, but the difference is insignificant. They're both **creational patterns**. Creational patterns provide various object creation mechanisms, which increase flexibility and reuse of existing code.

This also tells you that the `AndroidInjector<T>` you're asking Android Dagger to generate for you will replace the existing `ActivityComponent`.

Now that you understand the background, it's time to write some code.

Create a new **di.activities.main** package in the **app** module and create a new file in it named **MainActivitySubcomponent.kt**, then ad the following code:

```
@Subcomponent(
  modules = [
```

```
      ActivityModule::class, // 1
    ]
)
@ActivityScope // 2
interface MainActivitySubcomponent :
AndroidInjector<MainActivity> { // 3

    @Subcomponent.Factory // 4
    interface Factory : AndroidInjector.Factory<MainActivity> // 5
}
```

This code contains some interesting things:

1. `MainActivitySubcomponent` is a `@Subcomponent` that uses `ActivityModule` because it gives Dagger information about how to create the objects `MainActivity` needs.
2. `MainActivitySubcomponent` is a `@Subcomponent` for the bindings with `@ActivityScope`.
3. You extend `AndroidInjector<MainActivity>`, which means you implicitly define `inject()` with a parameter of type `MainActivity`.
4. The `MainActivity` object is something you provide when you need an instance of the `MainActivitySubcomponent` implementation. This is why you define `@Subcomponent.Factory`.
5. `@Subcomponent.Factory` extends `AndroidInjector.Factory<MainActivity>`. In this way, you implicitly inherit the definition of the `create()` operation with a parameter of type `MainActivity`.

With this code, you tell Android Dagger that you need an injector for `MainActivity`.

Refactoring SplashActivity

Next, you'll do the same for `SplashActivity`. Just create a new package named **splash** in the existing **di.activities** and create **SplashActivitySubcomponent.kt** inside. Then, add the following code:

```
@Subcomponent(
    modules = [
      ActivityModule::class,
    ]
)
@ActivityScope
interface SplashActivitySubcomponent :
AndroidInjector<SplashActivity> {
```

```
  @Subcomponent.Factory
  interface Factory : AndroidInjector.Factory<SplashActivity>
}
```

As you see, the code is basically the same as what you wrote for `MainActivity`, but with a different generic type parameter value.

Cleaning up your code

Before continuing, you need to do some cleanup and refactoring. Specifically, you need to:

1. **Move** the existing **ActivityModule.kt** from the **di** package into **di.activities**. This puts all the code related to `Activitys` in the same place.
2. **Delete** the existing **ActivityComponent.kt** from the **di** package.

Now, you told Dagger which injectors you need for your `Activitys`. Before going further, take a moment to see how to use them.

Simplifying the code

Supposing that Dagger already generated `AndroidInjector<SplashActivity>` and `AndroidInjector<MainActivity>` for you, how would you use them? This is the main advantage of Android Dagger — it allows you to replace all the boilerplate related to the `inject()` invocation you saw earlier with a simple instruction.

To see this in action, open **MainActivity.kt** in the **ui.view.main** package and replace the existing code with:

```
class MainActivity : AppCompatActivity() {

  @Inject
  lateinit var mainPresenter: MainPresenter

  override fun onCreate(savedInstanceState: Bundle?) {
    AndroidInjection.inject(this) // HERE
    super.onCreate(savedInstanceState)
    setContentView(R.layout.activity_main)
    if (savedInstanceState == null) {
      mainPresenter.goToBusStopList()
    }
  }
}
```

Compare this code with what you had before and you'll see:

- The injection code is now a simple invocation of the static method, `inject()`, on an `AndroidInjection`, which passes the reference to `MainActivity`.
- You don't need a reference to `ActivityComponent` anymore. As you'll see soon, Dagger will manage `@Subcomponent` inheritance for you.
- Because of the previous point, you also removed the `activityComp` extension property

Of course, you can do the same thing for **SplashActivity.kt** in **ui.view.splash**, getting something like this:

```
class SplashActivity : AppCompatActivity() {
  // ...
  override fun onCreate(savedInstanceState: Bundle?) {
    AndroidInjection.inject(this) // HERE
    super.onCreate(savedInstanceState)
    makeFullScreen()
    setContentView(R.layout.activity_splash)
    splashViewBinder.init(this)
  }

  // ...
}
```

Think about all the code you had to write before — and now, there's just a single instruction for every injection target.

How AndroidInjection works

But how does `AndroidInjection`'s `inject()` work?

You can summarize its source code like this:

```
  fun inject(activity: Activity) { // 1
    val application = activity.application
    if (application is HasAndroidInjector) { // 2
      application.androidInjector().inject(activity) // 3
    } else {
      throw RuntimeException("Something wrong") // 2
    }
  }
```

There are many important things to note:

1. `inject()` has a parameter of type `Activity` that is a common abstraction for all the `Activitys`. Therefore, it includes both `MainActivity` and `SplashActivity`.
2. You use the `Application` object that must implement the `HasAndroidInjector` interface, which defines a single `androidInjector()` operation. In short, a `HasAndroidInjector` is any object that can provide an `AndroidInjector<Any>`. This tells you that, to make everything work, your `Application` needs to be a `HasAndroidInjector` and must then provide an implementation of `AndroidInjector<T>`. Otherwise, you'll get a `RuntimeException`.
3. If your `Application` is a `HasAndroidInjector`, it will provide the `AndroidInjector<Any>` you'll delegate the `inject()` invocation to.

The last point tells you what the next two steps you need to do are:

1. Make your `Application` a `HasAndroidInjector`.
2. When the `Application` returns `AndroidInjector<Any>`, you need to give the information about the specific `AndroidInjector<T>` to invoke for the injection target of type `T`.

Next, you'll start with Busso's `Application`, which you extended in **Main.kt**.

Setting up Application for Dagger Android

As you just learned, to make Android Dagger work, you need to make your `Application` implement `HasAndroidInjector` so it can provide an implementation of `AndroidInjector<Any>` to use in your `Activitys`.

To do this, open **Main.kt** in the main package for the app and change it like this:

```
class Main : Application(), HasAndroidInjector { // 1

  @Inject
  lateinit var dispatchingAndroidInjector:
DispatchingAndroidInjector<Any> // 2

  override fun onCreate() {
    super.onCreate()
    DaggerApplicationComponent
      .factory()
      .create(this, BussoConfiguration)
      .inject(this)
  }
  // 2
```

```
  override fun androidInjector(): AndroidInjector<Any> {
    return dispatchingAndroidInjector
  }
}
```

In this code:

1. `Main` now implements `HasAndroidInjector` and must define `androidInjector()`, returning the implementation of `AndroidInjector<Any>` to use for the actual injection.
2. The `AndroidInjector<Any>` you return is the same object Android Dagger injects as `DispatchingAndroidInjector<Any>`.

You also removed the reference to the `ApplicationComponent` and the `appComp` extension property, which you don't need anymore.

But where does `DispatchingAndroidInjector<Any>` come from? Dagger Android provides it when you add the following `@Module` to the dependency graph for `ApplicationScope`. Open **ApplicationModule.kt** in **di** for the **app** module and add the following definition:

```
@Module(
  includes = [
    LocationModule::class,
    NetworkModule::class,
    AndroidSupportInjectionModule::class // HERE
  ]
)
object ApplicationModule
```

AndroidSupportInjectionModule is the module you need to add if you're using the support library — which Busso does.

`Main` now implements `HasAndroidInjector` and provides the `AndroidInjector<Any>` you need to inject in Busso's `Activitys`.

This is an object of type `DispatchingAndroidInjector<Any>`, which you get from Android Dagger through injection. Look at the source code and you'll find that it contains a `Map` between the type of the injection target of type `T` and the `AndroidInjector.Factory<T>` to use for the actual injection. Does that ring a bell? :]

You already told Dagger which `AndroidInjector<T>` implementation you need by providing an `AndroidInjector.Factory<T>` for each injection target. What you're still missing is a way to bind the injection type `T` to it — which is **multibinding!**

Before implementing the multibinding, you need to do some cleanup. Open **ApplicationComponent.kt** in the **di** package and remove the following definition:

```
@ApplicationScope
interface ApplicationComponent {

  fun activityComponentBuilder(): ActivityComponent.Builder //
REMOVE!!
  // ...
}
```

You don't need this anymore because the `ActivityComponent` is now Dagger Android's responsibility.

As a quick status update, clean up all the imports to the definitions you deleted then build the app. You'll only have some errors in the `Fragments`, which you'll fix later.

Binding the injector to the specific injection target type

Dagger Android now knows which `AndroidInjector<T>` to create but it doesn't know how to bind the result to a specific type. In Chapter 14, "Multibinding With Map", you solved a similar problem using `@ClassKey`. You'll do the same when you work with Dagger Android.

Create a new file named **MainActivityModule.kt** in **di.activities.main** and add the following code:

```
@Module(
  subcomponents = [MainActivitySubcomponent::class] // 1
)
interface MainActivityModule {

  @Binds
  @IntoMap
  @ClassKey(MainActivity::class) // 2
  fun bindMainActivitySubcomponentFactory(
    factory: MainActivitySubcomponent.Factory // 3
  ): AndroidInjector.Factory<*>
}
```

In this @Module. you configure two important things:

1. Using the subcomponent attribute of @Module, you create an inheritance relationship between MainActivitySubcomponent and the @Component or @Subcomponent you add this @Module to, using the modules attribute.
2. Using multibinding, you add a new entry to a Map that has Class<T> as its key and AndroidInjector.Factory<*> as a value. In this specific case, you assign MainActivitySubcomponent.Factory as a value to the MainActivity::class key.

Adding the @Modules to ApplicationComponent

Now, according to what you did in step one above, you need to add MainActivityModule to the modules attribute of the @Component or @Subcomponent that you want to be MainActivitySubcomponent's parent. This is ApplicationComponent.

Before that, create a new file named **SplashActivityModule.kt** in **di.activities.splash** and add the following code:

```
@Module(
  subcomponents = [SplashActivitySubcomponent::class]
)
interface SplashActivityModule {

  @Binds
  @IntoMap
  @ClassKey(SplashActivity::class)
  fun bindSplashActivitySubcomponentFactory(
    factory: SplashActivitySubcomponent.Factory
  ): AndroidInjector.Factory<*>
}
```

Now, you're ready to add both @Modules to ApplicationComponent. Open **ApplicationComponent.kt** in **di** and add the following definitions:

```
@Component(
  dependencies = [NetworkingConfiguration::class],
  modules = [
    ApplicationModule::class,
    InformationPluginEngineModule::class,
    InformationSpecsModule::class,
    MainActivityModule::class, // HERE
    SplashActivityModule::class // HERE
  ]
)
@ApplicationScope
```

```
interface ApplicationComponent {
  // ...
}
```

Build the app now and you'll get an unexpected error with the following message:

```
error: [Dagger/MissingBinding] android.app.Activity cannot be
provided without an @Inject constructor or an @Provides-
annotated method.
public abstract interface ApplicationComponent {
                ^
      android.app.Activity is injected at

com.raywenderlich.android.ui.navigation.di.NavigationModule.prov
ideNavigator(activity)
```

What's happening? Why is the compiler complaining about the `Navigator` interface? This is related to the limitation you read about earlier. You'll fix it next.

Working around Dagger Android limitations

You've almost finished configuring Dagger Android for Busso's `Activitys`, but you got an annoying error on the `Navigator` interface. This is a consequence of the limitation you read about earlier: `Navigator` needs an `Activity` but you have a `MainActivity` and a `SplashActivity`, instead.

Dagger is picky with types, and you learned that even if `MainActivity` IS-A `Activity`, Dagger treats them as different types unless you use `@Binds` to make them equivalent.

However, you can't just connect the `MainActivity` to `Activity` with `@Binds` because sometimes, you need `SplashActivity` instead. One possible solution is to use **qualifiers** to indicate when you should use which activity.

Using qualifiers

Start by creating a new file named **NavigatorModule.kt** in the new **di.navigator** and add the following to it:

```
@Module
object NavigatorModule {
```

```
    @Provides
    @ActivityScope
    @Named("Main") // HERE
    fun providesMainActivityNavigator(owner: MainActivity):
Navigator =
      NavigatorImpl(owner)

    @Provides
    @ActivityScope
    @Named("Splash") // HERE
    fun providesSplashActivityNavigator(owner: SplashActivity):
Navigator =
      NavigatorImpl(owner)
}
```

Here, you're saying that the `Activity` the `Navigator` needs can be `MainActivity` or `SplashActivity`, depending on the qualifier you use when you declare the dependency.

This should be straightforward, but there's still a problem: `NavigatorImpl` isn't visible because of the work you did in the previous chapter with encapsulation and modularization. To make it visible, you need to **break encapsulation**.

Do this by opening **NavigatorImpl.kt** in **libs.ui.navigation** and removing the `internal` modifier, like this:

```
class NavigatorImpl(private val activity: Activity) : Navigator
{ // HERE
  // ...
}
```

After this change, you can compile `NavigatorModule` — but you still need to apply some changes.

Adding Qualifiers

First, open **ActivityModule.kt** in **di.activities** in **app** and replace the existing `NavigationModule` with `NavigatorModule`, like this:

```
@Module(
  includes = [
    NavigatorModule::class // HERE
  ]
)
interface ActivityModule {
  // ...
}
```

Then, you need to use the right qualifier in the right place. Open **SplashViewBinderImpl.kt** in **ui.view.splash** and add `@Named("Splash")`.

```
class SplashViewBinderImpl @Inject constructor(
  @Named("Splash") private val navigator: Navigator // HERE
) : SplashViewBinder {
  // ...
}
```

This means that the Navigator you use in `SplashViewBinderImpl` is the one using the `SplashActivity`.

Now, open **MainPresenterImpl.kt** in **ui.view.main** and add `@Named("Main")`, like this:

```
class MainPresenterImpl @Inject constructor(
  @Named("Main") private val navigator: Navigator // HERE
) : MainPresenter {
  // ...
}
```

There's one final place where you need to apply a fix. Open **BusStopListPresenterImpl.kt** in **ui.view.busstop** and make the following change:

```
@FragmentScope
class BusStopListPresenterImpl @Inject constructor(
  @Named("Main") private val navigator: Navigator, // HERE
  private val locationObservable: Observable<LocationEvent>,
  private val bussoEndpoint: BussoEndpoint
) : BasePresenter<View, BusStopListViewBinder>(),
  BusStopListPresenter {
  // ...
}
```

Build and run now and you'll only get the errors about `Fragments` — which you're about to address.

Reviewing what you achieved

You've just migrated Busso's `Activitys` to Dagger Android. It's hard to believe, because the app doesn't build successfully yet, but that's only because you still need to migrate the `Fragments`. You'll do that right after you summarize what you've done so far. You:

1. Told Dagger which `AndroidInjector<T>` to create for Busso's injection target. You did this by creating a `@Module` and a `@Subcomponent` for each target.
2. Used multibinding to map the class of the injection target, `T`, to the `AndroidInjector.Factory<T>`.
3. Prepared your `Application` to be a `HasAndroidInjector` making it able to provide the `AndroidInjector<Any>` to use in your `Activitys` through `AndroidInjection`.

That's a lot. The good news is, you don't have to learn anything new for `Fragments`. You just need to follow the same process.

Injecting Fragments

Busso doesn't build successfully yet because you still need to fix the `Fragments` for Dagger Android. The process is basically the same as you followed for the `Activitys`, but with some small but important differences.

For instance, in the case of `Activitys`, the `HasAndroidInjector` needs to be an `Application`. In the case of `Fragments`, the `HasAndroidInjector` is an `Activity`. Just code along and everything will be fine.

Creating @Subcomponents and @Modules for Fragments

Create a new package named **ui.fragments** and move the existing **FragmentModule.kt** into it. Now, create a new package called **di.fragments.busstop** and create a new file named **BusStopFragmentSubcomponent.kt** in it. Finally, add the following content:

```
@Subcomponent(
  modules = [
    FragmentModule::class
  ]
)
@FragmentScope
interface BusStopFragmentSubcomponent :
AndroidInjector<BusStopFragment> {

  @Subcomponent.Factory
  interface Factory : AndroidInjector.Factory<BusStopFragment> {

    override fun create(@BindsInstance instance:
BusStopFragment): BusStopFragmentSubcomponent // HERE
  }
}
```

The only difference is that you override `create()` to make the return type, `BusStopFragmentSubcomponent`, explicit.

In the same package, create a new file named **BusStopFragmentModule.kt** with the following code:

```
@Module(
  subcomponents = [BusStopFragmentSubcomponent::class]
)
interface BusStopFragmentModule {
```

```
  @Binds
  @IntoMap
  @ClassKey(BusStopFragment::class)
  fun bindBusStopFragmentSubcomponentFactory(
    factory: BusStopFragmentSubcomponent.Factory
  ): AndroidInjector.Factory<*>
}
```

This is the code that you're already familiar with. :]

Create a new **di.fragments.busarrival** and create the **BusArrivalFragmentSubcomponent.kt** inside, adding this code to it:

```
@Subcomponent(
  modules = [
    FragmentModule::class
  ]
)
@FragmentScope
interface BusArrivalFragmentSubcomponent :
AndroidInjector<BusArrivalFragment> {

  @Subcomponent.Factory
  interface Factory :
AndroidInjector.Factory<BusArrivalFragment> {

    override fun create(@BindsInstance instance:
BusArrivalFragment): BusArrivalFragmentSubcomponent
  }
}
```

In the same package, also create **BusArrivalFragmentModule.kt** and add this code:

```
@Module(
  subcomponents = [BusArrivalFragmentSubcomponent::class]
)
interface BusArrivalFragmentModule {

  @Binds
  @IntoMap
  @ClassKey(BusArrivalFragment::class)
  fun bindBusArrivalFragmentSubcomponentFactory(
    factory: BusArrivalFragmentSubcomponent.Factory
  ): AndroidInjector.Factory<*>
}
```

These `@Subcomponents` will replace the existing **FragmentComponent.kt**. You don't need it anymore, so **delete** it. This also deletes the include for `InformationPluginEngineModule.FragmentBindings`, which you need to move into **FragmentModule.kt**.

The code should now look like this:

```
@Module(includes =
[InformationPluginEngineModule.FragmentBindings::class]) // HERE
interface FragmentModule {
  // ...
}
```

Now that you've told Dagger which `AndroidInjector<T>` to create for Busso's `Fragments`, the next step is to simply the injection code.

Simplifying the Fragments' injection

`Fragments` need code that's similar to what you used for `Activitys`.

Open **BusStopFragment.kt** in **ui.view.busstop** and apply the following change:

```
class BusStopFragment : Fragment() {
  // ...
  override fun onAttach(context: Context) {
    AndroidSupportInjection.inject(this) // HERE
    super.onAttach(context)
  }
  // ...
}
```

Again, this is the code that you're already familiar with.

Next, open **BusArrivalFragment.kt** in **ui.view.busarrival** and do the same thing, like this:

```
class BusArrivalFragment : Fragment() {
  // ...
  override fun onAttach(context: Context) {
    AndroidSupportInjection.inject(this) // HERE
    super.onAttach(context)
  }
  // ...
}
```

Note here how you used `inject()` for `AndroidSupportInjection`. That's because you're using the support library for `Fragments` and the parameter for `inject()` must be of the right type.

`inject()` works the same way as its counterpart for `Activitys` does, so the next step is to make `MainActivity` an object of type `HasAndroidInjector` — just as you did for `Main`.

Setting up HasAndroidInjector for Fragments

`inject()` for `AndroidSupportInjection` follows the same logic you saw for the `AndroidInjection` and `Activitys`. To implement it, open **MainActivity.kt** in **ui.view.main** and apply the following changes:

```
class MainActivity : AppCompatActivity(), HasAndroidInjector
{ // 1

  @Inject
  lateinit var mainPresenter: MainPresenter

  @Inject
  lateinit var androidInjector:
DispatchingAndroidInjector<Any> // 2

  override fun onCreate(savedInstanceState: Bundle?) {
    AndroidInjection.inject(this)
    super.onCreate(savedInstanceState)
    setContentView(R.layout.activity_main)
    if (savedInstanceState == null) {
      mainPresenter.goToBusStopList()
    }
  }

  override fun androidInjector(): AndroidInjector<Any> =
androidInjector // 3
}
```

Just as you did for `Main`, you:

1. Implement `HasAndroidInjector`.
2. Inject an object of type `DispatchingAndroidInjector<Any>`.
3. Return the injected object from `androidInjector()`.

You're almost done. The last step is to configure the relationship between the `@Subcomponents` for the `Fragments` and those of the `Activitys`.

Configuring the @Subcomponents' relationships

For your last step, you need to set `@Subcomponents` related to `Fragments` as children of the one related to the `MainActivity`, which is the only one containing any `Fragments`.

To do this, open **MainActivitySubcomponent.kt** in **di.activities.main** and add `BusStopFragmentModule` and `BusArrivalFragmentModule` as values for its `modules` attribute, like this:

```
@Subcomponent(
  modules = [
    ActivityModule::class,
    BusStopFragmentModule::class, // HERE
    BusArrivalFragmentModule::class // HERE
  ]
)
@ActivityScope
interface MainActivitySubcomponent :
AndroidInjector<MainActivity> {

  @Subcomponent.Factory
  interface Factory : AndroidInjector.Factory<MainActivity>
}
```

You did it! You can finally build and run successfully, getting what's in Figure 16.1:

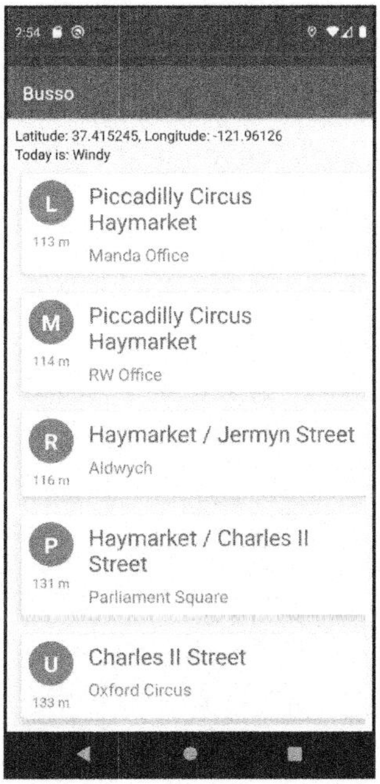

Figure 16.1 — The Busso App

Using Dagger Android utility classes

Dagger Android's goal was to help developers write less code, but frankly, at the moment, you're not sure it did that. You wrote a lot of boilerplate in different files, to save other boilerplate in `Activitys` and `Fragments`.

To improve this, Dagger Android provides some utility classes that, in most cases, help you write less code. In particular, Dagger Android provides:

- `DaggerApplication`
- `DaggerAppCompatActivity`
- `@ContributesAndroidInjector`

Next, you'll see the benefits of these tools.

Using DaggerApplication

`Main`, which is the `Application` for Busso, has quite a defined structure. It has to:

1. Implement `HasAndroidInjector`.
2. Define a property of type `DispatchingAndroidInjector<Any>`.
3. Provide an implementation for `androidInjector()`.

You can do the same thing by simply extending `DaggerApplication`.

Try this out by opening **Main.kt** and applying the following changes:

```
class Main : DaggerApplication() { // 1

  override fun applicationInjector(): AndroidInjector<out
DaggerApplication> { // 2
    return DaggerApplicationComponent
      .factory()
      .create(this, BussoConfiguration)
  }
}
```

In this code, you:

1. Extend `DaggerApplication` in **dagger.android.support**.
2. Implement the required `applicationInjector()`, returning the `DaggerApplicationComponent` implementation.

To make the second point work, you need your `ApplicationComponent` to be an `AndroidInjector<Main>`. So open **ApplicationComponent.kt** in **di** and change it like this:

```
// ...
@ApplicationScope
interface ApplicationComponent : AndroidInjector<Main> { // 1

  @Component.Factory
  interface Factory { // 2

    fun create(
      @BindsInstance application: Application,
      networkingConfiguration: NetworkingConfiguration
    ): ApplicationComponent
  }
}
```

In this case, it's important to note how:

1. `ApplicationComponent` now implements `AndroidInjector<Main>`.
2. `Factory` doesn't extend `AndroidInjector.Factory<T>` because you need an additional `NetworkingConfiguration` parameter.

Now, build and run and check that everything works as expected.

Using DaggerAppCompatActivity

Android Dagger provides the tools to reduce the boilerplate for `Activitys` as well. Open **MainActivity.kt** in **ui.view.main** and apply the following changes:

```
class MainActivity : DaggerAppCompatActivity() {

  @Inject
  lateinit var mainPresenter: MainPresenter

  override fun onCreate(savedInstanceState: Bundle?) {
    super.onCreate(savedInstanceState)
    setContentView(R.layout.activity_main)
    if (savedInstanceState == null) {
      mainPresenter.goToBusStopList()
    }
  }
}
```

As you see, `MainActivity` now extends `DaggerAppCompatActivity`, which takes care of all the injection boilerplate including the invocation to `AndroidInjection.inject()`.

Of course, you might need some more work, in case you already have a hierarchy for your app's `Activitys`.

Using @ContributesAndroidInjector with Activity

What you did with `DaggerApplication` and `DaggerAppCompatActivity` isn't much compared to what you can achieve with `@ContributesAndroidInjector`.

You've probably noticed how repetitive the code you wrote to create the `@Subcomponent` and `@Module` for each `AndroidInjector<T>` is. The question now is: Can you avoid that? In this case, the answer is yes.

Start by creating a new file named **ActivityBindingModule.kt** in **di** and add the following code:

```
@Module
interface ActivityBindingModule { // 1

  @ContributesAndroidInjector(  // 3
    modules = [
      ActivityModule::class,
      BusStopFragmentModule::class,
      BusArrivalFragmentModule::class
    ]
  )
  @ActivityScope // 4
  fun mainActivity(): MainActivity // 2

  @ContributesAndroidInjector(  // 3
    modules = [
      ActivityModule::class
    ]
  )
  @ActivityScope
  fun splashActivity(): SplashActivity // 2
}
```

In this code, you:

1. Define a simple Dagger `@Module`, implemented as an interface.
2. Create an abstract function that has the injection target type as the return type. In this case, `mainActivity()` returns `MainActivity` and `splashActivity()` returns `SplashActivity`.
3. Use `@ContributesAndroidInjector` to ask Dagger Android to generate the `@Subcomponent` and `@Module`, which, until now, you had to write yourself. The `@Modules` you define here become the `@Modules` you use in the related `@Subcomponents`.
4. Bind the object in the `@Subcomponent` to a `@Scope`.

You no longer need the previous definitions, so you can delete the following files:

- **MainActivityModule.kt**
- **MainActivitySubcomponent.kt**
- **SplashActivityModule.kt**
- **SplashActivitySubcomponent.kt**

As your final step, you just need to replace the previous `@Modules` with the new one in **ApplicationComponent.kt**, like this:

```
@Component(
  dependencies = [NetworkingConfiguration::class],
  modules = [
    ApplicationModule::class,
    InformationPluginEngineModule::class,
    InformationSpecsModule::class,
    ActivityBindingModule::class // HERE
  ]
)
@ApplicationScope
interface ApplicationComponent : AndroidInjector<Main> {
  // ...
}
```

Now, build and run to verify that everything works as expected.

Using @ContributesAndroidInjector with Fragments

`@ContributesAndroidInjector` also works for `Fragments`. To see how, create a new file named **FragmentBindingModule.kt** in **di** with the following code:

```
@Module
interface FragmentBindingModule {

  @ContributesAndroidInjector(
    modules = [
      FragmentModule::class
    ]
  )
  @FragmentScope
  fun busStopFragment(): BusStopFragment

  @ContributesAndroidInjector(
    modules = [
      FragmentModule::class
    ]
  )
  @FragmentScope
  fun busArrivalFragment(): BusArrivalFragment
}
```

This code has the same structure as **ActivityBindingModule.kt** except that it relates to `Fragments` instead of `Activitys`.

Now, just as you did for the `Activitys`, you can delete the following files:

- **BusStopFragmentModule.kt**
- **BusStopFragmentSubcomponent.kt**
- **BusArrivalFragmentModule.kt**
- **BusArrivalFragmentSubcomponent.kt**

Your last step is to fix how you use `FragmentBindingModule` in **ActivityBindingModule.kt**, by applying the following change:

```
@Module
interface ActivityBindingModule {

  @ContributesAndroidInjector(
    modules = [
      ActivityModule::class,
```

```
        FragmentBindingModule::class // HERE
      ]
    )
    @ActivityScope
    fun mainActivity(): MainActivity
    // ...
}
```

Congratulations! Busso is now a fully Dagger Android app.

Key points

- Android is responsible for the lifecycle of its standard components, like `Activitys`, `Services`, `BroadcastReceivers` and `ContentProviders`. This prevents you from using **constructor injection**.
- Dagger Android is Google's first solution for reducing the boilerplate code you need to write to inject into Android standard components. The next solution is **Hilt**, which you'll learn about in the rest of this book.
- Using Dagger Android requires a deep knowledge of Dagger and, specifically, how `@Subcomponents` and multibinding work.
- Dagger Android provides some utility classes to reduce the code you need to write.
- `@ContributesAndroidInjector` allows you to automatically generate the code for `AndroidInjector<T>`'s `@Subcomponent` and `@Module` for a standard component.

Wow! This has been intense, but you managed to learn everything you need about Dagger Android. Now you're ready for the next generation of dependency injection in Android: **Hilt**!

Chapter 17: Hilt — Dagger Made Easy

By Massimo Carli

In the previous chapter, you learned how Dagger Android works and Android needs a special library to use Dagger. You learned that Dagger can't instantiate Android standard components because their lifecycle is the responsibility of the Android system, which works as a container. Dagger Android has not been very successful but it taught Google lessons that they used when making architectural decisions for Hilt.

Dagger Android highlighted the most important topics to address:

- Make Dagger easier to learn and to use.
- Standardize the way developers create `@Scopes` and apply them to `@Components`.
- Make implementing tests easier.

You'll learn everything you need to know about testing with Hilt in this chapter, including:

- What Hilt's architectural decisions are.
- How to install Hilt in your app.
- What `@AndroidEntryPoint` is and how to use it.
- What a Hilt `@Module` is and how it differs from Dagger's.
- How to deal with different `@Scopes` with Hilt.
- Which tools Hilt provides to handle common use cases.

Of course, you'll put all these things to work in the Busso App.

> **Note**: At this time, Hilt is still in alpha release. Things might change in future versions of the library.

Hilt's architectural decisions

Looking at a high-level summary of what you've done in the Busso app is a useful way to understand the main architectural decisions Google made for Hilt. In Busso, you:

1. Created three different `@Scopes`: `@ApplicationScope` for objects that live as long as the `Application`, `@ActivityScope` for objects that live as long as a specific `Activity` and `FragmentScope` for objects that live as long as a `Fragment`.
2. Implemented a different `@Component` or `@Subcomponent` for each `@Scope`. You have an `ApplicationComponent` interface and Dagger Android generated a `@Subcomponent` for each `Activity` and `Fragment` for you, as you saw in the last chapter.
3. Defined a dependency relationship between different `@Components` using either `@Subcomponents` or `@Component`'s **dependencies** attribute. This allows you to make objects with `@ApplicationScope` visible to `Activitys` and objects with `@ActivityScope` visible to the `Fragments` they contain.
4. Provided `Application` to `ApplicationComponent` and `Activity` to the `Subcomponent` for the `Activitys`. You also added these objects to the corresponding dependency graph.
5. Defined different `@Modules` to tell Dagger how to bind a specific class to a given type.

To do this, you had to learn many different concepts and several ways to give Dagger the information it needs. As you'll learn in detail in this chapter, Hilt makes things much easier by:

1. Providing a predefined set of `@Scopes` to standardize the way you bind an object to a specific `@Component`'s lifecycle.
2. Doing the same for `@Components`. Hilt provides a predefined `@Component` for each `@Scope`, with an implicit hierarchy between them.

3. Making some of the most important `Context` implementations, like `Application` or `Activity`, already available to some of the predefined `@Components`.
4. Defining a new way to bind a `@Module` to a specific `@Component`. Now you install a `@Module` in one or more `@Components`.

This will become clearer when you start using Hilt for your Busso App.

Migrating Busso to Hilt

Migrating the Busso App to Hilt is a relatively smooth process — and it gives you an opportunity to experience Hilt's main concepts. You'll dive into those concepts more deeply later in the tutorial.

For your migration, you need to:

1. Install Hilt dependencies and plugins.
2. Enable Hilt in Busso's `Application`.
3. Use a predefined `@Scope` for the `ApplicationComponent`.
4. Migrate `Activitys` to Hilt using `@AndroidEntryPoint`.
5. In the same way, migrate `Fragments` to Hilt.
6. Install each `@Module` in the right `@Component` using `@InstallIn`.
7. Build, run and enjoy Busso.

Now — it's time to write some code!

> **Note**: As you already know, refactoring with Dagger means that you usually need to complete all the configurations before you can successfully build and run the app. This is also true in this case. However, it's good practice to try building the app at each step, anyway, allowing Dagger to generate what it can.

Installing what you need to use Hilt

Your first step is to install the Hilt plugin and dependencies in your app.

Start by opening the Busso App project in the **starter** folder of the materials for this chapter. This is the final project from the previous chapter, which uses Dagger Android. When you open the project, you'll have this structure:

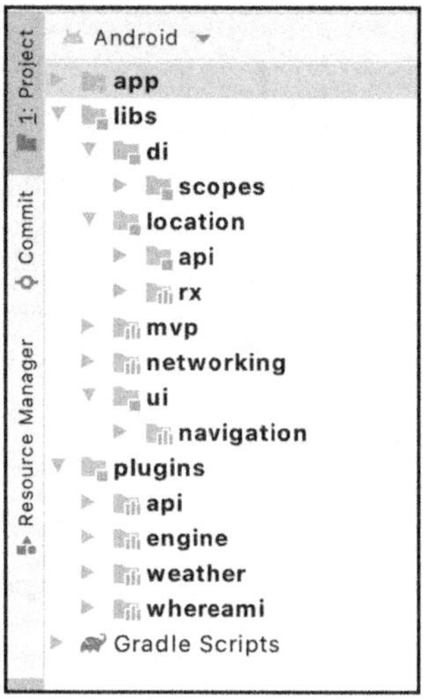

Figure 17.1 — Initial Project Structure

Now, open **build.gradle** in the main folder for the project, as in Figure 17.2:

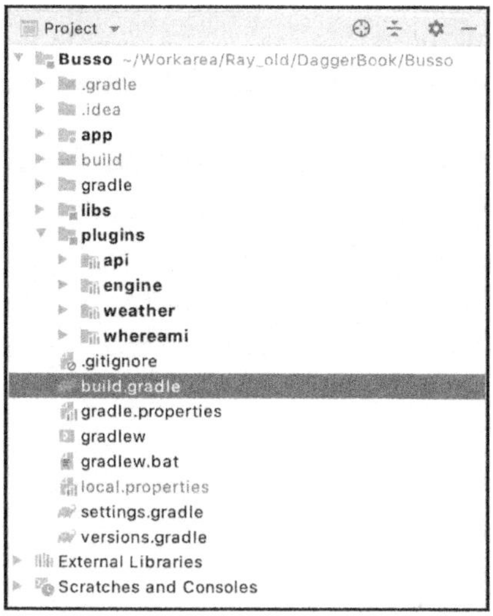

Figure 17.2 — build.gradle in the root of the Busso project

Then, apply the following changes:

```
buildscript {
  ext.kotlin_version = "1.4.20"
  ext.hilt_version = "2.28-alpha" // 1
  repositories {
    google()
    jcenter()
  }
  dependencies {
    classpath 'com.android.tools.build:gradle:4.1.1'
    classpath "org.jetbrains.kotlin:kotlin-gradle-plugin:
$kotlin_version"
    classpath "com.google.dagger:hilt-android-gradle-plugin:
$hilt_version" // 2
  }
}
// ...
```

In this Gradle file, you:

1. Include the definition of `ext.hilt_version` with the value of the latest version of Hilt.

2. Add `classpath` for Hilt's Gradle plugin.

Now, you have to apply the Hilt plugin to **build.gradle** for the modules that need it. For starters, open **build.gradle** from **app**, as in Figure 17.3:

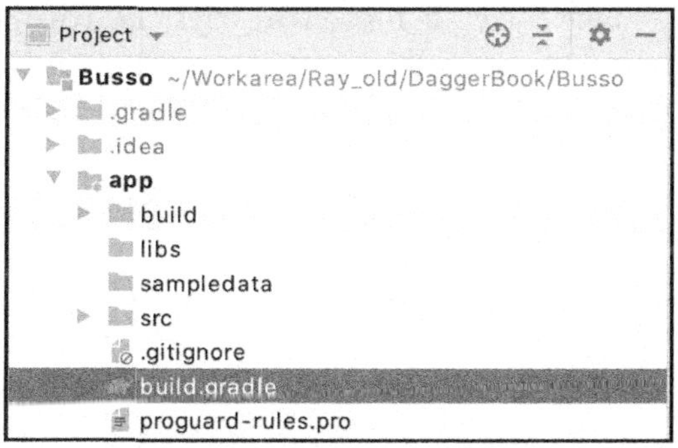

Figure 17.3 — build.gradle for the app module

Now, apply the following changes:

```
plugins {
  id 'com.android.application'
  id 'kotlin-android'
  id "kotlin-kapt"
  id "dagger.hilt.android.plugin" // 1
```

```
}
apply from: '../versions.gradle'

android {
  // ...
  compileOptions { // 2
    sourceCompatibility JavaVersion.VERSION_1_8
    targetCompatibility JavaVersion.VERSION_1_8
  }
  kotlinOptions {
    jvmTarget = '1.8'
  }
  // ...
}

dependencies {
  // ...
  // Hilt dependencies
  implementation "com.google.dagger:hilt-android:
$hilt_version" // 3
  kapt "com.google.dagger:hilt-android-compiler:
$hilt_version" // 4
  // ...
}
```

There are some interesting things to note in the Gradle file above. Here, you:

1. Add the plugin for Hilt. The plugin isn't necessary, and Hilt works without it, but it makes the developer experience better. For instance, it executes some bytecode transformations to make the code more IDE-friendly. This helps auto-complete the code without messing with auto-generated code. It also makes some code simpler. You'll see this later, when you work with `@HiltAndroidApp`.

2. Specify using Java 1.8, which Hilt requires. Busso already has the proper configuration in `compileOptions`.

3. Add the dependency to the Hilt library.

4. Indicate the specific library `kapt` uses for Hilt's annotation processor.

Now, sync the Busso project with the Gradle file and you're ready to use Hilt in your app. You just need a way to activate the Hilt plugin by providing an entry point to the Hilt world. You'll do this by using `Application`. In Busso, you'll find this class in **Main.kt**.

Enabling Hilt in Application

Building the Busso App now will give you some errors. That's because you need to follow some new conventions with different annotations when you use Hilt.

Your next step in migrating Busso to Hilt is to define the entry point for the entire dependency graph. You *must* do this in your app's `Application` implementation. If your app doesn't have an `Application` implementation, you need to create one.

Defining the entry point for the dependency graph

In Busso, you need to add your `Application` implementation in **Main.kt** in **app**. Open **Main.kt** and change the content of the file to this:

```
@HiltAndroidApp // 1
class Main : Application() // 2
```

Hey, where's all the code? Don't worry, one of the main benefits of Hilt is that you don't need all the previous code. Here, you:

1. Used `@HiltAndroidApp` to tell Dagger that this is the entry point for Busso's dependency graph.

2. Created `Main` as a simple `Application`.

Adding Application to the dependency graph

That looks good, but you might wonder if something's missing. In the previous implementation of `Main`, you had the following:

```
DaggerApplicationComponent
      .factory()
      .create(this, BussoConfiguration)
```

There, you created an instance of `ApplicationComponent` by passing the reference to:

- `Application`.
- `NetworkingConfiguration`.

That's how you added `Application` and `NetworkingConfiguration` to `ApplicationComponent`'s dependency graph. That made them automatically available for injection into any other object of the app.

With Hilt, on the other hand, you:

- Don't need to do anything for `Application`. Hilt guarantees it's automatically added to the dependency graph for `ApplicationComponent`, making it available for injection into any other object.
- Need to find a different way to tell Dagger which `NetworkingConfiguration` to use and how to add it to the dependency graph for `ApplicationScope`.

To address the second point, you need to tell Dagger:

1. How to bind `BussoConfiguration` to `NetworkingConfiguration`.
2. To add that implementation to the dependency graph for `ApplicationComponent`.

Adding a @Module

You already know how to solve the first point: you need a `@Module`. Open **ApplicationModule.kt** in **di** and add the following definition:

```
@Module(
  includes = [
    LocationModule::class,
    NetworkModule::class,
    AndroidSupportInjectionModule::class
  ]
)
object ApplicationModule {

  @Provides
  fun provideNetworkingConfiguration(): NetworkingConfiguration
=  // HERE
    BussoConfiguration
}
```

Here, you tell Dagger that whenever it needs `NetworkingConfiguration`, it'll use `BussoConfiguration`.

Binding @Module's objects to ApplicationComponent

Now, you need to bind the objects in this `@Module` to `ApplicationComponent`. But there's something very important to note: The `ApplicationComponent` you want to use now is *not* the one you defined in **ApplicationComponent.kt** in **di**.

Be brave and delete **ApplicationComponent.kt**, then apply the following change to **ApplicationModule.kt**:

```
@Module(
  includes = [
    LocationModule::class,
    NetworkModule::class,
    AndroidSupportInjectionModule::class
  ]
)
@InstallIn(ApplicationComponent::class) // HERE
object ApplicationModule {

  @Provides
  fun provideNetworkingConfiguration(): NetworkingConfiguration
=
    BussoConfiguration
}
```

You'll see this in more detail later. At the moment, you're using `@InstallIn` to tell Dagger that you want all the bindings you have in **ApplicationModule.kt** to be a part of the dependency graph for `ApplicationComponent`.

But which `ApplicationComponent` is that if you just deleted **ApplicationComponent.kt**? As you read earlier, Hilt has a set of predefined `@Components` — and `ApplicationComponent`, which you find in **dagger.hilt.android.components** — is one of those.

In this section, you did something very simple but powerful. You told Dagger:

1. To use `Main` as the entry point for Busso's dependency graph. You did this using `@HiltAndroidApp`.
2. That you want to use `BussoConfiguration` as the `NetworkingConfiguration` implementation.
3. That all the definitions you made in `ApplicationModule` will be part of the dependency graph for the predefined `ApplicationComponent`. You did this using `@InstallIn`, which you'll learn more about later.

You also learned that Hilt makes `Application` automatically available to the dependency graph for the `ApplicationComponent` — which also makes it available to all the other predefined Hilt `@Components`.

Using a predefined @Scope for ApplicationComponent

In the previous section, you learned that Hilt creates `ApplicationComponent` for you. You just need to tell it which objects to put into its dependency graph. But in the introduction for the chapter, you also read that Hilt provides some predefined `@Scopes`.

You'll learn about all the available `@Scopes` and `@Components` later. At the moment, it's important to know that the `@Scope` for `ApplicationComponent` is `@Singleton`. To migrate from the existing custom `@Scopes` in the **libs.di.scopes** module to Hilt's, make the following changes:

1. Delete **ApplicationScope.kt**, **ActivityScope.kt** and **FragmentScope.kt** from **libs.di.scopes**.
2. Add the Hilt dependencies in **build.gradle** for **libs.di.scopes**.
3. Fix the dependent modules using the Hilt `@Scopes` instead of the ones you just deleted.

> **Note**: Here, you're using **libs.di.scopes** as the module containing the dependencies for Hilt. This makes things easier to explain but, of course, you could also completely delete **libs.di.scopes** and fix all the dependencies in the other modules accordingly.

> **Note**: If you don't want to remove your custom `@Scopes`, Hilt provides you the `@AliasOf` annotation, which allows you to use your custom `@Scope` annotation in place of the ones Hilt provides. You'll see an example of this later.

After step 2, **build.gradle** for **libs.di.scopes** should look like this:

```
plugins {
  id 'com.android.library'
  id 'kotlin-android'
  id "kotlin-kapt"
  id "dagger.hilt.android.plugin"
}
apply from: '../../../versions.gradle'
android {
  compileSdkVersion compile_sdk_version
  buildToolsVersion build_tool_version
}
dependencies {
  api "javax.inject:javax.inject:$javax_annotation_version"
  implementation "org.jetbrains.kotlin:kotlin-stdlib:
$kotlin_version"

  api "com.google.dagger:hilt-android:$hilt_version"
  kapt "com.google.dagger:hilt-android-compiler:$hilt_version"
}
```

Of course, now you need to replace all the existing custom `@Scopes` with Hilt's. But don't worry about that, yet. At the moment, just replace the previous `@ApplicationScope` with `@Singleton`. You can find all the occurrences with a simple search:

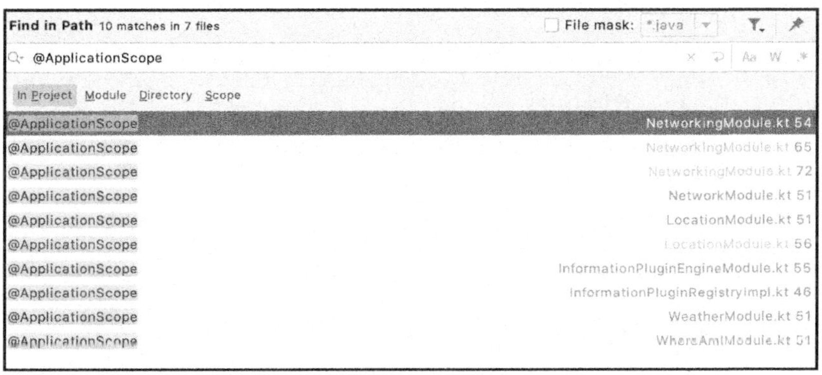

Figure 17.4 — @ApplicationScope usages

After you replaced all the `@ApplicationScopes` with `@Singletons`, you can start migrating Busso's `Activitys`.

Migrating Activitys to Hilt using @AndroidEntryPoint

In the previous section, you fixed most of the dependencies related to `ApplicationComponent` by using `@Singleton`. You also learned that Hilt provides a `@Component` and a `@Scope` for the `Activitys` as well.

This is true. Hilt provides `ActivityComponent` and `@ActivityScoped`. In Busso, you need to:

1. Delete the existing **ActivityBindingModule.kt** from **di**.
2. Tell Dagger that the objects in **ActivityModule.kt** should be installed in `ActivityComponent`.
3. Replace the custom `@ActivityScope` with `@ActivityScoped` (note the ending **d**).

After deleting **ActivityBindingModule.kt**, open **ActivityModule.kt** in **di.activities** and change it like this:

```
@Module(
  includes = [
    NavigatorModule::class
  ]
)
@InstallIn(ActivityComponent::class) // HERE
interface ActivityModule {
  // ...
}
```

Here, you're just using `@InstallIn` to install this `@Module`'s bindings in `ActivityComponent`.

Now, search for `@ActivityScope` and replace all the occurrences with `@ActivityScoped`, as in Figure 17.5:

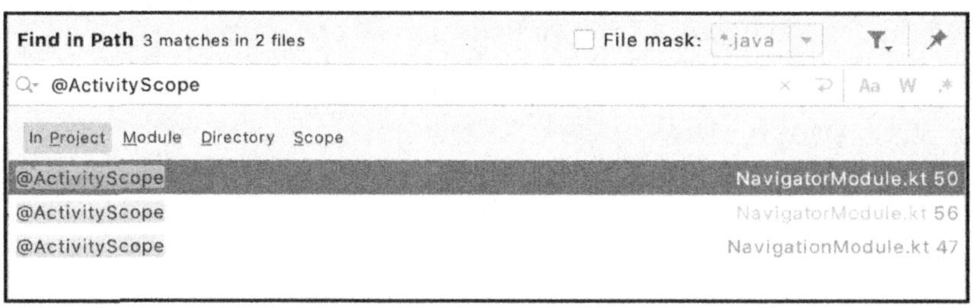

Figure 17.5 — @ActivityScope usages

After replacing those occurrences, there's one more step to complete your work with `Activitys`: You need to execute the injection in `MainActivity` and `SplashActivity`.

To do this, Hilt defines `@AndroidEntryPoint`, which allows you to **tag** a standard Android component as a possible dependency target.

Later, you'll see a detailed list of all the classes Hilt's `@AndroidEntryPoint` annotation supports. At the moment, you just need to open **SplashActivity.kt** in **ui.view.splash** and change it like this:

```
@AndroidEntryPoint // 1
class SplashActivity : AppCompatActivity() {
  // ...
  override fun onCreate(savedInstanceState: Bundle?) {
    // AndroidInjection.inject(this) // 2 TO DELETE
    super.onCreate(savedInstanceState)
    makeFullScreen()
    setContentView(R.layout.activity_splash)
    splashViewBinder.init(this)
  }
  // ...
}
```

In this case you:

1. Add `@AndroidEntryPoint`.
2. Remove the `AndroidInjection.inject()` invocation, which you don't need anymore.

In the same way, open **MainActivity.kt** in **ui.view.main** and apply the following changes

```
@AndroidEntryPoint // 1
class MainActivity : AppCompatActivity() { // 2
  // ...
}
```

In `MainActivity`'s case, you:

1. Added `@AndroidEntryPoint`.
2. Restored `AppCompatActivity` as the parent class for `MainActivity` in place of `DaggerAppCompatActivity`. Note that this implicitly removes the `AndroidInjection.inject()` invocation.

At this point, it's important to note that:

1. All the bindings you defined in `ActivityModule` are now available in `ActivityComponent`'s dependency graph.
2. `MainActivity` and `SplashActivity` are dependency targets for the `@ActvityScoped` objects in `ActivityComponent`.
3. The `@ActivityScoped` dependency targets can also access objects with `@Singleton` scope. Hilt implicitly manages dependencies between `@Components`.
4. Likewise, objects in the dependency graph for `@ApplicationComponent` access `Application`, and all objects in the dependency graph for `ActivityComponent` access `Activity`.

Now, it's time to migrate Busso's `Fragments` to Hilt. By now, you probably know how to do that. :]

Migrating Fragments to Hilt

In the previous step, you told Dagger which `@ActivityScoped` objects you want to inject in Busso's `Activitys`. Now, you have to do the same for `Fragments`. In this case, you'll need a `@Scope` and a `@Component` for `Fragments` that Hilt provides with:

1. **@FragmentScoped**
2. **FragmentComponent**

To use them, you just need to:

1. Delete **FragmentBindingModule.kt** in **di**.
2. Use `@InstallIn` to install `FragmentModule` in **di.fragments** in `FragmentComponent`.
3. Use `@AndroidEntryPoint` to tag `BusStopFragment` and `BusArrivalFragment` as dependency targets for injection.
4. Replace the existing `@FragmentScope` with `@FragmentScoped` (again, watch the final **d**).

After deleting **FragmentBindingModule.kt**, open **FragmentModule.kt** in **di.fragments** and change the `FragmentModule` definition to this:

```
@Module(includes =
[InformationPluginEngineModule.FragmentBindings::class])
@InstallIn(FragmentComponent::class) // HERE
interface FragmentModule {
  // ...
}
```

Now, open **BusStopFragment.kt** in **ui.view.busstop** and apply the following changes:

```
@AndroidEntryPoint // 1
class BusStopFragment : Fragment() {
  // ...
  /* START REMOVE
  override fun onAttach(context: Context) { // 2
    AndroidSupportInjection.inject(this)
    super.onAttach(context)
  } END REMOVE
  */

  // ...
}
```

Here, you need to do two very important things:

1. Add `@AndroidEntryPoint` to tell Hilt that `BusStopFragment` is a dependency target.
2. Remove the existing `inject()` invocation. Hilt will inject the objects you require into `BusStopFragment` for you.

Now, you need to do the same for `BusArrivalFragment`. Open **BusArrivalFragment.kt** in **ui.view.busarrival** and apply the same change:

```
@AndroidEntryPoint // 1
class BusArrivalFragment : Fragment() {
  // ...
  /* START REMOVE
  override fun onAttach(context: Context) { // 2
    AndroidSupportInjection.inject(this)
    super.onAttach(context)
  } END REMOVE
  */
  // ...
}
```

As your final step, you need to replace `@FragmentScope` with Hilt's `@FragmentScoped`, just as you did for `@ActivityScoped` and `@Singleton`. You can see this in Figure 17.6:

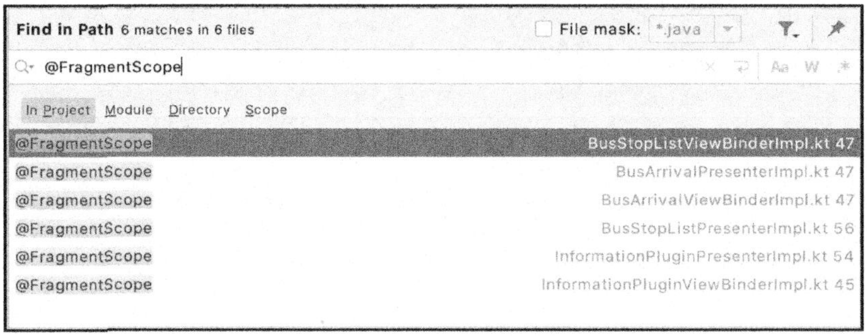

Figure 17.6 — @FragmentScope usages

Great job! You're almost done migrating Busso to Hilt. Now, you just need to check that you installed all the `@Modules` in the right `@Components` and do a bit of cleaning up.

Installing @Modules in @Components

Busso is a multi-module app that defines different `@Modules` in different Gradle modules. To complete the migration, you need to:

1. Install `NetworkModule`, `InformationPluginEngineModule` and `InformationSpecsModule` in `@ApplicationComponent`.
2. Fix the injection of the `Navigator` implementation.

These steps should be quite straightforward now. Open **NetworkModule.kt** in **network** and use `@InstallIn` to install it in the `ApplicationComponent`:

```
@Module(
  includes = [
    NetworkingModule::class
  ]
)
@InstallIn(ApplicationComponent::class) // HERE
object NetworkModule {
  // ...
}
```

Open **ApplicationModule.kt** in **di** and add the following definition:

```
@Module(
  includes = [
    LocationModule::class,
    NetworkModule::class,
    AndroidSupportInjectionModule::class,
    InformationPluginEngineModule::class // HERE ADD
  ]
)
@InstallIn(ApplicationComponent::class)
object ApplicationModule {
  // ...
}
```

In this case, it's important to note how `InformationPluginEngineModule` doesn't need to use `@InstallIn` itself. Hilt will install `InformationPluginEngineModule` in `ApplicationComponent` as part of `ApplicationModule`.

Now, you also need to install `InformationSpecsModule` by adding the following code in **InformationSpecsModule.kt** in **plugins**:

```
@Module(
  includes = [
    WhereAmIModule::class,
    WeatherModule::class
  ]
)
@InstallIn(ApplicationComponent::class) // HERE
object InformationSpecsModule
```

Fixing the Navigator injection

Build the app now and you'll get an error related to the `Navigator` implementation. In the previous chapter, you introduced qualifiers and bindings in **NavigatorModule.kt** in **di.navigator**. The good news is — you don't need these anymore. To fix the errors, you need to:

1. Delete **NavigatorModule.kt** in **di.navigator**.
2. Restore the use of `NavigationModule` in `ActivityModule` in place of the `NavigatorModule` you just removed.
3. Delete every use of the `@Named` qualifier for `Navigator`.

So delete **NavigatorModule.kt**, then open **ActivityModule.kt** in **di.activities** and apply the following change:

```
@Module(
  includes = [
    NavigationModule::class // HERE
  ]
)
@InstallIn(ActivityComponent::class)
interface ActivityModule {
  // ...
}
```

Here, you replaced `NavigatorModule` with `NavigationModule`. Next, delete the `@Named("Main")` and `@Named("Splash")` qualifiers in `MainPresenterImpl`, `BusStopListPresenterImpl` and `SplashViewBinderImpl`.

Here's how these classes will look now:

```
class MainPresenterImpl @Inject constructor(
  private val navigator: Navigator // HERE
) : MainPresenter {
  // ...
}
```

```
@FragmentScoped
class BusStopListPresenterImpl @Inject constructor(
  private val navigator: Navigator, // HERE
  private val locationObservable: Observable<LocationEvent>,
  private val bussoEndpoint: BussoEndpoint
) : BasePresenter<View, BusStopListViewBinder>(),
  BusStopListPresenter {
  // ...
}
```

```
class SplashViewBinderImpl @Inject constructor(
  private val navigator: Navigator // HERE
) : SplashViewBinder {
  // ...
}
```

For your last step, restore the encapsulation for **libs.ui.navigation** using the `internal` visibility modifier in the **NavigatorImpl.kt** file, like this:

```
// HERE
internal class NavigatorImpl(private val activity: Activity) :
Navigator {
  // ...
}
```

You did it! You can now successfully build and run Busso, ending up with what you see in Figure 17.7:

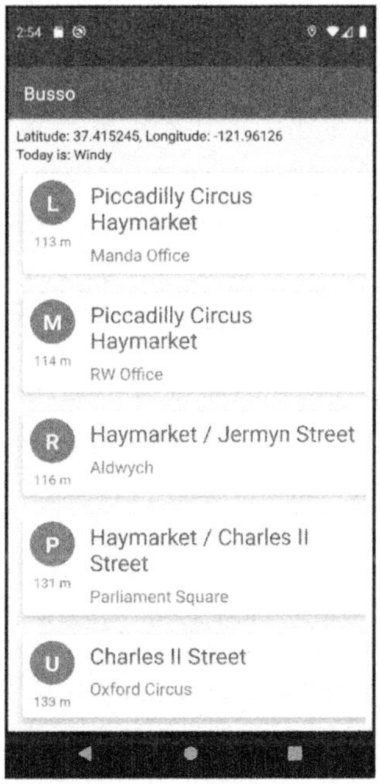

Figure 17.7 — The Busso App

It's now time for a short summary.

Reviewing your achievements

At this point, it's important to review what you learned while migrating Busso from using Dagger Android to Hilt. Here's what you discovered:

- Hilt provides a predefined set of `@Scopes` and `@Components` that already implement a dependency relationship. For instance, all the objects with `@Singleton` scope are visible to the `@ActivityScoped` objects.
- For `ApplicationComponent`, you use `@HiltAndroidApp` in your app's `Application`.
- You use `@InstallIn` to make the bindings in a specific `@Module` available to one or more `@Components`.
- Some of the `@Components` already provide `Context` implementations, like `Application` or `Activity`. For instance, the `NavigationModule` needs an `Activity`, which Hilt provides automagically.

You won't believe it but these are the main things you need to know to use Hilt in your app. Of course, you only saw a few of the `@Components` and `@Scopes` available. Now, you'll get a quick overview of everything Hilt provides.

Hilt's main APIs

While migrating Busso to Hilt, you learned that the main concepts you need to know are:

- Entry point and `@AndroidEntryPoint`.
- Generated `@Components` and `@Scopes`.

You already know how to use them. In the following sections, you'll just learn what's available.

Entry point using @AndroidEntryPoint

In this book, you referred to `Application`, `Activitys` and `Fragments` as **dependency targets**. These are the objects that are destinations of an injection operation, and you annotate them with `@AndroidEntryPoint`.

`Application` has a special meaning, so you use `@HiltAndroidApp`, instead. In Busso, you did this with `Application`, `Activitys` and `Fragments` but you can do the same with all the following classes:

- `Application`, by using `@HiltAndroidApp`
- `Activitys` that extend `androidx.activity.ComponentActivity`
- `Fragments` that extend `androidx.Fragment`
- `View`
- `Service`
- `BroadcastReceiver`

You might notice that this list doesn't match the Android standard components. It adds `Fragments` and `Views` but `ContentProvider` is missing. You might wonder when and how you could support more classes.

In theory, you should be able to use the existing entry points, but sometimes you need to handle third-party libraries or components that Hilt doesn't support yet.

As you'll learn in the next chapter, Hilt provides you with the APIs to create your own entry point, component and scope and integrate them with the ones you already have.

Using predefined @Components & @Scopes

In terms of `@Components` and `@Scopes`, Hilt provides what's shown in Figure 17.8:

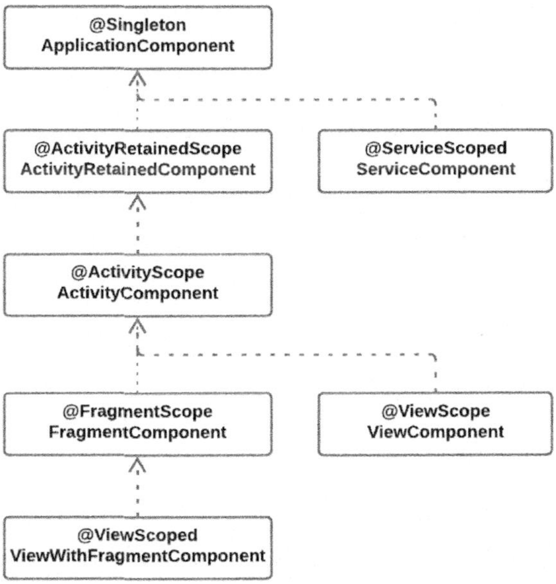

Figure 17.8 — Predefined @Components and @Scopes

In this dependency diagram, you find `ApplicationComponent` and `ActivityComponent`, along with their related `@Scopes`: `@Singleton` and `@ActivityScope`. Looking at the other `@Components`, it's worth saying more about:

- `ActivityRetainedComponent` with `@ActivityRetainedScoped`
- `ViewWithFragmentComponent` with `@ViewScoped`

`ActivityRetainedComponent` is similar to `ActivityComponent` but it uses a different lifecycle. It allows the bindings to survive configuration changes.

In this case, you need to take care that you don't have `Activity` as default binding, but rather `Application`, as in `ApplicationComponent`.

`ViewWithFragmentComponent` also allows you to optimize the lifecycle of `Views` when part of the `View` hierarchy is attached to a `Fragment`.

Finally, here are the default bindings for each predefined `@Component`:

- **ApplicationComponent**: `Application`
- **ActivityRetainedComponent**: `Application`
- **ActivityComponent**: `Application` and `Activity`
- **FragmentComponent**: `Application`, `Activity` and `Fragment`
- **ViewComponent**: `Application`, `Activity` and `View`
- **ViewWithFragmentComponent**: `Application`, `Activity`, `Fragment` and `View`
- **ServiceComponent**: `Application` and `Service`

When you need to decide which `@Scope` and `@Component` to use in your bindings, you need to consider:

- The **lifecycle** of the objects you inject.
- Which **default bindings** the specific `@Component` provides.

After that, you can apply the rules you just learned with the Busso App.

Hilt utility APIs

Hilt provides some utility APIs, which help migrate existing apps. The main ones are:

1. `@AliasOf`
2. `@ApplicationContext`
3. `@ActivityContext`

You'll see a simple example for each of those next.

Using @AliasOf

When you migrated Busso to Hilt, you deleted the custom `@Scopes` you implemented in the previous chapters. You deleted `@ApplicationScope`, `@ActivityScope` and `@FragmentScope` in favor of the predefined `@Singleton`, `@ActivityScoped` and `@FragmentScoped`.

Suppose you don't like `@Singleton` and want to keep the same naming convention by using `@ApplicationScoped`, instead.

You'd create a new file named **ApplicationScoped.kt** in **libs.di.scopes** with the following code:

```
@Scope
@MustBeDocumented
@Retention(AnnotationRetention.RUNTIME)
@AliasOf(Singleton::class) // HERE
annotation class ApplicationScoped
```

With this definition, you tell Dagger that `@ApplicationScoped` is just an alias for `@Singleton`. To prove this, just search for `@Singleton` and replace all the instances with the new `@ApplicationScoped`. After that, build and run the app as usual and it will work.

Of course, the best use case for `@AliasOf` is when you already have a lot of occurrences for a custom `@Scope` and you want to avoid replacing too much code.

Using @ApplicationContext

Another very useful tool from Hilt is related to `Context`. You've seen that some of the predefined `@Components` have an `Application` for default bindings, while others have an `Activity`. As you know, they're both implementations of the Android `Context` and if you want to distinguish one from the other, you use a qualifier. In this specific case, however, Hilt already provides the qualifier you need.

For instance, open **LocationModule.kt** in **libs.location.rx** and look at the following code:

```
@Module
class LocationModule {
  @ApplicationScoped
  @Provides
  fun provideLocationManager(application: Application):
LocationManager = // HERE
    application.getSystemService(Context.LOCATION_SERVICE) as
LocationManager
```

```
  // ...
}
```

Here, you used `Application` to get a reference to `LocationManager`. In this case, you really just need a `Context` and Hilt allows you to use that by applying the following change:

```
@Module
class LocationModule {
  @ApplicationScoped
  @Provides
  fun provideLocationManager(
    @ApplicationContext context: Context // HERE
  ): LocationManager =
    context.getSystemService(Context.LOCATION_SERVICE) as
LocationManager
  // ...
}
```

Here, you replaced `Application` with `Context`, using `@ApplicationContext` to tell Dagger that the `Context` you want is same as `Application`.

Using @ActivityContext

You can do the same when you need the `Context` of an `Activity`. In that case, you also have the opportunity to improve Busso's resource management.

Open **LocationModule.kt** in **libs.location.rx** and replace the current code with the following:

```
// 1
class LocationModule {

  @Module
  object ApplicationBindings { // 2
    @ApplicationScoped
    @Provides
    fun provideLocationManager(
      @ApplicationContext context: Context
    ): LocationManager =
      context.getSystemService(Context.LOCATION_SERVICE) as
LocationManager
  }

  @Module
  object ActivityBindings { // 3
    @ActivityScoped // 4
    @Provides
    fun providePermissionChecker(
```

```
      @ActivityContext context: Context // 5
    ): GeoLocationPermissionChecker =
      GeoLocationPermissionCheckerImpl(context)

    @Provides
    @ActivityScoped // 4
    fun provideLocationObservable(
      locationManager: LocationManager,
      permissionChecker: GeoLocationPermissionChecker
    ): Observable<LocationEvent> =
provideRxLocationObservable(locationManager, permissionChecker)
  }
}
```

As you see, this makes a few changes to `LocationModule`. In particular:

1. `LocationModule` is not a `@Module` anymore — it's just a container for a few other `@Module`s for bindings with different scopes.
2. `ApplicationBindings` is a `@Module` that contains the bindings with `@ApplicationScoped` or `@Singleton`.
3. `ActivityBindings` is the `@Module` containing the bindings with `@ActivityScoped`.
4. You now use `@ActivityScoped` for the `GeoLocationPermissionChecker` and `Observable<LocationEvent>`, whose optimal lifecycle is the same as `Activity`.
5. Use `@ActivityContext` to tell Dagger that the `Context` you require for `GeoLocationPermissionChecker` is `Activity`.

Updating where you had LocationModule

Now, you need to fix the places where you used `LocationModule`. Open **ApplicationModule.kt** in **di** and add the following definition:

```
@Module(
  includes = [
    LocationModule.ApplicationBindings::class, // HERE
    NetworkModule::class,
    AndroidSupportInjectionModule::class,
    InformationPluginEngineModule::class
  ]
)
@InstallIn(ApplicationComponent::class)
object ApplicationModule {
  // ...
}
```

Then, open **ActivityModule.kt** in **di.activities** and add the following definition:

```
@Module(
  includes = [
    NavigationModule::class,
    LocationModule.ActivityBindings::class // HERE
  ]
)
@InstallIn(ActivityComponent::class)
interface ActivityModule {
  // ...
}
```

Now, you can build and run Busso as usual and verify it works.

Key points

- The main goal of Hilt is to make Dagger easier to learn and to use.
- Hilt provides a predefined set of `@Components` and `@Scopes`.
- Using `@InstallIn`, you install the binding of a `@Module` in a specific `@Component`.
- Each predefined Hilt `@Component` provides a set of default bindings.
- There's an implicit hierarchy between Hilt's predefined `@Components`.
- `@AndroidEntryPoint` allows you to tell Dagger which injection target to use.
- `@AliasOf` simplifies the migration of existing apps to Hilt.
- Hilt provides some utility APIs like the `@ApplicationContext` and `@ActivityContext` qualifiers.

Congratulations! In this chapter, you learned the main concepts of Hilt, the new framework with the goal of simplifying Dagger usage in Android apps. However, Hilt is more than that. In the next chapter, you'll learn more about it — in particular, how to use customize it and how to use it with **Android architecture components**.

See you there!

Chapter 18: Hilt & Architecture Components

By Massimo Carli

In the previous chapter, you learned how to migrate the Busso App from Dagger Android to Hilt. You saw the main Hilt architectural decisions and how to apply them using new APIs like `@InstallIn` and `@AndroidEntryPoint`.

In this chapter, you'll learn more about Hilt, including how to:

- Use Hilt with other supported Android standard components, like `Services`.
- Create custom Hilt `@Endpoints` for currently unsupported Android standard components, like `ContentProviders`.
- Use Hilt with **ViewModel**s.

Throughout the chapter, you'll work with the **RayTrack** app. Don't worry about the amount of code the app has. It's purposely a complex app, to give you the opportunity to work with Hilt's architectural components. You'll only focus on the things that have to do with Hilt. To save space, you'll only see the most relevant parts of the code in this chapter.

> **Note**: An interesting exercise would be to simplify RayTrack's code. Check the project for the full code.

> **Note**: This chapter requires knowledge of the main Android Architecture Components, like **Lifecycle**, **ViewModel** and **LiveData**.

The RayTrack app

In this chapter, you'll work on RayTrack. Use Android Studio to open the **RayTrack** project in the **starter** folder for this chapter. You'll see the project structure shown in Figure 18.1:

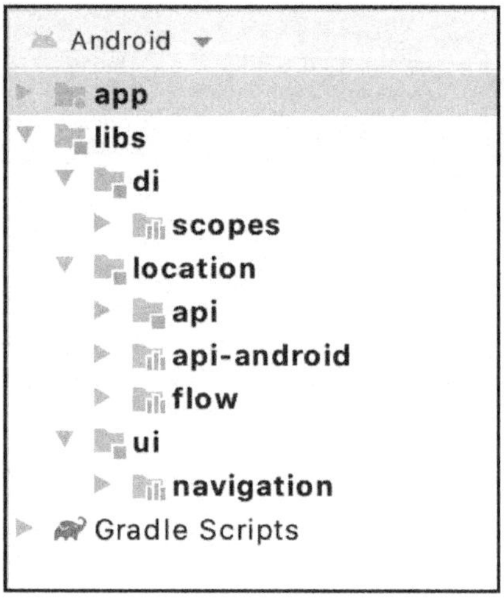

Figure 18.1 — Starting RayTrack project

RayTrack has some modules in common with Busso:

- **libs.di.scope**
- **libs.location.api**
- **libs.ui.navigation**

It also has some new modules:

- **libs.location.api-android**
- **libs.location.flow**

These are just a different implementation of the abstraction you have in **libs.location.api** for Android. They use Kotlin Flows and coroutines.

Build and run and you'll get, after the splash screen and permission request, something like in Figure 18.2:

Figure 18.2 — RayTrack in Action

Yeah, the UI isn't the best, but the **RayTrack app** does what you need. :] When you press the **Start Tracking** button, you start a **Foreground Service** that keeps track of your current location and stores it in a database. Pressing the **Stop Tracking** button while the tracking is running stops the service. While the service is running, you can also see the location in the notification area:

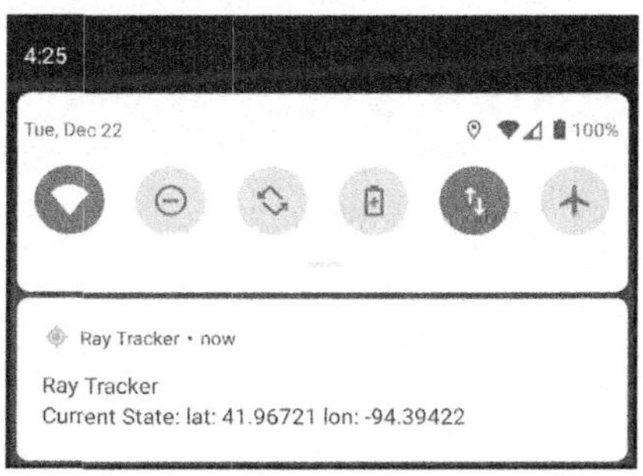

Figure 18.3 — RayTrack Notification

Selecting the notification area returns you to the list of locations shown in Figure 18.2. Finally, you can select the **Clear Data** button and delete the database content at any time.

Now that you know how RayTrack works, it's time to see how it's set up.

RayTrack's architecture

RayTrack consists of three main parts:

1. **Foreground service**: Tracks the location.
2. **RayTrackContentProvider**: Provides location data persistence.
3. **MainActivity**: Displays the location data on the screen.

Here's a detailed description of each of these important parts.

Tracking location data in the foreground

RayTrack uses `Service` to track the user's location. Because the user's location is sensitive data, Android requires you to implement this as a **foreground service** so the user always knows when it's running on their device.

This means that you have some specific constraints you must follow. For instance, you must display a **Notification** when `Service` is running. In Figure 18.4, you can see the architecture for this part of the RayTrack app:

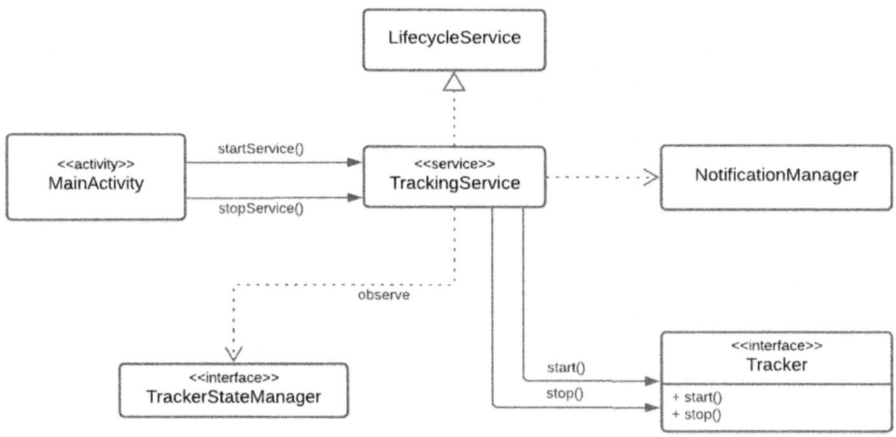

Figure 18.4 — The TrackingService

In the diagram, there are some important things to note:

1. `TrackingService` extends `LifecycleService`, which is a utility class Google provides for cases when you need your `Service` to be a `LifecyclerOwner`. You need this because `TrackerStateManager` exposes an interface based on **LiveData** that requires `LifecyclerOwner` to be observed.
2. You start and stop `TrackingService` directly from `MainActivity` using the classic `startService()` and `stopService()`.
3. To display the notification that Android requires when `TrackingService` is running, you need a dependency on `NotificationManager`.
4. An Android `Service` is an adapter between the Android environment and some thread that needs to live for a certain time. It's the ideal place to start long-living threads. In this case, `TrackingService` starts and stops `Tracker` and observes `TrackerStateManager` to update the information in `Notification`.
5. `Tracker` is the abstraction of the object responsible for the actual tracking of the location.

Looking at the diagram in Figure 18.4, you also understand which objects `TrackingService` depends on. It needs a reference to:

- `Tracker`
- `TrackerStateManager`

The good news is that you can use `Service` as an injection target for Hilt. To inject the required dependencies, you just need to do what's already in `TrackingService`.

Injecting dependencies

Open **TrackingService.kt** in **raytracker.service** and look at the following code:

```
@ExperimentalCoroutinesApi
@AndroidEntryPoint // 1
class TrackingService : LifecycleService() {

  @Inject
  lateinit var tracker: Tracker // 2

  @Inject
  lateinit var trackerStateManager: TrackerStateManager // 2
  // ...
}
```

In that code, you used:

1. `@AndroidEntryPoint` because `Service` is an Android Standard Component that Hilt supports.
2. `@Inject` for the property containing the reference to the dependent objects.

To understand where those dependencies come from, just click on the icons in Figure 18.5:

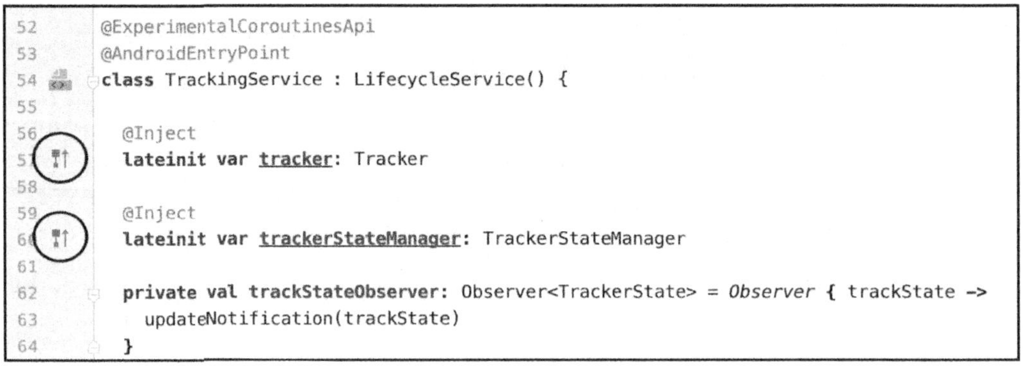

Figure 18.5 — Binding sources

In `Tracker`'s case, you'll see the following code from **TrackerModule.kt** in **di**:

```
interface TrackerModule {

  @Module(
      includes = [FlowLocationModule::class]
  )
  @InstallIn(ServiceComponent::class) // HERE
  interface ServiceBindings {
    @Binds
    fun bindTracker(
        impl: TrackerImpl
    ): Tracker
  }
  // ...
}
```

This shows how to use `@InstallIn` to install the `Tracker` implementation in the dependency graph for the `ServiceComponent`.

Now, open **TrackerImpl.kt** in **service** and look at the following code:

```
@ServiceScoped // HERE
class TrackerImpl @Inject constructor(
    private val trackerStateManager: TrackerStateManager,
    private val locationFlow: @JvmSuppressWildcards
Flow<LocationEvent>
) : Tracker, CoroutineScope {
  // ...
}
```

This is an example of `@ServiceScoped` as the `@Scope` for an object that lives as long as a `Service`.

Select the icon next to `TrackerStateManager` and you end up, once again, in **TrackerModule.kt** in **di**, where you have the following code:

```
interface TrackerModule {
  // ...
  @Module
  @InstallIn(ApplicationComponent::class) // HERE
  interface ApplicationBindings {
    @Binds
    fun bindTrackerStateManager(
        impl: TrackerStateManagerImpl
    ): TrackerStateManager
  }
}
```

In this case, `TrackerStateManager` needs to be in `ApplicationComponent` because it will contain the current state of the tracking. Look at **TrackerStateManagerImpl.kt** in **state** and see the following code:

```
@ApplicationScoped // HERE
class TrackerStateManagerImpl @Inject constructor(
    @ApplicationContext private val context: Context
) : TrackerStateManager {
  // ...
}
```

Here you just use `@ApplicationScoped`, which is the same `@AliasOf` for `@Singleton` that you used in the previous chapters.

`TrackingService` is an example of how to use Hilt with a `Service`. But what about a standard component that isn't supported yet? You'll see how to do that next.

Persisting location data

In the previous paragraph, you saw how to inject dependencies in `TrackingService`. You discovered that the dependency injection in a `Service` with Hilt is no different from the injection in an `Activity`, a `Fragment` or any other component Hilt supports.

You still use `@AndroidEntryPoint` to tag the `Service` as an injection target and `@Inject` to assign values to local properties. `Service` is an Android standard component that Hilt supports — but you're not always so lucky. At the moment, for example, Hilt doesn't support `ContentProviders`. However, Hilt gives you some tools to fix the problem.

To see how everything works you need to:

1. Understand `ContentProvider`'s role in RayTrack.
2. Enable the dependency injection in `ContentProvider` using `@EntryPoint`.

In the first case, a good UML diagram will help.

Understanding the role of ContentProvider in RayTrack

RayTrack uses a `ContentProvider` to persist location data. To understand how this works, look at the diagram in Figure 18.6:

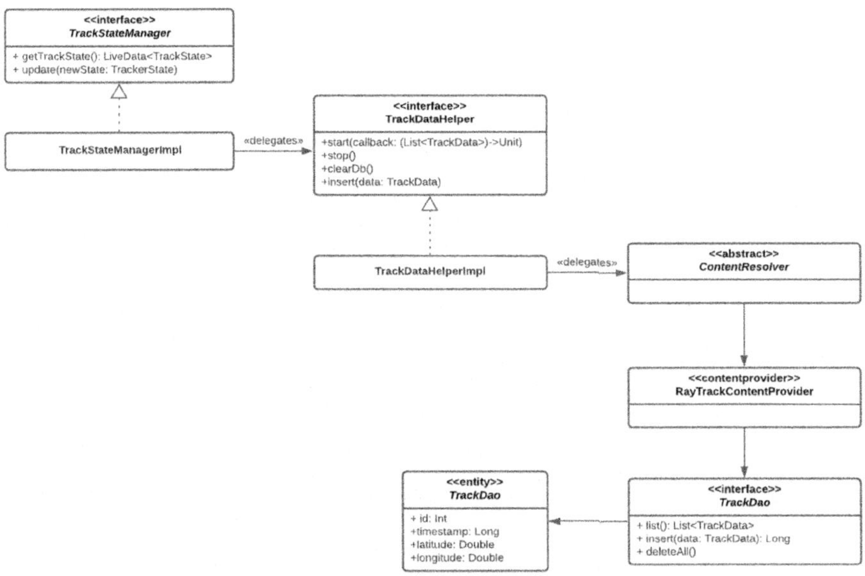

Figure 18.6 — RayTrack persistence

This diagram explains some interesting points:

1. `TrackStateManager` is the abstraction of the object responsible for maintaining `Tracker`'s state. This is the one that tells you if `Tracker` is running and what the user's current location is.
2. `TrackerStateManagerImpl` is the `TrackStateManager` implementation. Every time it receives a new `TrackState`, it delegates the persistence of the related `TrackData` to a `TrackDataHelper`.
3. `TrackDataHelper` is the abstraction of the object responsible for `TrackData`'s persistence.
4. `TrackDataHelperImpl` is the `TrackDataHelper` implementation that uses `ContentResolver` to persist the data into a `ContentProvider` in `RayTrackContentProvider`.
5. `RayTrackContentProvider` delegates the persistence operation to a `TrackDao` you define using the architecture component **Room**.

Open **RayTrackContentProvider.kt** in **repository.contentprovider** and notice how you only need to manage the dependency on the Room database:

```
class RayTrackContentProvider : ContentProvider(),
CoroutineScope {
  // ...
  private lateinit var trackDatabase: TrackDatabase
  private lateinit var trackDao: TrackDao

  override fun onCreate(): Boolean {
    trackDatabase = getRoomDatabase()
    trackDao = trackDatabase.trackDao()
    return true
  }

  private fun getRoomDatabase(): TrackDatabase = // HERE
      Room.databaseBuilder(
          context!!,
          TrackDatabase::class.java,
          Config.DB.DB_NAME
      ).fallbackToDestructiveMigration().build()
  // ...
}
```

At the moment, the relationship is a **composition** because you create the `TrackDatabase` instance in `RayTrackContentProvider` directly.

It would be nice to remove `getRoomDatabase()` and inject `TrackDatabase` directly using Hilt. You'll see how to do that next.

Creating a custom @EntryPoint

As you learned, Hilt doesn't support `ContentProviders` as a predefined `@AndroidEntryPoint` — but it gives you tools to work around that. That's what you'll do for `RayTrackContentProvider`.

> **Note**: In this case, you just need to inject `TrackDatabase`. This is a component that lives as long as the app, so it's in `ApplicationComponent`.

In this case, you need to:

1. Add the binding for `TrackDatabase` in the proper `@Component`.
2. Define an `@EntryPoint` that declares `TrackDatabase` as an object you can access from an unsupported component.
3. Access and use the object `@EntryPoint` exports in `RayTrackContentProvider`.

Adding bindings

To start, open **TrackDBModule.kt** in **di** and add:

```
@Module
@InstallIn(ApplicationComponent::class)
object TrackDBModule {

  @Provides
  fun provideTrackDatabase( // HERE
      @ApplicationContext context: Context
  ): TrackDatabase =
      Room.databaseBuilder(
          context,
          TrackDatabase::class.java,
          Config.DB.DB_NAME
      ).build()
  // ...
}
```

Here, the `TrackDBModule` installs bindings into `ApplicationComponent`. You're just providing `TrackDatabase` by using code similar to the one you had in `RayTrackContentProvider`.

Now, `TrackDatabase` is in the dependency graph for the app. You need to use it from `RayTrackContentProvider`.

Defining an entry point

Next, open **RayTrackContentProvider.kt** in **repository.contentprovider** and add the following code:

```
class RayTrackContentProvider : ContentProvider(),
CoroutineScope {

  @EntryPoint // 1
  @InstallIn(ApplicationComponent::class) // 2
  interface ContentProviderEntryPoint {

    fun trackDatabase(): TrackDatabase // 3
  }
  // ...
}
```

This is the definition of the `ContentProviderEntryPoint` interface that declares what `RayTrackContentProvider` needs from RayTrack's existing dependency graph. In this code, you used:

1. `@EntryPoint` to tell Hilt, and then Dagger, that this is the interface you want your custom component to use to access objects in the dependency graph.
2. `@InstallIn(ApplicationComponent::class)` to make the `@EntryPoint` Hilt creates for you as part of `ApplicationComponent`.
3. `trackDatabase()` to tell Hilt, and then Dagger, that the object you need is `TrackDatabase`.

Accessing TrackDatabase

Finally, you need to access `TrackDatabase` in `RayTrackContentProvider`. In **RayTrackContentProvider.kt** in **repository.contentprovider**, replace the existing `getRoomDatabase()` with:

```
  private fun getRoomDatabase(): TrackDatabase {
    val appContext = context?.applicationContext ?: throw
IllegalStateException() // 1
    val hiltEntryPoint =
        EntryPointAccessors.fromApplication( // 2
            appContext,
            ContentProviderEntryPoint::class.java) // 3
    return hiltEntryPoint.trackDatabase() // 4
  }
```

In this code, you:

1. Access `ApplicationContext`, throwing an exception if `Context` isn't available.
2. Use `fromApplication()` static function of `EntryPointAccessors` to access the reference to the `@EntryPoint` you defined in the same class.
3. Need to provide the class for `ContentProviderEntryPoint` to get an object of the right type.
4. Use `ContentProviderEntryPoint` to access the `TrackDatabase` reference.

It's important to note that `EntryPointAccessors` is a utility class that Hilt provides for cases where the bindings you need are in `@Components` that Hilt already supports. Other methods are:

- `EntryPointAccessors.fromActivity()`
- `EntryPointAccessors.fromFragment()`
- `EntryPointAccessors.fromView()`

In your case, you used `EntryPointAccessors.fromApplication()` because the binding for `TrackDatabase` is in `ApplicationComponent`.

> **Note**: To be picky, what you just did is not actually dependency injection. You still depend on the `EntryPointAccessors` and the injection **doesn't** come from outside. This is reminiscent of what happens with the **service locator** pattern.

It's important to say that, in `ContentProvider`'s case, you access a `TrackDatabase` object that has a binding in `ApplicationComponent`. As you'll see later, Hilt gives you the tools to create a custom `@Component` with a custom lifecycle. To do this properly, you need control over the creation and destruction of the custom `@Component` instance. This is something you don't have for `ContentProvider`. This isn't a problem, however, because you can assume that its lifecycle is the same as `ApplicationComponent`'s.

Great job! You managed to create a custom `@EntryPoint` for a `ContentProvider` you implemented in `RayTrackContentProvider`. Build and run and check that everything works as expected.

It's now time to see how `TrackData` displays onscreen.

Displaying the location data

RayTrack can display the location data on the screen. The diagram in Figure 18.7 describes the current architecture:

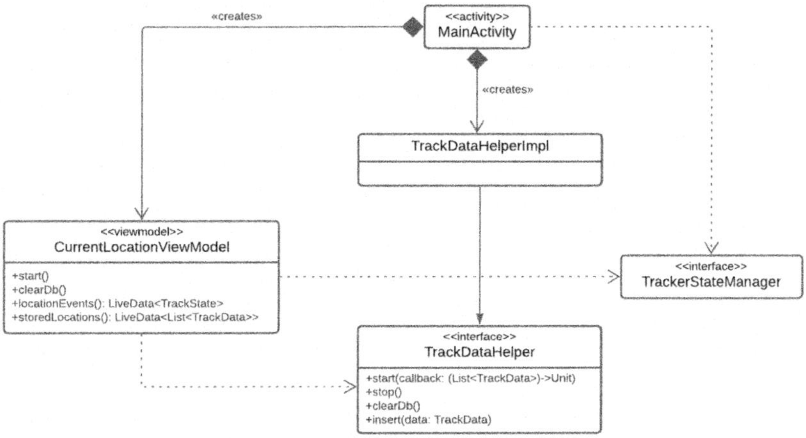

Figure 18.7 — Using CurrentLocationViewModel in MainActivity

In this diagram, you see some interesting points:

1. `MainActivity` depends on `TrackerStateManager`, `TrackDataHelperImpl` and `CurrentLocationViewModel`.
2. `CurrentLocationViewModel` depends on `TrackDataHelper` and `TrackerStateManager`.

The code in **MainActivity.kt** in **ui.main** shows something that the diagram already highlights:

```
@AndroidEntryPoint
class MainActivity : AppCompatActivity() {

  @Inject
  lateinit var trackerStateManager: TrackerStateManager // 2

  lateinit var locationViewModel: CurrentLocationViewModel

  override fun onCreate(savedInstanceState: Bundle?) {
    super.onCreate(savedInstanceState)
    setContentView(R.layout.activity_main)
    locationViewModel = CurrentLocationViewModel( // 1
        this.application,
        trackerStateManager,
        TrackDataHelperImpl(this) // 3
```

```
    )
    createNotificationChannel()
    startStopButton = findViewById(R.id.startStopTrackingButton)
    trackDataRecyclerView =
findViewById(R.id.location_recyclerview)
    initRecyclerView(trackDataRecyclerView)
    handleButtonState(locationViewModel.locationEvents().value)

handleTrackDataList(locationViewModel.storedLocations().value)
  }
  // ...
}
```

Here, `MainActivity`:

1. Creates the instance of `CurrentLocationViewModel`. As you learned in the first chapter of this book, this is a **composition relationship**, which you know isn't the best.
2. Depends on `TrackerStateManager` because `CurrentLocationViewModel` constructor needs it.
3. Creates an instance of `TrackDataHelperImpl` as the implementation of `TrackDataHelper` to pass to `CurrentLocationViewModel`.

There's definitely room for improvement here.

Your goal now is to inject `CurrentLocationViewModel` into `MainActivity`, as you do with other components. Hilt provides a new library to accomplish this. You just need to:

1. Add the dependency to the Hilt `ViewModel` support library.
2. Annotate your `ViewModel` implementation with `@ViewModelInject`.
3. Inject your `ViewModel` using `ViewModelProvider` or the `viewModels()` extension.

Now, you can migrate and replace the **composition relationship** with a simple dependency.

Adding VieModel support for Hilt

To add `ViewModel` support for Hilt, you need to extend the annotation processor. Open **build.gradle** for **app** and add the following dependencies:

```
// ...
dependencies {
  // ...
  // ViewModel Hilt support
  implementation "androidx.hilt:hilt-lifecycle-viewmodel:
$viewmodel_hilt_version" // 1
  kapt "androidx.hilt:hilt-compiler:$viewmodel_hilt_version" //
2
  // ...
}
```

> **Note**: `viewmodel_hilt_version` is already defined in **versions.gradle**. The current value is `1.0.0-alpha02` but you can update it if you need to.

Here, you just add the:

1. Dependency to the **hilt-lifecycle-viewmodel** library.
2. Extension to the annotation processor.

Now, sync Gradle for your project and you're ready to use `@ViewModelInject` in your code.

Using @ViewModelInject in your ViewModel implementation

Open **CurrentLocationViewModel.kt** in **ui.main** and look at the following header:

```
@ExperimentalCoroutinesApi
class CurrentLocationViewModel(
    application: Application,
    private val trackerStateManager: TrackerStateManager,
    private val trackDataHelper: TrackDataHelper
) : AndroidViewModel(application) {
  // ...
}
```

This defines all the `CurrentLocationViewModel` dependencies. Now, change it to the following:

```
@ExperimentalCoroutinesApi
class CurrentLocationViewModel @ViewModelInject constructor( //
HERE
    application: Application,
    private val trackerStateManager: TrackerStateManager,
    private val trackDataHelper: TrackDataHelper
) : AndroidViewModel(application) {
  // ...
}
```

Here, you just added `@ViewModelInject` to the primary constructor. In your case, all the parameters are already in the dependency graph for the app so you won't get any complaints when you build.

Injecting your ViewModel implementation in MainActivity

For your final step, you need to improve `MainActivity`. Open **MainActivity.kt** in **ui.main** and replace it with:

```
@ExperimentalCoroutinesApi
@AndroidEntryPoint
class MainActivity : AppCompatActivity() {

  //@Inject // REMOVE  1
  //lateinit var trackerStateManager: TrackerStateManager

  val locationViewModel: CurrentLocationViewModel by
viewModels() // 2

  private lateinit var trackListAdapter: TrackListAdapter
  private lateinit var trackDataRecyclerView: RecyclerView
  private lateinit var startStopButton: Button

  override fun onCreate(savedInstanceState: Bundle?) {
    super.onCreate(savedInstanceState)
    setContentView(R.layout.activity_main)
    /* // REMOVE 2
    locationViewModel = CurrentLocationViewModel(
        this.application,
        trackerStateManager,
        TrackDataHelperImpl(this) // 2
    )
     */
    createNotificationChannel()
    startStopButton = findViewById(R.id.startStopTrackingButton)
    trackDataRecyclerView =
findViewById(R.id.location_recyclerview)
```

```
    initRecyclerView(trackDataRecyclerView)
    handleButtonState(locationViewModel.locationEvents().value)

handleTrackDataList(locationViewModel.storedLocations().value)
  }

   // ...
}
```

Here, you:

1. Removed the trackerStateManager injection because you don't need it anymore. Hilt and Dagger will inject it in CurrentLocationViewModel for you.
2. Deleted the code to create CurrentLocationViewModel. This includes the creation of TrackDataHelperImpl, which Hilt and Dagger will also inject in CurrentLocationViewModel.
3. Used Kotlin delegation with viewModels(). It's smart enough to understand what locationViewModel's type is, so it knows which ViewModel to inject.

Now, build and run to check that everything works. The diagram in Figure 18.8 gives you a useful description of what you just did:

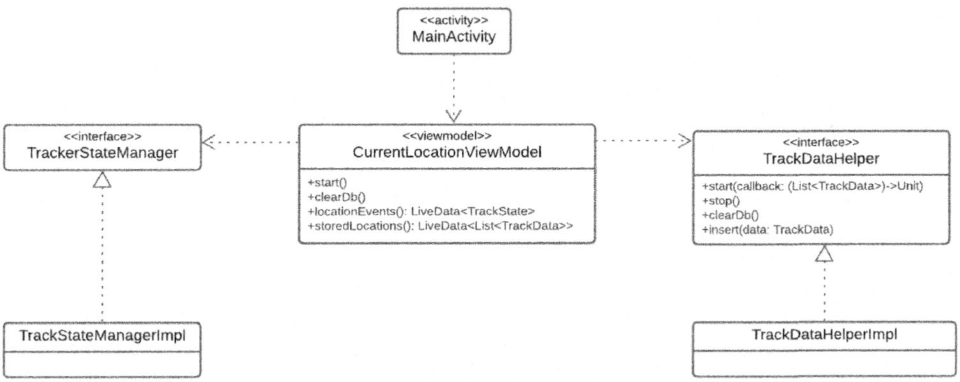

Figure 18.8 — Injecting CurrentLocationViewModel in MainActivity

As you can see, this is much better because:

1. MainActivity only depends on CurrentLocationViewModel.
2. CurrentLocationViewModel depends on the TrackerStateManager and TrackDataHelper abstractions.

Great job! You just removed all the **composition dependencies** and replaced them with **loosely coupled** dependencies.

Creating a custom @Component with @DefineComponent

Earlier, you learned that Hilt doesn't support all the Android standard components as `@AndroidEntryPoints`. That's why you had to use `@EntryPoint` with `RayTrackContentProvider`. In that case, you wanted to inject `TrackDatabase`, which is an object in `ApplicationComponent`, with `@Singleton` — or your alias, `@ApplicationContext` — scope.

However, Hilt provides the APIs to create your own `@Component` with a specific `@Scope` and its own lifecycle. It's worth mentioning that this is not something you should do very often because the existing `@Components` already cover most of the use cases.

A possible example is the **logged state** for a user in an app. You might have objects that need to be there only when the user is logged in to the app, and which you should remove if the user isn't logged in.

In **RayTrack**'s case, you'll define a new `@Component` for objects that need to exist only when the **Tracker** is running and there's something to display. This means that the `@Component` should exist only when there's an `Activity` to display locations from a running `Tracker`.

The steps you need to follow are:

1. Create a custom `@Scope`.
2. Create a custom `@Component` using `@DefineComponent`.
3. Add a `@DefineComponent.Builder`.
4. Manage the lifecycle for the `@DefineComponent`.
5. Add bindings to the custom `@Component` with `@EntryPoint`.
6. Use the custom `@Component` in your code.

It's time to dive in.

Creating a custom @Scope

Each `@Component` Hilt supports has a specific `@Scope`, so the custom `@Component` you'll create needs one as well. You already know how to do this. Just create a new package named **custom** in **di** and, inside, add a new file named **TrackRunningScoped.kt** with the following code:

```
@Scope
@MustBeDocumented
@Retention(AnnotationRetention.RUNTIME)
annotation class TrackRunningScoped
```

This is nothing different from what you did for other custom `@Scopes` in the previous chapters.

Creating a custom @Component using @DefineComponent

The next step is to create the custom `@Component`. In the same **di.custom** package, create a new file named **TrackRunningComponent.kt** and add the following code:

```
@DefineComponent(parent = ActivityComponent::class) // 1
@TrackRunningScoped // 2
interface TrackRunningComponent
```

In these few lines, there are some important things to note. Here, you use:

1. `@DefineComponent` to add a new `@Component` to the ones Hilt supports. Its **parent** attribute is fundamental because it allows you to choose **where** in the existing hierarchy to add your `@Component`. In this case, you're adding `TrackRunningComponent` as a child of `ActivityComponent`. You're extending the `@Component` hierarchy, as shown in Figure 18.9.

2. `@TrackRunningScoped` as the `@Scope` that binds objects to the lifecycle of `TrackRunningComponent`.

Extending the hierachy:

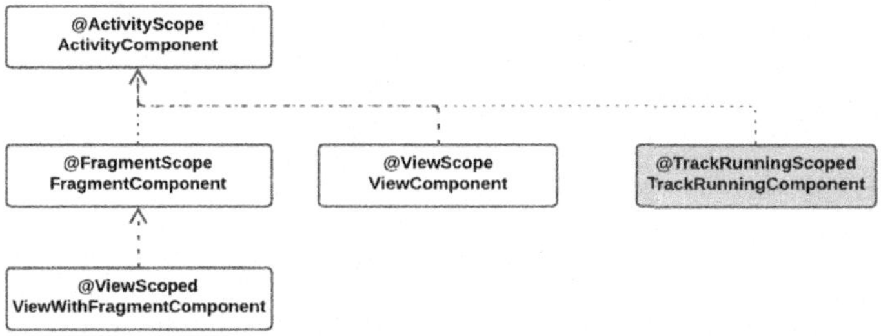

Figure 18.9 — Custom Component Hierarchy

Now, because you're responsible for creating and destroying the `TrackRunningComponent` implementation, Hilt requires you to provide a `Builder` for it.

Adding a @DefineComponent.Builder

Hilt requires you to manage the lifecycle of the custom `@Component` and wants you to provide a `Builder` to use to create the `@Component` instance. To do this, open **TrackRunningComponent.kt** and add the following code:

```
@DefineComponent(parent = ActivityComponent::class)
@TrackRunningScoped
interface TrackRunningComponent {

  @DefineComponent.Builder // 1
  interface Builder {
    fun sessionId(@BindsInstance sessionId: Long): Builder // 2
    fun build(): TrackRunningComponent // 3
  }
}
```

In this code, you:

1. Use `@DefineComponent.Builder` to define the abstraction of the `Builder` you'll use to create the specific `TrackRunningComponent` instance.

2. Provide an object that will be part of the `@TrackRunningComponent` dependency graph. In this case, it's a simple `Long` representing the concept of session. This is just an example. In your `@DefineComponent.Builder`, you might provide more objects, or none at all.

3. Define a `build()` that must have `TrackRunningComponent` as the return type. It's similar to `@Component.Builder` and `@Subcomponent.Builder`, which you learned about in previous chapters.

Now, you've created the `TrackRunningComponent` custom `@Component` with its own `@TrackRunningScoped`. For your next step, you need a way to manage its lifecycle.

Managing @DefineComponent's lifecycle

What differentiates each `@Component` from the others is its lifecycle. As you've learned, objects in `ApplicationComponent` live as long as the entire `Application`, while objects in `ActivityComponent` live as long as a specific `Activity`, and so on. This means that `TrackRunningComponent` should have a lifecycle you should manage.

In this case, you want to create `TrackRunningComponent` when `Tracker` is running and destroy it when it isn't running. To do this, you need:

1. An object that knows when to create and destroy the instance of `TrackRunningComponent`. You'll call this object **TrackRunningComponentManager**.
2. A `@Component` with a lifecycle longer than `TrackRunningComponent` that contains the `TrackRunningComponentManager` and uses it to create and destroy the custom `@Component`.

To do this, create a new file named **TrackRunningComponentManager.kt** in **di.custom** and add the following code:

```
@ActivityScoped // 1
class TrackRunningComponentManager @Inject constructor(
    private val trackRunnningBuilder:
TrackRunningComponent.Builder // 2
) {

  var trackRunningComponent: TrackRunningComponent? = null // 3

  fun startWith(sessionId: Long) { // 4
    if (trackRunningComponent == null) {
      trackRunningComponent = trackRunnningBuilder
          .sessionId(sessionId)
          .build()
    }
  }

  fun stop() {
    if (trackRunningComponent != null) {
      trackRunningComponent = null // 5
    }
  }
}
```

This code is very simple. In it, you:

1. Use `@ActivityScoped` to bind the lifecycle of `TrackRunningComponentManager` to `Activity`'s lifecycle. This needs to be the one you specify as `parent` in the `TrackRunningComponent` definition.
2. Inject the reference to `TrackRunningComponent.Builder`.
3. Define `trackRunningComponent`, which will contain the reference to the current `TrackRunningComponent` implementation instance.
4. Provide `startWith()` when you use `TrackRunningComponent.Builder`, which creates the `TrackRunningComponent` instance to store in `trackRunningComponent`.
5. Provide `stop()` to reset `TrackRunningComponent`.

You also add checks to avoid creating unnecessary `TrackRunningComponent` instances if you invoke `startWith()` multiple times.

Now, you need a place to put `TrackRunningComponentManager` and bind it to `TrackerState`. You'll use `MainActivity` for this. Open **MainActivity.kt** in **ui.main** and change it to:

```
@ExperimentalCoroutinesApi
@AndroidEntryPoint
class MainActivity : AppCompatActivity() {
  // ...
  @Inject
  lateinit var trackRunningComponentManager:
TrackRunningComponentManager // 1

  private fun handleButtonState(newState: TrackerState?) {
    with(startStopButton) {
      if (newState is TrackerRunning) {

trackRunningComponentManager.startWith(System.currentTimeMillis(
)) // 2
        text = getString(R.string.stop_tracking)
        setOnClickListener {
          stopService(Intent(this@MainActivity,
TrackingService::class.java))
        }
      } else {
        trackRunningComponentManager.stop() // 3
        text = getString(R.string.start_tracking)
        setOnClickListener {
          startService(Intent(this@MainActivity,
TrackingService::class.java))
        }
```

```
        }
      }
    }

    override fun onStop() {
      super.onStop()
      trackRunningComponentManager.stop() // 3
    }
    // ...
  }
```

You want to create `TrackRunningComponent` only when `Track` is running and an `Activity` wants to display some data. Because of this, you:

1. Inject `TrackRunningComponentManager` in `trackRunningComponentManager`.
2. When `Tracker` is running, you invoke `startWith()` on `trackRunningComponentManager`. You use `System.currentTimeMillis()` as the value for the `sessionId`.
3. When `Tracker` isn't running, you invoke `stop()` on `trackRunningComponentManager`.

Now, `TrackRunningComponent` is there only when you actually need it and removed when you don't. You created a place with a specific lifecycle where you might want to put objects you'll use only when `Track` is running and there's an `Activity` to display the locations.

Coming up, you'll see an example of how to use it.

Adding bindings to the custom @Component with @EntryPoint

For an example of a `TrackRunningScoped` object, think of a simple `Logger`.

> **Note**: The goal here is to show how bindings in custom `@Components` work. The specific object doesn't really matter.

Create a new package named **logging** and create a new file, **HiltLogger.kt**, with the following code:

```
@TrackRunningScoped // 1
class HiltLogger @Inject constructor() {
```

```
    fun log(message: String) {
      Log.d("HILT_LOGGING", "$this -> $message") // 2
    }
  }
```

This class:

1. Has `@TrackRunningScoped` scope.
2. Prints log messages with information about the instance.

Now, create a new file named **HiltLoggerEntryPoint.kt** in the same package with the following code:

```
@EntryPoint
@InstallIn(TrackRunningComponent::class) // HERE
interface HiltLoggerEntryPoint {

  fun logger(): HiltLogger
}
```

You already know how this code works. In this case, the only difference from the one you implemented above is that you're installing the binding into `TrackRunningComponent`. This means you can't use `EntryPointAccessors` because `TrackRunningComponent` isn't a `@Component` for an Android standard component.

Don't worry, Hilt provides an API for this. You'll see how to use it next.

Using the custom @Component in your code

Your final step is to use `HiltLogger` in `MainActivity`. Open **MainActivity.kt** in **ui.main** and apply the following change:

```
@ExperimentalCoroutinesApi
@AndroidEntryPoint
class MainActivity : AppCompatActivity() {
  // ...
  private fun handleButtonState(newState: TrackerState?) {
    with(startStopButton) {
      if (newState is TrackerRunning) {
        with(trackRunningComponentManager) {
          startWith(System.currentTimeMillis())
          with(newState.location) {
            EntryPoints.get( // HERE
                trackRunningComponent,
HiltLoggerEntryPoint::class.java
            ).logger().log("Lat: $latitude Long: $longitude")
          }
```

```
        }
        text = getString(R.string.stop_tracking)
        setOnClickListener {
          stopService(Intent(this@MainActivity,
TrackingService::class.java))
        }
      } else {
        // ...
      }
    }
  }
  // ...
}
```

Here, Hilt provides `EntryPoints` with a `get()` that has `TrackRunningComponent` as its first parameter and `@EntryPoint`'s type as its second parameter. This allows you to retrieve the reference to `HiltLogger` from the dependency graph for the `@Component` it belongs to — `TrackRunningComponent`.

Build and run now and check that everything works as expected.

To check the lifecycle for `TrackRunningComponent`, run the following steps:

1. Build and run.
2. Start the tracking.
3. Stop the tracking after a few seconds.
4. Start the tracking again.
5. Stop the tracking again after a few seconds.
6. Check Logcat and filter it using `HILT_LOGGING`.

You'll have something like this:

```
D/HILT_LOGGING: com...HiltLogger@32c174b -> Lat: 41.96721 Long:
-94.39422 // FIRST
D/HILT_LOGGING: com...HiltLogger@32c174b -> Lat: 41.96721 Long:
-94.39422
D/HILT_LOGGING: com...HiltLogger@32c174b -> Lat: 41.96721 Long:
-94.39422
D/HILT_LOGGING: com...HiltLogger@32c174b -> Lat: 41.96721 Long:
-94.39422
D/HILT_LOGGING: com...HiltLogger@2c5fa3a -> Lat: 41.96721 Long:
-94.39422 // SECOND
D/HILT_LOGGING: com...HiltLogger@2c5fa3a -> Lat: 41.96721 Long:
-94.39422
D/HILT_LOGGING: com...HiltLogger@2c5fa3a -> Lat: 41.96721 Long:
```

```
-94.39422
```

In this case, the `HiltLogger` instance during the first tracking was `@32c174b`. During the second, it was `@2c5fa3a`. That means that a new instance of `HiltLogger` was created at every session, as expected.

Key points

- Hilt currently doesn't support all the Standard Android Components as `@AndroidEntryPoints`.
- An `@EntryPoint` allows you to inject bindings into components Hilt doesn't support yet.
- You can create a custom `@Component` using `@DefineComponent`.
- `@DefineComponent` needs a parent that allows you to extend the default Hilt `@Component` hierarchy.
- Hilt provides a library to help you use dependency injection with `ViewModel`.

Congrats! In this chapter, you used some advanced Hilt APIs. You learned how to create custom `@Components` that extend the existing Hilt `@Component` hierarchy. You also learned how to use the libraries Hilt provides to manage dependency injection with `ViewModel`.

But Hilt can do even more. In the next chapter, you'll learn everything you need to know about testing. See you there!

Chapter 19: Testing With Hilt

By Massimo Carli

In Chapter 17, "Hilt — Dagger Made Easy", you learned that one of Hilt's main goals is to make testing easier. In the first chapter, you also learned that simplifying testing is also one of the main reasons to use **dependency injection**.

Using **constructor injection**, you can create instances of classes to test, then pass mocks or fakes directly to them as their primary constructor parameters. So where does Hilt come in? How does it make tests easier to implement and run?

To understand this, think about what Dagger and Hilt actually are. Dagger gives you a declarative way to define the dependency graph for a given app. Using `@Modules` and `@Components`, you define which objects to create, what their lifecycles are and how they depend upon one other.

Hilt makes things easier with a predefined set of `@Components` and `@Scopes`. In particular, using `@HiltAndroidApp`, you define the main `@EntryPoint` for the app bound to the `Application` lifecycle. You do the same with `ActivityComponent`, `ServiceComponent` and others you met in the previous chapters. In general, you define a **dependency graph** containing the instances of classes you inject.

Here's the point. The objects you use when you run a test are, in most cases, not the same objects you use when running the app. The dependency graph isn't the same.

Hilt gives you an easy way to decide which objects are in the dependency graph for the app and which objects are there for the tests.

In this chapter, you'll learn how Hilt helps you implement tests for your app. In particular, you'll see how to use Hilt to run:

- Robolectric UI tests
- Instrumentation tests

Hilt only supports Robolectric tests and instrumentation tests because with constructor injection, it's easy to implement unit tests without Dagger. You'll see how shortly.

To learn how to implement tests with Hilt, you'll work on the **RandomFunNumber** app. This simple app lets you push a button to get a random number and some interesting facts about that number. It's also perfect for learning about testing with Hilt.

> **Note**: As you know, Hilt is still in alpha version and so are its testing libraries. During this chapter, you'll implement some configuration caveats that need to be there to make the tests run successfully. Some of these solve bugs in the library that might be resolved by the time you read this chapter.

The RandomFunNumber app

In this chapter, you'll implement tests for RandomFunNumber. To start, use Android Studio to open the **RandomFunNumber** project from the **starter** folder in this chapter's materials. When you open the project, you'll see the structure in Figure 19.1:

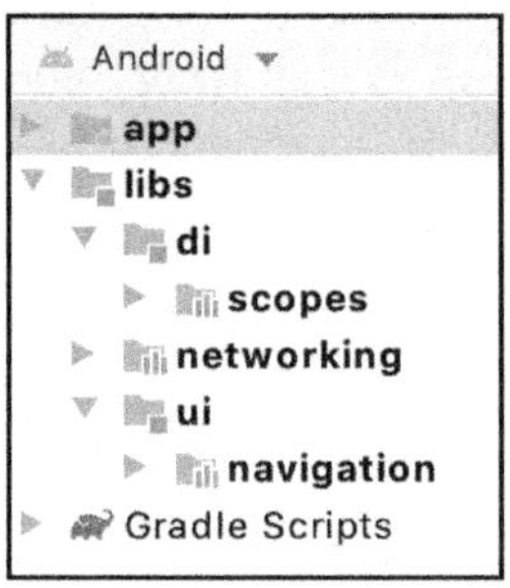

Figure 19.1 — Initial Project Structure

As you can see, this app uses some of the modules you already used in the previous chapters.

Build and run to see the screen in Figure 19.2:

Figure 19.2 — Initial Empty Screen

Click the **RANDOM NUMBER** button and you'll see a screen like in Figure 19.3:

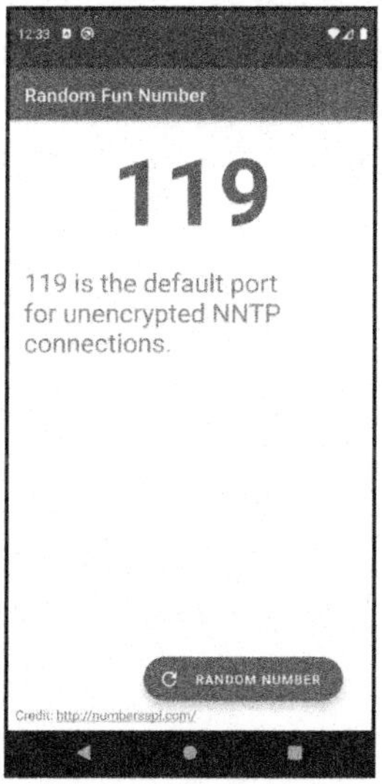

Figure 19.3 — A possible result

The output in your case is probably different because, when you press the button, you generate a random value and send a request to **numbersapi.com** to get some useful information about it. Every time you click the button, you'll get a different number and a different description.

This is a very simple app that contains everything you need to learn how to write tests using the tools and API Hilt provides. Before doing that, however, you'll learn about RandomFunNumber's:

- Architecture
- Hilt configuration

After you understand how the app works, you'll start writing tests.

RandomFunNumber's architecture

The class diagram in Figure 19.4 gives you a high-level description of RandomFunNumber's main components:

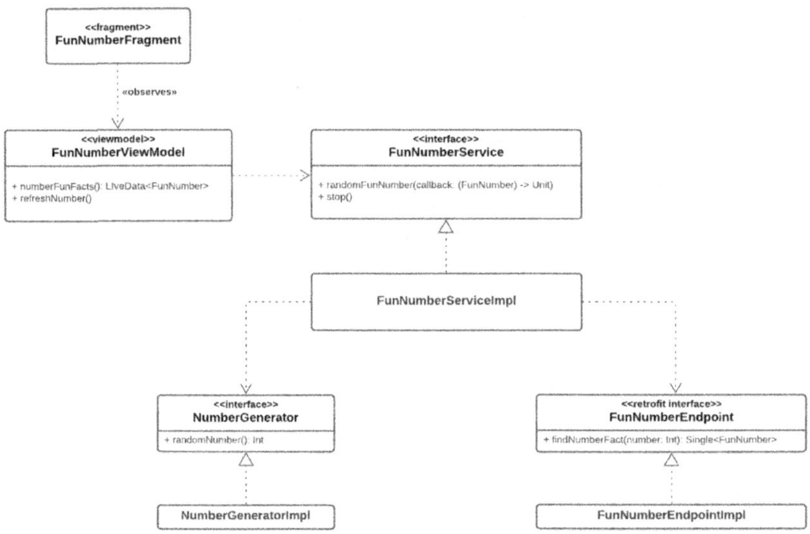

Figure 19.4 — RandomFunNumber class diagram

In this diagram, you see the components `FunNumberFragment` uses to implement the feature that gets the random value and fetches the text from the **numbersapi.com** service.

As you see:

1. `FunNumberFragment` delegates all the logic to a **ViewModel** you implemented in `FunNumberViewModel`.
2. `FunNumberViewModel` delegates the logic to a `FunNumberService` implementation.

3. `FunNumberServiceImpl` is the implementation of `FunNumberService` that uses a `NumberGenerator` to generate a random number, as well as the `FunNumberEndpoint` implementation **Retrofit** provides for the actual request to the server.

RandomFunNumber also contains:

- `SplashActivity` as the splash for the app.
- `MainActivity` as the container for `FunNumberFragment`.

Both use a `Navigation` implementation you find in **libs.ui.navigation**, which you already used in the app for the previous chapters.

Of course, RandomFunNumber uses Hilt. Next, you'll look at its configuration.

The Hilt configuration

RandomFunNumber only contains a few components. It has a relatively simple Hilt configuration, which you can see in the diagram in Figure 19.5:

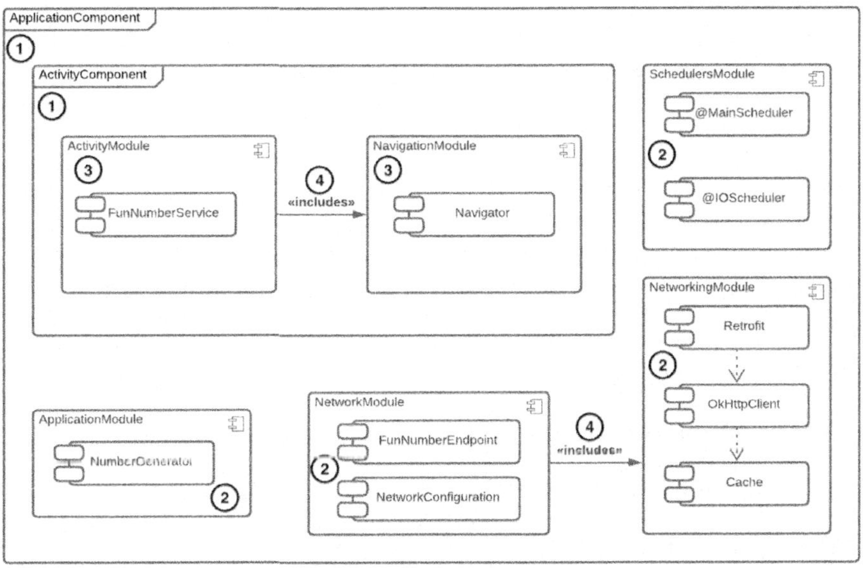

Figure 19.5 — RandomFunNumber dependency diagram

The diagram contains the `@Modules` and `@Components` for RandomFunNumber. In particular:

1. You use the predefined `ApplicationComponent` and `ActivityComponent`.
2. `ApplicationComponent` contains bindings from four different `@Modules`: `ApplicationModule`, `NetworkModule`, `NetworkingModule` and `SchedulersModule`.
3. `ActivityComponent` contains bindings from two different `@Modules`: `ActivityModule` and `NavigationModule`.
4. You include `NavigationModule` and `NetworkingModule` because their definitions are in different modules.

The code in the **starter project** in the materials for this chapter contains quite a few `@Modules`. One reason is **modularization**. For instance, `NetworkingModule` and `NavigationModule` are in the **libs.networking** and **libs.ui.navigation** modules.

Another reason is **testing**. As you'll see later, you'll replace **threading** during tests. That's why the `Scheduler`'s bindings are in `SchedulersModule` and not directly in `ApplicationModule`.

Now, it's time to implement the tests for RandomFunNumber.

Implementing RandomFunNumber's tests

You have the background you need to use RandomFunNumber to practice implementing tests with the utilities Hilt provides. In the following paragraphs, you'll learn how to:

- Structure your project for testing.
- Leverage constructor injection to implement a unit test.
- Use Robolectric and Hilt for UI testing.
- Implement UI instrumentation tests with Hilt and **Espresso**.

Keep in mind that most of the configurations are already in the starter project in the material for this chapter.

Defining the project structure for testing

Use Android Studio to open the starter project from the materials for this chapter. Next, select **Project View** and look at the **build types** for the **app** module in Figure 19.6:

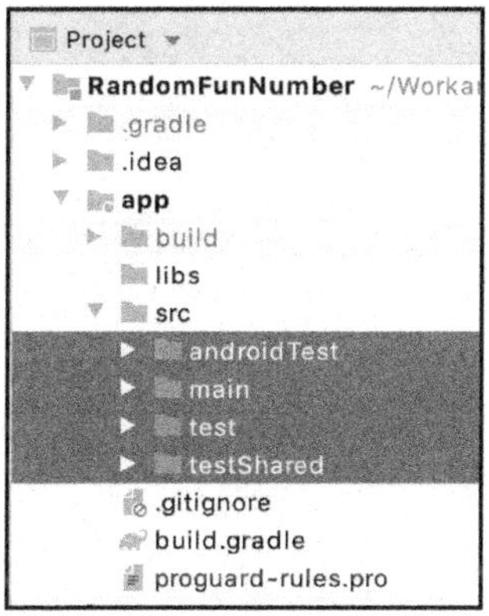

Figure 19.6 — App module build types

Highlighted in Figure 19.6, you have:

- **androidTest** for instrumentation tests.
- **main** for the main app code.
- **test** for unit and Robolectric tests.
- **testShared** for some code in common between **test** and **androidTest**.

You'll see each of these build types in detail in the following paragraphs. For the moment, just open **testShared** and look at its content:

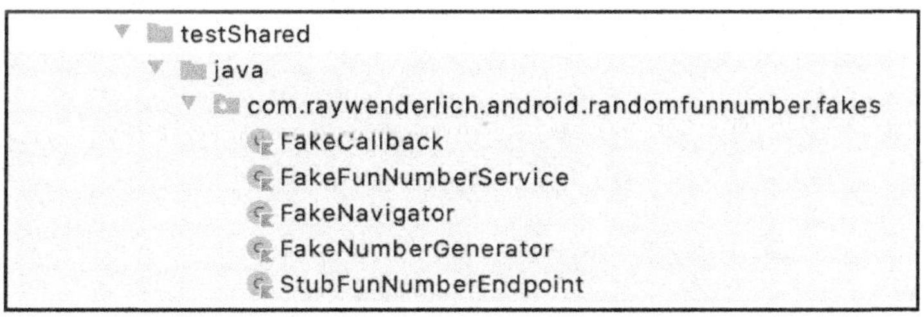

Figure 19.7 — Classes shared between tests

It contains some **fake**s and **stub**s you'll use in your tests.

> **Note**: If you want to learn more about fakes, mocks and stubs, Android Test-Driven Development by Tutorials (https://www.raywenderlich.com/books/android-test-driven-development-by-tutorials) is the right place for you.

Implementing unit tests with constructor injection

As you learned in the previous chapters of this book, **constructor injection** makes tests easier to write because you simply create an instance of the object to test and pass some fakes or stubs to it as parameters of its primary constructor.

With this kind of testing, there's not much benefit to using Dagger. To see this for yourself, you'll create a unit test for `FunNumberViewModel`.

Open **FunNumberViewModel.kt** in **ui.displaynumber** and click the class name, then press **Control-Enter**. This gives you the following pop-up:

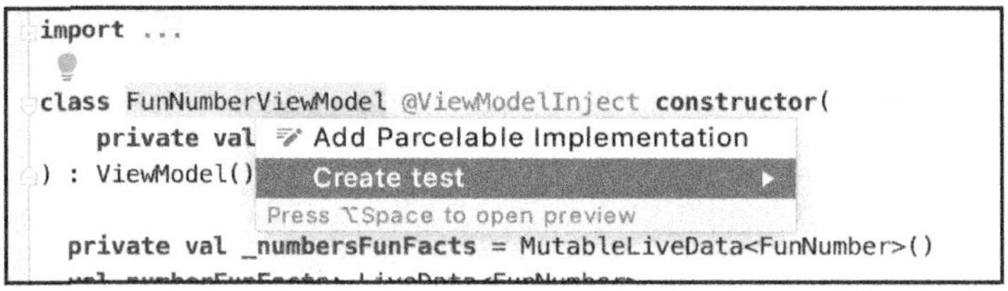

Figure 19.8 — Create a test for FunNumberViewModel

Select **Create test** and you'll end up with the dialog in Figure 19.9:

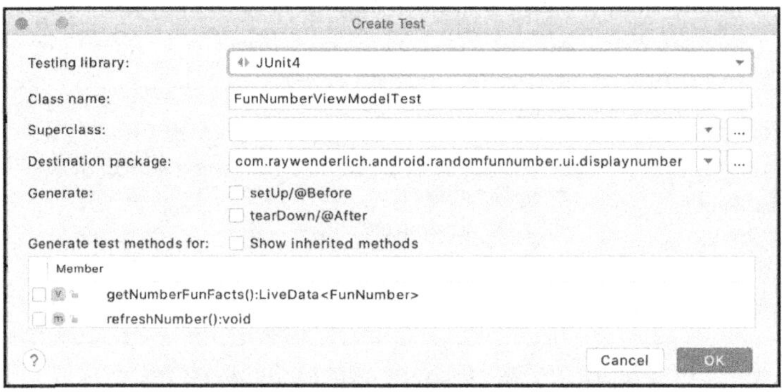

Figure 19.9 — Select the JUnit 4 option

Now, select **JUnit 4** for the testing library and click **OK** to get the screen in Figure 19.10:

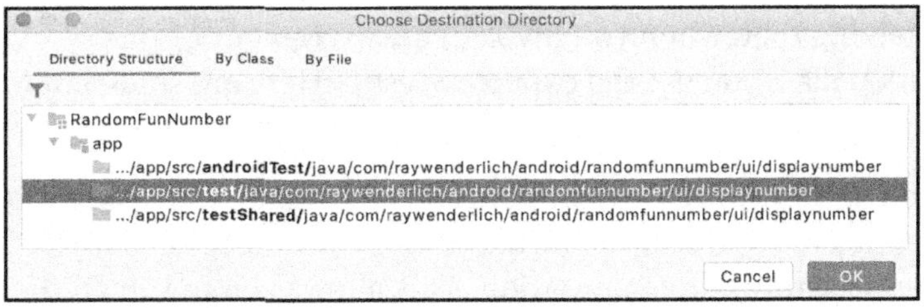

Figure 19.10 — Select the test building type

Select the **test** directory, as in Figure 19.10, and click **OK**. Android Studio will create a file with the following code:

```
class FunNumberViewModelTest {
}
```

Now, open the new **FunNumberViewModelTest.kt** and add the following code:

```
class FunNumberViewModelTest {

  @Rule
  @JvmField
  val instantExecutorRule = InstantTaskExecutorRule() // 1

  private lateinit var objectUnderTest: FunNumberViewModel // 2
  private lateinit var funNumberService: FakeFunNumberService //
3

  @Before
  fun setUp() {
    funNumberService = FakeFunNumberService()
    objectUnderTest = FunNumberViewModel(funNumberService) // 4
  }

  @Test
  fun `when refreshNumber invoked you observe FunNumber`() {
    val expectedFunNumber = FunNumber(
        88,
        "Testing Text",
        true,
        "default"
    )
    funNumberService.resultToReturn = expectedFunNumber
    objectUnderTest.refreshNumber() // 5
    val result =
objectUnderTest.numberFunFacts.getOrAwaitValue() // 6
    assertEquals(expectedFunNumber, result) // 7
```

```
    }
}
```

Here, you're testing that, when you invoke `refreshNumber()` on `FunNumberViewModel`, you get the expected result. Here are some important things to note:

1. As mentioned, threading is very important in general, especially when you work with `LiveData` or `Rx`. Here, you initialize `InstantTaskExecutorRule` to use `Scheduler`'s **instant** implementation. This allows you to run all the operations sequentially.

2. This is the property for the instance of the object to test. In this case, it's `FunNumberViewModel`.

3. `FunNumberViewModel` depends on `FunNumberService`. Here, you define the property that will contain the instance of the fake `FunNumberService`. Its code is in the **testShared** source folder.

4. In `@Before`, you initialize `FunNumberViewModel`, passing the fake `NumberService` implementation as a constructor parameter. This is the advantage of using **constructor injection**. You don't need Dagger here.

5. Here, you invoke `refreshNumber()` on the `FunNumberViewModel` instance you're testing. This uses the `FunNumberService` implementation you passed as a parameter.

6. `getOrAwaitValue()` is a utility extension function for `LiveData` that allows you to wait for the result. The source code is in **LiveDataTestUtil.kt** in the source folder for the **test** build type.

7. Finally, you check that your result is what you expected.

Now, run the test, selecting the´**Run 'FunNumberViewModelTest'** option shown in Figure 19.11:

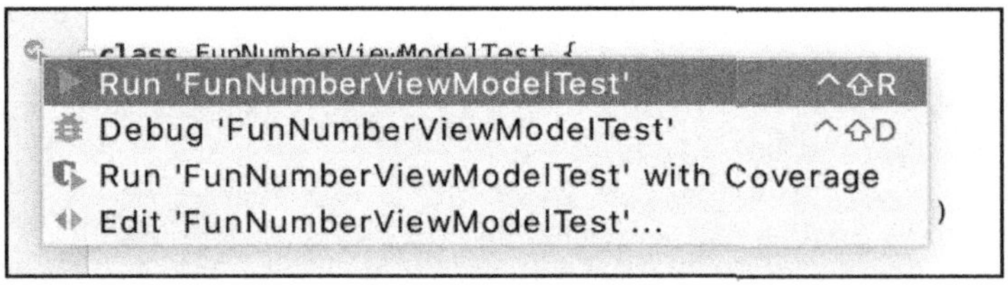

Figure 19.11 — Run FunNumberViewModelTest

The test runs successfully, as in Figure 19.12:

Figure 19.12 — FunNumberViewModelTest success

Aside from this specific test's functionality, there are three important things to note:

1. **Constructor injection** allows you to create the instance of the object under test by passing the reference to fakes or mocks as their primary constructor parameter.
2. You didn't use Dagger or Hilt at all.
3. There are no Android classes involved.

This is an example of the power of **dependency injection** — and, in particular, of **constructor injection**.

As mentioned above, `FunNumberViewModel` doesn't have any Android-specific dependencies. But how can you write tests that *do* involve Android-specific components, like `Activitys` and `Fragments`?

You have two options:

1. Use **Robolectric**.
2. Create an **instrumentation test**.

You're still working in the **test** build type, so it's time for Robolectric. :]

Using Robolectric & Hilt for UI tests

Robolectric (http://robolectric.org/) is a testing framework that lets you implement and run tests that depend on the Android environment without an actual implementation of the Android platform. This allows you to run UI tests on the JVM without creating instances of the Android emulator. In this way, tests run quickly and require fewer resources.

For your next step, you'll use Robolectric and Hilt to run tests for:

- MainActivity
- FunNumberFragment

Before the actual test implementation, however, you need to do some setup.

Installing the Hilt testing library for Robolectric

For your first step, you need to add the dependencies for Robolectric's Hilt testing library. Open **build.gradle** from **app** and add the following definition:

```
// ...
dependencies {
  // ...
  // Hilt for Robolectric tests.
  testImplementation "com.google.dagger:hilt-android-testing:
$hilt_version" // 1
  kaptTest "com.google.dagger:hilt-android-compiler:
$hilt_version" // 2
}
```

Here, you:

1. Add the dependency to use Hilt testing with Robolectric. This is a definition for the **test** build type.
2. Use `kaptTest` to install the **annotation processor** responsible for generating the testing code from the Hilt definition.

The version is the same as the main Hilt library's dependency has. Also, note how testing with Hilt requires you to install an annotation processor because it will have to generate some code.

Creating a MainActivity test with Robolectric & Hilt

Your first test will cover `MainActivity`. Open **MainActivity.kt** in the **ui** package of the **app** module and you'll see:

```
@AndroidEntryPoint // 1
class MainActivity : AppCompatActivity() {

  @Inject
  lateinit var navigator: Navigator // 2

  override fun onCreate(savedInstanceState: Bundle?) {
    super.onCreate(savedInstanceState)
    setContentView(R.layout.activity_main)
    if (savedInstanceState == null) {
      navigator.navigateTo( // 3
        FragmentDestination(FunNumberFragment(),
        R.id.anchor_point)
      )
    }
  }
}
```

This is a very simple `Activity` that:

1. Contains the `@AndroidEntryPoint` annotation that tags the `Activity` as a Hilt entry point.
2. Defines a `navigator` property you initialize using `@Inject`.
3. Uses `navigator` to display `FunNumberFragment`.

Next, you want to create a test that verifies that the navigator displays `FunNumberFragment` properly. Start by using the process shown in Figures 19.8-10, create a new **RoboMainActivityTest.kt** in the **test** build type.

Initially, your code looks like this:

```
class RoboMainActivityTest
```

Before you write the actual test, you need some initial configuration. Change the previous code to this:

```
@HiltAndroidTest // 1
@Config(application = HiltTestApplication::class) // 2
@RunWith(RobolectricTestRunner::class) // 3
class RoboMainActivityTest {

  @get:Rule
  var hiltAndroidRule = HiltAndroidRule(this) // 4

  @Before
  fun setUp() {
    hiltAndroidRule.inject() // 5
  }

  @Test
  fun whenMainActivityLaunchedNavigatorIsInvokedForFragment()
{ // 6
    assertTrue(true)
  }
}
```

This code contains a very important configuration you'll use in the following tests, as well. Here's what's going on:

1. You annotate the test with `@HiltAndroidTest`. This enables the Hilt annotation processor to generate the code to create the **dependency graph** for the test.
2. In **Main.kt** inside **app**, you used `@HiltAndroidApp` to tell Hilt which `Application` implementation to use. Now, you need to do the same thing for the tests. Hilt provides `HiltTestApplication` as the `Application` implementation for this purpose. Here, you use the Robolectric `@Config` annotation to do this, but you could get the same effect by editing **robolectric.properties**. You'll see how that works soon.
3. Due to bugs in the current library, you need to explicitly define `RobolectricTestRunner` as the `TestRunner` to use for running the tests in this file. You do this using `@RunWith`. If this bug has been fixed since the time of writing, you should remove this definition.

4. You create an instance of the `HiltAndroidRule` JUnit rule in `hiltAndroidRule`. This allows you to create and destroy the Hilt-provided dependency graph at each test execution.

5. You invoke `inject()` on `hiltAndroidRule` at the beginning of each test. As you'll see later, this injects objects from the Hilt test dependency graph into the test itself.

6. Define the function for the test in this file. At the moment, you're asserting something that you know is true, just to have something to run.

Before running this test, you need to open **robolectric.properties** from **resources** in the **test** build type. Its initial content is:

```
sdk=28
```

Robolectric requires this to avoid an annoying error on the API Level of the Android environment you're testing against. To avoid using what's at the previous point **2**, add the following line:

```
sdk=28
application=dagger.hilt.android.testing.HiltTestApplication #
HERE
```

Now, you can use Android Studio and run a successful test. Your next step is to implement the test.

Testing MainActivity with Robolectric & Hilt

In the previous section, you created an empty test to verify the Hilt configuration for Robolectric. Now, it's time to create the actual test.

To do this, you need to:

1. Configure the `ActivityScenario` API to launch `MainActivity`.
2. Replace the existing `Navigator` implementation with a **fake** one.
3. Write the actual test.

Configuring ActivityScenario

`ActivityScenario` is part of an API Google provides for testing `Activitys`. To use this, you need to add the following code to **RoboMainActivityTest.kt**, which you created earlier:

```
@HiltAndroidTest
@Config(application = HiltTestApplication::class)
@RunWith(RobolectricTestRunner::class)
class RoboMainActivityTest {

  @get:Rule(order = 0) // 2
  var hiltAndroidRule = HiltAndroidRule(this)

  @get:Rule(order = 1) // 2
  var activityScenarioRule: ActivityScenarioRule<MainActivity> =
      ActivityScenarioRule(MainActivity::class.java) // 1
  // ...
    @Test
  fun whenMainActivityLaunchedNavigatorIsInvokedForFragment() {
    activityScenarioRule.scenario // 3
  }
}
```

To use `ActivityScenario`, you need to:

1. Initialize a new JUnit Rule of type `ActivityScenarioRule<MainActivity>` in the `activityScenarioRule` property .
2. Use the `order` attribute for the `@get:Rule` annotation. You need this when you have more than one rule in the same file and you want to give them a specific execution order. `HiltAndroidRule` needs to be the first rule to run — setting `order = 0` allows you to ensure that it is.
3. Access the `scenario` property on the `activityScenarioRule` to launch the `Activity` you set as parameter type value in `ActivityScenarioRule<MainActivity>`. In this case, it's `MainActivity`.

Unfortunately, if you now run the test with Android Studio as you did before, you'll get the following error:

```
kotlin.UninitializedPropertyAccessException: lateinit property
navigator has not been initialized
```

Don't worry, this isn't your fault. :] This is a bug that, at the moment, prevents you from running this test from Android Studio.

Instead, just open a terminal and run the following command:

```
./gradlew testDebugUnitTest --tests "*.RoboMainActivityTest.*"
```

The test will successfully run.

It's an empty test, though. How can you test that `MainActivity` actually works? Look at its code and you see that `MainActivity` needs a `Navigator`.

Replacing the real Navigator with a fake

Now, you'll replace the actual `Navigator` implementation with a **fake** one. To achieve this, add the following code:

```
@HiltAndroidTest
@Config(application = HiltTestApplication::class)
@RunWith(RobolectricTestRunner::class)
@UninstallModules(ActivityModule::class) // 1
class RoboMainActivityTest {
  // ...
  @BindValue // 2
  @JvmField
  val navigator: Navigator = FakeNavigator() // 3

  @Test
  fun whenMainActivityLaunchedNavigatorIsInvokedForFragment() {
    activityScenarioRule.scenario
    val fakeNav = navigator as FakeNavigator
    assertNotNull(fakeNav.invokedWithDestination)
    assertTrue(fakeNav.invokedWithDestination is
FragmentDestination<*>) // 4
  }
}
```

This code contains everything you need to know about Hilt and testing. As you can see:

1. By using `@UninstallModules(ActivityModule::class)`, you're telling Hilt, and then Dagger, to literally **uninstall** all the bindings you defined in **ActivityModule.kt**. That file includes bindings for `NavigationModule`, adding one for the `FunNumberService` implementation. You don't actually need `FunNumberService` in this test, but you need to provide one to `Navigator`.

2. With `@BindValue`, you're binding an instance of `FakeNavigator` to the `Navigator` type. With this and the previous definitions, you've basically replaced the `Navigator` implementation in the **NavigationModule** module with the mock implementation.

3. `FakeNavigator` is a simple `Navigator` implementation that stores the reference to the `Destination` you use. The test consists of checking that you've used a `Destination` and that it's a `FragmentDestination`.

Now, run the test from the command line and check that it's successful.

Reviewing your achievements

Great! You implemented your first test using Hilt and Robolectric. You also learned that you can:

1. Use `HiltAndroidRule` to ask Hilt to generate a dependency graph to use when a test executes.

2. Uninstall the bindings you defined in one or more `@Modules` using `@UninstallModules`.

3. Replace one binding at a time using `@BindValue`.

Keep these points in mind because you'll use them many times in the following tests.

Implementing instrumented tests with Hilt & Espresso

In the previous section, you used **Robolectric** and **Hilt** to implement a UI test for `MainActivity`. Now, you'll try another option for testing with Hilt — running an instrumentation test with **Espresso**.

> **Note**: If you want to learn all about Espresso, Android Test-Driven Development by Tutorials (https://www.raywenderlich.com/books/android-test-driven-development-by-tutorials) is, again, a great resource.

> **Note**: In the **final** project in the materials for this chapter, you'll also find an instrumentation test for `MainActivity`. Implementing it is a useful exercise.

In this section, you'll create a more challenging test. This time, you'll test `FunNumberFragment`. Creating a test like this isn't obvious and it requires some preparation.

Usually, before you test a `Fragment`, you first launch an `Activity` as its container. With Hilt, the problem is that if the `Fragment` is an `@AndroidEntryPoint`, the same must be true for the container `Activity`. If you just use `ActivityScenario`, this doesn't happen automatically. You need to:

1. Add the testing Hilt dependencies for the instrumented test.
2. Create an `@AndroidEntryPoint` `Activity` to use as the container for the `Fragment` under test.
3. Implement a utility class to launch the `Fragment` under test into the Hilt-enabled `Activity`.
4. Create a custom `AndroidJUnitRunner` that uses `HiltTestApplication` instead of the one Android provides by default, then configure it in **build.gradle**.
5. Implement and run the instrumentation test.

It's important to do these tasks in sequence.

> **Note**: Don't worry if **FragmentTestutil.kt** in the **androidTest** build type doesn't compile at the moment. You'll fix it very soon.

Adding Hilt testing dependencies

To use the Hilt testing library in the instrumentation tests, you need to add the following definition to **build.gradle** in **app**:

```
// ...
dependencies {
  // Hilt for instrumented tests.
  androidTestImplementation "com.google.dagger:hilt-android-
testing:$hilt_version" // 1
  kaptAndroidTest "com.google.dagger:hilt-android-compiler:
$hilt_version" // 2
  // ...
}
```

In this case, you need to:

1. Add the dependency that lets you use Hilt testing in instrumentation tests. That's why the definition is for the **androidTest** build type.
2. Use `kaptAndroidTest` to install the annotation processor responsible for generating the testing code from the Hilt definition in instrumented tests.

Now, you're ready to use Hilt testing libraries in the instrumentation tests for RandomFunNumber.

Creating an Activity for testing

First, you need to create an empty `Activity` that uses `@AndroidEntryPoint`. Start by creating a folder for the **debug** build type at the same level as the existing ones. Create a **java** folder in it and add a package named **com.raywenderlich.android.randomfunnumber**. In that package, create a new file named **HiltActivityForTest.kt** and add the following code:

```
@AndroidEntryPoint // HERE
class HiltActivityForTest : AppCompatActivity()
```

Important here is the use of `@AndroidEntryPoint`, which Hilt requires for `Activitys` containing `@AndroidEntryPoint` `Fragments`. This is an `Activity` you need to launch from the instrumentation test.

To do this, create a file named **AndroidManifest.xml** in **debug** and add the following content:

```
<manifest xmlns:android="http://schemas.android.com/apk/res/
android"
  package="com.raywenderlich.android.randomfunnumber">

  <application>
    <activity
      android:name=".HiltActivityForTest"
      android:exported="false" />
  </application>
</manifest>
```

You'll end up with the file structure in Figure 19.13:

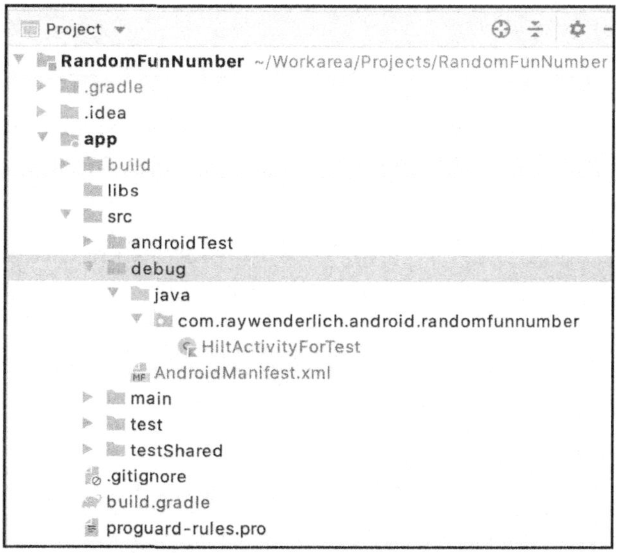

Figure 19.13 — Debug build type structure

Now, **FragmentTestutil.kt** in **androidTest** will successfully compile.

Implementing a utility to launch the Fragment

As mentioned earlier, you need a way to launch a `Fragment` using the `HiltActivityForTest` you implemented as its container.

> **Note**: Google already provides different versions of this utility in some Codelabs. They'll probably add it to a future release of the Hilt testing library.

Open **FragmentTestUtil.kt** in **util** in the **androidTest** build type and find the extension function with the following signature:

```
inline fun <reified T : Fragment> launchFragmentInHiltContainer(
    fragmentArgs: Bundle? = null,
    @StyleRes themeResId: Int =
R.style.FragmentScenarioEmptyFragmentActivityTheme,
    crossinline action: Fragment.() -> Unit = {}
) {
  // ...
}
```

The only thing you need to know is that you can now use `launchFragmentInHiltContainer()` to launch a `Fragment` that's an `@AndroidEntryPoint` for Hilt.

Implementing a custom AndroidJUnitRunner

As you learned when testing with Robolectric, you need to specify the `TestRunner` for your tests. To do this, you just need to create a custom `TestRunner` implementation.

Start by creating a new file named **HiltTestRunner.kt** in a new **runner** package in the **androidTest** build type and add the following code:

```
class HiltTestRunner : AndroidJUnitRunner() {

  override fun newApplication(
      cl: ClassLoader?,
      className: String?,
      context: Context?
  ): Application {
    return super.newApplication(
        cl,
        HiltTestApplication::class.java.name, // HERE
        context)
  }
}
```

Here, you override `newApplication()` by passing `HiltTestApplication::class.java.name` as the value for `Application` parameter.

Now, you need to set this as the default `TestRunner` implementation for instrumentation tests.

Open **build.gradle** and apply the following changes:

```
// ...
android {
  // ...
  defaultConfig {
    applicationId "com.raywenderlich.android.randomfunnumber"
    minSdkVersion 28
    targetSdkVersion 30
    versionCode 1
    versionName "1.0"
    testInstrumentationRunner
"com.raywenderlich.android.randomfunnumber.runner.HiltTestRunner
" // HERE
  }
  // ...
}
// ...
```

Here, you replaced the existing value for `testInstrumentationRunner` with `HiltTestRunner`'s full name. Now, it's finally time to write the instrumentation test for `FunNumberFragment`.

Implementing FunNumberFragment's test

You now have everything you need to implement the test for `FunNumberFragment`. Following the process in Figure 19.8-10, create **FunNumberFragmentTest.kt** in the **androidTest** build type and add the following code:

```
@HiltAndroidTest
@UninstallModules(ActivityModule.Bindings::class) // 1
class FunNumberFragmentTest {

  @get:Rule
  var hiltAndroidRule = HiltAndroidRule(this) // 2

  @BindValue
  @JvmField
  val funNumberService: FunNumberService =
FakeFunNumberService() // 3

  @Before
  fun setUp() {
    hiltAndroidRule.inject() // 4
  }

  @Test
  fun whenButtonPushedSomeResultDisplayed() {
    (funNumberService as FakeFunNumberService).resultToReturn =
```

```
        FunNumber(123, "Funny Number", true, "testValue")
    launchFragmentInHiltContainer<FunNumberFragment>() // 5
    onView(withId(R.id.refresh_fab_button)).perform(click()) //
6

onView(withId(R.id.fun_number_output)).check(matches(withText("1
23")))

onView(withId(R.id.fun_fact_output)).check(matches(withText("Fun
ny Number")))
  }
}
```

Other than `TestRunner`'s configuration, this test isn't much different from the one you implemented using Robolectric. Here, you:

1. Annotate the test class with `@HiltAndroidTest`.
2. Ask Dagger, through Hilt, to uninstall the bindings in `ActivityModule.Bindings`. These are the ones relating to `FunNumberService`.
3. Replace the `FunNumberService` implementation you just uninstalled with `FakeFunNumberService`.
4. Invoke `inject()` on the `hiltAndroidRule` to trigger the injection into the test.
5. Launch `FunNumberFragment` in `HiltActivityForTest` using `launchFragmentInHiltContainer()`.
6. Use Espresso to check that the `Fragment` displays what it gets from `FunNumberService`.

Now, use Android Studio to run the test and check that everything works as expected.

Great! You learned how to implement the configuration you need to use Hilt with an instrumented test. This example is similar to the one you implemented with Robolectric.

This is actually *almost* everything you need to know about Hilt and testing. There's just one more thing to cover, but you'll need a more complex example for it.

Replacing an entire @Module

In the previous example, you only replaced some of the bindings you installed as part of a `@Module`. For instance, in `RoboMainActivityTest`, you uninstalled `ActivityModule`, but you added a binding for `Navigator`.

In some cases, however, you need to replace an entire `@Module` with another. To see an example of this, create a new file named **FunNumberServiceImplHiltTest.kt** in the **business** package in the **androidTest** build type and add the following code:

```
@HiltAndroidTest
@UninstallModules( // 1
    SchedulersModule::class,
    NetworkModule::class,
    ApplicationModule::class)
class FunNumberServiceImplHiltTest {

  @Inject
  lateinit var objectUnderTest: FunNumberServiceImpl

  @Inject
  @IOScheduler
  lateinit var testScheduler: Scheduler // 2

  @BindValue
  @JvmField
  val funNumberEndPoint: FunNumberEndpoint =
StubFunNumberEndpoint() // 3

  @BindValue
  @JvmField
  val randomGenerator: NumberGenerator =
FakeNumberGenerator().apply { // 3
    nextNumber = 123
  }

  @get:Rule
  var hiltAndroidRule = HiltAndroidRule(this)

  @Before
  fun setUp() {
    hiltAndroidRule.inject()
  }

  @Test
  fun whenRandomFunNumberIsInvokedAResultIsReturned() {
    val fakeCallback = FakeCallback<FunNumber>()
    objectUnderTest.randomFunNumber(fakeCallback)
    (testScheduler as TestScheduler).advanceTimeBy(100,
TimeUnit.MILLISECONDS)
```

```
      val received = fakeCallback.callbackParameter
      Assert.assertNotNull(received)
      if (received != null) {
        with(received) {
          assertEquals(number, 123)
          assertTrue(found)
          assertEquals(text, "Number is: 123")
          assertEquals(type, "validType")
        }
      } else {
        Assert.fail("Something wrong!")
      }
    }

    @Module
    @InstallIn(ApplicationComponent::class) // 4
    object SchedulersModule {

      @Provides
      @ApplicationScoped
      @MainScheduler
      fun provideMainScheduler(): Scheduler =
  Schedulers.trampoline()

      @Provides
      @ApplicationScoped
      @IOScheduler
      fun provideIoScheduler(): Scheduler = TestScheduler()
    }
  }
```

This is the Hilt version of the test for `FunNumberServiceImpl`. You can find this class, as a unit test, in the **test** build type in the **final** project in the materials for this chapter.

The pattern is the same as you've seen in the previous examples. In this case, you:

1. Uninstall more than one `@Module` using a comma-separated list of `@Module`'s classes.
2. Use `@Inject` to get the reference to some objects in the testing dependency graph. In this case, you get the reference to `TestScheduler`, which you need for RxJava.

3. Use `@BindValue` to replace some of the objects in the testing dependency graph.

4. Replace the entire `SchedulersModule` with a new `SchedulersModule` you define in the same **FunNumberServiceImplHiltTest** file. In this case, you're replacing the `Schedulers` the app uses with the ones you need for the tests. In particular, you replaced `mainThread` with `Schedulers.trampoline()` and `io()` with `TestScheduler`.

In this example, you learned that you can replace the binding of an entire `@Module` by simply uninstalling the initial one and reinstalling a new one. You can define the testing `@Module` in the same file as the test or as an external file, depending on where you use the new `@Module`.

Key points

- Hilt provides a testing library for **Robolectric** and **instrumented** tests.
- You don't need Dagger to implement unit tests if you use **constructor injection**.
- Hilt allows you to replace parts of the app's dependency graph for testing purposes.
- Using `@HiltAndroidTest`, you ask Hilt to generate a dependency graph to use during the execution of a test.
- You can remove bindings from the dependency graph using `@UninstallModules` and replace some of them using `@BindValue`.
- You can replace all the bindings for a `@Module` by uninstalling it with `@UninstallModules` and installing a new `@Module`.

Great job! In this chapter, you saw how to modify the dependency graph of your app to make Robolectric and instrumentation tests easier to implement and run. You've now learned everything you need to know about Hilt.

This is the last chapter of this book that covers Dagger and Hilt. In the very final chapter, you'll see how you can implement dependency injection in the **Busso Server** back-end app.

Conclusion

Congratulations! After a long journey, you have learned a lot of concepts about dependency injection. You can implement dependecy injection manually, or you can use the Dagger and Hilt libraries provided by Google.

And, remember, if you want to further your understanding of Kotlin and Android app development after working through Dagger by Tutorials, we suggest you read the Android Apprentice and Kotlin Apprentice available on our online store:

- https://www.raywenderlich.com/books/android-apprentice
- https://www.raywenderlich.com/books/kotlin-apprentice

If you have any questions or comments as you work through this book, please stop by our forums at http://forums.raywenderlich.com and look for the particular forum category for this book.

Thank you again for purchasing this book. Your continued support is what makes the tutorials, books, videos, conferences and other things we do at raywenderlich.com possible, and we truly appreciate it!

Wishing you all the best in your continued Kotlin and saving data on Android.

– *The Dagger by Tutorials* book team

Section VI: Appendices

Appendix A: The Busso Server

By Massimo Carli

In this book, you learned everything you need to use Dagger and Hilt. You did this by working on several different apps, with Busso being the most complex of them. As mentioned in the first chapter, Busso needs a server: the **BussoServer**. This is a web application implemented using Ktor, which is the framework for implementing web services with Kotlin. In this last chapter, you'll look at how:

- The **BussoServer** works.
- To implement dependency injection on the server using **Koin**.

Koin (https://insert-koin.io/) is a dependency injection framework implemented in Kotlin. A complete description of the Koin framework would require another book. In this case, you'll just introduce dependency injection with Koin into the simple **BussoServer** app, to give you a look at a different approach.

The BussoServer app

As mentioned in the introduction, BussoServer is a Ktor (https://ktor.io/) app with the architecture in Figure 20.1:

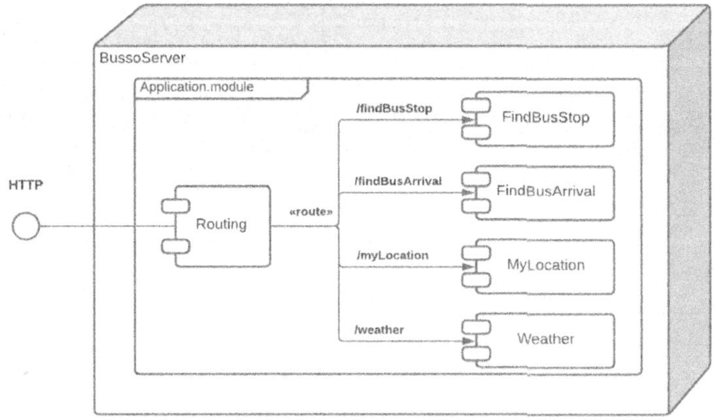

Figure 20.1 — BussoServer's High Level Architecture

To understand how this works, use IntelliJ and open the **BussoServer** project from the **starter** folder in the materials for this chapter. You'll see the structure in Figure 20.2:

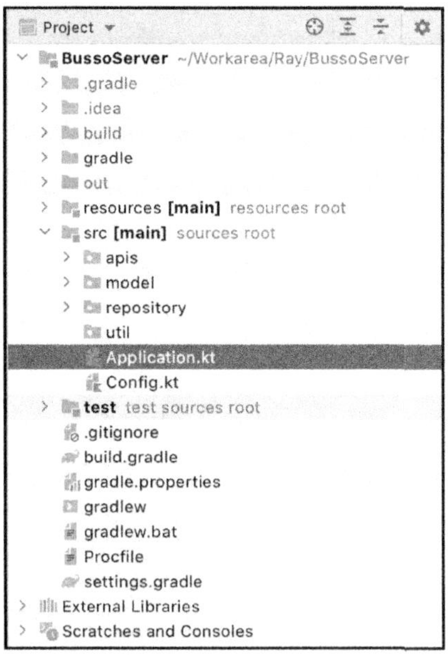

Figure 20.2 — BussoServer's Project Structure

Now, open **Application.kt** in the main package and look at its content:

```
// 1
fun main(args: Array<String>): Unit =
io.ktor.server.netty.EngineMain.main(args)

@KtorExperimentalLocationsAPI
@Suppress("unused") // Referenced in application.conf
fun Application.module() { // 2
  // 3
  install(Locations)
  // 4
  install(ContentNegotiation) {
    gson {
      setDateFormat("yyyy-MM-dd'T'HH:mm:ssZ")
    }
  }
  // 5
  routing {
    get("/") { // 6
      call.respondText("I'm working!!", contentType =
ContentType.Text.Plain)
    }
    // Features // 7
    findBusStop()
    findBusArrivals()
    myLocation()
    weather()
  }
}
```

This simple code is quite standard for Ktor. Here:

1. You define `main()` for the app by instantiating the engine that implements all the routing logic for the server. Here, you're using Netty (https://netty.io/).

2. The server engine needs some configuration that you put into a module. You usually provide this information using a `module()` extension function.

3. Ktor allows you to install and use different plugins for different purposes. In this case, you install the **Locations** feature. Despite its name, that feature has nothing to do with locations on a map. Rather, it gives you a type-safe way to define routing. You'll see this in action later. `Locations` is experimental and requires the `@KtorExperimentalLocationsAPI` annotation.

4. You use the **ContentNegotiation** feature, which allows you to manage JSON as the transport protocol. In this case, you use **Gson** as the parser.

5. The routing is the logic that maps a specific URI pattern to some logic. You define routings in a `routing` block.

6. Just for testing, if the server is up and running, you usually define a very simple endpoint for the root path /. In this case, you just return a simple text. Note how you send back content using `respondText()` on a `call` you get by invoking `get()` for a given path.

7. The remaining function allows you to install other endpoints for different paths. You'll see how to do this soon.

To launch the server locally, you just need to click on the **run** icon, as shown in Figure 20.3:

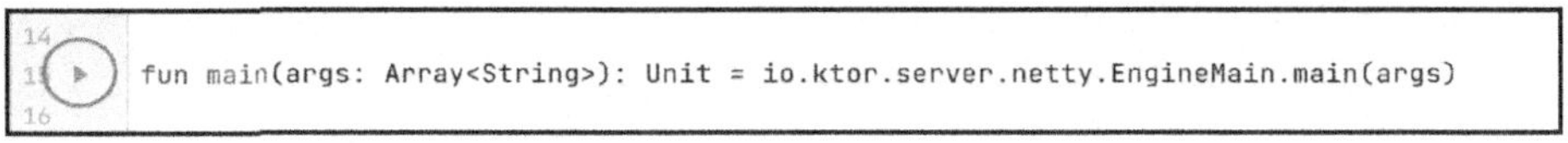

Figure 20.3 — Run BussoServer locally

You'll get an output ending with a log message similar to this:

```
2021-01-08 00:43:20.647 [main] INFO  Application - No
ktor.deployment.watch patterns specified, automatic reload is
not active
2021-01-08 00:43:21.393 [main] INFO  Application - Responding at
http://0.0.0.0:8080
```

Now, open the browser and access **http://127.0.0.1:8080**. You'll get the testing message that tells you that everything works, as in Figure 20.4:

Figure 20.4 — BussoServer is working

The routing is responsible for mapping a request path to some logic the server needs to execute to return a valid response. The **/findBusStop** endpoint is a good example of how this works.

How /findBusStop works

The `/findBusStop` endpoint is one of four endpoints **BussoServer** provides. It's the one responsible for returning the bus stop nearest to a given location. To see how it works, open **FindBusStop.kt** in the **api** package and look at the following code:

```
const val FIND_BUS_STOP = "$API_VERSION/findBusStop/{lat}/{lng}"
```

```
// 1
private val busStopRepository = ResourceBusStopRepository() // 2

@KtorExperimentalLocationsAPI
@Location(FIND_BUS_STOP) // 3
data class FindBusStopRequest(
  val lat: Float,
  val lng: Float
)

@KtorExperimentalLocationsAPI
fun Route.findBusStop() { // 4
  get<FindBusStopRequest> { inputLocation -> // 5
    // If there's a radius we add it as distance
    val radius = call.parameters.get("radius")?.toInt() ?: 0
    call.respond(
      busStopRepository.findBusStopByLocation( // 6
        inputLocation.lat,
        inputLocation.lng,
        radius
      )
    )
  }
}
```

The structure of this code is similar to that of the other endpoints. Here, you:

1. Define `FIND_BUS_STOP` with the path of the URL you invoke to access the endpoint. You pass the latitude and longitude in the input with the `lat` and `lng` query parameters.
2. Create `ResourceBusStopRepository`, which is the object you need to query the bus stop for a specific location. It's an implementation of the `BusStopRepository` interface that simply reads the result from a JSON file in the **resources** folder. At the moment, the query always returns the same result, but that doesn't matter for your purposes. :]
3. Use `@Location` to define `FindBusStopRequest` to encapsulate the input for the query.
4. Define `findBusStop()`. This is what you invoke in **Application.kt** to define the endpoint.
5. When you receive a request, the input parameters are encapsulated into `FindBusStopRequest`, which you receive as an implicit parameter for `get()`.
6. Invoke `findBusStopByLocation()` on `busStopRepository` to get the result you send back to the client using `respond()` on `call`.

Other than the specific logic, something might not look right in this code: In **2**, you create an instance of `ResourceBusStopRepository`. This is a **composition relationship**, which you've learned is something to avoid. Even worse, you have the same relationship in **FindBusArrival.kt**.

Check that out by opening **FindBusArrival.kt** to find the following:

```
const val FIND_BUS_ARRIVALS = "$API_VERSION/findBusArrivals/
{stopId}"
private val busArrivalRepository = RandomBusArrivalRepository()
private val busStopRepository = ResourceBusStopRepository()
// ...
```

How can you improve this? A very simple option is to use **Koin**.

Using Koin in BussoServer

Koin is a dependency injection framework completely implemented in Kotlin that doesn't have any type of code generation. It defines a **domain-specific language (DSL)** for managing dependency injection in different kinds of applications: Kotlin, Android, Ktor and others.

As mentioned, an in-depth exploration of Koin is outside the scope of this book. In this chapter, you'll just use it to fix the repository dependency. To do this, you need to:

1. Install the dependencies for Koin.
2. Look at the repository implementations you want to inject.
3. Create a module with the objects you want to inject.
4. Initialize Koin for Ktor.
5. Inject the repository implementation into `FindBusStop` and `FindBusArrival`.

This is a simple example, but it gives you an idea about how to use Koin and how it differs from Dagger and Hilt.

Installing Koin dependencies

Open **build.gradle** in Figure 20.5:

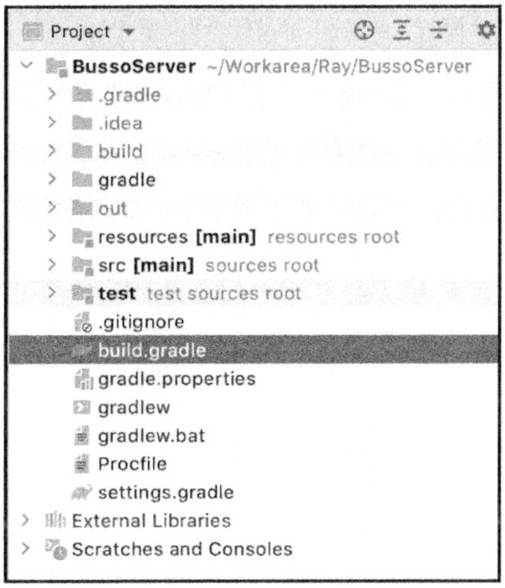

Figure 20.5 — Gradle file for BussoServer

Inside, add the following definition:

```
// ...

dependencies {
  // ...

  implementation "org.koin:koin-core:$koin_version" // 1
  implementation "org.koin:koin-ktor:$koin_version" // 2

  testImplementation "org.koin:koin-test:$koin_version" // 3

  // ...
}
// ...
```

Here, you just install the:

1. Core **Koin** library.
2. **Koin** library with some utilities for Ktor.
3. **Koin testing** library.

`koin_version` is already available in **gradle.properties**, along with other version variables. It's important to note that Koin doesn't need an annotation processor because it doesn't generate any code.

After you sync the BussoServer project with the Gradle file you just updated, you're ready to use Koin.

The repository implementations

BussoServer is a very simple app that uses the **repository pattern**. Look at the **repository** and **repository.impl** packages to see the definition in Figure 20.6:

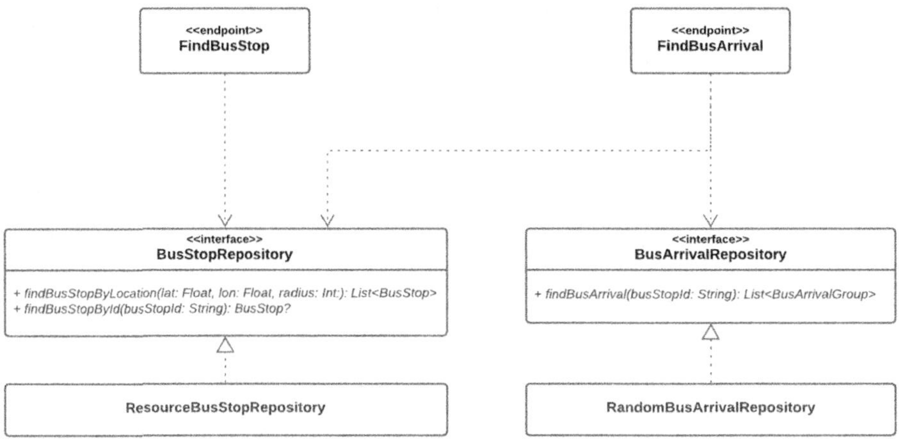

Figure 20.6 — Repositories dependency diagram

In this dependency diagram, note that:

1. There are two different repository abstractions: `BusStopRepository` and `BusArrivalRepository`.
2. `ResourcesBusStopRepository` is the implementation of `BusStopRepository`. `RandomBusArrivalRepository` is the implementation of `BusArrivalRepository`.
3. `FindBusStop` depends on `BusStopRepository`.
4. `FindBusArrival` depends on `BusStopRepository` and `BusArrivalRepository`.

It's important to note that, at this point, the relationships at points **3** and **4** are **compositions**. Your goal is to use **dependency injection** to make those dependencies **loosely coupled**.

Creating a Koin module

Think back to the definition of a Dagger `@Module`: a fundamental concept you use to tell Dagger how to create objects for a given type. Koin modules are similar.

To see this for yourself, create a new package named **di** and create a new file named **RepositoryModule.kt** in it with the following code:

```
val repositoryModule = module { // 1
  single<BusStopRepository> { ResourceBusStopRepository() } // 2
  single<BusArrivalRepository>
{ RandomBusArrivalRepository() } // 3
}
```

This code is very simple. It shows how to:

1. Define a module for the repositories in BussoServer by passing a block to the `module` where you define the bindings.
2. Create a binding between `BusStopRepository` and `ResourceBusStopRepository`. Using `single`, you tell Koin that you only have a single instance of `ResourceBusStopRepository` bound to the `BusStopRepository` type.
3. Do the same for the `BusArrivalRepository`. Every time you inject an object of type `BusArrivalRepository`, you'll use the instance of `RandomBusArrivalRepository` you created here.

Koin initialization in Ktor

Now, you need to tell Koin to use the bindings you just defined in `repositoryModule`. Open **Application.kt** and add the following definition:

```
@KtorExperimentalLocationsAPI
@Suppress("unused") // Referenced in application.conf
fun Application.module() {

  install(org.koin.ktor.ext.Koin) { // 1
    modules(repositoryModule) // 2
  }
  // ...
}
// ...
```

The code is straightforward. Here, you:

1. Use `install` to register the **Koin feature** with Ktor, just as you did for the `Locations` and `ContentNegotiation` features. It's important to use **org.koin.ktor.ext** as the Koin class' package.
2. Declare which modules to use. In your case, you use `modules()`, passing the reference to the `repositoryModule` you defined above.

Now that the implementations of the repositories are in BussoServer's dependency graph, you just need to inject them when needed.

Injecting the repository implementation

Earlier, you installed the `module` with the bindings for `BusStopRepository` and `BusArrivalRepository`. But how do you inject them? That's simple. Open **FindBusStop.kt** in the **apis** package and apply the following change:

```
const val FIND_BUS_STOP = "$API_VERSION/findBusStop/{lat}/{lng}"
// private val busStopRepository =
ResourceBusStopRepository() // DELETE 1

// ...

@KtorExperimentalLocationsAPI
fun Route.findBusStop() {

  val busStopRepository: BusStopRepository by inject() // 2

  get<FindBusStopRequest> { inputLocation ->
    // ...
  }
}
```

In this code, you need to:

1. Delete the initialization of the `busStopRepository` property with the instance of `ResourceBusStopRepository` that you now need to inject.
2. Use `inject()` to initialize the `busStopRepository` local variable of type `FindBusStopRequest`.

In this way, you inject the instance of `ResourceBusStopRepository`, which you defined in the module in `repositoryModule`, into `FindBusStop`.

Now, open **FindBusArrivals.kt** in the same **apis** package and add the following code:

```
const val FIND_BUS_ARRIVALS = "$API_VERSION/findBusArrivals/
{stopId}"
// private val busArrivalRepository =
RandomBusArrivalRepository() // DELETE 1
// private val busStopRepository =
ResourceBusStopRepository() // DELETE 1
// ...
@KtorExperimentalLocationsAPI
fun Route.findBusArrivals() {

  val busStopRepository: BusStopRepository by inject()  // 2
  val busArrivalRepository: BusArrivalRepository by inject() //
2

  get<FindBusArrivalsRequest> { busStopInput ->
    // ..
  }
}
```

In this code, you do the same for `RandomBusArrivalRepository`. Here, you:

1. Delete the initialization of `busArrivalRepository` and `busStopRepository` with instances of `RandomBusArrivalRepository` and `ResourceBusStopRepository`, respectively.
2. Use `inject()` to inject the instances from `repositoryModule`, just as you did for `FindBusStop` before.

Finally, run **BussoServer** to see that everything works as expected. To verify this, open the browser and access a URL like **http://localhost:8080/api/v1/findBusStop/1.0/2.0**.

You'll get what's shown in figure 20.7:

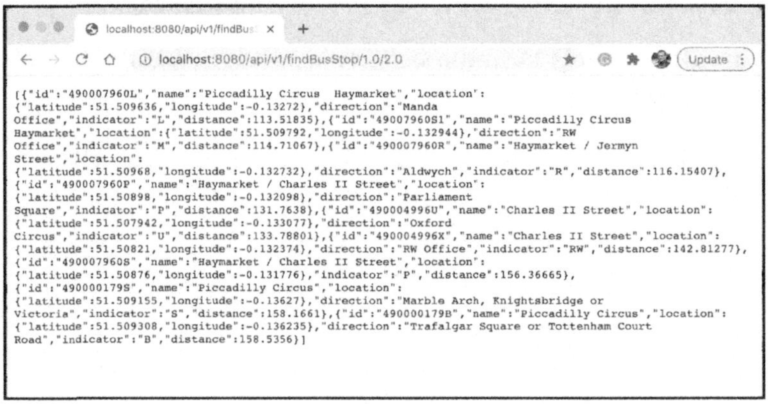

Figure 20.7 — Verify BussoServer is working

In this case, injecting the repositories is simple because `ResourceBusStopRepository` and `RandomBusArrivalRepository` don't have other dependencies. Next, you'll see a slightly more complicated example.

Adding other dependencies: Logger

In the previous section, you saw how to inject the implementation for two simple interfaces, `BusStopRepository` and `BusArrivalRepository`, which don't have dependencies.

Suppose you now want to add a simple logger to check that the instances you're using in the app are singletons or, using Koin language, are **single**. To do this, you just need to:

1. Add a new `Logger` abstraction with a simple implementation.
2. Create a `module` for the `Logger`.
3. Install the `module` for the `Logger` in Ktor.
4. Add the dependency to the `Logger` in `ResourceBusStopRepository` and `RandomBusArrivalRepository`.
5. Provide dependencies in modules.

Adding the Logger abstraction

You just want to see how dependency injection works with Koin, so all you need is a simple abstraction for the **Logger**. Start by creating a new package named **logging** in the **src** folder for **main** and create a new file named **Logger.kt** in it with the following code:

```
interface Logger {

  fun log(msg: String)
}
```

Now, you just need a very simple implementation. So in the same package, create a new file named **StdLoggerImpl.kt** and add the following code:

```
class StdLoggerImpl : Logger {
  override fun log(msg: String) {
    println(msg)
  }
}
```

This implementation uses the built-in function `print()` to write the log message to the standard output.

As you learned, you now need a module.

Creating a module for the Logger

To create a **module** for the `Logger`, create a new file named **LoggerModule.kt** in **di** with the following code:

```
val loggerModule = module { // 1
  factory<Logger> { StdLoggerImpl() } // 2
}
```

In this case, you:

1. Define `loggerModule` as a Koin `module` in the same way you did for the repositories.
2. Used `factory` instead of `single` to define the binding of the `Logger` type to an instance of `StdLoggerImpl`.

You could have used `single` again but you're using `factory` to show something different. In this case, you'll get a different instance of `Logger` every time you inject one.

Now, you need to install this module in Ktor.

Installing the module for the Logger in Ktor

Defining `loggerModule` doesn't install it in Ktor, but you already know how the installation works. Open **Application.kt** and add the following:

```
@KtorExperimentalLocationsAPI
@Suppress("unused") // Referenced in application.conf
fun Application.module() {

  install(org.koin.ktor.ext.Koin) {
    modules(repositoryModule)
    modules(loggerModule) // HERE
  }
  // ...
}
```

Here, you simply install `loggerModule` using `modules()`, as you did for `repositoryModule` earlier.

Great! Now, BussoServer knows that there's a `Logger` somewhere — but it doesn't know how to use it or which classes need it.

Creating dependencies

Suppose you now want to use the `Logger` in `ResourceBusStopRepository` and `RandomBusArrivalRepository`. To do this, you need to define the dependency by using — of course — constructor injection.

Open **ResourceBusStopRepository.kt** in **repository.impl** and apply the following change:

```
class ResourceBusStopRepository constructor(
  private val logger: Logger // 1
) : BusStopRepository {

  private val model: BusStopData

  init {
    logger.log("Initializing ResourceBusStopRepository:
$this") // 2
```

```
    val jsonAsText =
this::class.java.getResource(BUS_STOP_RESOURCE_PATH).readText()
    model = Gson().fromJson(jsonAsText,
BusStopData::class.java).apply {
      items.forEach { butStop ->
        this@apply.stopMap[butStop.id] = butStop
      }
    }
  }

  override suspend fun findBusStopByLocation(
    latitude: Float,
    longitude: Float,
    radius: Int
  ): List<BusStop> {
    logger.log("findBusStopByLocation on $this with lat:
$latitude lon: $longitude") // 3
    return mutableListOf<BusStop>().apply {
      (2..10).forEach {
        add(model.items[it])
      }
    }.sortedBy { busStop -> busStop.distance }
  }


  override suspend fun findBusStopById(budStopId: String):
BusStop? =
    model.stopMap[budStopId]
}
// ...
```

In this code, you:

1. Create the dependency on `Logger` by adding a parameter in the primary constructor.
2. Use `logger` when you initialize `ResourceBusStopRepository`.
3. Log a message every time you invoke `findBusStopByLocation`.

In all the logs, you also print the specific instance of `ResourceBusStopRepository` you're using. You'll use this to prove that `ResourceBusStopRepository` is actually a singleton.

Now, you need to do the same for the other repository. Open **RandomBusArrivalRepository.kt** and apply similar changes, like this:

```
/**
 * Number of arrivals for line
 */
```

```
fun arrivalNumberRange() = 0..nextInt(3, 10)
fun arrivalGroupRange() = 0..nextInt(1, 4)
// private val busStopRepository =
ResourceBusStopRepository() // DELETE 1

/**
 * Implementation for the BusArrivalRepository which returns
random values
 */
class RandomBusArrivalRepository constructor(
  private val busStopRepository: BusStopRepository, // 2
  private val logger: Logger // 3
) : BusArrivalRepository {
  override suspend fun findBusArrival(busStopId: String):
List<BusArrivalGroup> {
    logger.log("Invoking findBusArrival for id: $busStopId on
$this") // 4
    val busStop = busStopRepository.findBusStopById(busStopId)
    if (busStop == null) {
      return emptyList()
    }
    return mutableListOf<BusArrivalGroup>().apply {
      arrivalGroupRange().forEach {
        add(
          BusArrivalGroup(
            lineId = "1",
            lineName = lines.random(),
            destination = destinations.random(),
            arrivals = generateRandomBusArrival()
          )
        )
      }
    }
  }

}
```

In this code, you also see something you didn't know before. `RandomBusArrivalRepository` actually needs a `BusStopRepository` — so it depends on it. That's because you:

1. Delete the initialization of `busStopRepository` with a new instance of `ResourceBusStopRepository`, which must be injected.
2. Define the dependency on `BusStopRepository` by adding a parameter of the same type to its primary constructor.
3. Do the same for `Logger`.
4. Use the logger to print a message every time you use `RandomBusArrivalRepository`.

Build now and you'll get an error. You just added dependencies to ResourceBusStopRepository and RandomBusArrivalRepository, but Koin doesn't know who's providing those dependencies. You need to fix RepositoryModule.

Providing dependencies in modules

To resolve the dependencies, open **RepositoryModule.kt** in **di** and apply the following changes:

```
val repositoryModule = module {
  single<BusStopRepository> { ResourceBusStopRepository(get()) }
// 1
  single<BusArrivalRepository>
{ RandomBusArrivalRepository(get(), get()) } // 2
}
```

All you need to do is add get() every time you need to resolve a dependency. In this code, you use:

1. get() to resolve the dependency from ResourceBusStopRepository and Logger it requires as primary constructor parameter.
2. get() twice to resolve the dependency between RandomBusArrivalRepository and the two primary constructor parameters. Koin is smart enough to understand the parameters' types and to check if there's a module that provides a binding for them.

Now, build and run, checking that everything works as expected, as you did in Figure 20.7.

More interesting is to prove that the instance of the repositories is always the same at each request. Check in Logcat and you'll see something like this:

```
Initializing ResourceBusStopRepository:
com...ResourceBusStopRepository@6456c628
findBusStopByLocation on
com...ResourceBusStopRepository@6456c628 with lat:1.0 lon: 2.0
findBusStopByLocation on com..ResourceBusStopRepository@6456c628
with lat:1.0 lon: 2.0
findBusStopByLocation on com..ResourceBusStopRepository@6456c628
with lat:1.0 lon: 2.0
```

As you see, ResourceBusStopRepository is a singleton.

Key points

- **BussoServer** is Busso's server app. It's a Ktor app.
- You can use dependency injection on a Ktor server using Koin, a fully Kotlin solution without code generation.
- Like Dagger, Koin allows to install the definition of **modules** you need as a Ktor feature.
- Using `inject()` as a property delegate, you can inject dependencies into a dependency target.
- Using `get()`, you can manage transitive dependencies between different objects.
- This chapter only scratches the surface of Koin as an example of an alternative framework for dependency injection in Kotlin.

Appendix B: Assisted Injection

By Massimo Carli

Dagger and Hilt are libraries in continuous evolution. Google and Square, with the help of the open-source community, keep improving them, both by creating new features and by improving the performance of the existing ones.

One of Dagger's new improvements is **assisted injection**, which Google added in version 2.31. In this appendix, you'll learn:

1. What assisted injection is.
2. How to implement it with `@Assisted`, `@AssistedInject` and `@AssistedFactory`.

To do this, you'll work on the **RandomFunNumber** app.

What is assisted injection?

In this book, you learned all about **dependency injection**. You saw several examples of how dependency injection can improve the maintainability and testability of your code. You also learned that **constructor injection** is the best type of injection because it allows you to provide dependencies at the exact moment you create an instance of an object.

It's not unusual to see code like this:

```
class MyService @Inject constructor( // 1
    private val dep1: Dependency1, // 2
    private val dep2: Dependency2, // 2
    private val dep3: Dependency3  // 2
) : Service
```

Here, you define:

1. `MyService` as an implementation of the `Service` interface, and you annotate its primary constructor with `@Inject`. This tells Dagger how to create an instance of `MyService` to use anywhere you need an object of type `Service`.
2. The dependencies of `MyService` as primary constructor parameters. In this case, `MyService` needs objects of types `Dependency1`, `Dependency2` and `Dependency3`.

By also telling Dagger how to provide objects of type `Dependency1`, `Dependency2` and `Dependency3`, you know Dagger will create the instance of `MyService` for you every time you need a `Service`.

This is very cool, but sometimes you need something a bit different. To understand what, return to RandomFunNumber to see a practical example.

An example of constructor injection

Open the **RandomFunNumber** project from the **starter** folder of the materials for this appendix. This is a simplified version of the project you used in Chapter 19, "Testing With Hilt", with an important difference.

Figure 21.1 — The RandomFunNumber app

In **versions.gradle**, the version of the Hilt library is now **2.31.2-alpha**. It depends on version **2.31.2** of Dagger:

```
hilt_version = "2.31.2-alpha"
```

This is important because assisted injection was introduced in Dagger 2.31, so you need to use at least that version.

Now, open **FunNumberServiceImpl.kt** in the **business** package and look at the following code:

```
class FunNumberServiceImpl @Inject constructor( // 1
    private val numberGenerator: NumberGenerator, // 2
    private val funNumberEndpoint: FunNumberEndpoint // 2
) : FunNumberService {
  // ...
}
```

This is an example of **constructor injection**, where you:

1. Use `@Inject` to tell Dagger to use the **primary constructor** to create the instances.
2. Define the dependencies on `NumberGenerator` and `FunNumberEndpoint`.

Next, open **ActivityModule.kt** in **di** to find the following definition:

```
  // ...
    @Binds
    @ActivityScoped
    fun bindFunNumberService( // HERE
        impl: FunNumberServiceImpl
    ): FunNumberService
  // ...
```

This code just says that every time you need to inject an object of the type `FunNumberService`, Dagger will create an instance of `FunNumberServiceImpl` to handle the dependencies you saw earlier.

With this configuration, Dagger provides **all** the dependencies for you. But what if you want to provide a different dependency every time you need a `FunNumberServiceImpl`? That's where assisted injection comes in handy.

Providing dependencies with assisted injection

Suppose you want to provide a different `NumberGenerator` implementation every time you need a `FunNumberServiceImpl`. One way to achieve this is to use a **custom qualifier**.

However, while that would work, it would be quite verbose. Assisted injection is an elegant alternative.

To use this, you need:

1. `@AssistedInject` in place of `@Inject` for `FunNumberServiceImpl`.
2. `@Assisted` to tell Dagger which dependency you'll provide it.
3. `@AssistedFactory` to define the **Factory** that binds type `FunNumberService`.
4. To inject the `Factory` wherever you need a `FunNumberService` and provide the proper dependency.

Now, you're ready to code along and add assisted injection to RandomFunNumber.

Replacing @Inject with @AssistedInject

For your first step, you'll inform Dagger that you want to use assisted injection, and will therefore provide some of the dependencies you need for a specific binding.

To do this, open **FunNumberServiceImpl.kt** in **business** and apply the following change:

```
class FunNumberServiceImpl @AssistedInject constructor( // HERE
    private val numberGenerator: NumberGenerator,
    private val funNumberEndpoint: FunNumberEndpoint
) : FunNumberService {
  // ...
}
```

This code replaces `@Inject` with `@AssistedInject`. This tells Dagger that you'll explicitly provide some of the dependencies you define as primary constructor parameters.

However, the code above doesn't tell Dagger which dependencies you'll provide. For that, you need `@Assisted`.

Using @Assisted

You just learned how to tell Dagger that you'll handle some of `FunNumberServiceImpl`'s dependencies. Now, you need to declare which dependencies you'll provide.

In the same **FunNumberServiceImpl.kt** in **business**, add the following definition:

```
class FunNumberServiceImpl @AssistedInject constructor(
    @Assisted private val numberGenerator: NumberGenerator, //
HERE
```

```
    private val funNumberEndpoint: FunNumberEndpoint
) : FunNumberService {
  // ...
}
```

When you add the import for `@Assisted`, you'll probably see two different options. That's because there's an `@Assisted` in the **dagger.assisted** package and another in **androidx.hilt**. The source code in the latter has a comment saying that it'll be replaced with the former. Therefore, the one in **dagger.assisted** is the right one to import in your class.

In this code, you use `@Assisted` for the primary constructor parameter of type `NumberGenerator`. With this, you tell Dagger that, when it's time to create the object to bind to `FunNumberService`, you'll explicitly provide the dependency of type `NumberGenerator`.

But how can you do this? You need a **Factory**.

Using @AssistedFactory

So far, you've told Dagger that:

1. You want to do part of its job by providing some of the dependencies for `FunNumberService`'s binding.
2. You'll provide the dependency for the parameter of type `NumberGenerator`.

Now, you need a way to pass the binding: a Factory.

To add this, create a new file named **FunNumberServiceFactory.kt** in **business** and add the following code:

```
@AssistedFactory // 1
interface FunNumberServiceFactory { // 2

  fun create(
      numberGenerator: NumberGenerator // 3
  ): FunNumberServiceImpl // 4
}
```

In this code, you:

1. Use `@AssistedFactory` to tell Dagger to generate this interface of the `Factory` for you and create the object to bind `FunNumberServiceImpl`.
2. Define `Factory` as an interface.

3. Need a `create` operation that has the `@Assisted` dependencies as its parameters. Earlier, you told Dagger that you'll provide the dependency for `NumberGenerator`. This parameter is how you do that.

4. Return an object of type `FunNumberServiceImpl`. This last point is fundamental. The returning type is not the type of the `FunNumberService` abstraction, but the type of `@AssistedInject`, which is its implementation.

Because of the last point, you can open **ActivityModule.kt** in **di** and change it to this:

```
@Module(includes = [
  NavigationModule::class
])
@InstallIn(ActivityComponent::class)
object ActivityModule
```

In this code, you deleted the bindings for:

1. `FunNumberService`, because you'll provide it through `FunNumberServiceFactory`.
2. `NumberGenerator` because you'll provide this information explicitly — as you'll see in a bit.

Now that you've defined `FunNumberServiceFactory`, Dagger will also create the binding for you. This means you don't need to add this definition to any `@Module`. You can now simply `@Inject` the `FunNumberServiceFactory` where you need it — in this case, in `FunNumberViewModel`.

Using FunNumberServiceFactory in FunNumberFragment

You now need to inject `FunNumberServiceFactory` where you need a `FunNumberService`.

Do this by opening **FunNumberFragment.kt** in **ui.displaynumber** and apply the following changes:

```
@AndroidEntryPoint
class FunNumberFragment : Fragment() {

  private lateinit var funNumberTextView: TextView
  private lateinit var funFactTextView: TextView
```

```
  @Inject
  lateinit var funNumberServiceFactory:
FunNumberServiceFactory // 1
  private lateinit var funNumberService: FunNumberService // 2

  override fun onCreateView(inflater: LayoutInflater, container:
ViewGroup?, savedInstanceState: Bundle?): View? {
    val ctx = container?.context ?:
IllegalStateException("Context not available")
    funNumberService = funNumberServiceFactory.create(object :
NumberGenerator { // 3
      override fun randomNumber(): Int = 28
    })
    return LayoutInflater.from(ctx as
Context).inflate(R.layout.fragment_show_number, container,
false).apply {
      // ...
    }
  }

  override fun onStop() {
    funNumberService.stop()
    super.onStop()
  }
}
```

In this code, you:

1. Use `@Inject` to get the reference to `FunNumberServiceFactory` into the `funNumberServiceFactory` property.
2. Define `funNumberService` to store the reference to the `FunNumberService` instance you'll — theoretically — create later.
3. Invoke `create()` on the `funNumberServiceFactory` to create the `FunNumberServiceImpl` instance, passing the reference to a new `NumberGenerator` implementation you'll create locally.

> **Note**: In this code, you're only practicing how to use assisted injection. The instance of the `NumberGenerator` implementation you create here doesn't matter.

Now, run the app. Everything works as expected:

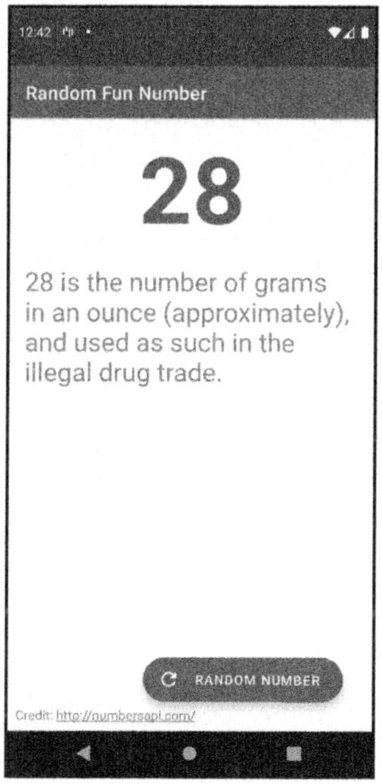

Figure 21.2 — The RandomFunNumber app

Limitations to assisted injection in Dagger

Congratulations! You've added assisted injection to the RandomFunNumber app. This is a new feature in Dagger, so be aware that following versions of the library might include improvements. At the moment, it has some limitations, including:

1. `FunNumberServiceFactory` defines `create()`, which has `FunNumberServiceImpl` as return type. That's because it must be the type of the class whose primary constructor you annotated with `@AssistedInject`. It would be nice to have the `FunNumberService` abstraction as the return type instead.

2. At the moment, `@AssistedInject` cannot use `@Scopes`.

Key points

- Dagger has offered assisted injection since version 2.31.0.
- `@AssistedInject` allows you to tag the primary constructor with `@Assisted` parameters.
- To create an instance of `@AssistedInject`, you need an `@AssistedFactory`.

Printed in Great Britain
by Amazon

36544935R00302